FUELING MEXICO

Around the 1830s, parts of Mexico began industrializing using water and wood. By the 1880s, this model faced a growing energy and ecological bottleneck. By the 1950s, fossil fuels powered most of Mexico's economy and society. Looking to the north and across the Atlantic, late nineteenth-century officials and elites concluded that fossil fuels would solve Mexico's energy problem and Mexican industry began introducing coal. But limited domestic deposits and high costs meant that coal never became king in Mexico. Oil instead became the favored fuel for manufacture, transport, and electricity generation. This shift, however, created a paradox of perennial scarcity amidst energy abundance: every new influx of fossil energy led to increased demand. Germán Vergara shows how the decision to power the country's economy with fossil fuels locked Mexico into a cycle of endless, fossil-fueled growth – with serious environmental and social consequences.

GERMÁN VERGARA is Assistant Professor of History at the Georgia Institute of Technology.

Studies in Environment and History

Editors

J. R. McNeill, *Georgetown University*
Ling Zhang, *Boston College*

Editors Emeriti

Alfred W. Crosby, *University of Texas at Austin*
Edmund P. Russell, *Carnegie Mellon University*
Donald Worster, *University of Kansas*

Other Books in the Series

FUELING MEXICO

Energy and Environment, 1850–1950

GERMÁN VERGARA

Georgia Institute of Technology

CAMBRIDGE
UNIVERSITY PRESS

CAMBRIDGE
UNIVERSITY PRESS

University Printing House, Cambridge CB2 8BS, United Kingdom

One Liberty Plaza, 20th Floor, New York, NY 10006, USA

477 Williamstown Road, Port Melbourne, VIC 3207, Australia

314–321, 3rd Floor, Plot 3, Splendor Forum, Jasola District Centre, New Delhi – 110025, India

79 Anson Road, #06–04/06, Singapore 079906

Cambridge University Press is part of the University of Cambridge.

It furthers the University's mission by disseminating knowledge in the pursuit of education, learning, and research at the highest international levels of excellence.

www.cambridge.org
Information on this title: www.cambridge.org/9781108831277
DOI: 10.1017/9781108923972

First published 2021

A catalogue record for this publication is available from the British Library.

ISBN 978-1-108-83127-7 Hardback

Contents

Figures and Tables

Figures

Tables

Acknowledgments

I like to think that this book, while clearly academic, is also a personal story. I was born and raised in Mexico City. On many occasions, as I sat down to write (and rewrite) it, I recalled my teenage impressions of the place – of its enormity, its beauty and ugliness. At eighteen, I used to climb to the rooftop of the tall apartment building where my family lived and look out on the city. On clear days, when rain and wind dissipated the brown smog that typically blanketed the Valley of Mexico, I could see the vastness of the city extending all the way to the foothills of the mountain ranges in the southwest. It never ceased to amaze me, this juxtaposition between endless "asphalt jungle" and verdant foothills and sierras. Looking back, I'm left to wonder how much of my academic work was influenced by the conflicting awe and alarm I felt looking out over Mexico City. Years later, after living in Europe and in different parts of the U.S., I found myself coming back to similar questions about my hometown. How had modern Mexico City – and modern Mexico – come to be? Why had it changed so dramatically from the time my parents were young to my own youth? Could a city of such proportions continue to exist in its present form long-term? How could those forests survive next to one of the biggest cities in the world? This book represents my answer to these questions.

But no matter how personal its origins, writing a book requires the support and collaboration of many people. The relationship between the author and this larger group is not unlike that between passengers on a train: a few people will make the entire trip with you, while others hop on or off along the way. It can be a solitary journey at times, but one is rarely ever alone. Just as a train ride would be impossible without railway workers, stations, tracks, and power, writing a history book is hard to imagine without colleagues, a home institution, library and archival collections, and a network of family and friends. May these acknowledgments convey the gratitude I feel towards the people who joined me on this ride.

This book originated as a doctoral dissertation supervised by Margaret Chowning and Mark Healey at the University of California, Berkeley. To both, my most heartfelt thanks. They read and commented on numerous iterations of the text as it evolved over the years, and supported its completion in more ways than I can name here. One could not ask for more committed, generous, and better academic advisors and friends. Other Berkeley colleagues and fellow grad students also gave their valuable feedback, including David Tamayo, Pablo Palomino, Sarah Hines, and Mark Brilliant. Carolyn Merchant read the full dissertation and provided insightful suggestions. My deepest thanks to all.

As a postdoctoral fellow at Brown University, Robert Self, Nancy Jacobs, Daniel Rodríguez, Cynthia Brokaw, and the late Douglas Cope generously read and offered advice on parts of the manuscript. I'm also grateful for the ways in which they welcomed and supported me during my time at Brown. Nancy Jacobs and James Green went beyond the call of duty when they helped me refine job talks based on the project and (in the case of James) kindly wrote letters of recommendation. Brown's Cogut Center funded summer research and provided an opportunity to present and discuss some of the material contained in this book. Fellow postdocs Claire Sagan, Iris Montero, and Nicole Burrows shared meals, drinks, and comradeship along the way. Brown's library and their efficient librarians were a wonderful resource to have during the early stages of revising the manuscript. Rafael Ortega and Mariana Sabino were excellent and reliable research assistants in Mexico and Austin, respectively.

Many thanks go to my colleagues in the School of History and Sociology at Georgia Tech for their support during the writing and revision process (listed in no specific order): Eric Schatzberg, Todd Michney, Kate Brown, Dan Amsterdam, Allen Hyde, Sherie Randolph, John Tone, John Krige, Laura Bier, Kristie Macrakis, Jennifer Singh, Johnny Smith, Billy Winders, Amy D'Unger, Willie Pearson, Mary McDonald, Hanchao Lu, Karla Gerona, and Douglas Flamming. A special thanks to Steve Usselman for his guidance, advice, and mentorship. Matt Ventresca and Katie Hemsworth offered friendship, excellent banter, and Canadian warmth. Both my home department and Georgia Tech's Ivan Allen College of Liberal Arts provided essential research funds that allowed me to visit archives and library collections and access critical information in the late stages of the writing process. I would also like to thank the librarians at Georgia Tech who determinedly chased obscure volumes and articles when I needed them most.

I feel much gratitude to John Tutino, whose generous and thorough feedback substantially improved the manuscript. Matthew Vitz also went out of his way to carefully read the entire manuscript at a critical moment. Margaret Chowning gave me much needed advice as I finished revising the text. Ted Beatty organized a workshop at the University of Notre Dame's history department in the fall of 2019 that gave me the chance to discuss the project with a knowledgeable and sympathetic audience. Some of their comments helped me rewrite parts of chapter 4. Ted, Jaime Pensado, and Jorge Puma made me feel at home during my visit. Of course, any mistakes, omissions, or errors in judgement that remain in the book are my sole responsibility.

José Galindo, Michael Ducey, and Yamil Cano all helped me obtain access to the building in Poza Rica housing the fabulous mural by artist Teodoro Cano that graces the cover of this book. Alberto Velázquez León took the expert photograph. My gratitude to all.

It has been a great pleasure to work with Cambridge University Press. John R. McNeill, co-editor of the series in environmental history and a leading figure in the field, generously supported the manuscript. His sustained interest in the book has meant more to me than he probably knows. Senior editor Lucy Rhymer expertly directed and oversaw the publication process from beginning to end. Natasha Whelan, Raghavi Govindane, and Sue Clements did their jobs with great professionalism and efficiency, making my life easier along the way. Heather Dubnick (unaffiliated with Cambridge) created the index.

No one shared this train ride with me longer than my family. Without their support and love over the years, the trip would have proved over-whelming – at times, they were the tracks, the engine, and the fuel that kept me going. To my mother Marcela, my father Juan Manuel, my aunt Adriana, my brother Juan Manuel, my sister-in-law Lucero, their wonder-ful daughter Lucía, and my dear late grandmother Pina, I could not have done this without you. Terri, Mark, and Hannah welcomed me into their home, fed me organic veggies grown in their own backyard (without any fossil-fuel inputs), and kept me supplied with mandarins and coffee during key moments in the revision process. To all of you, thank you.

Finally, I owe an enormous debt of gratitude to Beth Stemen, who patiently edited multiple drafts of this book. She read every word with care, engaging both the arguments and the prose. She helped to polish the text and cut thousands of words in order to keep the book within reasonable limits. In a real sense, this book is also hers.

Energy, Environment, and History

It was the best of times, it was the worst of times . . .
Charles Dickens, *A Tale of Two Cities*

Picture Mexico in 1850. The majority of Mexicans lived in villages and practiced some form of agriculture and animal husbandry: slash and burn in the tropical lowlands; rain-fed agriculture in the temperate central highlands and the Bajío;[1] and a mix of ranching and limited irrigation in the arid north. Humans and animals powered every stage of food production. Urban centers were small, few, and far between. Of the country's seven and a half million people, no more than one in twenty lived in a city. Trade and travel depended on human and animal muscle power. Manufacturing took place in small urban workshops or river-powered factories. Like other agrarian societies, population and economic growth were slow and subject to periodic declines. Despite enormous disparities between regions, classes, genders, and races, all mid-nineteenth-century Mexicans lived in a world of low energy consumption where life's necessities came from the land. But if preindustrial Mexico was not a paradise of plenty, neither did its people live in harmony with their surroundings. Deforestation, pollution, and environmental degradation were common but largely limited to specific areas like mining regions. In short, 1850s Mexico was an agricultural society under tight energy constraints, where economic activity, cultural practices, attitudes towards nature, and urban and population growth depended on the diffuse flow of the sun's energy.

One hundred years later, the Mexico of the mid-nineteenth century was wholly transformed. By 1950, Mexico had undergone a fossil fuel revolution that turned the former agrarian country into a rapidly industrializing nation. Beginning in the 1880s, various environmental, political, and social

---

[1] Located in north-central Mexico with an important history of agricultural and mining production dating back to colonial times.

I

pressures prompted Mexican industry to power parts of production with coal. Vast oil deposits discovered in northern Veracruz in the early twentieth century further accelerated the country's transition to fossil fuels. By the mid-twentieth century, fossil fuels had become the cornerstone of Mexico's society and economy. From cigarettes, cotton cloth, and steel; to trains, cars, and the tracks and roads they rode on; to the electricity that powered industrial machinery and lighted houses and buildings across the country, fossil fuels underwrote the nation's growth. Cities now concentrated about 40 percent of the population in fossil-fueled economic hubs. Mexico City alone housed around four million people, and some 60,000 civilian cars and thousands of buses transporting more than 1,000,000 passengers daily had replaced most of the draft animals that had once clomped through the streets. Urban and rural areas were now connected by a road network totaling over 21,000 km, almost as large as the country's railroad system. In the countryside, food production was rapidly mechanizing with the onset of Mexico's Green Revolution: over 20,000 tractors ploughed land increasingly dependent on petrochemical fertilizers.

Fossil fuels underpinned the longest economic boom in Mexico's history, the country's *trente glorieuses* averaging 7 percent growth annually between 1940 and 1970. But this fossil-fueled revolution was a gamble. While it brought great economic benefits to substantial sectors of Mexico's population, it left many others behind. It also caused massive environmental change as well as unsustainable demographic, urban, and economic growth that has persisted into the present.

How and why did this century-long transformation occur? To answer these questions, *Fueling Mexico* goes back to the 1830s, when Mexican officials and elites began industrializing parts of the country using water and wood for fuel. By the 1880s, this industrial model confronted an energy, ecological, and social bottleneck. Factories exploited most available river water yet suffered shortages during the drought season. Wood-burning steam engines depleted many forests, to the great concern of conservationists and government officials. Peasant communities clashed with factories over these scarce resources. In the midst of a railroad construction boom following just a few decades of industrialization, Mexican elites found themselves short on energy. But what could power Mexican industry if not wood and water? Looking to their peers in the north and across the Atlantic, the nation's political and economic leaders seemed to find the answer.

Starting in the 1880s, Mexican industrialists began supplementing wood and water with coal. There was just one problem: Mexico was not a coal country. This coal mainly came from abroad or from distant domestic deposits in Mexico's north, making it expensive. Railroads and important industries adopted coal but continued championing a cheaper and more abundant fossil energy source. Cue oil. Unlike coal, oil was plentiful in Mexico. After 1900, oil gradually became the favored fuel for manufacture, transport, and electricity generation, displacing – though not eliminating – coal. By the 1950s, fossil fuels – oil, coal, and natural gas – formed the bedrock of Mexico's economy and society.

For over a century, successive Mexican governments and industrial elites fostered the transition to fossil fuels. They were convinced that fossil energy would overcome the environmental, energy, and social limits to growth of wood- and-water-based industrialization. Yet the shift failed to truly solve Mexico's energy problems. Rather, it resulted in a paradox of perennial scarcity amidst energy abundance: every new influx of fossil energy into the economy encouraged new applications. This led to increased demands, prompting the quest for and consumption of even more fossil fuels. Fossil power locked Mexico into a cycle of endless, fossil-fueled growth – with profound environmental and social consequences.

Mexico and Energy

By placing the fossil fuel energy transition at the center of Mexico's modern history, this book moves beyond traditional scholarly approaches and reconceptualizes critical junctures in Mexican history. Discussion of Mexico's oil history has focused on topics such as production, oil's role as an export commodity, labor struggles, and contentious relations between Mexican governments and oil multinationals.[2] The few existing analyses of coal tend to fall into the arena of labor and economic history.[3] (Virtually no historical scholarship exists on natural gas.) While important, these approaches largely overlook two crucial elements: the significance of

---

[2] An overview of this literature is Marcelo Bucheli, "Major Trends in the Historiography of the Latin American Oil Industry," *The Business History Review* 84, no. 2 (2010): 339–62.

[3] See Roberto R. Calderón, *Mexican Coal Mining Labor in Texas and Coahuila, 1880–1930* (College Station: Texas A&M University Press, 2000); Camilo Contreras, "Geografía del mercado de trabajo en la cuenca carbonífera de Coahuila," *Frontera Norte* 13, no. Esp (2001); Camilo Contreras and Moisés Gámez, *Procesos y espacios mineros. Fundición en el centro y noreste de México durante el Porfiriato* (Tijuana: El Colegio de la Frontera, 2004); Ma. Teresa Sánchez, "La minería del carbón y su impacto geográfico-económico en el centro-oriente y noreste de Coahuila, México," *Investigaciones Geográficas. Boletín del Instituto de Geografía*, no. 31 (1995): 93–112; Juan Luis Sariego, *Enclaves y minerales en el Norte de México: Historia social de los mineros de Cananea y Nueva Rosita 1900–1970* (México, D. F.: CIESAS – Centro de Investigaciones y Estudios Superiores en Antropología Social, 2010).

domestic consumption and the underlying unity in the history of these energy sources.[4] Between the 1880s and the 1950s, Mexico's consumption of fossil fuels followed an upward trend, moving the country from an energy regime based on solar energy accumulated in plants and human and animal muscle to one based on ancient sunlight concentrated in fossil fuels. This shift to coal, oil, and natural gas became the main agent of environmental, economic, and social change in Mexico from the late nineteenth into the twentieth century. This book shows that the introduction of coal in the 1880s, the adoption of oil in the first half of the twentieth century, and the consumption of natural gas beginning in the 1940s were all part of the same process – Mexico becoming a fossil-fueled society.

Habitual periodizations of modern Mexico include political and social events like the outbreak of the Mexican Revolution in 1910; the 1929 foundation of the PRI party and one-party system that ruled Mexico until 2000; and the nationalization of the oil industry in 1938. From the standpoint of energy and environmental history, however, the 1880s marked the real turning point in Mexico's modern history, when certain industries began using coal as fuel. Analyzing Mexico's history from this perspective underlines a fundamental continuity between people and movements that the historical literature traditionally contrasts. From the 1880s on, many Mexicans – including most members of the elite, some middle sectors, revolutionaries, and post-revolutionary regimes – agreed that fossil fuels represented the country's ticket to modernity and industrial prosperity. (Those who disagreed, like the Huastec indigenous people of northern Veracruz, were ignored or repressed.) The violent political, social, and cultural disputes that characterized twentieth-century Mexico often reflected different views on how the benefits and burdens of a fossil-fueled society should be shared.

An energy-centric approach sheds new light on pivotal events in Mexican history. Inasmuch as scholars have discussed the role of energy sources during the Mexican Revolution, they have largely focused on how revolutionary factions used oil export revenues to fund their military actions and governments.[5] But deeper connections were at play. By the time the 1910 Revolution broke out, Mexico's energy revolution had been underway for over

---

[4] On consumption, there are exceptions. See, for instance, María del Mar Rubio, "Oil and Economy in Mexico, 1900–1930s," *JEL* N5, no. Q33 (2005); Luz María Uthoff, "La industria del petróleo en México, 1911–1938: del auge exportador al abastecimiento del mercado interno. Una aproximación a su estudio," *América Latina en la Historia Económica*, no. 33 (2010): 7–30.

[5] Linda B. Hall and Don M. Coerver, "Oil and the Mexican Revolution: The Southwestern Connection," *The Americas* 41, no. 2 (1984): 229–44; Francis Galan, "There Will Be Blood: Oil, Rebels, and Counterrevolution in the Gulf of Mexico Borderlands, 1900–1920," in *New Frontiers in Latin American Borderlands* (Newcastle upon Tyne: Cambridge Scholars Publishing, 2012), 7–19.

two decades. The wrenching social and economic dislocations that led to the Mexican Revolution were partly driven by fossil-fueled technologies in manufacturing, transport, and mining. During the war, coal and oil fueled the railroads that transported armies and materiel. In turn, the armed conflict shaped the pace and direction of Mexico's energy transition by severely disrupting coal mining while leaving the oil industry virtually intact, accelerating the transition to oil as the country's main source of energy. Take another example: oil's role in the political maneuverings of the country's postrevolutionary regimes.[6] Yes, oil revenues padded the state's coffers and helped solidify government legitimacy. But that is not the only story of oil in twentieth-century Mexico. Fossil fuels directly powered unprecedented industrial and economic growth between 1940 and 1970, the so-called Mexican economic miracle. This epic period of growth dramatically transformed Mexico's society – for better or worse – by the increasing exploitation of fossil fuels. Indeed, the miracle's rapid growth introduced fossil fuels to virtually every aspect of Mexico's society by fostering patterns of urban, population, and economic growth that required ever more energy.

By focusing on energy, the book deliberately downplays certain actors and events typically featured in modern Mexican history, instead directing attention to underexamined figures and moments. Every self-respecting historian writing about oil in Mexico is more or less obligated to examine the Cardenista period (1934–40) and the oil expropriation from US and British oil corporations. This book does neither. From the perspective of Mexico's shift to oil energy, the Cardenista expropriation marked no significant change. Mexico's upward trend of oil consumption preceded the expropriation and continued after it, unabated. One could argue that the expropriation simply made official the fact that Mexico ran on oil. While Cárdenas's vision of a modern, prosperous Mexico may have differed from those of peers and predecessors, he never questioned that oil would power this vision. The book spends little time with these well-examined topics in favor of those previously overlooked, including the expansion of the oil pipeline network, the growth of motor traffic and the road system, and industrial patterns of fossil energy consumption.

Although vast, the historiography on Mexico lacks a systematic account of the role energy sources played in the country's industrialization.[7] Historians have examined in detail the development of specific sectors

---

[6] Jonathan C. Brown and Alan Knight, eds., *The Mexican Petroleum Industry in the Twentieth Century* (Austin: University of Texas Press, 1992).

[7] An overview of the historiography on Mexican industrialization is Aurora Gómez Galvarriato, "Industrialización, empresas y trabajadores industriales, del Porfiriato a la Revolución: La nueva historiografía," *Historia Mexicana* 52, no. 3 (2003): 773–804. For examples of historians of Mexico's

like textiles and steel; regional industrialization; the role of preindustrial artisanal traditions; banking and early manufacturing; the emergence of an industrial working class; the political economy of industrialization; industrialization and economic "backwardness"; and the general history of industry over the centuries.[8] The historiography's lack of a methodical consideration of energy and industrialization is all the more remarkable considering that records show nineteenth- and twentieth-century Mexicans were very concerned with it. Scholars of industrialization elsewhere in the world have written extensively about the critical connection between energy and industry since the nineteenth century.[9] Given that

industrialization who discuss energy, see Edward Beatty, *Technology and the Search for Progress in Modern Mexico* (Berkeley: University of California Press, 2015); Gustavo Garza, *El proceso de industrialización en la ciudad de México, 1821–1970* (México, D. F.: El Colegio de México, Centro de Estudios Demográficos y de Desarrollo Urbano, 1985); Dawn Keremitsis, *The Cotton Textile Industry in Porfiriato, Mexico, 1870–1910* (New York: Garland Publishers, 1987).

[8] The literature on Mexican industrialization is too vast to fully list here. Some prominent examples are: Edward Beatty, *Institutions and Investment: The Political Basis of Industrialization in Mexico before 1911* (Stanford: Stanford University Press, 2001); William E. Cole, *Steel and Economic Growth in Mexico* (Austin: University of Texas Press, 2014); Susan M. Gauss, *Made in Mexico: Regions, Nation, and the State in the Rise of Mexican Industrialism, 1920s-1940s* (University Park: Penn State University Press, 2011); Aurora Gómez Galvarriato, *La industria textil en México* (México, D.F.: Instituto Mora: Colegio de Michoacán: Colegio de México: Instituto de Investigaciones Históricas-UNAM, 1999), and *Industry and Revolution: Social and Economic Change in the Orizaba Valley, Mexico* (Cambridge, Massachusetts: Harvard University Press, 2013); Stephen H. Haber, *Industry and Underdevelopment: The Industrialization of Mexico, 1890–1940* (Stanford: Stanford University Press, 1989); Luis Jáuregui and Ma. Eugenia Romero, eds., *La industria mexicana y su historia: siglos XVIII, XIX, XX* (México, D.F.: Facultad de Economía, Universidad NacionalAutónoma de México, 1997); John Lear, *Workers, Neighbors, and Citizens: The Revolution in Mexico City* (Lincoln: University of Nebraska Press, 2001); Robert A. Potash, *Mexican Government and Industrial Development in the Early Republic: The Banco de Avío* (Amherst: University of Massachusetts Press, 1983); Armando Razo, *Social Foundations of Limited Dictatorship: Networks and Private Protection during Mexico's Early Industrialization* (Stanford: Stanford University Press, 2008); Francisco Rodríguez Garza, *Protoindustrialización, industrialización y desindustrialización en la historia de México* (México, D. F.: Universidad Autónoma Metropolitana, Unidad Azcapotzalco, División de Ciencias Sociales y Humanidades, Coordinación de Difusión y Publicaciones: Ediciones y Gráficos Eón, 2009).

[9] Dolores Greenberg, "Reassessing the Power Patterns of the Industrial Revolution: An Anglo-American Comparison," *The American Historical Review* 87, no. 5 (1982): 1237–61, and "Energy Systems and Social Change," *Science* 220, no. 4603 (1983): 1265; Louis C. Hunter, *A History of Industrial Power in the United States, 1780–1930* (Charlottesville: Published for the Eleutherian Mills-Hagley Foundation by the University Press of Virginia, 1979); William Stanley Jevons, *The Coal Question: an Enquiry Concerning the Progress of the Nation, and the Probable Exhaustion of Our Coal-Mines* (London: Macmillan, 1865); Astrid Kander, Paolo Malanima, and Paul Warde, *Power to the People: Energy in Europe over the Last Five Centuries* (Princeton: Princeton University Press, 2013); Kenneth Pomeranz, *The Great Divergence: China, Europe, and the Making of the Modern World Economy* (Princeton: Princeton University Press, 2000); Rolf Peter Sieferle, *The Subterranean Forest: Energy Systems and the Industrial Revolution* (Cambridge: The White Horse Press, 2001); Theodore Steinberg, *Nature Incorporated: Industrialization and the Waters of New England* (Cambridge: Cambridge University Press, 2003); Edward A. Wrigley, *Energy and the English Industrial Revolution* (Cambridge: Cambridge University Press, 2010);

new forms of power needed to mechanize production were central to industrialization everywhere,[10] the history of Mexico's industrialization warrants detailed appraisal of the energy it exploited. Building on the solid scholarship on Mexico's industrialization, *Fueling Mexico* seeks to provide such an account.

Centering energy in Mexico's industrialization shifts the scale of analysis in novel ways. The energy transitions happened first at the local level, so the story of Mexico's industrialization shifts perspective from the nation-state to subnational regions such as the Valley of Mexico or Monterrey. This regional unit of analysis illuminates the similarities between the trajectories of Mexico's industrializing regions and those in Europe and the USA. It was not Britain, the USA, or Mexico, but London and the Midlands, the Northeast, and Mexico City and the Monterrey area that first adopted fossil fuels for industrial power. A regional focus also challenges narratives that starkly oppose European and US industrial "success" to Mexican or Latin American "failure," which only become convincing at the national level.[11] A regionally based approach makes it easier to examine these transitions on their own terms and understand them as part of a multifaceted global process of industrialization.[12] The Valley of Mexico, along with other *regions* within Mexico and Latin America, was

---

[10] Kenneth Pomeranz defines "industrialization" as the increased use of "energy from sources that never were, or have not recently been, alive (for instance, coal, moving water, electricity and so on, rather than muscle or wood) in manufacturing, transportation, and other parts of life." See "Introduction: What Is 'Industrialization' and What Does It Have to Do with the 'Pacific World'?," in *The Pacific in the Age of Early Industrialization* (Farnham, Surrey; Burlington: Ashgate, 2009), XIII.

[11] Victor Bulmer-Thomas, *The Economic History of Latin America since Independence* (New York: Cambridge University Press, 2014); John H. Coatsworth and Alan M. Taylor, eds., *Latin America and the World Economy since 1800* (Cambridge: Harvard University/David Rockefeller Center for Latin American Studies, 1998); Stephen H. Haber, ed., *How Latin America Fell Behind: Essays on the Economic Histories of Brazil and Mexico, 1800–1914* (Stanford: Stanford University Press, 1997).

[12] Pomeranz identifies two basic paths to industrialization. One was the "North Atlantic path" of Western Europe, the USA, and Canada. Following Kaoru Sugihara's essay "Agriculture and Industrialization: The Japanese Experience," Pomeranz characterizes the North Atlantic path by "exceptionally favorable ratios of land and other resources to population, as well as by the growth of markets and (after about 1750) increasingly rapid technological changes. High labor productivity in both agriculture and industry was partly a result of these ratios and of labor-saving technologies that were selected to exploit them." By contrast, the "East Asian path was different, in part because of very different factor endowments. Labor-absorbing innovations were often critical to raising living standards – for example, double-cropping, breeding silkworms so that they would need maximum attention during the off-season for rice, creating higher-quality cloth through more complex kinds of weaving and so on." Pomeranz suggests that Latin America's path, at least along the Pacific, more closely resembled Southeast Asia, featuring raw material exports, enclave economies, and cheap labor. See Pomeranz, "Introduction: What Is 'Industrialization' and What Does It Have to Do with the 'Pacific World'?," in *The Pacific in the Age of Early Industrialization*, XVII–XXXIV, XLIII–XLVIII.

as much a part of the global industrial revolution as the Midlands, the Ruhr or New England.

Mexico's energy transition to fossil fuels is a story about Mexico, but it is not an exclusively Mexican story. Similar transitions took place elsewhere in the world, including most of Europe, the rest of North America, and parts of Latin America and East Asia. In all cases, industrial growth and its need for vast amounts of cheap energy primarily drove the shift to fossil fuels. Mexico's adoption of fossil fuels followed analogous stages to those abroad, moving from wood and water to coal and then to oil (and natural gas, to a lesser degree). In Mexico, as elsewhere, stages overlapped substantially, with earlier sources of energy coexisting beside new ones. Regional particularities aside, fossil-fueled industrialization worldwide happened roughly over the same period, followed a similar sequence, and was shaped by analogous factors. Energy thus highlights Mexico's connection to the rest of the world as well as the connection between national and global history.

Energy and History

Historians have been trying for several decades to understand how energy sources and transitions shape historical change. Carlo Cipolla's *The Economic History of World Population* was one of the first studies to explicitly frame its narrative from the perspective of energy use.[13] Others, especially US scholars, studied the environmental, social, and economic impact of successive energy sources from the late eighteenth to the late twentieth century, both nationally and in specific cities or regions.[14] The work of Vaclav Smil stands out for its sheer volume, scope, and commitment to interdisciplinarity. Combining insights from energetics, Earth and environmental science, and history, Smil has surveyed the manifold implications of humanity's energy habits in many geographical contexts over the past 40 years.[15]

---

[13] Carlo M. Cipolla, *The Economic History of World Population* (Baltimore: Penguin Books, 1970).

[14] A pioneering US work is Sam H. Schurr et al., *Energy in the American Economy, 1850–1975* (Baltimore: Johns Hopkins, 1960). See also Hunter, *A History of Industrial Power in the United States, 1780–1930*; Martin V. Melosi, *Coping with Abundance: Energy and Environment in Industrial America* (Philadelphia: Temple University Press, 1985); David E. Nye, *Consuming Power: A Social History of American Energies* (Cambridge, Massachusetts: MIT Press, 1999); Harold L. Platt, *The Electric City: Energy and the Growth of the Chicago Area, 1880–1930* (Chicago: University of Chicago Press, 1991); Theodore Steinberg, *Nature Incorporated: Industrialization and the Waters of New England*.

[15] Particularly relevant are Vaclav Smil, *Energy in World History: Essays in World History* (Boulder: Westview Press, 1994), *Enriching the Earth: Fritz Haber, Carl Bosch, and the Transformation of World Food Production* (Cambridge, Massachusetts; London: The MIT Press, 2004), *Energy Transitions:*

Interest in energy history grew rapidly from the 1990s onward, no doubt due to energy's significance to industrial civilization and increased awareness of climate change. Some scholars studied the impact that fuelwood and coal availability had on the timing and development of British and German industrialization.[16] Others explored why parts of western Europe industrialized while regions in Asia with similar levels of economic development did not.[17] Some authors focused on specific fuels or regions, emphasized infrastructure's role in energy transitions, examined energy over the *longue durée*, or explained the shift to fossil energy as a result of capitalist efforts to control labor.[18] Others underlined the role of coal in achieving sustained economic growth during industrialization, previously unattainable under the "organic energy regime."[19]

This connection between fossil energy and modern economic growth has been the focus of a burgeoning literature, only partially written by historians and published within the last two decades.[20] Innovative and often of excellent quality, this work frequently examines the economics of energy transitions, particularly the relationship between increased energy consumption – mostly coal- and-oil-based – and economic growth over time.[21] Such an emphasis has supported the development of sophisticated

History, Requirements, Prospects (Santa Barbara: Praeger, 2010), and *Energy and Civilization: A History* (Cambridge, Massachusetts: The MIT Press, 2017).

[16] Sieferle, *The Subterranean Forest.*   [17] Pomeranz, *The Great Divergence.*

[18] Barbara Freese, *Coal: A Human History* (Cambridge: Perseus, 2003); James C. Williams, *Energy and the Making of Modern California* (Akron: University of Akron Press, 1997); Christopher F. Jones, *Routes of Power: Energy and Modern America* (Cambridge: Harvard University Press, 2014); Jean-Claude Debeir, Jean-Paul Deléage, and Daniel Hémery, *In the Servitude of Power: Energy and Civilisation through the Ages* (London; Atlantic Highlands: Zed Books, 1991); Andreas Malm, *Fossil Capital: The Rise of Steam Power and the Roots of Global Warming* (London; New York: Verso, 2016).

[19] Wrigley, *Energy and the English Industrial Revolution.*

[20] See Kathleen Araújo, "The Emerging Field of Energy Transitions: Progress, Challenges, and Opportunities," *Energy Research & Social Science*, 2014, 112–21; Arnulf Grübler, "Energy Transitions Research: Insights and Cautionary Tales," *Energy Policy* 50 (2012): 8–16; Benjamin Sovacool, "What Are We Doing Here? Analyzing Fifteen Years of Energy Scholarship and Proposing a Social Science Research Agenda," *Energy Research & Social Science* 1 (2014): 1–29; Daniel Spreng, "Transdisciplinary Energy Research-Reflecting the Context," *Energy Research & Social Science* 1 (2014): 65–73.

[21] Robert C. Allen, "Backward into the Future: The Shift to Coal and Implications for the Next Energy Transition," *Energy Policy* 50 (2012): 17–23; Carlo Bardini, "Without Coal in the Age of Steam: A Factor-Endowment Explanation of the Industrial Lag Before World War I," *The Journal of Economic History* 57, no. 3 (1997): 633–53; Mauricio Folchi and Mar Rubio, "El consumo de energía fósil y la especificidad de la transición energética en América Latina, 1900–1930" (III Simposio Latinoamerican y Caribeño de Historia Ambiental, Carmona, 2006); Roger Fouquet, "The Slow Search for Solutions: Lessons from Historical Energy Transitions by Sector and Service," *Energy Policy* 38 (2010): 6586–96; Maria Froeling, "Energy Use, Population and Growth, 1800–1970," *Journal of Popular Economics* 24 (2011): 1133–63; Ben Gales et al., "North versus South: Energy

quantitative historical series on energy production and consumption for individual countries and regions, above all western Europe.[22]

Energy humanities take a different approach to the study of energy.[23] Scholars in this emerging field also emphasize that key elements of modern societies – increasing urbanization, economic growth, and the massive expansion of global trade – were enabled by an equally massive influx of cheap energy from fossil fuels. But they are particularly attentive to how energy regimes mold human social relations and cultural practices that, in turn, shape energy use. Energy humanities frequently critiques energy research that narrowly privileges technical aspects; instead, it emphasizes the role of social structures and cultural practices in shaping energy systems. Energy humanities scholars also tend to call into question the foundations of modern energy systems. They point out that the fossil-fueled growth upon which modern industrial societies depend is unsustainable and inequitable. Taking cues from ecological economists, energy humanists criticize the "growth dogma" and desire for and possibility of endless growth on a finite planet.

Fueling Mexico draws on several insights from this sizable scholarship on energy. The book supports the broad claim that global energy transitions to fossil fuels have been a driving force behind environmental, social, and

---

Transition and Energy Intensity in Europe over 200 Years," *European Review of Economic History* II (2007): 219–53; Iñaki Iriarte-Goñi and María-Isabel Ayuda, "Not Only Subterranean Forests: Wood Consumption and Economic Development in Britain (1850–1938)," *Ecological Economics* 77, no. 77 (2012): 176–84; José Jofré González, "Patrones de consumo aparente de energías modernas en América Latina, 1890–2003" (PhD Dissertation, Universitat de Barcelona, 2012); Kander, Malanima, and Warde, *Power to the People*; Astrid Kander, "Economic Growth and the Transition from Traditional to Modern Energy in Sweden," *CAMA Working Paper*, no. 65 (September 2013): 1–35; Nuno Luis Madureira, "The Iron Industry Energy Transition," *Energy Policy* 50 (2012): 24–34; Paolo Malanima, "Energy Crisis and Growth, 1650–1850: The European Deviation in a Comparative Perspective," *Journal of Global History* I (2006): 101–21, and "Energy in History," in Mauro Agnoletti and Simonee Neri Serneri, eds., *The Basic Environmental History* (New York: Springer, 2014); María del Mar Rubio, et al., "Modern Energy Consumption and Economic Modernization in Latin American and the Caribbean between 1890 and 1925" (Working Paper); Rubio and Mauricio Folchi, "Will Small Energy Consumers Be Faster in Transition? Evidence from the Early Shift from Coal to Oil in Latin America," n.d.; Rubio, "Energía, economía y CO2: España, 1850–2000," *Cuadernos Económicos*, no. 70 (n.d): 52–75; Rubio et al., "Energy as an Indicator of Modernization in Latin America, 1890–1925," *Economic History Review* 63, no. 3 (2010); David Stern and Astrid Kander, "The Role of Energy in the Industrial Revolution and Modern Economic Growth," *The Energy Journal* 33, no. 3 (2012): 125–52; Paul Warde, *Energy Consumption in England & Wales, 1560–2000* (Roma: Consiglio nazionale delle ricerche, Istituto di studi sulle società del Mediterraneo, 2007).

[22] Kander, Malanima, and Warde, *Power to the People*.

[23] Dominic Boyer and Imre Szeman, eds., *Energy Humanities: An Anthology* (Baltimore: Johns Hopkins University Press, 2017).

economic change worldwide in the past century. It also echoes other scholars by carefully considering the political, cultural, social, and economic forces at play in the transition and presenting a multicausal explanation of change over time. In so doing, the book is especially indebted to environmental historians who combine cultural and materialist approaches to the study of the past.[24] *Fueling Mexico*'s focus on the connection between fossil fuels and modern growth – and the latter's long-term unsustainability – reflects the influence of both historians and energy humanities scholars.

Yet the book departs from this literature in various ways. It is the first energy history of a country other than the USA and those of Western Europe, the focus of an overwhelming majority of similar studies. The Mexican case helps us better understand what the fossil fuel transition looked like beyond the so-called global north.[25] It highlights how a country could fully shift to fossil energy while following a distinct industrial path, challenging the notion of a single pattern of energy transition and industrialization based on Europe or the USA. *Fueling Mexico* underlines the role of contingency and human agency in energy transitions, departing from the tendency of some energy scholarship to portray such shifts as mechanical and deterministic. It allows the book to showcase the central role of politics in some energy transitions and demonstrates how profoundly state power shaped the timing and trajectory of Mexico's energy shift. Additionally, *Fueling Mexico* takes a different methodological approach than other studies in energy history. The majority of scholarship on energy transitions has concentrated on national or global patterns of energy consumption, partly because much of it derives data from national government-compiled statistics. By contrast, *Fueling Mexico* bases its account on a variety of archival, published, quantitative, and qualitative sources. It uses those sources to tell the story of Mexico's transition from a regional perspective while firmly situating it within a national, global, and long-term history of energy.

---

[24] On debates about materialist and culturalist perspectives in environmental history, see Isenberg's introductory essay in Andrew C. Isenberg, *The Oxford Handbook of Environmental History*, 2014, 1–20.

[25] This does not mean that Mexico's case illustrates transitions in the "global south." Not only do Mexico and Latin America form part of the "West," but their history differs substantially from that of the "global south." See Marcello Carmagnani, *The Other West: Latin America from Invasion to Globalization* (Berkeley: University of California Press, 2011); Jose C. Moya, "Introduction," in *The Oxford Handbook of Latin American History* (Oxford: Oxford University Press, 2011), 2–24.

Environment and Latin America

Much like Robert Paine's concept of keystone species – those that play an oversized role in a given ecosystem, shaping its structure and the relative abundance of other species – environmental histories have often understood energy as a "keystone" factor whose various manifestations and forms of exploitation lead to significant environmental impacts.[26] This is particularly evident in the discipline's global incarnation. Various global environmental historians place changes in energy use at the fore of their narratives. In his book *Something New under the Sun: An Environmental History of the Twentieth Century* (Norton, 2001), John R. McNeill connected the dramatic environmental changes of the twentieth century to the transition from a "somatic energy regime" to one based on fossil energy.[27] But these global accounts have few archive-based historical monographs on energy to draw from. The handful that exist deal mostly with Europe and the USA, not Latin America, Africa, or Asia. Understanding this critical global dynamic between energy and environmental change will require many fine-grained, archive-based case studies of regions and countries around the world. This book aims to fill the gap.

Studies of energy and transitions also hold promise for a deeper understanding of environmental history. As this book demonstrates, the two are intimately linked, particularly on the subject of fossil fuels. Coal, oil, and natural gas give humans the capacity to radically transform our local and global environments, and many contemporary environmental issues are linked in one way or another to their exploitation. The environmental history of Latin America boasts many remarkable studies of European colonialism, forest conservation, export commodities, plantations, urbanization, water and land reform, and disease, but none on energy transitions.[28] This book examines

[26] R. T. Paine, "A Note on Trophic Complexity and Community Stability," *The American Naturalist* 103, no. 929 (1969): 91–3; L. Scott Mills, Michael E. Soulé, and Daniel F. Doak, "The Keystone-Species Concept in Ecology and Conservation," *BioScience* 43, no. 4 (1993): 219–24.

[27] Other examples: Edmund Burke III, "The Big Story: Human History, Energy Regimes, and the Environment," in *The Environment and World History* (Berkeley: University of California Press, 2009), 33–53; Anthony N. Penna, *The Human Footprint: A Global Environmental History* (Chichester, West Sussex: Wiley-Blackwell, 2014); I. G. Simmons, *Global Environmental History* (Chicago: University of Chicago Press, 2008). Big history frequently uses energy as a narrative framework. See David Christian, *Maps of Time: An Introduction to Big History* (Berkeley: University of California Press, 2004).

[28] A sample of this literature is: Christopher R. Boyer, *Political Landscapes: Forests, Conservation, and Community in Mexico* (Durham: Duke University Press, 2015); Alfred W. Crosby, *The Columbian Exchange: Biological and Cultural Consequences of 1492* (Westport: Greenwood Press, 1972); Reinaldo Funes Monzote, *From Rainforest to Cane Field in Cuba: An Environmental History since 1492* (Chapel

environmental change in a prominent Latin American country from an energy perspective.

Until recently, historians of Mexico and Latin America viewed energy largely as an export commodity, not as an energy source shaping historical change within those societies. This perspective marks much of the vast literature on Mexico's oil industry and other oil-producing countries, like Venezuela. This historiography tends to present Latin America's oil industry as enclaves within their countries of origin, connected to domestic politics and society through export revenues. It has generally shown less interest in how oil consumption molded broader environmental, social, and cultural change within those countries. The scant scholarship on coal almost exclusively examines labor issues. Two exceptions are Myrna I. Santiago, *The Ecology of Oil: Environment, Labor, and the Mexican Revolution, 1900–1938* (Cambridge, 2009) and Miguel Tinker Salas, *The Enduring Legacy: Oil, Culture, and Society in Venezuela* (Duke, 2009). Santiago's book was the first to explore the environmental impact of Mexico's oil industry and connect it to the history of labor and indigenous people. Tinker Salas illustrated how Venezuela's oil industry (American- and British-owned before nationalization in 1976) profoundly transformed its society, culture, and politics. We must now look at how the transition to a fossil fuel energy regime changed the basic design of Latin American countries and radically altered their historical paths. This literature must also consider all fossil fuels together, instead of focusing on individual energy sources like oil and coal. Energy-focused history is particularly suited to showing the complex interaction between environment and society, a key goal of environmental history.

Hill: University of North Carolina Press, 2008); Thomas M. Klubock, *La Frontera: Forests and Ecological Conflict in Chile's Frontier Territory* (Durham: Duke University Press, 2014); Elinor G. K. Melville, *A Plague of Sheep: Environmental Consequences of the Conquest of Mexico* (Cambridge, England; New York: Cambridge University Press, 1994); Shawn W. Miller, *Fruitless Trees: Portuguese Conservation and Brazil's Colonial Timber* (Stanford: Stanford University Press, 2000); John Soluri, *Banana Cultures: Agriculture, Consumption, and Environmental Change in Honduras and the United States* (Austin: University of Texas Press, 2006); Emily Wakild, *Revolutionary Parks: Conservation, Social Justice, and Mexico's National Parks, 1910–1940* (Tucson: University of Arizona Press, 2011); Matthew Vitz, *A City on a Lake: Urban Political Ecology and the Growth of Mexico City* (Durham: Duke University Press, 2018); Mikael D. Wolfe, *Watering the Revolution: An Environmental and Technological History of Agrarian Reform in Mexico* (Durham: Duke University Press, 2017). For an overview of Latin American environmental history: Mark Carey, "Latin American Environmental History: Current Trends, Interdisciplinary Insights, and Future Directions," *Environmental History* 14, no. 2 (2009): 221–52.

Book Organization

The organization of the book reflects its overarching argument that from roughly 1850 to 1950, Mexico moved from an energy regime dominated by the flow of the sun's energy to one mainly powered by fossil fuels.

The chapters in the book follow a chronological sequence, albeit with substantial overlap. This overlap echoes the book's contention that the transition's various stages were characterized by the coexistence of different energy sources. Chapter 1 introduces the basic patterns in mid-nineteenth-century Mexico's energy regime. After a brief overview of Mexico's longer history, it presents a panoramic view of Mexican society in the 1850s and analyzes the relationship between economic activity, environmental conditions, and the country's energy regime, which depended on the annual solar cycle. It sketches the basic contours of Mexico's pre–fossil fuel era, providing a baseline against which the social, economic, and environmental developments examined in subsequent chapters can be gauged.

Chapter 2 tracks the early stages of what I call embedded industrialization based on waterpower and increased use of biomass. After mid-century, certain regions of the country began to mechanize manufacturing and mining with wood-burning steam engines and waterwheels. The state-promoted construction of a vast railroad network in the 1880s further accelerated industrialization. By the late 1880s, embedded industrialization and long-established activities, particularly silver mining, began approaching ecological limits to growth. The most easily accessible forests dwindled at alarming rates and no more rivers could be harnessed for waterpower. Embedded industrialization also faced social constraints: peasant communities clashed with factories and railroads over water and wood. The increased strain on nonfossil energy sources motivated Mexico's state and economic elites to search for new ways to power industry. Due to its prestige and connection to European and US industrialization, coal became the favored alternative.

Chapter 3 examines Mexico's transition to coal between the 1880s and 1910s. State officials, newspapermen, and industrialists viewed coal as crucial to becoming a modern and prosperous nation. Mounting concerns over rampant deforestation from embedded industrialization and railroad expansion prompted Mexican conservationists to promote coal as a way of protecting the nation's forests. In response, the Mexican state surveyed its territory and discovered the largest deposits along the Mexico–USA border. By combining domestic production and imports, Mexico's economy partially shifted to coal. Coal would play the role of "energy bridge" between embedded and oil-based industrialization.

Chapter 4 shows how state power and industrial interests turned oil into Mexico's most important energy source in the first half of the twentieth century. In the 1890s, Mexico imported US crude and refined it domestically to be used as a source of artificial illumination and an industrial lubricant. Reliance on imported oil ended when domestic production on a commercial scale began after 1901. By 1921, Mexico was the second largest oil producer in the world after the USA, representing one-quarter of total global output that year. By the 1930s, Mexico's electricity generation, industries, railroads, and automobiles all relied on oil to various degrees. By mid-century, the majority of energy consumed in Mexico derived from oil and increasing amounts of natural gas (typically mixed with oil in underground deposits).

Chapter 5 tells the story of how, with the full support of the state and amidst a new push to further industrialize, fossil fuels powered virtually every aspect of life in Mexico by the 1950s. Transport systems became increasingly energy intensive. Vehicles with internal combustion engines drove down asphalt roads. Cars reshaped Mexico's culture, class, and gender divisions, and the way people experienced the nation's territory and environments. Mexican cities entered a period of exponential physical and demographic growth, their layouts rapidly reorganized to accommodate increasing numbers of motorized vehicles. Industrial manufacture and electricity generation used fossil fuels at virtually every stage of production and distribution, while the Mexican food system underwent a Green Revolution featuring fossil-fueled agriculture.

The conclusion compares the Mexican case with energy transitions to fossil energy throughout the world. It also looks at the transition's contradictory effects on Mexico. While Mexico became a middle-income country with a fairly diversified industrial base, the transition set Mexico on a path of dependency on nonrenewable energy, uncontrollable urban growth, and accelerated environmental change. I suggest that a historical perspective on Mexico's energy transition provides valuable insights into current issues; as we try to imagine the feasibility of building a post–fossil fuel world, we may find it useful to revisit the factors that came together to get countries like Mexico to where they are today.

CHAPTER I

1850s: Solar Society

The energy of the universe is constant.
Rudolf Clausius, *The Mechanical Theory of Heat,* 1867

From the small villages that domesticated maize, beans, and squash some 7,000 years ago, to the Aztec empire of 1500, to the colonial possession that declared independence from the Spanish crown in 1821, the region we now call Mexico has sustained many human societies. Some lived off hunting and the collection of plants, nuts, and roots for centuries, perhaps millennia, and continued doing so into the mid-nineteenth century. Others built large cities featuring massive structures and long, straight thoroughfares. A few organized some of the world's first capitalist economies, mining vast amounts of silver that shaped global trade. The majority organized themselves in small rural communities that cultivated maize, beans, and squash, the trinity of Mesoamerican staples. But regardless of when, where, or how these societies lived, all subsisted within the energy constraints of the sun's cycles and rhythms – the solar energy regime. Such was the case for every human society until the emergence of coal as the basis of eighteenth-century British life.

Like their predecessors, the diverse populations that made up Mexican society in the mid-nineteenth century depended on the flow of light energy from the sun to produce food to feed animals and humans – the sources of all labor and transport. Sunlight set the hydrological cycle that regulated running water for irrigation and waterwheels. Life in 1850s Mexico was characterized by almost complete dependence on local environmental conditions. Even in the richest ecosystems, energy was scarce, so growth was exceptional and reduced to brief spurts.[1] The prohibitive energetics of

---

[1] Historians tend to project rapid economic growth – characteristic of industrial societies often considered "natural" – backwards into the past, asking why growth didn't happen in past societies, instead of asking why growth happened at all. See E. A. Wrigley, *Energy and the English Industrial Revolution* (Cambridge: Cambridge University Press, 2010), chapter 1.

transportation meant that little more than luxury items or low-bulk valuable items like silver could be carried overland beyond a few dozen kilometers. Overusing any given local resource faced relatively quick penalization. Overexploitation of forests for the increased production of iron could only be sustained for a short period before wood scarcity set in. By land, wood could only be transported over 30 or so kilometers before costs became exorbitant (with the exception of all-important fuelwood, for which mines often paid handsomely). Even if forests were abundant beyond that boundary, communities still experienced wood scarcity.

But things were beginning to change. The limits of the old energy regime were expanding through a combination of increased waterpower and the introduction of steam power. Until the advent of the steam engine in eighteenth-century Britain, the only way humans could put to work the solar energy stored in plants was through biological converters (animals and people). When Mexico's mining companies and factories introduced steam power to their operations, wood became a fuel to generate work for the first time.[2] Nevertheless, the mid-nineteenth century marks a transitional moment in Mexican history. If we were to take a snapshot of this moment, the constraints of the solar energy regime still shaped every aspect of society. Yet new ways of extracting and transforming energy were spreading, setting in motion a series of developments that would transform Mexican society over the following decades. During the 1850s, Mexico existed on the boundary between two ages.

To understand this critical moment, the chapter presents a panoramic view of mid-nineteenth-century Mexico. It emphasizes the material and environmental conditions across the country, paying particular attention to energy use. The chapter analyzes the relationship between economic and political institutions, cultural practices, and the country's solar energy regime. Through this snapshot, the chapter seeks to sketch the basic contours of Mexico's pre–fossil fuel era, providing a baseline against which the energy, social, economic, and environmental changes and continuities examined in subsequent chapters can be easily assessed.

The Basics

Before turning to our story, however, a word on key concepts used throughout this chapter. The notion of energy is frequently discussed

---

[2] That said, steam engines were scarcely employed in the 1850s, which limited their impact on production.

throughout this chapter – indeed, throughout this entire book. What is energy exactly? It is best thought of as a flow. Through thermonuclear reactions, the sun radiates thermal energy that plants (autotrophs or primary converters) transform into chemical energy, building the basis of most life processes on our planet.[3] Other organisms such as animals (heterotrophs or secondary converters) consume plants or other animals and transform chemical energy into life-sustaining heat. A small percentage of this energy is converted into mechanical energy, or work. Solar radiation also drives the hydrological cycle of evaporation, condensation, precipitation, and runoff. The sun heats surface ocean water until it evaporates, rising into the atmosphere as water vapor. At certain heights, the moist air cools and loses its capacity to retain water vapor, which initiates the condensation process. Clouds form and are transported by wind currents around the globe, where they return water to the surface as precipitation. Water on the ground can either return to the atmosphere as transpiration, empty as runoff into lakes, rivers, and oceans, or seep into the earth as groundwater. Finally, the sun's uneven heating of the earth causes air to move, creating wind. During daytime, the air heats faster over land than over water. Warm air expands and rises, leaving cooler ocean air rushing inland in its place. At night, this process reverses, as air over land cools faster. Chemical energy, the hydrological cycle, and wind currents were all components of the solar energy regime under which Mexican society operated well into the nineteenth century.

Another important aspect of solar radiation is what ecologists call the net primary productivity of ecosystems.[4] Every organism uses energy to grow and reproduce. Plants, the basis of both terrestrial and maritime ecosystems, use energy in biomass production, growth, and reproduction. They capture a mere 0.1 percent of light that reaches the earth, converting it into plant tissue and chemical energy.[5] The net primary productivity (NPP) is the energy that remains after these processes and is stored as organic matter. NPP in Mexico is highly variable, but it averages 3 tons per hectare

---

[3] Thermonuclear reactions at the sun's core fuse hydrogen atoms into heavier helium atoms, releasing lost mass into space as radiant energy. On general energetics, see Howard T. Odum and Elisabeth C. Odum, *Energy Basis for Man and Nature* (New York: McGraw-Hill, 1976).

[4] David Pimentel and Marcia H. Pimentel, *Food, Energy, and Society* (Boca Raton: CRC Press, 2007), 4–20.

[5] Solar irradiation varies globally. Mexico receives a daily average of 5 kWh/m², double that of Germany and similar to some regions in Africa, the Andes, and Oceania. Within Mexico, the arid northwest has the highest solar insolation, while the central highlands and the tropical lowlands of the southeast receive less. See Sergio Romero, et al., "Energy in Mexico: Policy and Technologies for a Sustainable Future" (México, D. F.: USAID; Wilson Center, Mexico institute; ITAM, 2013).

annually. Given the country's total territory of 197,255,000 hectares, Mexico's entire vegetative cover produces some 591,765,000 tons annually. Assuming 4,200 kcal per kg of biomass, all of Mexico's ecosystems thus produce 2,485,413,000,000,000 kcal per year. This *annual energy flow* represented the theoretical limit of energy available to mid-nineteenth-century Mexican society.

Of course, human beings had to share this flow with countless other animals and could tap into only a fraction of it. Agriculture represented the basic way to appropriate some of this flow. Like every other farming system around the world, mid-nineteenth-century Mexican agriculture sought to control and harvest as much incoming solar energy as possible for human needs. It concentrated solar energy in crops to sustain human and animal labor, which performed a wide variety of tasks: making shoes in small workshops; extracting ore from deep shafts in industrial-scale mining operations; and building towns and cities and the roads connecting them.

All of these basic processes lay at the heart of Mexico's mid-nineteenth-century energy system. Scholars refer to this energy system as the solar energy regime, the biological *ancién regime*, the somatic energy regime, or the organic energy regime. All four terms are useful but emphasize different aspects of energy use. The terms "biological" and "organic" underline the importance of organic components like plants and animals for the societies that depended on them. That said, they implicitly suggest that the fossil fuel energy regime under which we currently live is not organic. This is misleading: both coal and oil derive from fossilized vegetable matter,[6] which is organic. The term "somatic" draws attention to human and animal muscle's capacity to do work but overlooks the importance of hydraulic and eolic (wind) power to some societies living under this regime. The term "solar" avoids both problems and reminds the reader of the non–fossil fuel basis of these societies.[7] As such, I will use the concept of "solar energy regime" moving forward.[8]

Mexico's solar energy system had specific ecological and technological characteristics. By far the most important energy source was food, a form of

---

[6] Oil is also derived from zooplankton.

[7] Of course, all energy sources, including fossil fuels, ultimately derive from sunlight.

[8] Edmund Burke III, "The Big Story: Human History, Energy Regimes, and the Environment," in *The Environment and World History* (Berkeley: University of California Press, 2009), 33–53; John R. McNeill, *Something New under the Sun: An Environmental History of the Twentieth-Century World* (New York: W.W. Norton & Company, 2001); Rolf Peter Sieferle, *The Subterranean Forest: Energy Systems and the Industrial Revolution* (Cambridge: The White Horse Press, 2001); Vaclav Smil, *Energy in World History. Essays in World History* (Boulder: Westview Press, 1994); Wrigley, *Energy and the English Industrial Revolution*.

chemical energy that humans and animals converted and transformed into Mexico's main source of mechanical power: muscle. Another source of energy was water, transformed by nonbiological converters like the water-wheel into mechanical energy that moved mills, spindles, and so on. Wind went to work at sea, moving sail ships along Mexico's coasts. Wood was the main source of heat energy, although dung and cornstalks substituted in some wood-scarce regions.[9] A small number of steam engines burned wood and small amounts of imported coal in mines and textile factories (and one or two ships), but they represented a marginal percentage of Mexico's overall energy output.

The Longer History

Mexico's history, of course, did not begin in 1850. Timeframes and period-izations are contested historical constructs. Still, historians have to start their stories somewhere. While this chapter offers a snapshot of the country in the mid-nineteenth century, this picture must be historically context-ualized to avoid misleading. A succinct overview of the fundamental ecological transformations that marked New Spain after 1500 and Mexico before 1850 will ensure that.

In the early sixteenth century, what is today Mexico encompassed three distinct regions: the north populated by hunter-gatherers and a few cultiva-tors; the tropical lowlands dominated by slash-and-burn farmers; and the Mesoamerican highlands with a maize-based civilization of family producers and large polities. While all indigenous societies shaped their environments, the latter inhabited a "sculptured landscape," none more so than in the Valley of Mexico, where there were large urban centers with whitewashed walls like Texcoco. The surrounding countryside was dotted with villages and heavily cultivated with maize fields (*milpas*), some of them flanked by rows of maguey plants to protect from wind and soil erosion. In the middle were five interconnected lakes. The two lakes furthest north (Zumpango and Xaltocan) and the two in the south (Chalco and Xochimilco) were fresh-water lakes located at a slightly higher elevation that drained into the saline waters of Lake Texcoco. Crisscrossing the lakes, a series of structures both connected and divided them. There were dikes that regulated the water level of the lakes and prevented flooding as well as keeping Lake Texcoco's more

---

[9] William W. Carpenter, *Travels and Adventures in Mexico: In the Course of Journeys of Upward of 2500 Miles, Performed on Foot; Giving an Account of the Manners and Customs of the People, and the Agricultural and Mineral Resources of That Country* (New York: Harper & Brothers, Publishers, 1851), 147.

saline eastern waters from mixing with its less brackish western waters, known as the lake of Mexico. There were also long, wide causeways linking all the main population centers with the largest urban conglomeration in the valley, Tenochtitlan. Located on an artificially expanded island on the western fringe of Lake Texcoco with a population of about 200,000, Tenochtitlan was one of the largest cities in the world. The valley in which it sat was one of the most humanized landscapes in the Americas. It had been so for centuries, if not millennia.[10]

European arrival initiated a process of incalculable consequences for the whole of the western hemisphere: the Columbian Exchange. Two halves of the world separated since the land bridge of Beringia that had been submerged by the North Pacific sometime in the tenth millennium BCE came together on October 12, 1492. The exchange was an unequal affair. The influx of organisms from east to west was far larger than that from west to east, with Europeans bringing domesticated animals (horses, cattle, goats, pigs, and sheep), plants (wheat, rye, barley, oranges, sugarcane, and coffee, among others), and, most ominously, pathogens (smallpox, influenza, chickenpox, measles, and whooping cough). The flow from west to east included maize, potatoes, tomatoes, beans, squash, tobacco, pea-nuts, cassava, pineapple, peppers, and cotton. American plants would change the world, but among the animals domesticated in the Americas, only the turkey became important elsewhere.[11]

Eurasian animal domesticates had no equivalent in the Americas. Although key species for the trajectory of human history such as horses and camels originally evolved in the Americas, they became extinct by the end of the last Ice Age, around 11,000 BC, along with some 70 percent of all large mammals. This megafauna extinction likely resulted from human predation and climate change. When these large animals disappeared, the indigenous population lost a number of potential domesticates, with important long-term consequences for different aspects of their civilizations, including the dominance of human muscle, food production, and warfare.[12]

---

[10] The term "sculptured landscape" comes from T. M. Whitmore and B.L. Turner, *Cultivated Landscapes of Middle America on the Eve of Conquest* (Oxford; New York: Oxford University Press, 2001), 2. A masterful description of the Valley of Mexico during early Spanish rule is Charles Gibson, *The Aztecs under Spanish Rule; a History of the Indians of the Valley of Mexico, 1519–1810* (Stanford: Stanford University Press, 1964), chapter 1.

[11] The key work on the Columbian Exchange is, of course, Alfred Crosby, *The Columbian Exchange: Biological and Cultural Consequences of 1492* (Westport: Greenwood Press, 1972).

[12] See Paul S. Martin, "Pleistocene Overkill," *Natural History* 76, no. 10 (1967): 32–8. On the consequences of the megafauna extinctions for the indigenous population of the Americas, see Jared M. Diamond's controversial work *Guns, Germs, and Steel: The Fates of Human Societies*

While, early on, domesticated animals numbered no more than a few horses, cattle, pigs, sheep, and goats, within decades their populations exploded into thousands of semi-feral roaming animals. It has been argued that Spaniards prevented animal populations, sheep in particular, from reestablishing a sustainable population in parts of central Mexico after their numbers crashed by artificially overstocking the region. This led to permanent degradation of landscapes, like those of the Valle del Mezquital, which was transformed within a century from a rich agricultural land into an impoverished and arid region of scrub vegetation. Other scholars have criticized this analysis for using a single factor (overgrazing) to explain a highly complex process like land degradation. There is evidence, too, that suggests Spaniards were aware of the danger of overgrazing and took steps to mitigate it, particularly through transhumance. Terrace abandonment due to native demographic collapse has also been signaled as an important cause behind massive soil erosion in places like the Valle del Mezquital. Climate change, specifically the relatively cool and dry period known as the Little Ice Age (roughly from 1400 to 1800), may have played an important role in the environmental changes attributed to the "plague" of sheep. In any case, there is little doubt that the introduction of livestock into the Americas and into what is today Mexico deeply shaped the landscape.[13]

While the prehistoric extinction of the megafauna and the sixteenth-century introduction of Eurasian domesticates had great environmental impacts on the Americas, the arrival of Europeans and their diseases caused perhaps the largest demographic collapse in recorded history. Wave after wave of epidemic outbreaks of smallpox, measles, mumps, influenza, and other diseases decimated native populations, whose almost complete isolation from the Old World for millennia left them without immunity and highly vulnerable to these diseases. Moreover, most human diseases were of

---

(New York: W.W. Norton & Co., 1998), part 1. An important exception to megafauna extinctions across the Americas is the camelids of South America; the llama and the alpaca became important domesticates in pre-Columbian Andean civilizations.

[13] On the impact of livestock in central Mexico, see Elinor G. K. Melville, *A Plague of Sheep: Environmental Consequences of the Conquest of Mexico* (Cambridge: Cambridge University Press, 1994). For an opposing view, see Karl W. Butzer and Elisabeth K. Butzer, "The Natural Vegetation of the Mexican Bajío: Archival Documentation of a 16th-Century Savanna Environment," *Quaternary International* 43144 (1997): 161–72. For a detailed review of the Melville–Butzer debate, see Richard William Hunter, *People, Sheep, and Landscape Change in Colonial Mexico the Sixteenth-Century Transformation of the Valle del Mezquital* (Baton Rouge: Louisiana State University, 2009), chapter 1. A colonial account of the demographic explosion among introduced herbivores is José de Acosta, *Historia natural y moral de las Indias, en que se tratan de las cosas notables del cielo, y elementos, metales, plantas y animales dellas: y los ritos, y ceremonias, leyes y gobierno, y guerras de los indios* (México: Fondo de Cultura Económica, 1962), libro 4, capítulo XXXIII.

zoonotic origin (animal-borne), derived from the close contact between humans and domesticated animals. Native Americans arrived in the Americas before any large animal had been domesticated, with the exception of the dog, and thus received little exposure to zoonotic diseases prior to the Columbian Exchange. In addition, the ancestors of the indigenous populations had crossed Beringia when climatic conditions were very cold, which killed off most pathogens. In all, between 1492 and 1650 perhaps as many as 90 percent of the indigenous population in parts of the New World succumbed to disease. For example, the population of the Basin of Mexico – which included the valley of the same name plus adjacent areas – declined from 1–1.2 million in 1519 to only about 100,000 people in 1650. Only in the twentieth century did the local human population again reach the one-million watermark.[14]

Human depopulation changed everything. In a society overwhelmingly dependent on human labor, muscle power became scarce. A rapidly declining indigenous population in the tropical lowlands was replaced by enslaved Africans. In the Mesoamerican highlands, Spanish authorities concentrated, with the mediation of local elites, the remaining indigenous population in landed republics. Dwindling numbers made it impossible to maintain large infrastructure works like the complex hydraulic system in the lakes of the Valley of Mexico, leading to recurrent flooding and centuries-long drainage projects. Labor-intensive *chinampas* declined in number and area. On the other hand, demographic collapse made land plentiful. Radical changes ensued. Villages became self-sufficient and enjoyed a large degree of political and cultural autonomy, although many partook in the commercial economy as seasonal laborers for cash wages (necessary for maintaining ritual life and paying taxes). Old World fruits and livestock increased the chemical energy at their disposal. Provisioned by large estates devoted to commercial crops like wheat, urban centers became manufacturing and financial centers and seats of political and judicial power mediating social conflict. Native and mixed-race migrants, vast herds of livestock (cattle, sheep, and horses), and some

---

[14] A classic analysis of indigenous demographic collapse in central Mexico is Sherburne Friend Cook and Woodrow Wilson Borah, *The Indian Population of Central Mexico, 1531–1610* (Berkeley: University of California Press, 1960). See also Rebecca Storey, "Population Decline during and after Conquest," in Deborah L. Nichols, ed., *The Oxford Handbook of Mesoamerican Archaeology* (Oxford; New York: Oxford University Press, 2012). By comparison, one of the other great demographic cataclysms in human history, the Black Plague, had an average mortality rate of "only" around 50 percent. See John Aberth, *The Black Death: The Great Mortality of 1348–1350: A Brief History with Documents* (Bedford/St. Martin's: Palgrave Macmillan, 2005), 3.

Europeans pushed the frontier north of Mesoamerica into the vast arid plateau.[15]

These newcomers built a highly commercialized economy organized around the extraction and export of silver in the Bajío and the far north. Chinese demand and an emerging global trade increasingly dominated by Europeans drove silver mining across this vast region. Urban centers like Querétaro provided mines with textiles and manufactures crafted in their many *obrajes*, workshops, and, in the eighteenth century, huge factories (tobacco, for example). Cash wages were the norm. Large haciendas and ranchos supplied the silver economy with leather products, tallow, fuel-wood, and animals as muscle power to move complex machinery and winches. It was one of the earliest capitalist societies anywhere, whose main product, silver, profoundly influenced the early modern world.[16]

By 1800, these two core areas of New Spain, the central highlands and the Bajío-North, were among the richest in the Americas. They were also highly urbanized and featured several important cities, including Mexico City. The largest in the western hemisphere at the time, Mexico City was the financial and trade center linking the north's mining economy with the world of relatively autonomous peasant communities, commercial estates, and *chinampa* agriculture in the central highlands. Sustained by the enormous flow of silver and connected to global circuits of trade, this urban, commercial world came crashing down in the second decade of the nineteenth century when an explosive mix of population growth, overexploitation, and a political vacuum created by Napoleon's invasion of Spain erupted in a devastating war and popular insurgency. The country became independent in 1821.[17]

The postindependence decades saw a number of conflictive changes. Silver production fell by half and only began to recover in the 1840s.[18] The commercial economy suffered, especially mines and large estates, but not communities that depended mostly on subsistence farming, which enjoyed renewed autonomy and abundant harvests.[19] Exports and trade declined,

---

[15] This analysis is based on personal communication with John Tutino. For a detailed account of the changes described here, see John Tutino, *The Mexican Heartland: How Communities Shaped Capitalism, a Nation, and World History, 1500–2000* (Princeton: Princeton University Press, 2018), chapters 1 and 2.

[16] See John Tutino, *Making a New World: Founding Capitalism in the Bajío and Spanish North America* (Durham: Duke University Press, 2011), part 1.

[17] Tutino, *The Mexican Heartland*, chapters 4 and 5.

[18] Enrique Cárdenas, "A Macroeconomic Interpretation of Nineteenth-Century Mexico," in Stephen Haber, ed., *How Latin America Fell Behind: Essays on the Economic Histories of Brazil and Mexico, 1800–1914* (Stanford: Stanford University Press, 1997), 65–92.

[19] Tutino, *The Mexican Heartland*, chapters 6 and 7.

hurting fiscal revenues and leading to recurrent rounds of loan acquisitions, crippling debt, defaults, and political instability. Some cities, like Querétaro, lost population. Others, like Mexico City, generally maintained the level of urbanization that had existed under Spanish rule. Importantly, Mexico's textile sector began mechanizing in the 1830s – one of the earliest in the world to do so – and continued growing throughout the century and beyond.[20] In 1846, war broke out between Mexico and an expanding USA, with disastrous results for Mexico. The country lost its vast northern territories, which contained enormous agricultural, mineral, forest, and, crucially, coal and oil resources, all of which would play a central role in the rise of the USA as an industrial power by the last quarter of the nineteenth century. In essence, the war transferred huge energy resources from Mexico to the USA, with long-term implications for both countries and the world.[21]

The Mexico of the 1850s emerged from these changes. On the one hand, the country's elites kept developing a mechanized textile industry as they continued the search for alternatives to the silver economy of the past. On the other, Mexico was a more agrarian, less commercial, less dynamic nation than its 1800 predecessor. Food production was both the main occupation of the vast majority of the population and its main energy source.

Food Energy

In the mid-nineteenth century, over ninety percent of Mexicans farmed.[22] Most of this population were subsistence farmers who depended on human and animal muscle and weather patterns to produce food. These farmers consumed the majority of their produce, selling the rest in town and city markets. Commercial farming units included ranchos and haciendas,

---

[20] Armando Razo and Stephen Haber, "The Rate of Growth of Productivity in Mexico, 1850–1933: Evidence from the Cotton Textile Industry," *Journal of Latin American Studies* 30, no. 3 (1998): 481–517.

[21] I thank John Tutino for this insight. A recent account of the war is Peter Guardino, *The Dead March: A History of the Mexican-American War* (Cambridge: Harvard University Press, 2017).

[22] Jesús Hermosa, *Manual de geografía y estadística de la república mejicana* (Paris: Librería de Rosa y Bouret, 1859), 83. Mexico's total population was estimated at 8,396,524 in 1861. See José María Pérez Hernández, *Estadística de la república mejicana. Territorio, población, antigüedades, monumentos, establecimientos públicos, reino vegetal y agricultura, reino animal, reino mineral, industria fabril y manufacturera, artes mecánicas y liberales, comercio, navegacion, gobierno, hacienda y crédito público, ejército, marina, clero, justicia, instruccion pública, colonias militares y civiles* (Guadalajara: Tipografía del Gobierno, 1862), 65.

which sold most of what they produced to mines, towns, and cities. In 1850, Mexico had some 14,500 ranchos and about 3,400 haciendas.[23]

Food production varied substantially by location. At the time, observers identified three broad agroecological and climatic regions within Mexico's territory.[24] First was the "hot country" (*tierra caliente*). This region encompassed the tropical lowlands along the Gulf of Mexico, the Pacific coast, and the Yucatan Peninsula. Some interior areas with a hot but dry climate, like the Tierra Caliente of Michoacán, also fit the label. In parts of these tropical lowlands, such as Yucatán, peasants practiced shifting agriculture, an itinerant form of farming that involved using the same plot of land for several years, then opening up a new patch in the forest once the former was exhausted.

The system was relatively straightforward. First, peasants cut down the forest in the middle of the dry season in January and February.[25] Forest cutting in Mexico's lowlands was energy intensive, representing about one-third of the work involved in shifting agriculture. Peasants then let the vegetation dry out until the end of the dry season (April–May) before burning it. The ashes fertilized the thin and nutrient-poor tropical soil. At the beginning of the rainy season (May–June) farmers planted maize, beans, squash, and sweet potatoes using a wooden planting stick (*coa*).[26] A first maize harvest took place in November and a second in February.

Field size was normally limited to 3 to 5 hectares, since the extreme thinness of the soils made plowing impossible, and cultivation depended entirely on human muscle. Productivity was relatively high for the first 2 or 3 years – about 1 metric ton per hectare – but typically declined by half after only 2 years, when another patch had to be cleared. The entire cycle took about 15 years to complete, at which point the farmer returned to the original plot, now covered in secondary-growth forest.

Although yields were low compared with more intensive forms of food production like irrigated agriculture or the *chinampa* system, the energy returns for shifting agriculture – the ratio of energy output (crops) to energy input (labor) – were probably high. Recent estimates for shifting cultivators in Amazonia indicate a ratio of 13.9, similar to that of wet rice

[23] Pérez Hernández, *Estadística de la República Mejicana*, 52–3.
[24] A classic description is Alexander von Humboldt, *Ensayo político sobre el reino de la Nueva España*, 4 vols. (Paris: Casa de Rosa, Gran Patio del Palacio Real, 1822), vol. 1, 70–6.
[25] The description of shifting cultivation and all figures used for my estimates are taken from José M. Regil and Alonso M. Peón, "Estadística de Yucatán," *Boletín de la Sociedad Mexicana de Geografía y Estadística* 3 (1853): 237–336. While men did most planting and crop maintenance, forest cutting involved the entire family, including children and sometimes neighbors.
[26] The *coa*'s point was often hardened with fire and, when available, tipped with iron.

cultivation in the Philippines.[27] This type of farming, however, typically supported very low population densities; areas characterized by this form of food production were among the most sparsely populated in Mexico.[28] Shifting cultivation could only feed a limited number of nonproducers, or city residents. Mérida, then the largest city in Mexico's entire tropical lowlands, had a mere 25,000 inhabitants. Yucatec farmers were frequently unable to feed the area's population, forcing the state to import grain from across Mexico or abroad.[29] Shifting cultivation also required large territories. While Yucatec farmers cultivated some 3,400 km² annually, the whole cycle required 51,000 km² or almost 40 percent of the state's territory. It is unsurprising that the encroachment of commercial agriculture on seemingly empty forest could easily threaten peasant livelihoods and prompt a violent reaction.[30] Furthermore, scarce population in agrarian societies was historically associated with forced labor. Mid-nineteenth-century Yucatán is a good example of this.[31] From an energy perspective, Yucatán's infamous coercive labor systems can be considered attempts to secure and control a crucial source of mechanical energy: human bodies.

While the transition between *tierra caliente* and *tierra templada* was fairly obvious to observers and travelers, the difference between *tierra templada* and *fría* was subtler and more arbitrary.[32] Combined, these two

---

[27] Tropical farmers worldwide practiced versions of shifting cultivation. There is debate about the system's energy efficiency. Anthropologists tend to portray it as an energy-efficient form of producing food with high energy returns. Some critics point out that when one considers the energy contribution of burned biomass, the system's overall efficiency declines. See David G. McGrath, "The Role of Biomass in Shifting Cultivation," *Human Ecology* 15, no. 2 (1987): 221–42.

[28] 1850s Yucatan, which included the present-day states of Yucatán, Quintana Roo, and Campeche, had 600,000 inhabitants and a population density of about 5 persons per square kilometer. See Regil and Peón, "Estadística de Yucatán." On population density for shifting cultivators, see Vaclav Smil, "World History and Energy," in *Encyclopedia of Energy* (Amsterdam; Boston: Elsevier, 2004).

[29] Mérida's status as a quasi-port city meant it could access food beyond its hinterland when shipping it by sea.

[30] See Gilbert Joseph, "From Caste War to Class War: The Historiography of Modern Yucatán (c. 1750–1940)," *Hispanic American Historical Review* 65, no. 2 (1985): 111–34.

[31] Yucatec elites thought as much. See Regil and Peón, "Estadística de Yucatán."

[32] "Temperate country" for mid-nineteenth-century Mexicans could refer to Jalapa, a town nestled in the eastern Sierra Madre at 1,300 masl (meters above sea level), with luxuriant vegetation and forests, an average annual temperature of 18 Celsius, and rainfall of 1,600 mm annually. It could also refer to Saltillo, located in the semi-arid central plateau between the eastern and western Sierra Madres at 1,600 masl, with an average annual temperature of 19 Celsius and averaging 500 mm of rainfall annually. In practice, most land within a range of 1,000 to 2,000 masl was considered "temperate," although places at lower elevations, like Monterrey (540 masl), could also fall under this category, and regions above the upper limit, like the Valley of Mexico, were included, too. The belt of land above 2,500 masl and up to the edge of the tree line was the cold region. Thus, the temperate and cold areas encompassed the massive parallel Sierra Madres running through Mexico from north to south, the volcanic range crisscrossing them in an east–northwest direction to form the central highlands, and the semi-arid plateau extending north of the latter to the US border.

geographics made up two-thirds of the country, included the most productive agricultural lands, and supported the largest populations.[33]
Particularly fertile were the valleys of the central highlands and the area
to the north, known as the Bajío. While the Bajío only came under
cultivation during Spanish rule using animals and European irrigation
technologies, the intermontane central valleys had produced most of the
food in what is now Mexico since pre-Columbian times. These places
concentrated most of mid-nineteenth-century Mexico's energy in the form
of food and human and animal biological converters.[34] Agriculture in the
state of Querétaro and the Valley of Mexico illustrates how systems of food
production worked in the Bajío and the central highlands.

In 1850, Querétaro was one of Mexico's wealthiest states.[35] It enjoyed
a relatively robust system of food production reliant on human muscle,
many draft animals, and even water-powered machinery. With 180,000
people living in one of the smallest territories in the country, Querétaro's
population density was three times that of Yucatan. About 70 percent of
the state was under exploitation. Land ownership primarily consisted of
haciendas and ranchos, which controlled 39 percent of the territory, while
pueblos owned a mere 2 percent.[36] The overwhelming majority of farmers
practiced rain-fed agriculture.[37] Less than half of 1 percent of land was
irrigated, mostly belonging to haciendas. Tens of thousands of oxen,
horses, mules, and donkeys pastured on roughly 30 percent of the state's
land.[38] These animals moved winches (*malacates*) in mines, pulled plows in

---

[33] Five states – Guanajuato, Jalisco, México, Puebla, Querétaro, plus the Valley of Mexico – concentrated 45 percent of the country's population. See Pérez Hernández, *Estadística de la República
Mejicana*, 63.

[34] Environmental boundaries were determined by technology, population level, social organization,
forms of resource use, and other factors. The flexibility of these boundaries is attested by the much
larger and denser populations of pre-Columbian societies in the central highlands of Mexico on the
eve of the Spanish invasion.

[35] "Notas estadísticas del Departamento de Querétaro," *Boletín de la Sociedad Mexicana de Geografía
y Estadística* 3 (1852): 169–236. This source calculated the state's area at 856 square leagues or
15,180 km^2 (the present-day estimate is 11,699 km^2). My estimations of agricultural productivity
and energy flows rely on these figures and are therefore mere approximations.

[36] The state had 124 haciendas and 398 ranchos at the time, but over the next two decades experienced
a process of land concentration by haciendas and a decline in the number of ranchos. See
Marta García, *Querétaro: historia breve* (México, D. F.: FCE, 2010), 203–6.

[37] Catalina Rodríguez and Beatriz Scharrer, "La agricultura en el siglo XIX," in *La agricultura en tierras
mexicanas desde sus orígenes hasta nuestros días* (México, D. F.: Conaculta, 1991), 217–54.
Simon Miller, "The Mexican Hacienda between the Insurgency and the Revolution: Maize
Production and Commercial Triumph on the Temporal," *Journal of Latin American Studies* 16,
no. 2 (1984): 309–36.

[38] It is unclear how grazing land was distributed, but it's safe to assume haciendas and ranchos
controlled much of it.

fields, and carried loads on roads. Draft animals in mid-nineteenth-century Querétaro produced the energy output of 270,000 men.[39] They were so important that a "hacienda or rancho without pastureland [was] considered of little value."[40] The period's ratio of farmed land to pasture in Querétaro reveals one major energy constraint all agrarian societies faced: more land allotted to raising draft and burden animals meant less land for feeding human beings. In turn, feeding animals and human beings directly threatened woodlands, the main source of heat energy. In other words, if one wanted more wood to, say, increase iron production, it was at the expense of growing food to feed humans and animals. One simply could not augment all forms of energy simultaneously. For an agrarian society such as mid-nineteenth-century Querétaro, "the problem of energy utilization was one of alternative land uses."[41]

Querétaro farmers developed ingenious strategies for expanding the number of farm animals without expanding the amount of land under cultivation. Much like their European counterparts, Querétaro farmers grazed animals in the forest for half of the year, effectively making forest ecosystems "subsidize" human husbandry. During the rainy-summer season, livestock was brought to forested areas to feed on plants like *quelite* and *romerillo*.[42] During the dry-winter season, livestock depended on a mix of cultivated and wild crops like clover (*trébol*), wild oats, nopal cactus, mesquite, and maize and bean stalks. Alfalfa, wheat, and barley straw were reserved for time spent in pens. While it is hard to estimate its impact, this practice undoubtedly deprived forests of litter and essential nutrients and likely reduced the forest's biomass capacity.

[39] In 1850, there were 26,035 oxen, 9,017 horses, 3,544 mules, and 3,510 donkeys. I assume that 1 horse's energy output equals 10 men; 1 ox's, 6 men; 1 mule's, 5 men; and 1 donkey's, 2 men. I follow Astrid Kander and Paul Warde, *Number, Size, and Energy Consumption of Draught Animals in European Agriculture*, Working Paper, March 2009.

[40] "Notas estadísticas del Departamento de Querétaro."

[41] Sieferle, *The Subterranean Forest*, 25. This constraint played out even at the level of crops themselves. The maize plant grown at the time, unlike more modern, "high-yielding" varieties, devoted much of its energy to developing large stalks and husks. Farmers in Mexico grew this type of maize because these parts, which could not be directly consumed by humans, were essential fodder for animals. The high-yielding, short-stalk varieties that exist today are only viable in a society where animals do not play the role of power source. See David Clawson and Don Hoy, "Mexico: A Peasant Community that Rejected the 'Green Revolution'," *The American Journal of Economics and Sociology* 38, no. 4 (1979): 371–87. In 2016, only 6.7 percent of Querétaro's territory was pasture. See INEGI, *Anuario estadístico y geográfico de Querétaro 2017* (Aguascalientes: INEGI, 2017).

[42] *Quelite* is a generic term for various plants of the genera *Amaranthus* and *Chenopodium*. *Romerillo* is a common name for *Asclepias linaria*, *Baccharis sarothroides*, and *Bidens alba*. On the Bajío's original vegetation, see Butzer and Butzer, "The Natural Vegetation of the Mexican Bajio."

Figure 1.1 Zapotec peasant in Oaxaca with wooden plough and oxen, the most
common draft animal in nineteenth-century Mexico, ca. 1870.
Source: Fototeca INAH.

The final piece in Querétaro's agrarian system was farm technology.[43]
Farmers used a variety of technologies to increase production. The wooden
plough was a fundamental instrument, tipped in iron or with an iron-tipped
moldboard. In Mexico, a yoke of two oxen was common (see Figure 1.1). The
yoke was driven by one man (*gañán*) followed by another who cast the seeds
into the ground (*sembrador*). In general, Querétaro's cultivated areas had
light soils,[44] so it is possible a yoke could plow more land daily than the
typical 0.4 hectares of land that a team of two oxen could plow in the heavy
soils of northern Europe, but we simply lack the information to say this with
certainty. Normally, haciendas owned both ploughs and oxen and provided
them to sharecroppers,[45] but with only 124 recorded haciendas in the state at
the time compared with 8,000 ploughs, it appears that this technology was
widely available.[46] Shovels, hoes, wagons, digging sticks, pitchforks, and

[43] "Notas estadísticas del Departamento de Querétaro."
[44] Pheozems and vertisols, with some heavier luvisols in the south. See INEGI, *Anuario Estadístico
y Geográfico de Querétaro 2017*, map 12.
[45] Miller, "The Mexican Hacienda between the Insurgency and the Revolution."
[46] The figure is from an 1840s state census. See "Notas estadísticas del Departamento de Querétaro."

sickles were also common. Some haciendas (Tequisquiapan, for example) introduced locally made, likely water-powered machines to winnow and shell maize and wheat. They also employed threshing machines to separate straw from wheat grain. Estimates suggest that these machines reduced production costs by 35 percent. But mechanical winnowers and threshers were only accessible to heavily capitalized haciendas, so their impact on overall farm productivity in the state likely remained small.

Rain-fed agriculture in the Valley of Mexico (and across much of the *tierra templada* and *fría*) looked fairly similar to that practiced in Querétaro. What was unique to the Valley of Mexico was the wet, raised-bed agriculture system known as *chinampas*. Though diminished from its heyday in the early sixteenth century, when it covered over 100 square kilometers, *chinampa* agriculture remained important in mid-nineteenth-century Mexico. Once widespread across the lake system, by the nineteenth century, *chinampas* were largely confined to the shores of lakes Chalco and Xochimilco and the towns of Santa Anita, Ixtacalco, and Mexicalzingo. Like their colonial predecessors, nineteenth-century chinamperos first located an underwater mound (*cimiento*) by sounding out the bottom of the canal with an oar. Once found, peasants fenced the mound with reeds.[47] They then piled up alternating layers of lake mud and aquatic vegetation, known in Nahuatl as *atapalácatl*, until the mound was some 20–25 centimeters above water level. Willow trees or *huejote* were planted along the edges of the *chinampa* in order to stabilize the soil. The size of *chinampa* plots varied widely, from a few meters to the size of several modern soccer fields.[48]

Chinampas produced several crops annually and were never left fallow. With the exception of a few vegetables – radish, turnip, and carrot – most plants were first grown in nursery beds (*almácigos*) and then transplanted to the main *chinampa*. Maize continued to be the most important crop cultivated in *chinampas*, both for local consumption and for market in Mexico City and other large population centers in the valley. Tomatoes, chili pepper, cabbage, cauliflower, lettuce, green tomatoes, Brussels sprouts, onion, spinach, and celery were also grown. Yields were sustained over time by adding aquatic vegetation and lake mud before every planting.[49] In the early sixteenth

---

[47] *Chinampa* comes from the Nahuatl *chinamitl*, meaning "cane enclosure."

[48] The largest were up to 900 meters long and 6 meters wide, or 5,400 square meters, with most measuring about 90 square meters. See Miguel Santamaría, *Las chinampas del Distrito Federal: informe rendido al señor Director General de Agricultura* (Mexico: Impr. y Fototípia de la Secretaría de Fomento, 1912), 18. A singles tennis court is 195 square meters, or 24 meters long by 8 meters wide.

[49] Santamaría, *Las chinampas del Distrito Federal*, 15–16. Although published in the early twentieth century, Santamaría based his work on interviews with old peasants ("cultivadores ancianos"). It is reasonable to assume that this information can also be applied to the nineteenth century. See also

century, *chinampa* agriculture yielded on average 3 tons of maize per hectare and supported over 170,000 people with per capita annual consumption around 160 kilograms. Assuming a population of 200,000 for Tenochtitlan in 1519, *chinampas* provided 85 percent of the food requirements of the Mexica capital.[50] This was an extraordinary level of productivity, matched only by twentieth-century farming methods using mechanization and synthetic fertilizers. There is evidence that such levels of *chinampa* productivity remained stable as late as the nineteenth and early twentieth centuries.[51]

Given that most energy in agrarian societies came from food, how much surplus a farming system could produce mattered greatly. How much of this surplus the state or urban elites could force subsistence farmers to give up – an inherently political question – also mattered. Surplus food determined the size (and location) of nonfarming populations, meaning cities and towns.[52] Around 1860, Mexican farmers produced enough food for a mere 10 percent of the total population to live in cities (Table 1.1). This urban population was not homogeneously distributed across Mexico but concentrated in areas with the richest farmland in the country.

With a population of about 200,000 residents, it is no coincidence that Mexico City was by far Mexico's most populated urban center in the 1850s (Puebla came in a distant second with 70,000 inhabitants). No other region in the country surpassed the Valley of Mexico's productive system of *chinampas* and rich alluvial plains.[53] As the largest market in the nation, Mexico City also attracted producers from outside the valley. Mexico's very high land

Antonio García Cubas, *Geografía e historia del Distrito Federal* (México: Antigua Imprenta de Murguía, 1894), 19.

[50] The estimate for pre-Hispanic *chinampa* productivity is in William Sanders, "The Agricultural History of the Basin of Mexico," in *The Valley of Mexico: Studies in Pre-Hispanic Ecology and Society* (Albuquerque: University of New Mexico Press, 1976), 101–60. A detailed description of late colonial *chinampa* agriculture can be found in José Antonio de Alzate y Ramirez, *Gacetas de literatura de México*, vol. 2 (Puebla: Reimpresas en la Oficina del Hospital de San Pedro, 1831), 382–95. A description of colonial *chinampa* agriculture in the Valley of Mexico is Gibson, *The Aztecs under Spanish Rule*, 320–1. Gibson observes that *chinampa* agriculture was still practiced in reduced areas in the salt lakes (including Texcoco) during colonial times. See also Teresa Rojas Rabiela, *La agricultura chinampera: compilación histórica* (Chapingo: Universidad Autónoma Chapingo, 1983).

[51] Rojas Rabiela claims that early twentieth-century *chinampas* yielded an unlikely average of 5–6 tons per hectare, almost twice as much as the 3 tons per hectare proposed for pre-Hispanic *chinampa* agriculture. Even if Rojas Rabiela's figure is inaccurate, it suggests that *chinampa* productivity did not decline over time. See Rojas Rabiela, "Ecological and Agricultural Changes in the Chinampas of Xochimilco-Chalco," in *Land and Politics in the Valley of Mexico: A Two Thousand-Year Perspective* (Albuquerque: University of New Mexico Press, 1991).

[52] Not all nonfarming populations lived in cities; these included several thousand miners, mule train drivers, and so on.

[53] William Sanders estimated an average yield of 1,400 kg per hectare of alluvial land in the Valley of Mexico during pre-Hispanic times. See Sanders, "The Agricultural History of the Basin of Mexico," 144.

Table 1.1 *Estimate of rural and urban population in Mexico, 1856*

Type of Population	Number	Percentage
Rural	7,443,309	90.3
Urban	804,351	9.7
Total	8,247,660	100

Source: Jesús Hermosa, *Manual de geografía y estadística de la República Mexicana*, 1857, 83.

transportation costs at the time limited the amount of food that could reach Mexico City, or any city, from other regions. But Mexico City's lake system – which connected the downtown area and rich hinterland in the south and southeast of the valley – made it the country's only noncoastal major city with access to cheap water transportation.[54] By contrast, the average population size for other capital cities in 1850 Mexico was 24,000 inhabitants. A city's population in mid-nineteenth-century Mexico, then, indicated the productivity of its agrarian hinterland and the city's capacity to access its surplus. As following chapters illustrate, cities played a central role in Mexico's energy transition to fossil fuels, so this national urban geography based on local agrarian productivity had long-term implications.

The solar energy regime also shaped how urban spaces were utilized and limited the size they could achieve.[55] In the 1850s, Mexico City had an area of about 10–11 km², large by contemporary standards.[56] Although

[54] This hinterland provided mid-nineteenth-century Mexico City residents with an annual bounty of 17,000 head of cattle, 280,000 sheep (*carneros*), 60,000 pigs, 1,260,000 chickens, 125,000 ducks, 250,000 wild turkeys, 65,000 pigeons (*pichones*), 140,000 quails and partridges (*codornices y perdices*), 118,000 three-fanega maize *cargas* (16,284,000 kilograms, assuming 138 kilograms per *carga*), 130,000 wheat flour *cargas* (20,930,000 kilograms), 300,000 pulque *cargas*, 12,000 aguardiente barrels, and over 68,000 kilograms of oil. See Marcos Arróniz, *Manual del viajero en Méjico, ó, compendio de la historia de la Ciudad de Méjico, con la descripcion e historia de sus templos, conventos, edificios públicos; las costumbres de sus habitantes, etc., y con el plan de dicha ciudad* (Paris: Librería de Rosa y Bouret, 1858), 39. Notice the importance of meat for urbanites' diet. Given that people and animals competed for food in agrarian societies, overpopulation usually meant giving up meat. A plant-based diet can feed about eight times the population of a meat-based one. The abundance of meat in mid-nineteenth-century Mexico City suggests relatively low population pressure. See Sieferle, *The Subterranean Forest*, 18.

[55] Sieferle calls this principle the "minimization of transport." See Sieferle, *The Subterranean Forest*, 45.

[56] Mexico City and its metropolitan area covered some 1,500 km² in the early twenty-first century, 150 times more than its nineteenth-century predecessor. López Rosado estimated (without citing sources) that in 1858, Mexico City had an area of 8.5 square kilometers, increasing to 40.5 square kilometers by 1910, a growth of 4.7 times in half a century. He gives a population figure of 200,000

minuscule compared with its present-day size (about 1,500 km²), it was extremely difficult for a city relying on transport by humans and draft animals to expand beyond the boundaries that both could traverse efficiently in a short period. Such constraints had many repercussions for urban life. For one, it forced people of different classes to live in close proximity. A recurring theme in the period's travel literature is the disgust elites felt sharing urban spaces with *léperos* (urban underclass) and other members of the lower classes. Small cities also shaped routines of everyday life. Work and private life often existed under the same roof. Workshops and stores typically devoted the first floor to business and the second to living quarters. Under the solar energy regime, cities concentrated energy in every form, from animal and human bodies to food resources and material goods.[57] To keep the circulation of energy efficient, urban spaces had to remain small.

In sum, food production was the basis of mid-nineteenth-century Mexican society. While some indigenous groups in the north still subsisted as hunter-gatherers,[58] the vast majority of Mexicans depended on agriculture. From an energy perspective, hunter-gatherers largely tapped the flow of solar energy without regulating it. Agriculturalists, on the other hand, controlled this flow. They replaced an enormous variety of natural vegetation with a few selected plants, concentrating dispersed energy into their crops. Like farmers in other agrarian societies, Mexican food producers managed a number of constraints and risks. Some of these constraints were more or less fixed, such as the amount of land that could be cultivated using animal power. Others were cyclical in nature, like devastating El Niño–induced droughts.[59] Population growth was relatively slow and fluctuated depending on harvests, epidemics, natural disasters, and war.[60]

Forests

Photosynthesis is the basis of life on earth. Plants, trees, and phytoplankton (aquatic plants) are the only organisms capable of photosynthesizing or

---

in 1858 and 471,000 in 1910. See Diego G. López Rosado, *Historia del abasto de productos alimenticios en la Ciudad de México* (México, D. F.: Fondo de Cultura Económica, 1988), 152.

[57] A demographic analysis of cities in nineteenth-century Mexico is Richard E. Boyer, "Las ciudades mexicanas: perspectivas de estudio en el siglo XIX," *Historia Mexicana* 22, no. 2 (1972): 142–59.

[58] E. Lamberg, "Inspección de las colonias militares de Chihuahua," in *Boletín de la Sociedad Mexicana de Geografía y Estadística*, vol. III (México, 1852), 19–25.

[59] Blanca Mendoza et al., "Historical Droughts in Central Mexico and Their Relation with El Niño," *Journal of Applied Meteorology* 44, no. 5 (2005): 709–16.

[60] María Eugenia Romero and Luis Jáuregui, "México 1821–1867. Población y crecimiento económico," *Iberoamericana* III, no. 12 (2003): 25–52.

fixing incoming solar radiation for their own growth. They sustain the majority of multicellular life-forms, which eat either plants or plant-eaters. Plants and trees capture less than 1 percent of all the solar radiation that reaches earth, and only a fraction of that amount is transformed into plant tissue. This all means that the total amount of plant matter in any given place sets a *limit* to the energy that can be harvested. Such a limit imposes ecological constraints on societies that use wood for heat energy. A close look at wood use in households, factories, mines, and other mid-nineteenth-century industries will illustrate this connection.

Although pre-Columbian indigenous civilizations proved perfectly capable of overexploiting forests, the real assault on Mexico's forests began with colonial mining.[61] Over three centuries, successive cycles of expansion, stagnation, decline, and renewed growth on a larger scale – coupled with colonial mining of silver, gold, and other metals – took a considerable toll on Mexico's forests. The central highlands, the two Sierra Madres, and the northern plateau's "mining belt" were particularly hard-hit. One study suggests that under Spanish rule, some 315,000 km^2 of pine-oak and mesquite forest – an area slightly larger than Italy – may have been cut in the mining belt to meet the voracious fuel demands of smelting and refining.[62] Another estimate proposes a much smaller overall impact of colonial mining, about one fourth of the deforested area.[63] Despite disagreement, it is clear that the silver currency that powered the global economy of the early modern period, filled the coffers of European merchants, and circulated in distant Chinese markets[64] literally consumed Mexico's forests. If one considers the deforestation caused by other fuel-hungry industries like iron and glass, along with the comparatively less demanding expansion of agriculture and animal

[61] Sherburne Friend Cook, *The Historical Demography and Ecology of the Teotlalpan* (Berkeley: University of California Press, 1949), 31–3.

[62] Daviken Studnicki-Gizbert and David Schechter, "The Environmental Dynamics of a Colonial Fuel-Rush: Silver Mining and Deforestation in New Spain, 1522 to 1810," *Environmental History* 15 (2010): 94–119. One potential problem: Studnicki-Gizbert does not consider the average biomass productivity of different types of Mexican forests, which directly influences the forest area that needed to be cut for fuelwood production. He also assumes that charcoal making in Mexico always caused deforestation, ruling out possible forms of sustainable wood harvesting.

[63] See Saúl Guerrero, "The Environmental History of Silver Refining in New Spain and Mexico, 16c to 19c: A Shift of Paradigm" (PhD Dissertation, McGill University, 2015), 554. Guerrero claims that some 70,000 km^2 were deforested during colonial times. Another important study favoring smaller areas of deforestation is Robert C. West, *The Mining Community in Northern New Spain: The Parral Mining District* (Berkeley: University of California Press, 1949), 45–6.

[64] Richard von Glahn, "Foreign Silver Coins in the Market Culture of Nineteenth-Century China," *International Journal of Asian Studies* 4, no. 1 (2007): 51–78.

husbandry, the true scale of New Spain's deforestation comes further into focus.[65]

It is very likely, then, that Mexico's independent history began with large parts of its territory deforested. "Forest" and "wood," however, are generic terms that obscure a huge diversity of types, conditions, histories, ecologies, and energy densities.[66] Where were Mexico's forests located in 1850? What type of forests were they? What was their extension and condition? A combination of altitude, latitude, precipitation, tempera- ture, and soil composition determine forest type.[67] In broad terms, this means that vegetation is typically more abundant in areas of Mexico closer to the equator and decreases as one moves north. Mexico's tropical lowlands came in two basic forms: 1) an evergreen rainforest with a tall canopy (up to 40 meters), average rainfall of over 2,000 mm annually, and high temperatures year-round and 2) a dry, deciduous tropical forest with a lower canopy (up to 20 meters) and a stark divide between rainy and dry seasons. These dry forests extended along Mexico's Pacific coast and into the Yucatan Peninsula, shading into thorny woodland and eventually a scrub forest in northern latitudes. Mexico's highlands sup- ported montane forests, mostly fir, pine-oak, and oak forests. About a third of Mexico's territory, mostly northern, was occupied by xero- phytic brush vegetation, which turned into grasslands in areas with higher precipitation and adequate conditions.[68] Of course, these "theor- etical" forest zones were heavily modified by human action by 1850, some

[65] On Mexico's colonial forest history, see Antony Challenger, *Utilización y conservación de los ecosistemas terrestres de México: pasado, presente y futuro* (México, D.F.: Comisión Nacional para el Concimiento y Uso de la Biodiversidad, 1998); Andrés Lira, "Los bosques en el virreinato (apuntes sobre la visión política de un problema)," *Relaciones* 11, no. 41 (1990): 117–27; Manuel Lucena Giraldo and Luis Urteaga, *El bosque ilustrado: estudios sobre la política forestal española en America* (Madrid: Instituto Nacional para la Conservación de la Naturaleza: Instituto de la Ingeniera de España, 1991).

[66] *Monte* and *bosque* were originally Spanish colonial legal terms, not necessarily descriptive categories of vegetative cover (much like "woodland" and "forest" in most of Western Europe). Spanish forest codes typically used *monte* to refer to any wooded area. See *Real ordenanza para el gobierno de los montes y arbolados de la jurisdicción de marina* (Madrid: Imprenta Real, 1803). See also Paul Warde, "Fear of Wood Shortage and the Reality of the Woodland in Europe, c. 1450–1850," *History Workshop Journal*, no. 62 (Autumn 2006): 28–57.

[67] Latitude influences how much sunlight a given place receives for photosynthesis. Temperature decreases by roughly 1 °C per 100 meters and affects plant growth. Soil composition is closely related to climate.

[68] Overviews of Mexico's vegetation types are Jerzy Rzedowski, *Vegetación de México* (México, D. F.: Conabio, 2006); SEMARNAT, *Atlas Geográfico del Medio Ambiente y Recursos Naturales* (México, D. F.: SEMARNAT, 2006). Philip L. Wagner, "Natural Vegetation of Middle America," in *Handbook of Middle American Indians. Volume One: Natural Environment and Early Cultures* (Austin: University of Texas Press, 1964).

even largely products of it. Consider the scrublands that cover vast areas in the mining belt of northern Mexico, once populated by a variety of dry oak, poplar, and willow forests; most were felled to fuel silver mining.[69] Other forest types regrew following heavy human disturbance, including tropical forests in the Maya area, but with concentrations of plant species useful to human beings that would not occur in the absence of anthropogenic influence.

Although there is little information for accurately estimating forest cover in Mexico by the mid-nineteenth century, it is possible to make some rough calculations. One source from the early 1860s suggested that about 14–15 percent of the country's total area was devoted to agriculture, 9–10 percent was fallow farmland, 8–9 percent was pasture and meadows, 6–7 percent was partially wooded (*montes*), a mere 4 percent was forest (*bosques*), and the remaining 55–60 percent consisted of human settlements, uncultivated or unmanaged land, rivers, and lakes.[70] Woodland and forest may have covered 10–15 percent or roughly 200,000–300,000 km² of Mexico in the middle of the nineteenth century (Table 1.2).[71]

Limited forest cover in densely populated areas created severe problems for mid-nineteenth-century Mexico's wood-based civilization. Various nonfuel uses exerted constant pressure on local timber stands. While typically walled with lime-mortared stones, wealthy homes required large amounts of timber for flooring and roofing. The poor also used wood for the frames of their homes when it was available. As mentioned before, most farming implements were made of wood, as was complex machinery like waterwheels. Some waterwheels had enormous dimensions, a testament not only to wood's versatility but to sophisticated wood craftsmanship. Wooden coaches were also common, although by the mid-nineteenth

---

[69] Daviken Studnicki-Gizbert, "Exhausting the Sierra Madre: Mining Ecologies in Mexico over the Long Durée," in John R. McNeill and George Vrtis, eds., *Mining North America: An Environmental History since 1522* (Berkeley: University of California Press, 2017), 19–46.

[70] Pérez Hernández, *Estadística de la República Mejicana*, 58–9. Emiliano Busto, *Estadística de la República Mexicana. Resúmen y análisis de los informes rendidos á la Secretaría de Hacienda por los agricultores, mineros, industriales y comerciantes de la República y los agentes de México en el exterior, en respuesta á las circulares de 1° de Agosto de 1877* (México: Imprenta de Ignacio Cumplido, 1880), vol. II, 422. Busto agrees with Pérez Hernández regarding forest cover but almost triples the area for woodland (*montes*) at 16 percent of Mexico's total area. (A typo in Busto's original suggests he took the forest figure from Pérez Hernández.)

[71] For comparison, in 2002 Mexico's forests represented 34 percent of its total area. See SEMARNAT, *Atlas geográfico del medio ambiente y recursos naturales*, 10. At 10–15 percent forest cover, Mexico fared better than most of Europe, where forest covered around 6 percent of western and central Europe in 1850. See Jed O. Kaplan, Kristen M. Krumhardt, and Niklaus Zimmermann, "The Prehistoric and Preindustrial Deforestation of Europe," *Quaternary Science Reviews* 28, no. 27 (2009): 3016–34. See also Warde, "Fear of Wood Shortage."

Table 1.2 *Estimate of distribution of land cover in Mexico, ca. 1860*

Type of Land Cover	Area (km²)	Percentage
Forest	83,825	4.0
Woodland	142,345	6.8
Cultivated	326,025	15.7
Fallow	215,600	10.4
Grassland and Meadows	196,630	9.5
No Cultivation	1,099,385	53.2
Total	2,063,810[72]	100

Source: Hernández, *Estadística de la República Mexicana,* 58–9.[73]

century US-made coaches became popular. In short, wood was easily the most important construction material for mid-nineteenth-century Mexicans.

But wood's most important role was as a source of heat energy.[74] Virtually every Mexican household cooked using wood or charcoal in iron stoves or with iron or copper-made pots. Peasants everywhere made tortillas by placing flat iron griddles (*comal*) over a wood or charcoal open fire. Meat was also roasted over open flame. Only in wood-poor areas did the rural population resort to using animal dung, corn husks, dry maguey leaves, or any combustible material available.[75] We lack precise figures for domestic fuel consumption in mid-nineteenth-century Mexico, especially rural consumption. Still, it is likely that people in the countryside survived with 1–2 kg of

---

[72] Mexico's actual total area is 1,973,000 km²; Pérez Hernández overestimated its area by 90,810 km².

[73] Given that figures for the vast tropical lowland forests were nonexistent at the time, the area Pérez Hernández included under "forest" or "woodland" likely referred to the temperate forests of the central highlands and the Sierra Madres and the arid woodland that covered most of the Bajío and northern and western Mexico – all woods historically exploited since colonial times. It is also possible that Pérez Hernández considered the southern and lowland dry and humid tropical forests, wetlands, and mangrove forests, which lay beyond 1850 Mexico's core agrarian nucleus, as "uncultivated." While covering tropical forests of a later period, see Herman W. Konrad, "Tropical Forest Policy and Practice During the Mexican Porfiriato, 1876–1910," in Harold K. Steen and Richard P. Tucker, eds., *Changing Tropical Forests: Historical Perspectives on Today's Challenges in Central and South America* (Durham: Duke University Press, 1992).

[74] And light. Urban lighting depended on turpentine (*trementina*), an oil derived from pine resin. See "Alumbrado de trementina," *El Monitor Republicano,* January 13, 1850.

[75] Sociedad Mexicana de Geografía y Estadística, *Boletín de la Sociedad Mexicana de Geografía y Estadística,* vol. II (México: Sociedad Mexicana de Geografía y Estadística, 1850), 375.

wood daily, if figures for urban and statewide consumption are any indication.[76] Residents in the city of Querétaro, by contrast, had access to about 2–2.5 kg of wood per day.[77]

It is possible to roughly calculate mid-nineteenth-century Mexico's domestic fuel consumption and its environmental impact. Most sources agree that the country's population in the 1850s hovered around eight million. If we take an average daily consumption of 2 kg of wood per capita, Mexico's population used some 16,000 metric tons of wood every day or 5,840,000 metric tons annually. Assuming an average annual growth of 600 metric tons of wood per square kilometer, Mexicans in the 1850s required the yearly product of 9,733 km^2 of forest or an area somewhat smaller than the state of Querétaro to cook their meals, warm themselves, and otherwise cover their domestic needs. This represented between 3.2 and 4.8 percent of Mexico's total forest area at the time. Such a vast extension of forest, of course, was only needed if people were harvesting their forests sustainably, that is, restricting themselves to extracting their forests' annual growth. A significantly smaller territory would have been needed if people had simply clear-cut. Many mines had

---

[76] Sherburn Cook estimated that a five-member family in early sixteenth-century Mexico consumed 10 kg of firewood daily. See Cook, *The Historical Demography and Ecology of the Teotlalpan*, 32. This conforms with average fuel consumption in northern Europe, which ranged from 1 kg daily in Mediterranean regions to 3 kg in northern latitudes. See Warde, "Fear of Wood Shortage." Rural Mexicans in 2010, many of whom continued using fuelwood, consumed a daily average of 2.4 kg of wood per capita, ranging from 1.4 kg in semiarid regions to 2.9 kg in tropical humid areas. See Miguel Caballero Deloya, "La verdadera cosecha maderable en México," *Revista Mexicana de Ciencias Forestales* 1, no. 1 (2010): 5–16. This all suggests that a similar level of fuelwood consumption has persisted among rural Mexicans for over 400 years.

[77] Querétaro's population was about 27,000 (down from over 50,000 in 1800); the inhabitants consumed 7,590 metric tons of charcoal in 1844. That represented 0.3 kg of charcoal per person. Assuming a ratio of 20 percent of wood to charcoal, every urban resident could access about 1.4 kg of wood as charcoal. Records also put statewide consumption of fuelwood in 1844 at 149,873 metric tons, or about 0.8 kg per capita. Thus, urban residents in Querétaro consumed on average 2–2.5 kg of wood daily, either as fuelwood or as charcoal. If we suppose a similar consumption level across the entire state, its 180,000 inhabitants required 360,000 kg of wood (as fuelwood or charcoal) or 360 metric tons *daily* – 131,400 metric tons per year. When one converts this figure into forest area, Querétaro's population required the annual growth of 219 km^2 of forest every year simply to meet domestic needs. All figures come from "Notas estadísticas del Departamento de Querétaro." The conversion formula is 1 *carga* = 138 kg; 55,000 charcoal *cargas* = 7,590 metric tons; and 1,086,034 *cargas de leña* = 149,873 metric tons. For converting metric tons of wood into forest area, I assume an average annual wood growth or net primary productivity of 6 metric tons per hectare or 600 metric tons per square kilometer. Of course, annual wood growth varies substantially depending on forest type; here I use the average for temperate oak and pine-oak forests, characteristic of Mexico's central highlands and the *monte* of northern Mexico. Leopoldo Galicia et al., "Perspectivas del enfoque socioecológico en la conservación, el aprovechamiento y pago de servicios ambientales de los bosques templados de México," *Madera y Bosques* 24, no. 2 (2018) offers a range between 5.8 and 10.7 metric tons of wood per hectare annually for Mexico's temperate forests.

the financial means to bring fuel over long distances, and itinerant industries like ironworks could move to a new area once local forest was depleted. But most communities in Mexico were attached to their land and depended on local forests. They probably sought to ensure the long-term availability of woods and avoided clear-cutting unless necessary.

Woods, especially fuelwood, were also necessary for a variety of manufacturing and extractive industries in mid-nineteenth-century Mexico. Ironworks, glassworks, and saltworks all required large amounts of wood energy. Throughout the colonial period and until the mid-nineteenth century, Catalan forges produced virtually all of Mexico's iron.[78] In these forges, an open charcoal fire melted the iron ore. A trompe, a device in which water fell through perforated pipes to produce an air blast, intensified the heat of the open fire. Workers then used a waterwheel-powered hammer to work the mass of wrought iron into bars, which merchants sold at local markets for approximately 6 to 8 cents per kilogram.[79] Due to the exorbitant cost of transporting wood and charcoal over long distances, ironworks were typically located in mountainous, forested regions close to their fuel sources. Indian and peasant charcoal makers would enter the forest, where they felled, cut, and split the trees.[80] After cutting the wood into small pieces, the charcoal makers stacked them in mounds. Leaving the center of the mound hollow to serve as a chimney, they covered it with leaves or grass and dirt to seal it. The charcoal makers then burned the mound and, in a process that could take up to 2 weeks, controlled the fire, making certain no holes emerged in the structure. Human porters or donkeys then transported the charcoal in bags to furnaces.[81]

---

[78] Estanislau Tomás, "The Catalan Process for the Direct Production of Malleable Iron and Its Spread to Europe and the Americas," *Contributions to Science* 1, no. 2 (1999): 225–32; Gerardo Sánchez Díaz, "Los orígenes de la industria siderúrgica mexicana. Continuidades y cambios tecnológicos en el siglo XIX," *Tzintzun: Revista de Estudios Históricos*, 50 (2009): 11–60.

[79] In the Valley of Mexico, many ironworks remained small well into the twentieth century. One ironworks founded in 1904 in Mexico City was worth only 20,000 pesos, had 50 workers, and exploited only 15 horsepower. See "La Secretaría de Fomento remite boletas para recoger datos relativos a la estadística industrial del Distrito" 1907, Secretaría de Gobierno del D.F., Estadísticas, caja 1, exp. 31, AHDF. The description of Catalan forges is based on John Birkinbine, *Industrial Progress of Mexico* (Philadelphia: no publisher identified, 1909), 13–15.

[80] Some indigenous communities in central Mexico were largely charcoal-makers. In San Bernabé, a typical mountain peasant community in the Valley of Mexico, 62 percent of males made charcoal in the late 1860s. See "Padrón de los habitantes del pueblo de San Bernabé de la Municipalidad de San Ángel" (1868), Tlalpan, Estadísticas, caja 89, exp. 3, AHDF.

[81] "Charcoal in Mexico," *Journal of the United States Association of Charcoal Iron Workers*. 3, no. 1 (1882): 8–11. See also Patricia Fournier, "Indigenous Charcoal Production and Spanish Metal Mining Enterprises: Historical Archaeology of Extractive Activities and Ecological Degradation in Central and Northern Mexico," in Marcos de Souza and Diogo Costa, eds., *Historical Archaeology and Environment* (Cham: Springer, 2018), 87–108.

In the mid-nineteenth century, a traditional ironworks consumed 6.3 metric tons of charcoal (32 tons of fuelwood) to produce 1 ton of pig iron. A Catalan forge in Durango in the 1830s consumed in 1 week the same amount of wood that 19 hectares of forest yielded in a year.[82] Put another way, a typical ironworks in mid-nineteenth-century Mexico could, in a single year, exhaust the entire annual wood growth of a forest area equivalent to Mexico City's total surface area in the 1850s (about 10 km^2). In some cases, the real consumption would have been much lower, since some ironworks operated for about half of the year. Nevertheless, Lucas Alamán, the great Mexican historian and statesman, noted in the 1840s that "the consumption of fuel by ironworks requires that woodlands *be carefully managed* or soon these establishments will run out of charcoal."[83]

The production of wood-fired iron faced clear environmental limits. Suppose a total of 200,000 km^2 of forest in mid-nineteenth-century Mexico. Assuming a very rough annual average productivity of 600 metric tons of wood per square kilometer, such a forest area yielded some 180,000,000 metric tons of dry wood annually. Even if the *entire* annual forest yield of Mexico had been harvested to fuel ironworks (which obviously never happened), total production would have been 5,625,000 metric tons of pig iron, well below present-day outputs. As an essential component of industrialization, these estimates illustrate the clear limits to large-scale iron production under Mexico's solar energy regime.[84]

But Mexico's largest consumer of fuelwood, both historically and in the 1850s, was mining. There were hundreds of mines all over Mexico, the majority of them located in the traditional mine belt of colonial origin. This included Zacatecas, Guanajuato, Real de Catorce in San Luís Potosí,

[82] Federico Weidner, *El Cerro del Mercado de Durango. Compendio de noticias mineralógicas, orognósticas, históricas, estadísticas y metalúrgicas de dicho cerro y la Ferrería de San Francisco* (México: Imprenta de Andrade y Escalante, 1858), 30. The ironworks manufactured a maximum 3.6 metric tons of pig iron weekly by burning 23 metric tons of charcoal (or 115 metric tons of wood).

[83] Approximately five units of wood produced one unit of charcoal. The Lucas Alamán quote comes from Horacio Labastida, *Documentos para el estudio de la industrialización en México. 1837–1845* (México, D. F.: Secretaría de Hacienda y Crédito Público: Nacional Financiera, 1977), 34.

[84] This estimate follows Edward Wrigley's discussion of energy limits in "organic societies." "The heat output," writes Wrigley, "from the combustion of dry wood is 4,200 kcal/kg compared with 8,000 kcal/kg in the case of bituminous coal." Wrigley argues: "[i]f half the land surface of Britain had been covered with woodland; it would only have sufficed to produce perhaps 1 ¼ million tons of bar iron on a sustained-yield basis." See *Energy and the English Industrial Revolution*, 16. Estimates on wood consumption in nineteenth-century Mexican ironworks come from Labastida, *Documentos para el estudio de la industrialización en México, 1837–1845*, 221. For comparison, in 2015 and 2016 Mexico produced 7,581,577 and 6,969,582 metric tons of iron, respectively. See "Anuario Estadístico de la Minería Mexicana" (México, D. F.: Servicio Geológico Mexicano, 2017), 36.

the Pachuca area mines, and Taxco, in Guerrero. Most mines were relatively small, worked by about a dozen miners, and yielded modest outputs. Human and animal muscle provided mechanical energy and wood supplied heat. Technological inputs included simple tools and the ubiquitous horse-powered winch (*malacate*) for draining mines. A few mines, however, were large-scale operations with thousands of miners. These also used steam engines, which had a gargantuan appetite for fuel. Take the famous Real del Monte, a highly productive mine in Hidalgo, northeast of Mexico City.[85] In the 1820s, the mines came under the control of British investors, who sought to make them profitable again following the production collapse during the wars of independence. The British introduced some of the first steam engines in Mexico to drain flooded tunnels. In 1834 alone, Real del Monte in combination with one refining hacienda devoured a forest some seven times the area of Mexico City.[86] Charcoal consumption must have risen further when the company acquired a 400-horsepower steam engine in 1853, a veritable giant at the time.[87] Other major mining

[85] Hidalgo state produced 2,400 metric tons of silver between 1667 and 1806, devouring 2,700 to 4,000 km² of forest. Silver figures come from Studnicki-Gizbert. Contrast with Guerrero, "The Environmental History of Silver Refining in New Spain and Mexico," 538. Guerrero's calculations are almost certainly too low. He assumes (p. 167) that 0.4 hectares of forest produced 1 ton of charcoal (18.5 m³ (925 kg) of wood), and 1 ton of charcoal produced 1 kg of silver, while 1 hectare of forest produced 2.5 tons of charcoal. He then adopts a very low wood-to-charcoal conversion rate of 10 percent, meaning that 10 units of wood equaled 1 unit of charcoal (sometimes he uses a more typical 5:1 ratio). Based on these assumptions, Guerrero implicitly proposes an average annual wood growth of 25 tons per hectare, an exceptionally high figure only second-growth patches of tropical rainforest or some contemporary tree plantations can yield. It's unlikely that any temperate forest or dry woodland in the mining belt was so productive during the colonial period; the net primary productivity of Mexico's temperate forests today ranges between 5 and 10 tons per hectare. In other words, even when one uses a conversion of 5 units of wood for 1 of charcoal, Guerrero is still assuming 12.5 tons of wood per hectare, a productivity level above any temperate forest in Mexico today.

[86] The steam engines required 34,204 metric tons of fuelwood (*leña*) – 57 km² of forest – while the refining hacienda (hacienda de beneficio) consumed 138 metric tons of charcoal weekly (7,176 metric tons annually), equaling 12 km² of forest. See Rafael de Armenta, "Consumo de leña en las minas de Real del Monte," *Boletín de la Sociedad Mexicana de Geografía y Estadística* II (1870 [1834]): 509. According to Real del Monte's own records, in a typical month in 1830, fuelwood represented 13 percent of the company's expenditures (including cutting and transportation costs), second only to piecework. See "Real del Monte Mining Company Expenditures and Returns" (April 7, 1830), José Villegas Collection on Mining. MSS 758. Special Collections & Archives, UC San Diego. By the late 1840s, Real del Monte faced serious fuelwood shortages. See Robert Randall, *Real del Monte: A British Silver Mining Venture* (Austin: University of Texas Press, 2014), 162–4.

[87] Typical steam engines at the time delivered a few dozen horsepower. William Parish Robertson, *A Visit to Mexico, by the West India Islands, Yucatan and United States: With Observations and Adventures on the Way* (London: Simpkin, Marshall & Co., Stationers' Hall Court, 1853), 175. Robertson suggests that tree plantations existed on the mine's estate for fuel. In 1850, 41 censused mines worked in the State of Mexico, including Real del Monte, the largest, which consumed 10,027 metric tons of charcoal and 114,373 pesos of fuelwood (which, assuming a price of approximately

operations had similar fuel needs. The nearby Mineral del Chico, Hidalgo, consumed the yield of some 90 km² of forest in 1849 to fuel production.[88] Fresnillo, in Zacatecas, required 89 km² annually in the 1840s. Even relatively small operations like the mines of Anangueo, Michoacán, used almost 13 km² of forest annually.[89]

As more mines adopted steam engines, fuel consumption rose accordingly. Mexico's steam engines, like their British counterparts, were first used to drain flooded mines. It is possible a steam engine was operating in the mines of Real de Catorce as early as 1819. Santiago Smith Wilcox, the first US consul in Mexico City, obtained rights to import steam engines in 1821.[90] In 1823, one Juan Black imported one of these devices into Mexico for the Temascaltepec mine, west of Mexico City.[91] More reliable reports indicate that steam engines came to Real de Catorce between 1819 and 1823.[92] Whatever the exact date, it is clear that steam engines were introduced in Mexico only a handful of years later than in Peru, the first territory in Spanish America to use the technology.[93] With 40 horsepower, the Temascaltepec engine operated 8 pumps that drained 3,153 cubic meters of water every 24 hours. For comparison, a *malacate* could draw about 900

2.4 pesos per metric ton, was equivalent to 47,655 metric tons). Charcoal supplies alone required 88 km² of forest and fuelwood 79 km². The census data is in Sociedad Mexicana de Geografía y Estadística, *Boletín de La Sociedad Mexicana de Geografía y Estadística*, vol. II (México: Sociedad Mexicana de Geografía y Estadística, 1850), 247. The price estimate comes from data included in Juan Burkhart, "Memoria sobre la explotación de minas en los distritos de Pachuca y Real del Monte de México," *Anales de la Minería Mexicana* (1861): 106–7.

88 If practice at Mineral El Chico was standard in mid-nineteenth-century Mexico, mines favored clear-cutting over sustainable wood harvest. At El Chico, "the wood to buttress the shafts and to make fuel is abundant, but it will disappear in a few years, as it already has in Pachuca, because the forests are cut without replanting a single tree for their reproduction." See Sociedad Mexicana de Geografía y Estadística, *Boletín de la Sociedad Mexicana de Geografía y Estadística*, II (1850): 264.

89 Ibid., 267; 292–302; 318.

90 Emilio del Castillo Negrete, *México en el siglo XIX, o sea su historia desde 1800 hasta la época presente* (México: Las Escalerillas, 1887), vol. 12, 465, claims that the Mexican government gave Willcox exclusive rights to import steam engines into the country (apparently, he never did). This privilege was later reversed over concerns that the monopoly might slow steam engine adoption across Mexico.

91 "Máquina de vapor en el mineral de Temascaltepec, Estado de México," *El Sol*, August 6, 1824.

92 Clara Bronstein, "La introducción de la máquina de vapor en México" (Tesis de Maestría, UNAM, 1965), 132–9. Strictly speaking, these were not Mexico's first steam engines (there seems to have been a model steam engine in the Palacio de Minería in the early nineteenth century.) See Bronstein, 94–5. Colonial authorities in the 1720s and 1730s tried and failed to introduce a Newcomen atmospheric engine to drain flooded mines. See Carlos Sempat Assadourian, "La bomba de fuego de Newcomen y otros artificios de desagüe: un intento de transferencia de tecnología inglesa a la minería novohispana, 1726–1731," *Historia Mexicana* 50, no. 3 (2001): 385–457.

93 "Máquina de vapor en el mineral de Pasco, Perú," *Gaceta Extraordinaria del Gobierno de México*, April 16, 1817, tomo VIII, núm. 1059.

cubic meters within the same period.[94] Later reports from the 1830s and 1840s on the mines of Fresnillo, Zacatecas suggest that despite an enormous initial cost, sometimes running up to half a million pesos, a steam engine's operating cost could be less than half that of horse-powered *malacates*. Not to mention that steam engines could reach depths of 800 to 875 meters, far beyond the *malacate*'s reach.[95] But even a medium-sized machine like the Temascaltepec engine burned through 17 metric tons of wood daily, a rate that devoured some 10 km^2 of forest to keep running year-round.[96]

The enormous energy requirements of steam engines concerned many Mexicans during the first half of the nineteenth century. Some found them ill-suited to a fuel-poor country like Mexico, which had neither vast forests like the USA nor rich coal deposits like Great Britain. The renowned Spanish mining engineer Fausto de Elhuyar, founder and director of New Spain's College of Mines (*Colegio de Minería*) and longtime royal mine supervisor, adamantly opposed adopting steam engines in Mexico. When the Spanish crown consulted him in the early nineteenth century about a plan to introduce steam engines to revive New Spain's mining industry, Elhuyar rejected the idea on grounds that the country lacked enough fuel. He claimed that steam engines were unviable in Mexico due to lack of coal and widespread deforestation, especially around mining centers. He favored animal-powered *malacates* to drain mines; though not very efficient or applicable to deep mines, *malacates* were cheap and easy to use. Aware that his opposition might be overridden, Elhuyar emphasized the necessity of implementing forest conservation measures in case steam engines came to New Spain. He also called for locating coal deposits as soon as possible.[97] Elhuyar's proposition to conserve forests while simultaneously pushing coal as an alternative to wood would emerge time and again in similar discussions over the next century.

[94] F. J. Down, *Embracing a Sketch of the Most Thrilling Incidents in the History of Ancient Mexico and Her Wars, the Present State of the Country, and Its Mines; a Full Account of the War Between the United States and Mexico* (New York: 128 Nassau-Street, 1850), 96. In this case, twelve horses moved each *malacate*, likely in shifts to keep the *malacate* working night and day. As this mine needed several *malacates* operating simultaneously to keep the mines dry, it probably employed dozens if not hundreds of horses. These expensive animals frequently represented a substantial percentage of a mine's total operating cost.

[95] Sociedad Mexicana de Geografía y Estadística, *Boletín de la Sociedad Mexicana de Geografía y Estadística*, II: 292–302. Half of expenses went to cover the astronomical cost of transporting these machines overland by oxcart from the port of Veracruz to Fresnillo, over 1,000 km away.

[96] "Máquina de vapor en el mineral de Temascaltepec, Estado de México," *El Sol*, August 21, 1824.

[97] Bronstein, "La introducción de la máquina de vapor en México," 89–114. Elhuyar's opposition was maybe self-serving: he had recently invented (or improved) a water-powered machine that drained mines. Additionally, Elhuyar did not seem to know of Watt's much more fuel-efficient steam engine.

Fuel scarcity was not the only concern among steam's opponents. During the 1820s, steam engines were located in distant mines in the countryside, far from most urban residents. In the following decade, however, several factories and urban establishments began adopting these devices. Some town dwellers decried their presence, deeming them noisy and potentially dangerous. Angry residents of an urban neighborhood where a steam-powered textile factory was being built complained that

> in addition to [the steam engine] being very annoying to the people of this neighborhood due to the great noise it will make, which will certainly hurt one's ears whether one is on the same street or three blocks away, it is frightening because it has happened that engines blew up entire city blocks, killing everyone living there and some who were close by, as was the case up north.[98]

Their "just and rational fears" of steam engines seemed to have little sway with officials and industrialists, who viewed the machines as beacons of progress. In fact, the government granted privileges and tax exemptions to businessmen who introduced or invented new industrial technologies. One San Luis Potosí entrepreneur requested such prerogatives to establish a steam engine at a chocolate factory. The editors of the *Gaceta de San Luís* (the *San Luis Gazette*) opposed the businessman's request on the grounds that the steam engine, which had been imported from France, would economically devastate the large number of chocolate dealerships (*expendios*), not to mention the countless number of women who manually ground chocolate (*molenderas*).[99] Indeed, many poor people initially viewed steam engines as a threat to their very livelihoods. Beyond being noisy and dangerous, other critics claimed that steam engines could contaminate or taint food.[100]

Still, everybody seemed to agree these engines represented a turning point. For the first time in history, heat could be turned into motion. Under the solar energy regime, people viewed energy not as different manifestations of the same underlying reality but as a set of discrete sources.[101] With the invention of the steam engine (and later the internal

[98] "Vecinos se oponen a instalación de una fábrica textil movida por máquina de vapor," *El Mosquito Mexicano*, December 9, 1834.

[99] "Oposición a uso de máquina de vapor para hacer chocolate por afectar clases menesterosas," *El Cosmopolita*, September 11, 1839. *Molenderas* sometimes ground their chocolate at home and then brought it to customers. Other times, they ground chocolate at their customers' homes (usually wealthy patrons.)

[100] "Máquina de vapor para moler chocolate," *El Siglo Diez y Nueve*, September 23, 1842.

[101] Sieferle, *The Subterranean Forest*, chapter 1.

combustion engine and electric motors and turbines), the gates that had previously cordoned off different energy forms were lifted. As scholars have pointed out, it is no coincidence that a unified concept of energy as a single entity converted into different forms only emerged after the creation of the steam engine, the first nonbiological converter.[102]

Aware of their enormous power, industries beyond mining began using steam engines in the 1840s. Textile factory owners were among the first converts. Both cotton and wool manufacturers employed them.[103] But steam remained an unlikely option, for it required an enormous financial investment. In places like Puebla, then the center of Mexico's textile industry with its abundant water resources, most industrialists in the 1840s continued privileging cheaper waterpower. Out of the 21 textile factories located in Puebla in 1843, 18 used waterpower while the remaining 3 employed mule-powered machinery.[104]

Despite cost and opposition, steam engines found various applications in Mexico. In 1843, engineers used steam engines to remove water from the foundations of the new dock at the port of Veracruz.[105] As early as the 1830s, some people in Mexico realized that these devices could be used in transportation. Likely, they had attended exhibitions demonstrating steam's versatility and potential. One such exhibition featured a steam-powered coach running on a small, circular track laid in the patio of a Mexico City building. For only two reales (a quarter of a peso), visitors could admire "one of the greatest inventions of human ingenuity."[106] Almost three decades before Mexicans successfully established a national railroad network in the late 1870s, a few steamships transported passengers and goods along Mexico's coast and even on the lakes and canals of the Valley of Mexico.[107] (Figure 1.2). Accounting for mines, factories, and a handful of steamboats, there may have been up to 100 steam engines in Mexico by the 1850s.

---

[102] Allen MacDuffie, *Victorian Literature, Energy, and the Ecological Imagination* (Cambridge, England: Cambridge University Press, 2014), part 1.

[103] "Máquina de vapor en el mineral de Plateros, Zacatecas," *El Registro Oficial. Periódico Oficial del Estado de Durango*, March 30, 1845; "Informe de D. Pedro de Baranda sobre la fábrica de tejidos de algodón que tiene establecida en el Distrito de Valladolid," *El Siglo Diez y Nueve*, August 22, 1844. Dirección General de la Industria Nacional, *Memoria sobre el estado de la agricultura e industria de la República en el año de 1844* (México: José M. Lara, 1845), 20.

[104] Estevan de Antuñano, "Estado de la industria manufacturera de algodones en Puebla, nacida en dicha ciudad el año de 1835," *El Siglo Diez y Nueve*, March 28, 1843.

[105] "Máquina de vapor para construir muelle en el puerto de Veracruz," *El Siglo Diez y Nueve*, June 6, 1843.

[106] "Exhibición de carruaje movido por máquina de vapor," *El Fénix de la Libertad*, October 18, 1833.

[107] "Navegación por vapor en el Canal de La Viga," *El Siglo Diez y Nueve*, May 15, 1849; "Navagación por vapor en el Valle de México," *El Siglo Diez y Nueve*, September 28, 1852. Steamboats continued operating on the valley's lakes until the 1890s.

Figure 1.2 Steamboat *La Esperanza* on the Canal de la Viga. This canal connected the valley's southern lakes with Mexico City. The lithography was made from a balloon. Source: Manuel Arróniz, *Manual del viajero en Méjico*, 1858, 52.

Steam engines required heavy fuel inputs, putting further pressure on forests. How much fuel, then, did mid-nineteenth-century Mexico consume between wood and charcoal for all manufacturing and extractive purposes? The short answer is that we do not know. There were no reliable statistics for this type of consumption in mid-nineteenth-century Mexico. That said, we can use proxy figures to gauge the overall impact industry had on forests. The most accurate data is for all-important silver production. Between 1851 and 1860, Mexico produced a total of 4,569,500 kg of silver.[108] Silver production burned through a forest the size of the state of Tlaxcala every year and consumed the yield of a forest area larger than the state of Puebla in those 9 years.[109] After adding in ironworks, glassworks,

[108] Secretaría de Industria, Comercio y Trabajo, *Anuario de Estadística Minera* (México: Talleres Gráficos de la Nación, 1923), 42.
[109] Studnicki-Gizbert and Schechter, "The Environmental Dynamics of a Colonial Fuel-Rush." About 1,000 kg (1 metric ton) of charcoal produced 1 kg of pure silver. Assuming a ratio of five

and the many other industries that required heat energy in their productive process, there is no doubt this total figure would be substantially higher.

The combined pressure on Mexico's forests from traditional industries (iron) and new technologies (steam engines) inspired a growing interest in coal. As early as 1829, the state government of Nuevo León granted a concession to one Juan Woodbury and one Juan Cameron to exploit iron and coal deposits in the state. These individuals also obtained permits to import machinery, presumably steam engines for mines.[110] From the 1830s, newspapers reported coal deposits discovered across the country, emphasizing their significance by claiming that no other fuel was "more appropriate for the steam engines that are currently employed to drain mines."[111] Enthusiasm for coal came from the common view that coal would reduce dependence on Mexico's depleted forests[112] along with the conviction that Mexico required large quantities of coal to enter what industrialist Estevan de Antuñano called the "English stage" of industrialization.[113] Production needed investment, and investment depended on legislation. When, in 1841, General D. Vicente Filisola requested that the Mexican government grant him monopoly rights to exploit coal across Mexico for 10 years, a government-appointed committee refused. Members justified their decision on the grounds that coal was essential for "the progress of arts" (industry) and that England, the world's "leading manufacturing nation," never allowed coal monopolies in its territory.[114] This laissez-faire approach, however, failed to increase Mexico's coal production. By the late 1840s, the government decided to exempt imported coal from duties, a practice that would continue for decades.[115] By the early 1850s, coal was present in ironmaking and as a fuel for steam engines

units of wood per one unit of charcoal and an average productivity of 600 tons of wood for Mexican forests per km^2, the wood yield of 38,079 km^2 was harvested in those 9 years to produce Mexico's silver.

[110] "Concesión a los ciudadanos Juan Lucio Wodbury y Juan Cameron para la explotación de minas de fierro y carbón de piedra" (October 4, 1829), Fondo: Capital del Estado; Sección: Reglamentos, decretos y circulares; Colección: Impresos II; Volumen: 6; Exp: 4, AHM.

[111] "Descubrimiento de mina de carbón de piedra en Carácuaro, Michoacán y origen del carbón de tierra," *El Gladiador*, May 23, 1831. There is a reference to coal use in Guanajuato in 1805, which, if correct, would be the earliest in Mexico. See Sociedad Mexicana de Geografía y Estadística, *Boletín de la Sociedad Mexicana de Geografía y Estadística*, II: 27.

[112] ". . . la explotación de minas de carbón [es] el único medio de acelerar la reparación de los bosques que han sido devastados." "Utilidad de las plantas," *El Mosaico Mexicano*, January 1, 1840.

[113] Estevan de Antuñano, *Pensamientos para la regeneración industrial de México* (México, D. F., M. Porrúa, 1955 [1837]), 85–6.

[114] "Petición de monopolio y extracción de carbón mineral," *Semanario de la Industria Mexicana*, June 15, 1841.

[115] Mexican officials considered coal essential for locomotives. See Secretaría de Fomento, *Colección de leyes, decretos, disposiciones, resoluciones y documentos importantes sobre caminos de fierro, años de 1824 a 1870*, vol. 1 (México: Imprenta de Francisco Díaz de León, 1882), 32.

in mines and for the handful of steamboats that called at Mexican ports.[116] Overall consumption probably did not exceed a few thousand metric tons annually.

In sum, mid-nineteenth-century Mexico found itself in an unenviable situation. Centuries of silver mining, iron production, and agricultural expansion and animal husbandry (especially goat and sheepherding) had caused substantial deforestation, especially in the central highlands and the mining belt. The total forest area in the mid-nineteenth century was between 200,000 and 300,000 km², representing 10–15 percent of Mexico's territory. While several European countries featured territories with a mere 6 percent forest cover, Mexico's forested area was minuscule compared with that of the USA.[117] But Mexico seemed to have little coal to supplement wood, as opposed to European countries and the USA. Put simply, Mexico was attempting to develop its industry with relatively scarce wood supplies and little to no coal. Forests provided almost all the heat energy and an increasing share of mechanical energy for steam engines. Combined, domestic and industrial consumption probably exploited the annual yield of 10,000–15,000 km² of forest, or anywhere between 3 and 7.5 percent of the country's total forest area. While many peasant communities were forced to harvest wood on a more or less sustainable basis to maintain forest cover, between a third and a half of all Mexican forest was likely clear-cut. Most of the clear-cutting came from mines and factories, which could afford fuelwood transported from distant sources. There is little doubt that overall pressure on forests in mid-nineteenth-century Mexico was considerable and made other sources of energy attractive.

Water and Wind

Water and wind were subordinate sources of energy in mid-nineteenth-century Mexico. While waterpower played an important role on land, wind power was rare. Waterwheels were common in haciendas and various workshops and factories, especially modern textile establishments. They milled grain, powered hammers in foundries and ironworks, and moved mechanical looms. Haciendas and ranchos used *norias* to irrigate land. Windmills were virtually nonexistent in Mexico, but wind worked at sea,

---

[116] "Entradas al puerto de Acapulco. Importación de carbón inglés," *Periódico Oficial del Gobierno de los Estados Unidos Mexicanos*, April 21, 1852.

[117] United States Department of Agriculture, "US Forest Resource Facts and Historical Trends" (Forest Service, August 2014), 7. In 1850, 45 percent of US territory was classified as forest.

where, with the exception of some steamboats, sailboats comprised the majority of the country's small merchant fleet.

Where was Mexico's water? Once again, geography was not kind to Mexicans. Most water was abundant where human population was not, particularly the southeastern tropical lowlands. Water scarcity marked the densely populated central highlands and the northern mining belt. Fifty-four percent of the country's runoff comes from just three rivers: the Grijalva-Usumacinta, the Papaloapan, and the Coatzacoalcos.[118] All three drain parts of the southeastern Mexican tropical lowlands. The biggest river system in central-western Mexico is the Lerma-Santiago, beginning in an area west of Mexico City and flowing into Lake Chapala, the country's largest freshwater lake, and the Pacific. This system traverses 58 basins and its total annual flow represents only 3.4 percent of the nation's water.[119] Great seasonal variations mean that most of this flow occurs during the rainy months between May and September.[120] In other words, the majority of Mexico's mid-nineteenth-century population, towns, and cities were located in a region characterized by mountainous terrain, numerous small basins, and relatively low-volume rivers that run high for just a few months of the year. The vast, semiarid region north of Mexico City was even less fortunate. Excluding the Sinaloa River and the Bravo-Conchos systems, rivers in the north were few and meandered across vast, largely empty desert landscapes.

These factors make it clear why the majority of the country's water-driven machinery was located in farms, mines, workshops, and factories in central, western, and north-central Mexico. They also explain why water was a relatively subordinate energy source, especially compared with western Europe and the eastern USA. Since medieval times, several European societies had relied on waterpower for a variety of tasks, including grain milling, wood sawing, and operating heavy hammers in foundries and workshops. As early as the eleventh century, there was 1 water-powered mill

---

[118] Mexico contains 37 hydrological regions with a total runoff of 378,311 hm³ (cubic hectometers). Rivers and streams represent only 22.1 percent of the 1,489 billion m³ of precipitation that falls in Mexico; 73.1 percent evaporates back into the atmosphere, and 4.8 percent percolates through soil and accumulates in underground aquifers. See Comisión Nacional del Agua, *Atlas del agua en México* (México, D. F.: CONAGUA, 2011), 22–8. A mid-nineteenth-century description of Mexico's rivers and lakes is Brantz Mayer, *Mexico, Aztec, Spanish and Republican: A Historical, Geographical, Political, Statistical and Social Account of That Country from the Period of the Invasion by the Spaniards to the Present Time, with a View of the Ancient Aztec Empire and Civilization, a Historical Sketch of the Late War, and Notices of New Mexico and California* (Hartford: S. Drake, 1852), book IV, 17–21.

[119] Comisión Nacional del Agua, *Atlas del agua en México*, 22.

[120] In the Lerma-Santiago hydrological region, 64 percent of precipitation falls from July to September. Comisión Nacional del Agua, *Atlas del agua en México*, 32.

for every 350 people in England. The three early nineteenth-century New England industrial centers, Lowell, Lawrence, and Manchester, derived their energy from the Merrimack river.[121] Places like Puebla, which had both a large population *and* water, were the closest Mexican equivalents and became industrial and manufacturing leaders in the 1830s and 1840s. The productivity of the state's numerous water-powered textile factories was unsurpassed in Mexico at the time.[122] But even in Puebla, most cloth was woven by hand using the 30,000 or so individual looms, also called *malacates*.[123]

Originally introduced by the Spanish soon after conquest, waterwheels became common in both Spanish and indigenous settlements.[124] Some early colonial mills employed undershot waterwheels, which move in the opposite direction to the running water. This model was relatively inefficient at harnessing the kinetic energy of water and required high-speed running water to operate properly. Depending on local conditions, other mills preferred horizontal waterwheels (*rodeznos*), which were technically simple (no complex gears) and needed only a small volume of water.[125] Another available model was the overshot wheel, the most efficient of which could convert up to 85 percent of water's kinetic energy to mechanical energy. Here, water was diverted from a river or stream into a channel or, typically, an aqueduct and then fed through flumes into buckets at great

[121] Smil, *Energy in World History*, 108; Smil, "World History and Energy."

[122] At *La Constancia Mexicana*, the state's largest and first mechanized textile establishment in Mexico, 113 water-driven looms churned out 600 pieces of cloth weekly (312,000 annually), enough to clothe about 15 percent of the state's 660,000 inhabitants in the 1840s. These power looms were about six times more productive than a person. Data on La Constancia comes from Antuñano, "Estado de la industria manufacturera de algodones en Puebla, nacida en dicha ciudad el año de 1835." Puebla's estimated population in the 1840s is in INEGI, *Estadísticas históricas de México: Población* (Aguascalientes: INEGI, 2008), 102. A piece of cloth (*pieza de manta*) typically measured one *vara* (0.8 meters); an average Pueblan in the 1840s needed three per year. A weaver and an assistant produced two pieces of *manta* weekly, a third of a water-powered loom's production. See Jan Bazant, "Industria algodonera poblana de 1803-1843 en números," *Historia Mexicana* 14, no. 1 (1964): 131–43.

[123] Estevan de Antuñano, "Documentos para la historia de la industria algodonera de México, en lo fabril y en lo agrícola, o sea narraciones y cálculos estadísticos sobre ella," *El Siglo Diez y Nueve*, March 28, 1843.

[124] On the colonial history of waterwheels, see Magdalena García, "El dominio de las 'aguas ocultas y descubiertas': hidráulica colonial en el centro de México, siglos XVI-XVII," in *Mestizajes tecnológicos y cambios culturales en México* (México, D. F.: CIESAS; Miguel Ángel Porrúa, 2004), 93–128. The oldest waterwheel reference dates back to the first century BCE in the eastern Mediterranean, though the technology was likely much older. See Smil, *Energy in World History*, 103, and Terry S. Reynolds, *Stronger than a Hundred Men: A History of the Vertical Water Wheel* (Baltimore: Johns Hopkins University Press, 1983).

[125] Víctor Gómez, "Los molinos del Valle de México. Innovaciones tecnológicas y tradicionalismo (Siglos XVI–XIX)" (PhD Dissertation, UAM-Iztapalapa, 2008), 161–4.

speed. Since the wheel's movement was generated by the weight of the water, overshot wheels could be located on slow-flowing rivers, greatly expanding their range and applications.

In Mexican haciendas and pueblos, the waterwheel was used for milling wheat (not maize). One Hacienda de los Hornos in Chihuahua, owned by Don Leonardo Zuloaga, had a water-powered mill with an overshot waterwheel and two grindstones that could grind 2.7 metric tons of wheat every 24 hours. The water was carried into a canal – presumably from a storage pond, reservoir, or spring that ensured a reliable water supply – and fell from a height of 2.4 to 2.7 meters, filling the buckets and moving the wheel downwards.[126] Wheels like this probably delivered some 15 to 25 horsepower, if 1880s reports are any indication.[127] This was modest compared with later wheat mills. If it operated year-round without interruption (unlikely), the Zuloaga mill would produce 985.5 metric tons of wheat compared with the 5,000 metric tons of wheat that an enormous, electric 500-horsepower mill in Sonora could grind in a year by the early twentieth century.[128] Waterwheels in mid-nineteenth-century Mexico were commonly wood, given the paucity of iron in Mexico.[129] It seems that craftsmen preferred mesquite for its durability and ubiquity in Mexico's arid plateaus and highlands.[130] Less iron also forced craftsmen to rely on nonmetals for watermill parts, including the runner stones, which were kept in place with tight leather strips, much to the amazement of foreign observers.[131]

In industry, waterwheels powered looms and various types of machines that beat, crushed, ground, and sawed cloth, leather, ores, wood, and many other materials. We already mentioned water's role in the mechanized and modern textile industry that expanded in central Mexico between the 1830s and the 1850s. In general, the trend was a transition from muscle power

---

[126] "Un nuevo molino de agua en Chihuahua," *El Museo Mexicano*, January 1, 1844.

[127] *Memoria de la Secretaría de Fomento* (México: Oficina Tipográfica de la Secretaría de Fomento, 1887), vol. 5, 475–9. The three waterwheels in this description were located in the northeastern state of Tamaulipas on sugarcane haciendas. All were overshot wheels 5.7–6.50 meters in diameter, moved by 230–448 liters of water per second, falling from 6 meters and producing 15–24 horsepower.

[128] Gómez, "Los molinos del Valle de México," 192.

[129] Some industrial and agricultural enterprises refused to purchase iron-made machinery for fear of being unable to replace broken parts. See Severo Cosío, "Fundería de fierro en las minas de Proaño, Aguascalientes," *El Siglo Diez y Nueve*, April 21, 1856.

[130] By mid-century, wholly iron-made waterwheels were available in Mexico, advertised as "modern" over their "primitive" wooden predecessors. See "Para los industriales, dueños de trapiches, molinos a la moderna," *El Siglo Diez y Nueve*, October 27, 1852.

[131] Gómez, "Los molinos del Valle de México," 165.

(human and animal) to waterpower. Consider the mountainous, water-rich area southwest of Mexico City. Traditionally a fruit-producing area, the foothills became the locus of an incipient industrial corridor by the mid-nineteenth century. Scattered throughout the Valley of Mexico, most manufacturing establishments were located in the southwest, particularly along rivers. Heavy rainfall during the rainy season, sometimes three times as much as in the valley's drier northern areas, meant an abundant supply of water. Water-powered machinery quickly became widespread in the region. Out of 17 textile factories established here in the early 1840s, 8 were powered by human muscle, 5 by water, 2 by mules, and 1 by steam. A decade later, most of these factories used water. Waterpower led to increased factory size and productivity over time. In 1843, La Magdalena, one of the region's biggest textile factories, had 8,400 spindles and 90 water-powered mechanical looms (*telares de poder*), producing under 9,000 cotton cloth pieces a year. A decade later, La Magdalena increased its number of spindles to 8,472, but now had 326 mechanical looms. As a result, production skyrocketed to over half a million pieces of cotton cloth annually.[132]

Waterpower production capacity had limits. The Valley of Mexico's clear division between rainy and dry seasons produced enormous variations in the water volume that rivers and streams carried downhill throughout the year. It was common for mills to stop working altogether for extended periods. Some factory owners tried solving this problem by building reservoirs, which often caused conflict with local inhabitants who used water for irrigation and domestic consumption.

Despite these drawbacks, water's relative cheapness as an energy source and the familiarity of Mexican craftsmen with waterwheels and milling technology (as opposed to, say, steam engines), made waterpower highly attractive to certain users. Gunpowder factories, for example, were still relying on waterwheels by the mid-nineteenth century, and some of these became increasingly large, powerful, and

[132] Secretaría de Fomento, *Anales del Ministerio de Fomento, Indústria, Agrícola, Minera, Fabril, Manufacturera y Comercial, y estadística general de la República Mexicana* (Mexico: Impr. de F. Escalante y Comp., 1854), vol. 1, 6. Early 1840s data are in Labastida, *Documentos para el estudio de la industrialización en México*, 81. On La Magdalena and other textile mills in the Valley's southwest, see Mario Camarena Ocampo, "Fábricas, naturaleza y sociedad en San Ángel (1850–1910)" and Mario Trujillo Bolio, "Producción fabril y medio ambiente en las inmediaciones del Valle de México, 1850–1880," in Alejandro Tortolero, ed., *Tierra, agua y bosques: historia y ambiente en el México central* (Ciudad de México; Guadalajara, Jalisco, México: Centre français d'études mexicaines et centraméricaines: Instituto de Investigaciones Dr. José María Luis Mora: Potrerillos Editores; Universidad de Guadalajara, 1996).

complex.[133] One wheel installed in an undefined location in the 1820s powered two gears that moved four large, bronze cones each weighing over half a ton. These cones rotated on a platform crossed by a canal holding charcoal, saltpeter, and sulfur. Grooves surrounded the cones into which the ground paste flowed. A skilled worker then added water to moisten the mixture, a critical step that determined the final quality of the gunpowder. This water-powered gunpowder mill could grind the paste in 6 hours, a tremendous gain over the 24 hours required using muscle power. It also seems to have improved the quality and potency of the gunpowder and reduced human labor by three-fourths, highly appealing from the factory owner's perspective.[134]

In industry, waterpower and animal power were inversely proportional: the more abundant water was, the less likely it was that a mine or factory would rely on animal-driven machinery. The famous German writer Carl Sartorius, who spent most of his adult life in Mexico, confirmed this when he visited the foundries that processed ore from the Fresnillo mines, in Zacatecas. "These immense works [foundries]" – Sartorius wrote – "employ thousands of men and thousands of beasts of draft and burden because all the machines, due to the lack of water, must be set in motion by mules. This remark applies specifically to Zacatecas and its environs, for other areas, although not all, have waterpower."[135]

Perhaps windmills could have solved this quandary, but this ancient technology was nearly absent in Mexico.[136] Geography and environmental conditions were partly to blame. Although Mexico has substantial inland wind resources, most of them are concentrated in present-day Oaxaca, in the southeast.[137] Here, the Isthmus of Tehuantepec, Mexico's narrow waist separating the Gulf of Mexico from the Pacific by just 220 km, creates an enormous wind funnel. Warm marine currents in the Gulf of Mexico produce differences in temperature and pressure, generating constant

---

[133] Yolanda Terán Trillo, "Maderos impelidos por la fuerza del agua. Molinos del periodo virreinal," *Boletín de Monumentos Históricos*, núm. 27 (May 1, 2013): 99–110.

[134] "Rueda hidráulica en fábrica de pólvora," *El Sol*, November 15, 1825.

[135] Carl Christian Sartorius, *Mexiko. Landschaftsbilder and Skizzen aus dem Volksleben* (Darmstadt: Gustav Georg Lange Verlag, 1859), 345.

[136] On the windmill's history see Adam Lucas, *Wind, Water, Work: Ancient And Medieval Milling Technology* (Leiden; Boston: BRILL, 2006), 101–3. As late as 1903, Mexican windmills were imported from countries like the USA. See *Directorio general de la República Mexicana* (México: Ruhland & Ahlschier, 1903), 504.

[137] Present-day estimates place the total at about 40,000 to 60,000 MW, 35,000 of which may be in the Isthmus alone. See Mercedes Canseco, "Energías renovables en América Latina" (Madrid: Fundación Ciudadanía y Valores, 2010), 7; Sergio Romero, et al., "Energy in Mexico: Policy and Technologies for a Sustainable Future," 194.

strong wind from October to April.[138] The Isthmus, however, lacked a strong manufacturing or mining tradition and had few inhabitants in 1850. But unlucky geography cannot be the whole explanation, because Zacatecas is also among the best endowed with wind resources in the country.[139] So why didn't mining exploit this energy source using windmills? Perhaps people were simply unfamiliar with the technology or its applications. Or if they knew it, they maybe associated it with draining waterlogged or marshy soils to create farmland, not a problem in arid Zacatecas. Perhaps windmill intermittency discouraged industries that required machinery to operate without interruptions.

Whatever the reasons, wind was only used as an energy source along the coasts of Mexico. In 1852, of the 839 ships that called at Mexican ports, 73 percent were sailboats (frigates, brigantines, and schooners) and 27 percent used steam. Only 8 percent were Mexican, while 52 percent sailed under the American flag, followed by the English (13 percent) and French banners (8 percent).[140]

In sum, while water was a relatively minor power source compared with muscle and wood, it played important roles in farming and manufacturing in Mexico by mid-century. Waterwheels and new water turbines transformed the kinetic energy of running or falling water into mechanical energy for textile looms, hammers, grindstones, factories, mines, wheat mills, and various types of workshops across the country. Like other technologies, water-driven machinery was concentrated in areas with the largest population and human economic activity, particularly the central highlands and the mining belt in the center-north. Wind was of negligible relevance on land but powered most of Mexico's small naval fleet.

Transport

Like other societies under the solar energy regime, mid-nineteenth-century Mexico faced a "transportation problem."[141] Overland transportation confronted clear energy limits, dependent as it was on muscle. Costs became prohibitive for many enterprises after a relatively short distance, especially

---

[138] Jorge Gutiérrez, "Energía renovable en el siglo XXI" (Monterrey, México: Senado de la República, 2001), 71.

[139] Q. Hernández-Escobedo, F. Manzano-Agugliaro, and A. Zapata-Sierra, "The Wind Power of Mexico," *Renewable and Sustainable Energy Reviews* 14, no. 9 (2010): 2830–40.

[140] Juan Nepomuceno Almonte, *Guía de forasteros y repertorio de conocimientos útiles* (México, 1852), 558.

[141] Sieferle, *The Subterranean Forest*, 57.

bulky, low-cost goods like grain and wood.[142] A pack of mules covered 20 to 30 kilometers daily, and in the highlands it cost 12–14 cents to transport one load (*carga*) of 138 kilograms (12 *arrobas*) 4 kilometers (1 *legua*), or 3.5 cents per kilometer. Thus, transportation costs for daily necessities like firewood (38 cents per *carga*) exceeded the item's price after 10–15 kilometers. Similarly, it only took a few dozen kilometers before items like grain and wood required more energy to haul than they contained. Only high-priced, low-volume goods like precious metals and luxury commodities remained profitable after long-distance transportation.[143]

Poor road conditions exacerbated the energy constraints of muscle-based land transportation. The main colonial roads from Veracruz to Mexico City and the one linking the latter city with Santa Fe, New Mexico fell into disrepair after decades of neglect. Other regions, including parts of the all-important northern mining belt, relied on poor-quality roads largely used by mule trains, horseback riders, or foot travelers – hardly fit for carts or coaches. On May 22, 1822, English engineer Robert Phillips and a Mexican colonel named Martínez departed from the port of Altamira, in Tamaulipas, with 14 four-wheel, ox-drawn wagons loaded with parts for a 36-inch steam engine. Their destination? The mine in La Concepción, Real de Catorce. After taking the only road north through Saltillo before veering south, the party covered some 800 km to arrive in Real de Catorce on November 11, almost 6 months later. The travelers braved high temperatures, broken wheels, and water scarcity. Most stretches of road were in bad shape. At points, the roads became narrow passages carved into mountainsides. Other times, the party hauled the machinery over rivers, at one point requiring the assistance of fifty Indigenous Mexicans and twenty yokes of oxen, and constructing a provisional dam to slow water flow. The terrain shattered wheels, and impromptu forges were built to mend them,

---

[142] Pérez Hernández, *Estadística de la República Mejicana*, 40–1. A *carga* or mule load was a measure of the weight one mule could carry. By comparison, it cost only 7–8 pesos to transport 1 ton of cargo from Panama to Acapulco, or from Acapulco to San Francisco. On a straight line, the distance from Panama to Acapulco is 3,000 km. Thus, it cost 7–8 pesos to transport 1,000 kg of cargo over 3,000 km by water. Hauling the same cargo overland would cost 756 pesos.

[143] This partly explains silver's preeminent economic role in New Spain and independent Mexico. It also underlines the enormous geographical obstacles Mexico faced when it began industrializing. Poor transportation and rugged topography became standard explanations for Mexican *atraso* (backwardness): John H. Coatsworth, "Obstacles to Economic Growth in Nineteenth-Century México," *The American Historical Review* 83, no. 1 (1978): 80–100. Missing in this argument is the acknowledgement that Mexico's "transportation problem" was typical of any society under the solar energy regime, which in the mid-nineteenth century included the entire world with the exception of regions with coal-based railroad transportation in Europe and the eastern USA.

contributing to delays. When the party finally arrived at their destination, they found the machinery badly damaged from travel. Phillips spent another 2 years making repairs before testing it, only to learn it needed iron pumps from the USA and another voyage to retrieve them. The steam engine finally began draining the mine in late November 1826, four and a half years after the initial trip.[144]

As English diplomat H. G. Ward pointed out, the condition of Mexico's roads rendered wheat grown in the highlands an "article of luxury" to residents of the port of Veracruz: "For strange as the assertion may appear, in the present state of the roads it would be easier, and cheaper, for towns upon the Eastern and Western coasts to draw their supplies from the United States, or California, by sea, than from the nearest corn lands on the tableland."[145] It cost half the price to ship wheat from Ohio to Veracruz than to import it from the wheat haciendas of Atlixco, Puebla, 300 km away (Table 1.3).

Unfortunately for Mexico, the country had few navigable rivers, and most could only be cruised by boats and ships with a small draft. The only rivers capable of carrying large ships flowed through the scantily populated tropical lowlands.[146] The exception was the Valley of Mexico. Here, the movement of people and goods depended on water transportation in the bottomlands, where large canoes crisscrossed the lakes and canals linking

Table 1.3 *Estimate of cost of cargo transport by land and water in Mexico, 1862*

Type of Transport	Weight (metric tons)	Distance (km)	Cost
Overland (Mule)	1	100	21.70 pesos
Water	1	100	27 cents

Source: José María Pérez Hernández, *Estadística de la República Mexicana*, 1862, 40–1.

[144] H. G. Ward, *Mexico in 1827* (London: Henry Colburn, 1828), 528–47. Tellingly, Phillips's trip to Cincinnati on the Mississippi River only took a little over 2 weeks.

[145] Ward, 47. "Corn" was generic for grain.

[146] Fewer than a third of Mexico's rivers were navigable by small ships. Pérez Hernández, *Estadística de la República Mejicana*, 24. A few steamers operated on the Pánuco River and along the Veracruz coast. See Miguel Lerdo de Tejada, *Cuadro sinóptico de la Republica Mexicana en 1856, formado en vista de los últimos datos oficiales y otras noticias fidedignas* (México: Imprenta de Ignacio Cumplido, 1856), 62–4.

Mexico City with its hinterland.[147] Lakes and canals made accessing urban consumers easy and cheap. The lake system represented essential transport until the late nineteenth century, when most of it was finally drained. Only after the arrival of railroads later in the century would water cease to be the valley's cheapest option for transport.[148]

Conclusion

For millennia, societies inhabiting present-day Mexico lived under the solar energy regime. These societies depended predominantly on the solar energy stored in plants. This presented limits to population sizes and their capacity to transform the environment. That said, the region's history from pre-Hispanic times until the middle of the nineteenth century was highly eventful from an environmental standpoint. There were phases of intense modification followed by recovery periods, and moments of acute exploitation and irreparable damage followed by permanent abandonment. In the absence of draft animals, Mesoamerican indigenous civilizations developed complex societies powered by human muscle. Humans were the main energy converters of chemical energy stored in plants into mechanical energy.

Then came the Columbian Exchange with the introduction of live-stock and diseases from the Old World. New pathogens wiped out most of the indigenous population and set the stage for the emergence of New Spain, with a heartland around Mexico City and a northern area centered around the Bajío and mining provinces. The former became a society of peasant communities with substantial ecological and food autonomy, commercial estates, and urban centers that channeled silver wealth into the global economy. The latter formed a highly commercial, manufacturing, capitalist economy organized around silver extraction,

---

[147] There were 81,217 canoes in 1861. See Hernández Pérez, *Estadística de la República Mejicana*, 171.

[148] Estimates for transport costs in preindustrial Europe are in Sieferle, *The Subterranean Forest*, 2001, 59. According to Pérez Hernández, a railroad from Mexico City to the villa de Guadalupe (4 kilometers) already existed in the early 1860s. A second linked Mexico City and Tacubaya (6 kilometers). The railroad from Mexico City to Veracruz was 26.4 km, although only one-third of tracks were operational. Within Mexico City, there were 640 carretas and 366 carretones for freight transport. Horses could also be rented for 5 pesos a day. There were 419 rental horses in the early 1860s. See *Estadística de la República Mejicana*, 37, 42. The figures for Mexico City's *cargadores* by the mid-nineteenth century are in Jesús Hermosa, *Manual de geografía y estadística de la República Mejicana*, 186. Perhaps not coincidentally, the valley's lake drainage project was finally accomplished – after almost 300 years of effort – only after railroads were introduced, a connection the literature on this topic overlooks. This suggests that an energy perspective may shed new light on even thoroughly studied topics such as the draining of the Valley of Mexico's lakes.

which deforested much of the region. Livestock expanded the limits of New Spain's solar energy regime, replacing humans in many tasks that required high energy expenditure. Then came waterpower, first introduced under Spanish rule, which increased the amount of energy available for manufacturing. After the silver economy collapsed with popular insurgency in 1810, Mexico's elites began promoting an incipient water-and-muscle-based industrialization process in parts of the country in the 1830s – radically early by global standards. The loss of vast northern territories to an expanding USA severely diminished Mexico's energy resources after 1848.

Mexico entered the 1850s with a less commercial economy, a shrunken territory, limited energy resources, and reliance on food energy and muscle power. That said, it was successfully developing a mechanized textile industry, reviving its mining sector, and amassing steam engines. First introduced in the 1820s to drain flooded mines, these devices made it possible for the first time to transform heat into motion. But the vast majority of these machines in Mexico used wood as fuel. Unlike, say, Britain, where they burned coal, steam engines in Mexico continued to depend on the amount of biomass available at any given location. Steam engines remained tied to local environmental conditions, operating under the constraints of the solar energy regime. This basic fact held enormous implications over the following decades as steam engine use in Mexico boomed with increased industrialization and the rapid expansion of the country's railroad system in the 1870s and 1880s. This multiplied the effect on Mexico's forests, depleted over centuries of silver mining. Forests began shrinking perceptibly in many regions, raising concern among state officials and industrialists over Mexico's long-term industrial potential.

The environmental, energy, and social conditions of the mid-nineteenth century emerged from the complex conditions of Mexico's previous centuries, which would deeply shape Mexico's energy history moving forward. To paraphrase that famous Marxist dictum, people in Mexico would make their own history, but not under the environmental and energy conditions of their choosing.[149] At the same time, changes in the types of energy exploited and the manner of their use would dramatically transform those initial circumstances.

---

[149] John R. McNeill, *Something New Under the Sun: An Environmental History of the Twentieth-Century World* (New York: W. W. Norton & Company, Inc., 2000), 194.

CHAPTER 2

The Nature of Capitalist Growth

There always will be limits to growth.
Donella H. Meadows, *Thinking in Systems*

In 1862, a man named Don Miguel Ramos requested from Mexico City Council's Petitions Committee a license to install a steam engine in his textile wool factory. A few months later, Ramos installed a 4-horsepower steam engine in an inner patio of his property. The committee sent an inspector to examine the machine, and the inspector reported that it was solidly built, its cylinder-walls had the appropriate thickness, and it featured a security valve. The inspector also confirmed that the steam engine was placed far enough from areas of heavy traffic within the building in the event of an explosion.[1] This may all seem mundane protocol, and that is precisely what makes it remarkable. By the early 1860s, acquiring and installing a steam engine in Mexico had become a fairly common process for both entrepreneurs and municipal authorities. Even a modest establishment like Ramos's could purchase one.

Over the following decades, an increasing number of small businesses, including bakeries, chocolate factories, workshops, and sawmills, switched to steam. Some mechanized stages of production for the first time, while others added steam to a partially mechanized set of procedures already in place. Most of these establishments initially adopted steam to complement waterpower. Water remained a cheap and common energy source. But given how heavily flows fluctuated between wet and dry season, waterpower was also unreliable.

Mexico's largest industrial establishments also introduced steam power to production. Mining companies employed steam engines as early as the 1820s to drain water from shafts, a problem so severe that it paralyzed many

[1] "Licencia para máquina de vapor," *El Siglo Diez y Nueve*, March 28, 1862; "Permiso al C. Miguel Ramos para poner una máquina de vapor para tejer hilaza," *El Siglo Diez y Nueve*, June 13, 1862.

mines by the end of the colonial period. After the mid-nineteenth century, an increasing number of mining companies introduced steam power into processing the ore itself, modifying a system dating back to the sixteenth century.[2]

With the construction of a vast railroad network in the early 1880s, transportation too became powered by steam. By the end of that decade, steam-powered railroads connected a large, mountainous country with a historically poor road system under a relatively unified web of lines. This groundbreaking transportation network set the stage for a manufacturing, export, and mining boom that would last until the outbreak of the Mexican Revolution of 1910.

The widespread application of steam engines, reliant almost exclusively on fuelwood until coal became more common in the 1880s, had enormous environmental effects. Combined with mining, population growth, and agricultural clearance, steam engines provoked a full-blown wood crisis by the 1880s. Increased deforestation most acutely affected central and northern Mexico, where mining and industry, population, and railroad expansion were most concentrated. Though there were still vast tracts of forest in the country, especially in the tropical lowlands, areas near urban centers and mining regions, along with lands crossed by railroad lines, experienced wood scarcity by the last quarter of the nineteenth century.

As the wood crisis intensified, so did anxieties over deforestation. Numerous government officials and Mexican elites called for urgent solutions. But life without the steam engine was out of the question. In order to protect developing industries and continue railroad expansion, officials and influential thinkers decided that forest conservation, reforestation programs, and the adoption of coal would mitigate the wood crisis without sacrificing industrial progress. The switch to coal after 1880 would have a long-term impact, as it marked the beginning of Mexico's transition to fossil fuels.

---

[2] Consider Real del Monte in Hidalgo. Until then, the company had used the centuries-old patio system that combined mercury and silver ore in large pools where humans and horses trampled it, invented by Spanish merchant Bartolomé de Medina in the mid-sixteenth century in nearby Pachuca. The new system replaced muscle with mechanized barrels moved by wood-powered steam engines. See Juan Burkhart, "Memoria sobre la explotación de minas en los distritos de Pachuca y Real del Monte de México," *Anales de la Minería Mexicana*, January 1, 1861. Ironically, Medina's system became widespread in colonial Mexico because it required less fuelwood, already scarce in some mining regions. See Julio Sánchez Gómez, "La lenta penetración de la máquina de vapor en la minería del ámbito hispano," *Arbor*, no. 149 (1994): 203–41.

The Power to Produce

Into the 1880s, waterpower remained important in Mexico wherever water was available and the topography rugged. Additionally, there existed a tradition of craftsmen who possessed the right skills to build and repair waterwheels.[3] Such conditions occurred in the central highlands and parts of western and southern Mexico. Certain sectors such as the textile industry, which required lots of power at certain stages of manufacturing, continued to use waterpower. As late as 1877, close to 40 percent of Mexico's textile factories relied exclusively on waterpower (Table 2.1). In some states where water resources supported an important textile industry, such as Jalisco in western Mexico, this figure went up to 60 percent.[4]

Mexican hydraulic technology became increasingly sophisticated during the late nineteenth century. Gone were the days when waterwheels were made of wood with a few iron parts protecting friction-prone areas. Wheels also grew larger, some by monumental proportions. The Hércules factory, one of the largest textile factories in Mexico, located in the state of Querétaro, owned one of the tallest overshot wheels in the world (Figure 2.1), 14 meters in diameter (the size of a modern Ferris wheel) and fully metal. The wheel and the beautiful stone factory in which it was located became an 1880s tourist attraction. Visitors eager to admire these symbols of progress came so frequently that the factory's managers were said to keep a clerk present to

Table 2.1 *Cotton and wool textile factories in Mexico by motive power, 1877*

Type of Factory by Motive Power	Number	Percentage
Steam and Water	52	53.6
Water	36	37.1
Steam	9	9.2
Total	97	100

Source: Emiliano Busto, *Estadística de la República Mexicana*, vol. 1, 1880, 82–4.

[3] Luis Robles Pezuela, *Memoria presentada á S.M. el Emperador por el Ministro de Fomento Luis Robles Pezuela de los trabajos ejecutados en su ramo el año de 1865* (México: Imprenta de J.M. Andrade y F. Escalante, 1866), 82.

[4] Emiliano Busto, *Estadística de la República Mexicana*, vol. 1, parte tercera, 76, 82.

Figure 2.1 Overshot waterwheel in the Hércules textile Factory, Querétaro, 1906.
Source: Fototeca INAH.

show the gardens, the artificial ponds surrounded by European-style statues, and, of course, the state-of-the-art machinery, including the waterwheel.[5]

Water turbines also helped to ensure that waterpower persisted in the age of steam. Developed originally in France in the 1820s and refined in the USA in the 1840s,[6] water turbines could achieve efficiencies of up to

---

[5] Lorenzo Castro, *The Republic of Mexico in 1882* (New York: Thompson & Moreau, 1882), 231. The Hércules waterwheel's size comes from David A. Wells, *A Study of Mexico* (New York: D. Appleton and Company, 1887), 151–2.

[6] Edward W. Constant, "Scientific Theory and Technological Testability: Science, Dynamometers, and Water Turbines in the 19th Century," *Technology and Culture* 24, no. 2 (1983): 183–98.

75 percent and deliver twice the horsepower with the same amount of water as used for a waterwheel. By the 1870s, buyers in Mexico could purchase one from Europe or the USA through one of Mexico City's import houses, which routinely ran advertisements in local newspapers showing off their steel-made merchandise.[7]

In some cases, waterpower remained the preferred option when alternatives, especially steam, were too expensive. The Piedra Azul ironworks, located on the banks of the Tunal River, 8 km south of Durango in northern Mexico, powered its bellows and hammers with two overshot wheels, one undershot wheel, and one turbine.[8] The quantities of pine and oak charcoal needed weekly to feed its blast, heating, and puddling furnaces, sinking fires, and smith fires traveled far from the mountains of the Sierra Madre on the backs of burros.[9] After spending up to 2 weeks making charcoal in distant forests, Indigenous Mexicans loaded burros with sacks carrying about 100 kg of fuel in total. It took three full days to reach the ironworks; by then, much of the charcoal had been damaged and reduced in size in transit. The price of charcoal fetched at the ironworks, though cheaper than elsewhere in Mexico, coupled with the required volume to make Piedra Azul iron exceedingly expensive.[10] Under such conditions, wood-fired steam engines simply did not compete with waterpower.

[7] Pablo Leautaud, "Agente general para toda clase de maquinarias de los Estados Unidos y Europa," *La Voz de México*, May 11, 1871. Not all water turbines were imported; in the late 1870s, haciendas in the Bajío were replacing old waterwheels with turbines, some locally made. See Busto, *Estadística de la República Mexicana*, 1880, vol. 3, 10.

[8] On the Piedra Azul ironworks, see Gerardo Sánchez Díaz, "Los orígenes de la industria siderúrgica mexicana: continuidades y cambios tecnológicos en el siglo XIX," *Tzintzun*, no. 50 (2009): 11–60. See also Leonidas Le Cenci Hamilton, *Hamilton's Mexican Handbook; a Complete Description of the Republic of Mexico, Its Mineral and Agricultural Resources, Cities, and Towns of Every State, Factories, Trade, Imports and Exports, How Legally to Acquire Property in Mexico, How to Transact Business under Mexican Laws, Railroads and Travelling in the Republic, Tariff Regulations, Duties, Etc ...* (London: Sampson Low, Marston, Searle, and Rivington, 1884), 175–6.

[9] Eighty metric tons in the 1850s, but down to 30 by the early 1880s under a more efficient system. The first figure comes from Federico Weidner, *El Cerro de Mercado de Durango con su corte geológico* (México, 1878), 29; the second from Hamilton, *Mexican Handbook*, 175–6.

[10] At Piedra Azul, charcoal cost 10–13 pesos per metric ton. Elsewhere, the price oscillated around 15 pesos per ton. I estimated the price of charcoal at Piedra Azul from Weidner, *El cerro de Mercado de Durango con su corte geológico*, 7; and the average price from Ministerio de Fomento, "Situación de las minas en México y puertos para la exportación de metales preciosos," *Diario del Imperio*, December 27, 1865. At 336 pesos per metric ton in the mid-1880s, Piedra Azul iron sold for almost double the iron from Mazatlan's coastal ironworks, which accessed cheap imported coal from Britain. Due to its price, Piedra Azul's iron could only be marketed in Durango itself. For Modesto Bargalló, expensive fuel explained the persistent economic problems of Piedra Azul. See Modesto Bargalló, *La minería y la metalurgia en la América española durante la época colonial* (México, D. F.: Fondo de Cultura Económica, 1955), 355.

In spite of waterpower's obvious advantages – relatively low cost, easy assembly and repair, and the kinetic potential of Mexico's numerous mountain rivers – it had several important drawbacks.[11] First, it could only power machinery close to the waterwheels. As a rule of thumb, the bigger the machine, the closer its location needed to be to the energy source. This necessary setup meant limitations to industrial design and factory layout, which were not always the most convenient or efficient arrangements for other steps in the productive process. Second, waterpower was often unreliable. Large parts of Mexico experience a stark contrast between the rainy and dry seasons; as such, rivers tend to be seasonal or carry different volumes of water during the year. When water volume was at its minimum (usually between September and April), industrial production could be severely affected and sometimes halted completely. Establishments also had to share their water with other users, including farmers and peasants, who used it for irrigation, and urban residents, who depended on rivers for most of their drinking water. Water-powered industrialization could be a zero-sum game, with one's consumption happening at the expense of another. When water-powered establishments returned used water to its river or canal, it was typically heavily polluted. Some owners created reservoirs to ensure water availability year-round, which decreased river flow and diverted larger volumes of water over time.[12] Water-dependent establishments were also located in rural and mountainous areas instead of urban areas, the main centers of consumption for industrial products. These limitations pushed industrialists, mining companies, workshops, and other ventures after 1860 to increasingly power their establishments with wood-powered steam engines.

The "Wings of Progress"

In 1869, the liberal newspaper *El Siglo XIX* ecstatically reported that a steam engine built by the mining company Real del Monte was now draining the flooded tunnels of a local mine. "The regularity [of the steam engine] is

[11] Relatively low cost does not mean free or even cheap. Factory owners paid rent for the water they used, which could be high enough to request exemptions from municipal authorities. See "Lorenzo Oliver pide sea eximido del pago de renta del agua que mueve su máquina de fundir plomo" (February 13, 1860), Fondo: Monterrey, Nuevo León y Coahuila; Sección: Ayuntamiento: Colección: Civil: Volumen: 271: Exp. 66, AHM. Municipal waterpower fees had been an established practice in Monterrey since the opening of its first mechanized textile factory in 1854. See "El gobierno aprueba el anterior permiso" (May 23, 1854), Fábricas Pioneras, exp. 12, AEGS.

[12] See the case of the Belén Mill in "Molino de Belén," Aguas, Molino de Belén 1735–1903, tomo 1, exp. 4, 12/Aguas, Gobierno del Distrito, tomo 18, 1898, exp. 1256, AHDF.

magnificent," it declared, explaining to readers that the contraption pulled up a leather bag (*tanate*) filled with water every 4.5 minutes from a depth of 400 meters. "Thanks to this resource," the newspaper stated, "1,000 men can now go back to work at this mine." "Steam [power]," it concluded, "is the wings of progress."[13] Two things stand out here. First, Real del Monte was building functioning steam engines as early as the 1860s.[14] Unfortunately, we do not know who designed and built this particular engine. Were they Mexican tinkerers and engineers? Or perhaps English machine-makers? (Real del Monte was British owned until 1848.) Whatever the case, importation was no longer the only way of acquiring a steam engine in Mexico.[15] Second, the note illustrates the *deus ex machina* role steam played in Mexico's industrialization. Steam solved Mexican mining's centuries-long drainage problems seemingly overnight. While steam engines were often installed to complement rather than replace water and muscle power, their effect was nonetheless revolutionary.

By 1880, virtually all of Mexico's mining districts had adopted steam engines in some capacity.[16] The list included crown jewels like Zacatecas and Fresnillo in the state of Zacatecas, Real de Catorce in San Luís Potosí, Chihuahua, and the Pachuca and Real del Monte districts in the state of Hidalgo.[17] Even fuel- and water-deprived Guanajuato, which mostly relied on muscle power, had five steam engines by 1880: four in the famous

---

[13] "Máquina de vapor para drenar la mina de Carretera, Real del Monte," *El Siglo Diez y Nueve*, September 10, 1869.

[14] This is about a decade before the Fundición Sinaloa, one of the most important manufacturers of steam engines in Mexico, built one. See Miguel Ángel Aviles-Galán, "A Todo Vapor: Mechanization in Porfirian Mexico: Steam Power and Machine Building, 1862 to 1906" (PhD Dissertation, University of British Columbia, 2010), 68. But it is a few years *after* the Apulco ironworks, 70 km away from Real del Monte, built a steam engine. While Apulco built the engine's body, it borrowed the valve system for steam distribution from an older engine, possibly made abroad. Real del Monte acquired the Apulco engine and became a frequent client of the ironworks for precision tools and machinery. See "Ministerio de Fomento. Situación de las minas en México y puertos para la exportación de metales preciosos," *Diario del Imperio*, December 27, 1865, 721.

[15] Typically, from Cornwall. See "Conditions of contract for an 85-inch cylinder steam engine, boilers, pumps, and other machinery for the Real del Monte Mining Company, Mexico," (February 18, 1857), José Villegas Collection on Mining. MSS 758. Special Collections & Archives, UC San Diego.

[16] Neither muscle nor waterpower disappeared. Energy sources and converters tend to coexist over long periods of time rather than simply displacing each other.

[17] For Chihuahua, see "La minería en Chihuahua," *El Siglo Diez y Nueve*, March 24, 1863; On Pachuca, see Ramón Almaraz, *Memoria de los trabajos ejecutados por la Comisión Científica de Pachuca en el año de 1864* (México: J.M. Andrade y F. Escalante, 1865), 91–5. Real del Monte had eleven steam engines around 1860; see Burkhart, "Memoria sobre la explotación de minas en los distritos de Pachuca y Real del Monte de México," 86. Fresnillo introduced its first engine in 1838, followed by three more later; see Busto, *Estadística de la República Mexicana*, vol. 2, 342–4. For Zacatecas, see *Anales del Ministerio de Fomento de la República Mexicana* (México: Imprenta de Francisco Díaz de León, 1881), vol. 5, 318. For Real de Catorce, see Busto, *Estadística de la República Mexicana*, vol. 3, 307.

Valenciana mine and the other in a hacienda de beneficio.[18] But steam engines also became common in innumerable smaller mining operations scattered from Sonora and Chihuahua in the north to Guerrero in the south. This region formed an imaginary parallelogram some 2,500 km long and 450 km wide at its girth in Zacatecas, Guanajuato, and San Luís Potosí, largely enclosed within the Sierra Madres. One nineteenth-century observer described this territory as the "historic mines of Mexico," noting that most dated back to colonial times.[19]

Since emerging in Mexico in the early 1820s, steam engines in mining were used exclusively to drain silver mines. This changed after 1860 as mines expanded steam's applications. Real del Monte led the way: in the 1850s, it replaced the colonial patio system of refining silver with a German procedure that mixed silver ore and mercury in steam-powered barrels, known as pan amalgamation.[20] This new system, according to one qualified observer, more efficiently processed even very low-grade silver ore.[21] After centuries of production, the silver content in old deposits had grown extremely low; the only way to keep them profitable was through increased energy inputs. Steam engines augmented the power needed to drain flooded mines or work low-quality more efficiently. Alternatives typically involved purchasing dozens or hundreds of horses and mules (and paying to feed, house, and care for them) or obtaining more waterpower, which was often scarce or required a lengthy legal process to secure water rights.[22]

---

[18] Busto, *Estadística de la República Mexicana*, vol. 2, 64, 76.

[19] Charles Bunker Dahlgren, *Historic Mines of Mexico. A Review of the Mines of that Republic for the Past Three Centuries. Comp. from the Works of von Humboldt, Ward, Burkart, Egloffstein, Reports of the United Mexican Mining Association, the Files of the "Minero Mexicano," and Geographical Society of Mexico, and Reports of Various Engineers of Mines and Mining Companies* (New York: Printed for the author, 1883), 13.

[20] Marvin D. Bernstein, *The Mexican Mining Industry, 1890–1950: A Study of the Interaction of Politics, Economics, and Technology* (Albany: State University of New York, 1964), 20.

[21] Burkhart, "Memoria sobre la explotación de minas en los distritos de Pachuca y Real del Monte de México," 85.

[22] The Pachuca mines in 1863 employed 963 horsepower, of which 522 was steam (54.2 percent), 32 was water (3.3 percent), and 409 was horses and mules (42.4 percent). For Pachuca, steam proved cheaper than muscle and water was scarce. One horse provided about 75 percent of one steam horsepower. Fuelwood for one 30-horsepower steam-powered winch in Pachuca cost M$65 weekly. Thirty steam horsepower replaced forty horses, which cost the company M$80 weekly. See Manuel Rivera Cambas, *Memoria sobre el mineral de Pachuca* (México: Impr. de. J. M. Andrade y F. Escalante, 1864), 21–2. John Buchan, director of Real del Monte in 1848 under English ownership, claimed that in the 1840s the company had three steam engines working nonstop to keep the mines dry at an annual cost of $90,000. Replacing these engines with horsepower would have required at least 180 winches moved by 7,000 horses and 2,000 men with an expenditure of $2 million. See Buchan's full report in William Parish Robertson, *A Visit to Mexico, by the West India Islands, Yucatan and United States: With Observations and Adventures on the Way* (London: Simpkin, Marshall & Company, 1853), 243–4.

But steam power came at the price of increased fuel consumption. Until the 1880s (when coal became relatively common), most steam engines burned fuelwood.[23] While generalizations are impossible given variations in size and energy requirements, even small steam engines needed constant supplies of fuelwood and charcoal. A 52-horsepower steam engine could consume up to 1650 metric tons of wood per year – the annual wood yield of about 3 km² of forest. A 360-horsepower engine could consume the annual yield of 7 km² of forest per year.[24] Though it is unknown how many steam engines operated at the thousands of silver mines across Mexico during the nineteenth century's last decades, their fuel consumption was undoubtedly considerable.[25] While visiting Real del Monte in 1864, engineer José Romero saw 150,000 *cargas* of fuelwood (about 20,700 metric tons) piled up in the Guajolote ranch for the company's steam engines.[26] That amount of wood alone would have required harvesting 35 km² of forest. Mines and refining haciendas in Mexico adopted steam engines despite wood scarcity and the long distances over which it was carried – in the case of Pachuca, as far as 20 kilometers away.[27] There was simply no better technology for extracting and processing their product.

Silver mining companies and associate refining haciendas (haciendas de beneficio) were historically the largest consumers of fuelwood and charcoal from the early colonial period until the early nineteenth century. As mines flooded and exhausted the most valuable ore, their impact on forests diminished. By draining mines and making it economically viable to process low-quality ore, steam engines revitalized the industry. They also multiplied silver mining's impact on forests, turning the industry into a forest juggernaut by the end of the nineteenth century. Between 1872 and 1902, Mexico produced a total of 16,631,983 kg of silver. Following a dip in output around 1870, silver production rose steadily for the following two decades, making silver mining the largest cause of deforestation in Mexico in the last quarter of the nineteenth century (Figure 2.2).

---

[23] In the case of Real del Monte, the delay was probably related to imported coal's high price. In 1896, Texas cannel coal fetched $12.25 (M$23.3) per metric ton in Pachuca. See "Real del Monte mine business correspondence," (1896–1899), José Villegas Collection on Mining. MSS 758. Special Collections & Archives, UC San Diego.

[24] Rivera Cambas, *Memoria sobre el mineral de Pachuca*, 16–18.

[25] One source recorded 2,819 mines and 300 metallurgical works in operation in Mexico in the late 1880s, mostly silver mines: "Foreign Mining News. Mexico," *The Engineering and Mining Journal* 46, no. 14 (October 6, 1888): 290–1.

[26] Almaraz, *Memoria de los trabajos ejecutados por la Comisión Científica de Pachuca en el año de 1864*, 133.

[27] Rivera Cambas, *Memoria sobre el mineral de Pachuca*, 33.

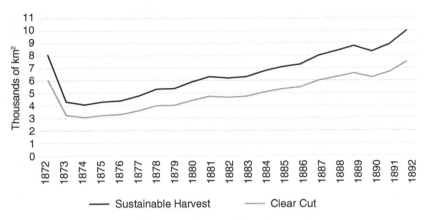

Figure 2.2 Estimated forest area harvested for silver production, 1872–92.
Source: INEGI, *Estadísticas históricas de México*, 1986, 437–8.

The chart plots two estimates. The black line shows the amount of forest needed for any year's production of pure silver between 1872 and 1892 if wood was *harvested sustainably*, that is, if only a forest's annual wood growth was harvested without clear-cutting it. Under this method, meeting the production demands of silver in 1872 would have required some 8,000 km^2 of a temperate forest's annual yield. By 1892, this figure would have grown to 10,000 km^2. The gray line tracks the area required for any given year if forest was clear-cut. It would have been smaller compared with the sustainable method – perhaps by 20–25 percent or 1,600–2,000 km^2 – simply because more wood was extracted from any given patch of forest.[28] Clear-cutting reduced the aggregated area but had detrimental environmental effects, since it largely eliminated forest cover. The total clear-cut forest area for 1872 and 1892, then, would have been approximately 6,000 km^2 and 7,500 km^2, respectively.[29]

[28] Olli Tahvonen and Janne Rämö, "Optimality of Continuous Cover vs. Clear-Cut Regimes in Managing Forest Resources," *Canadian Journal of Forest Research* 46, no. 7 (2016): 891–901.

[29] I make several assumptions to calculate forest area that require clarification. First, these are simple approximations. I claim no precision but, rather, offer a range of possibility. Following Daviken Studnicki-Gizbert and David Schechter, I assume that 1 kg of pure silver required about 1 metric ton of charcoal to produce. I also consider that one unit of charcoal required on average five units of fuelwood. A second key premise is that 1 km2 of temperate forest in Mexico yielded an average 600 tons of fuelwood. Studnicki-Gizbert and Schechter assume a higher, but sound, yield per square km of about 1,000 metric tons, which would reduce my proposed deforestation figures by 40 percent. Finally, I assume that 100 percent of silver fuel between 1872 and 1892 came from wood, which was not the case, but we simply do not know how much coal was used in silver mining during this period. Large mining districts like Pachuca and Real del Monte began using coal from

Which estimate is more likely? In forests belonging to mining companies and those on public lands, probably clear-cutting. We simply lack precise, numerical information about the cutting practices of fuelwood and charcoal makers who supplied the silver mining industry in nineteenth-century Mexico. However, a fair amount of circumstantial and anecdotal evidence suggests that indigenous charcoal makers (*indios carboneros*) sometimes simply cut as much wood as they could carry on their donkeys and mules.[30] From 1872 to 1892, silver production would have required sustainably harvesting 138,600 km^2 of forest (a bit larger than England) or 103,951 km^2 of clear-cut forest (about the size of the US state of Kentucky). If clear-cutting was the norm, silver production alone may have cleared or severely depleted between a third and half of Mexico's temperate forests and woodlands between 1872 and 1892.

What holds true for those woods does not necessarily reflect forest use elsewhere. There is substantial evidence that forests under peasant control were subject to a large degree of regulation. This is particularly true of many indigenous pueblos in central Mexico with titled claims over forests, land, and water from the colonial period. Some communities specialized in woodcutting and charcoal making, overseeing who made charcoal and how they made it.[31] They issued permits that allowed charcoal makers to use dead wood only (*palo muerto*) and fined the cutting of entire trees.[32] These local regulations sometimes echoed elite ideas about forests, such as their ability to attract rains and improve public health by purifying the air. They considered forests essential for rain-fed agriculture, the basis of their subsistence.[33] Of course, abuses happened. Local authorities sometimes sold permits to outsiders, and accusations of embezzlement were common. Local forest regulations, particularly those issued by municipal authorities, often attacked poor communities, especially their poorest members. The goal

---

Europe, the USA, and Coahuila in the 1880s. See Elvira Eva Saavedra Silva and María Teresa Sánchez Salazar, "Minería y espacio en el distrito minero Pachuca-Real del Monte en el siglo XIX," *Investigaciones Geográficas*, no. 65 (2008): 82–101. The estimates by Studnicki-Gizbert and Schechter are in Daviken Studnicki-Gizbert and David Schechter, "The Environmental Dynamics of a Colonial Fuel-Rush: Silver Mining and Deforestation in New Spain, 1522 to 1810," *Environmental History* 15 (2010): 94–119.

[30] "Sigue la tala al monte hasta que los indios vean desaparecer el agua y con ella la agricultura e industria" (June 1864), San Ángel, Montes, exp. 49, AHDF.

[31] "Padrones del municipio de San Ángel" (1845), San Ángel, Estadística, exp. 4, AHDF.

[32] "Permisos para fabricación de carbón en los bosques de San Nicolás y La Magdalena" (1864), Montes de Tlalpan, Municipio de San Ángel, exp. 39, AHDF.

[33] "Varios vecinos de San Bartolo quejándose del pago de un censo y talamiento del monte ordenados por el Regidor López y abusos del Auxiliar, todo en copias pues los orginales obran en la Prefectura" (1878), San Ángel, Gobierno, exp. 83, AHDF.

seemed to be curtailing peasant forest use to secure urban water supplies and industrial fuel. The poor complained that richer community members flouted regulations when they cut large amounts of wood to make charcoal for factories and grazed animals in communal forests, which prevented forest regeneration. They argued that regulations largely affected poorer peasants lacking connections and political power to subvert them.[34] In sum, there were two main types of forests: those owned by mining companies located in public lands and those controlled by pueblos and municipalities. Clear-cutting and haphazard exploitation seems to have been normal in the former; regulated use (not necessarily more sustainable or equitable) characterized the latter.

Factories and Workshops (Plus a Camel)

Steam power gained popularity in a wide variety of manufacturing establishments between the 1860s and the 1880s. From large textile factories to small workshops, steam supplemented unreliable water flow and muscle power, the latter coming from peasants-turned-factory-workers unaccustomed to harsh industrial labor regimes. Steam engines also allowed some textile factories to relocate to urban areas with a large pool of potential customers, almost "freeing" textile factories from their surrounding environment – I say "almost" because they continued relying on wood and charcoal. Despite these advantages, steam engines had a clear downside: they burned large amounts of fuelwood, a pricey and often scarce commodity.[35] Many textile factory owners thus viewed steam power initially as a complement to water and muscle, not their replacement. By the late 1870s, over half of Mexico's textile factories depended on a mix of steam and water, while 9 percent relied exclusively on steam. The Hércules textile factory illustrates some of these trends (Figure 2.3).

The Hércules textile factory was established in Querétaro in 1866, costing an impressive $4,000,000 pesos. Its stone buildings were surrounded by carefully tended gardens with artificial ponds adorned by $15,000-peso statues imported from Italy, including the god Hercules. In the 1880s, this lavish factory had 21,000 spindles and 700 looms, the latter manufactured in

---

[34] "Escrito de varios vecinos del pueblo de La Magdalena pidiendo se modere una disposición de la Prefectura sobre prohibición de cortar madera en los montes y hacer carbón. Se formó un reglamento y se mandaron seis inspectores de montes" (1877), San Ángel, Gobierno, exp. 77, AHDF.

[35] High prices weren't necessarily a sign of wood scarcity or local deforestation. Sometimes, fuel prices went up when wood and charcoal peddlers avoided areas for fear they would be conscripted by the army, a constant threat for many poor Mexicans throughout the nineteenth century. See "Carestía de carbón," *La Unidad Católica*, July 17, 1861.

Figure 2.3 Hércules textile factory, Querétaro, 1883. Notice the smokestack towering
over the large building complex.
Source: Fototeca INAH.

New Jersey and New England. Daily output amounted to 1,500 pieces of
manta – coarse, unbleached cotton cloth that poor Mexicans used for their
clothes – which sold at $4 per piece of 32 *varas*.[36] The factory, operating at
night as a giant wheat mill, depended on a mix of steam, water, and muscle
power. A Corliss engine from Providence, Rhode Island burning fuelwood at
$16 per cord provided steam with the help of English-made steam boilers.
For water, a small stream with a high fall moved an iron overshot wheel
(shown earlier). Muscle power came from humans and horses. Work for
both was punishing; shifts were 16 hours long, starting at daybreak and
ending at 9:30 p.m., with a half-hour breakfast and a 1-hour main meal at 2
p.m. For such long hours, spinners made 37–50 cents daily and weavers
6–7 pesos weekly, while mules and horses were "paid" in straw, corn husks,
and some grain.[37] Steam gave the factory flexibility and avoided the risk of
a complete and costly shutdown associated with dependence on one energy
source. It also made human labor more expendable.

---

[36] One *vara* equaled 0.8 meters. See *Sistema métrico-decimal: tablas que establecen la relación que existe
entre los valores de las antiguas medidas mexicanas y las del nuevo sistema legal, formadas en el Ministerio
de Fomento, conforme a la ley de 15 de marzo de 1857* (México: Imprenta de J.M. Andrade y F.
Escalante, 1857), 21.

[37] Wells, *A Study of Mexico*, 151–4; Castro, *The Republic of Mexico in 1882*, 231.

After 1860, workshop and small-business owners also found steam power attractive. Steam engine makers and importers focused on providing industry with small but potent steam engines (stationary and mobile) that could be easily transported on Mexico's notoriously poor roads to customers nationwide.[38] In turn, Mexicans and Mexico-based businesses adapted steam engines to a wide variety of tasks, including production of tortillas, candy, chocolate, lead pipes, burnished marble, and soda salts.[39] Even small firms otherwise reliant on muscle power, including one particularly strange case of a match maker who distributed his product to Mexico City stores via camel, acquired steam engines.[40] As the technology became common after 1860, a market for its sale and purchase developed, especially through newspaper ads. "Steam engine with 30 HP for sale with its boilers; it can be seen on Revillagigedo street, number 30," read one title.[41]

In the 1860s, mobile steam engines debuted in Mexico to address one of Mexico's greatest age-old problems: Mexico City's recurrent flooding.[42] The city began flooding periodically under Spanish rule due to a series of poor decisions regarding the indigenous hydraulic infrastructure and deforestation in the surrounding mountains for timber. Disastrous flooding returned every 20 to 30 years throughout the colonial period and into the nineteenth century, despite numerous efforts to drain the valley's lakes.[43] In 1861, city authorities paid contractor Juan Adorno a handsome 10,000 pesos to build about a dozen mobile steam engines to desilt the city's open drains (*atarjeas*). The task of making the engines was entrusted to a "skilled [Mexican] mechanic." The goal was to combat flooding by

[38] "Fábrica de maquinarias, Juan White," *El Siglo Diez y Nueve*, February 18, 1873.

[39] "Ayuntamiento de México. Máquina de vapor para hacer tortillas," *Diario del Imperio*, September 2, 1865; "Apertura de la dulcería 'El Fiel Pastor,'" *La Voz de México*, January 3, 1874; "Fábrica de chocolate con máquina de vapor," *La Voz de México*, December 1, 1878; "A los arquitectos y hacendados," *El Pájaro Verde*, March 7, 1867; "Máquina de vapor para cortar y bruñir mármol," *La Sociedad*, March 9, 1867; "Industria nacional. Fabricación de sales de sosa en Guadalupe Hidalgo," *La Voz de México*, April 12, 1871.

[40] "Introducción de máquina de vapor a la fábrica de cerillos 'La Esperanza,'" *La Voz de México*, October 9, 1881. Unfortunately, we know nothing else about the camel, including how it came to Mexico.

[41] "Se vende una máquina de vapor," *La Sociedad*, January 1, 1866.

[42] On Mexico City's colonial history of flooding and drainage, see Vera S. Candiani, *Dreaming of Dry Land: Environmental Transformation in Colonial Mexico City* (Stanford: Stanford University Press, 2014).

[43] On late nineteenth-century plans to combat flooding and drain the lakes, see Matthew Vitz, *A City on a Lake: Urban Political Ecology and the Growth of Mexico City* (Durham: Duke University Press Books, 2018), chapter 1. Flooding persists to this day. See Patricia Romero Lankao, "Water in Mexico City: What Will Climate Change Bring to Its History of Water-Related Hazards and Vulnerabilities?," *Environment and Urbanization* 22, no. 1 (2010): 157–78.

dredging the city's numerous open drains, an unpleasant job that had previously fallen to men who waded naked in water up to their necks. The plan appeared ineffective when another flood hit the city 4 years later. This time, a city official visited the city's myriad workshops looking for a steam engine to drain the inundated streets. He found plenty, but all were too small and modest for the task. A team of mules powering a pump was used in the meantime. The following year, another contractor replaced the mules with a steam-powered pump, apparently with some success.[44]

In 1868, the Ministry of Development decided to scale up these efforts, utilizing a steam-powered dredge on an iron-deck boat 2.5 meters wide by 15 meters long with a shallow draft of only half a meter to remove the accumulated silt of the San Lázaro canal.[45] Built in London under the supervision of Mexican engineer Miguel Iglesias, the dredge was part of a larger plan to mechanize Mexico City's perpetual war against water.[46] Through a cylinder and shaft, the engine powered a wheel featuring several 1-cubic-meter buckets. These raked silt from the bottom of the canal, lifted it, and discharged the muck onto a canoe below. Once this filled up, workers unloaded the silt onto the canal's edge while another canoe assumed position beneath the wheel. A portable hoist on the edge of the canal directed the boat's movements through a chain. Apart from extracting 400 tons of mud in 12 hours, the 6-horsepower engine did not interrupt navigation in the rest of the canal (when humans did the work, the area being serviced was temporarily closed and kept dry using dikes). The boat carrying the engine was also small enough to cross under the many bridges spanning the canal, the longest and most important waterway in the Valley of Mexico connecting downtown Mexico City with the eastern lake system. The hope was that dredging would facilitate San Lázaro's ability to expel the city's filthy floodwaters into the lakes, thus "avoiding the fermentation that result from their stagnation, the accumulation of organic substances, and the gas emissions that poison us," as one Mexico City newspaper put it.[47] Steam promised to relieve Mexico City of both chronic flooding and epidemic disease.

---

[44] Francisco Vera, "Limpia y reparación de la ciudad con máquinas de vapor," *El Siglo Diez y Nueve,* October 9, 1861. "Fuerza motriz para desaguar la Ciudad de México," *Diario del Imperio,* November 9, 1865. "Inundación de las calles de México y uso de máquinas para remediarla," *Diario del Imperio,* November 9, 1865. "Desagüe de la ciudad de México con máquina de vapor," *La Sociedad,* January 22, 1866. "Valle de México," *La Sociedad,* May 23, 1866.
[45] "Draga de vapor para limpiar el canal de San Lázaro," *El Siglo Diez y Nueve,* June 13, 1868.
[46] Other English-made steam engines were already deployed at pumping stations to accelerate the drainage process.
[47] "Draga de vapor para limpiar el canal de San Lázaro."

Steam engines also expanded into the countryside. People used steam power to saw wood and remove pips from cotton on the banks of the Papaloapan River in southern Veracruz.[48] Further south, in the Yucatan Peninsula, sugar haciendas readily adopted steam engines for their mills.[49] All-important henequen haciendas followed suit, often with fanfare. One Yucatec bigwig debuted steam engines at his henequen hacienda with a lavish banquet and the local bishop's blessing. Installed by the hacienda owner's "mechanic" son, the engines mechanized two key steps in henequen (*Agave fourcroydes*) cultivation and processing: pumping groundwater for irrigation and crushing and scraping the leaves.[50] As more henequen haciendas adopted steam engines, workers who could operate them became valuable.[51] The following steps – washing the fibers, drying them in the sun, and compressing them into bales for export to fiber-hungry markets in the USA, Canada, and Europe – were still done by hand. In subsequent decades, steam-powered mechanization coexisted alongside the harshest labor regimes, including slavery.[52] The "wings of progress" did not lift everyone.

From mining to making henequen, steam power found many applications in Mexico. In all cases, steam's motive power applied itself directly to axles, shafts, and wheels, circumscribing steam's reach to its immediate surroundings. By the 1880s, wood-fired steam engines became widely adopted for electricity generation. This dramatically expanded steam's capacity to perform work at a distance or produce light, its most common function during that decade. The first instance of steam-generated electricity in Mexico dated back to 1852 with the country's first telegraph line between Veracruz and Mexico City. Starting with a few hundred kilometers in the 1850s, Mexico's telegraph network exploded over the following decades, reaching 28,560 kilometers by 1889.[53] In 1879, La Americana, a textile factory

---

[48] "La costa de Sotavento en el estado de Veracruz. Máquinas de vapor para aserrar y despepitar algodón," *El Siglo Diez y Nueve*, June 6, 1868.

[49] "Máquina de vapor para fabricar azúcar en el municipio de Espita, Yucatán," *La Razón del Pueblo. Periódico Oficial del Estado de Yucatán*, December 29, 1871; "Máquina de vapor en la hacienda Santa María de Fermín Irabien para elaborar azúcar," *La Razón del Pueblo. Periódico Oficial del Estado de Yucatán*, January 12, 1872; "Ingenio de azúcar en Campeche con máquina de vapor," *La Voz de México*, May 15, 1874.

[50] "Máquina de vapor para la raspa del henequén en la hacienda de Tecoh," *La Razón del Pueblo. Periódico Oficial del Estado de Yucatán*, April 29, 1870.

[51] "Raspadores de henequén en máquina de vapor," *La Razón del Pueblo. Periódico Oficial del Estado de Yucatán*, June 10, 1870.

[52] Sterling David Evans, *Bound in Twine: The History and Ecology of the Henequen-Wheat Complex for Mexico and the American and Canadian Plains, 1880–1950* (College Station: Texas A&M University Press, 2013), chapter 3.

[53] Alberto Best, *Noticia sobre las aplicaciones de la electricidad en la República Mexicana* (México: Imprenta de la Secretaría de Fomento, 1889), 76–7.

in the city of León in north-central Mexico, was the country's first to install electric lighting on its premises.[54] Other factories across Mexico followed suit. Steam-generated lighting shone brighter than kerosene lamps and gaslights and did not raise room temperatures like large gasoline burners used previously. Electricity was also the cheaper option (always fortunate). Wealthy families began illuminating their residences with electric light, making electricity a symbol of status and modernity. It is no coincidence that the first home electric system in Mexico was mounted in 1882 – only 2 years after Edison's company began the commercial manufacture of light bulbs – in the home of General Carlos Pacheco, the serving minister of the Ministry of Development (*Secretaría de Fomento*).[55] Fomento was charged with "modernizing" Mexico, and modernize it did. By 1889, most large cities and towns in Mexico had public electric lighting systems, with 66 power plants and 96 electric generators powering almost 6,000 streetlamps across the country. Wood-fired steam engines produced nearly 90 percent of this electricity, while water generated the rest.[56] This would change over the next decades with the shift to hydroelectricity, but steam's role in Mexico's early electricity generation is well attested.

The Power to Move

January 1, 1873 marks a key date in Mexico's modern history. On that day, President Miguel Lerdo de Tejada inaugurated the country's first long-distance railroad line, initiating the birth of mechanized transportation in Mexico and muscle-powered transportation's long decline.[57] The track, finished under the direction of British engineers and operated by the British-controlled Mexican Railway (*Ferrocarril Mexicano*), linked the port of Veracruz in the Gulf of Mexico with Mexico City, some 420 km away.

The inauguration was all the more significant for contemporaries because it marked the realization of a project begun in 1837. In that year, the Mexican government granted the first line concession to a Mexican

---

[54] Best, *Noticia sobre las aplicaciones de la electricidad*, 53.   [55] Ibid., 63.

[56] Ibid., 170–1. Steam-generated electricity's impact on Mexican forests was small compared with that of mines and factories. Guadalajara, a large city of 80,000 inhabitants in the 1880s, consumed no more than 2 km² of forest every year to illuminate its streets for 5 or 6 hours per night. See Best, *Noticia sobre las aplicaciones de la electricidad*, 22.

[57] Gustavo Adolfo Baz and Eduardo L. Gallo, *Historia del ferrocarril mexicano: riqueza de México en la zona del Golfo á la Mesa Central, bajo su aspecto geológico, agrícola, manufacturero y comercial. Estudios científicos, históricos y estadísticos* (Mexico: Gallo y Compañia, editores, 1874), 18.

merchant from Veracruz, only 7 years after the South Carolina Canal and Railroad Company, the first steam-powered railroad in the USA, began operations. It failed and was followed by many other concessions given to successive investors, each of whom left behind little more than a few kilometers of poorly built track surrounded by rusting construction material.[58] The endless delays were partly due to chronic political instability and the tremendous environmental challenges of building a railroad that began at sea level and rose to over 2,000 meters within roughly 120 km.[59] Indeed, the planned route passed over some of the most rugged terrain in a country so mountainous that conquistador Hernán Cortés (in a poetic but likely apocryphal anecdote) once described it to Spanish monarch Charles I by crumpling a sheet of paper in his hand. Despite these difficulties, about half of the track was completed when the failed emperor Maximilian of Hapsburg succumbed to a liberal firing squad in 1867.[60]

While the main line inched forward, a few local tramways were established in urban areas. Until the late 1850s, the only form of public transit in Mexico was mule-drawn omnibuses linking principal cities and towns with nearby population centers.[61] Passengers boarded at the system's stations, boisterous and chaotic places where haughty middle-class passengers unable to afford their own carriages rubbed elbows with the *lépero* class or urban poor. Vendors screamed offers from the streets, horse riders caracoled their mounts, and pedestrians walked obliviously in front of the cars. After departing, the cars navigated roads with grooves 1 or sometimes 2 meters deep from the cars' thin wheels, rainy season downpours, and poor maintenance. Reportedly, omnibuses sometimes literally floated like boats across flooded stretches of the rain-soaked roads. Other times, cars would get stuck in mudholes so deep they covered the mules up to their necks. During the dry season, dust blown from road traffic often caked passengers, drivers, and mules in dirt.

[58] David Pletcher, "The Building of the Mexican Railway," *Hispanic American Historical Review* 30, no. 1 (1950): 26–62.

[59] Fuel availability was crucial when deciding where to build the first Veracruz–Mexico line. Juan Balbontín argued that planners chose the path through Orizaba instead of Jalapa because fuelwood (and water for engines) was more accessible and cheaper along this route. See Juan M. Balbontín, "Inauguración del ferrocarril de Veracruz," *El Siglo Diez y Nueve*, January 8, 1873.

[60] Baz and Gallo, *Historia del Ferrocarril Mexicano*, 17.

[61] Manuel Rivera Cambas, *México pintoresco, artístico y monumental: vistas, descripción, anécdotas y episodios de los lugares más notables de la capital y de los estados, aun de las poblaciones cortas, pero de importancia geográfica ó histórica* (México: Imprenta de la Reforma, 1880), 341–5.

In 1856 or 1857, the first animal-powered tramway on tracks connected the capital's downtown area with the nearby Tacubaya suburb. Through the 1860s, the system expanded, reaching the most important points in the east, west, and south of the Valley of Mexico. Steam locomotives operated on the longest stretches, but elevated fuel expenses prompted company owners to replace most engines with hundreds of mules and horses after a few years.[62] By 1880, Mexico City's urban and suburban tramways covered almost 100 km, mostly powered by animals.[63] While this was by far the most comprehensive tramway system in the country, virtually every major town and city claimed one by the early 1880s.[64] Animal-powered transport persisted for many years due to its low cost and the short distances covered by many urban and suburban lines.[65]

A construction boom followed the completion of the Veracruz–Mexico City trunk line in 1873. When Porfirio Díaz became president for the first time in 1876, the country's railway network totaled just 675 km. By 1880, it reached 1,079 km. A decade later, an iron and wood web of roads totaling 9,717 km crisscrossed the country, 92 percent of it powered by steam.[66] Between 1877 and 1892, Mexico built more kilometers of railroad track than any other nation in Latin America.[67] On the eve of the 1910 Revolution, Mexico boasted 19,797 km of railroad tracks, the third largest system in Latin America.[68]

---

[62] Ibid., 346. Some residents strongly opposed steam traction. They resented the noise of locomotives and worried about potential risks from their vibrations. See "Oposición al tren en Chalco," *La Sociedad*, February 22, 1866. Despite opposition, some longer lines in the Valley of Mexico continued using steam power for an indefinite amount of time, as persistent complaints against steam-powered locomotives suggest. See "Queja sobre el ferrocarril de Tlalpan," *La Voz de México*, November 10, 1870.

[63] Castro, *The Republic of Mexico in 1882*, 157.

[64] See Charles W. Zaremba, *The Merchants' and Tourists' Guide to Mexico* (Chicago: The Althrop Publishing House, 1883). On the Valley of Mexico's railroad network, see Antonio García Cubas, *Mexico: Its Trade, Industries and Resources* (Mexico: Typographical Office of the Department of Fomento, Colonization, and Industry, 1893),315–16.

[65] Secretaría de Fomento, *Álbum de los ferrocarriles* (México: Secretaría de Fomento, 1889), 176–7.

[66] Ibid., 171–8.

[67] Sandra Kuntz Ficker, *Historia mínima de la expansión ferroviaria en América Latina* (México, D. F.: El Colegio de Mexico, 2016), 345–52. Providing slightly different figures, contemporary observer Luís Pombo believed that from 1877 to 1892, Mexico built 10,204 km; Argentina, 9,108 km; and Brazil, 6,193. After Chile (1,020 km), no other Latin American country had more than a few hundred kilometers of track in 1892, while Honduras had none. See Luís Pombo, *México: 1876–1892* (México: Imprenta de "El Siglo Diez y Nueve," 1893), 77–8. US and British capital and government subsidies for each kilometer of track built funded most of the expansion. For US capital's role in Mexico's railroad development, see David M. Pletcher, *The Diplomacy of Trade and Investment: American Economic Expansion in the Hemisphere, 1865–1900* (Columbia: University of Missouri Press, 1998), chapter 3.

[68] Fred Wilbur Powell, *The Railroads of Mexico* (Boston: Stratford, 1921), 1.

The prize of this vast network was the Boston-based Mexican Central Railway, which began construction in 1880 and was completed in 1884. Well into the twentieth century, the Central was not only the largest railroad company in Mexico, but Mexico's largest company.[69] The company offers insight into the role railroads played in Mexico's 1880s energy crisis.

From its founding, the Central quickly became and remained one of the period's largest consumers of fuel in Mexico. Between 1882 and 1907, locomotive fuel represented the company's highest operating expense. In some years, fuel expenses could run up to 26 percent, hitting a 15 percent low at other times. Over 25 years, energy expenditures represented 14.2 percent of all the expenses, the largest single block for the company.[70]

When a reporter asked Daniel B. Robinson, the company's general manager, what he considered the greatest obstacle to the economical operation of railroads in Mexico, Robinson replied: "lack of [cheap] fuel."[71] Unsurprisingly, the company board and management consistently sought to lower energy costs, first by offsetting high fuel prices with cheap labor. According to Robinson, the company remained profitable due to Mexico's relatively inexpensive labor. This strategy was highly racialized and mostly affected Mexican workers, not the company's American workforce in Mexico, who earned similar salaries to their US counterparts. As Robinson unabashedly explained,

> [a]ll our general officers, heads of departments, conductors and engineers are Americans, and receive practically the same pay as those performing similar services in the United States. Our brakemen, firemen and common laborers are almost all Mexicans, whose work we were able to procure at from 40 to 50 cents a day. You will readily perceive that there is a great saving in this item enough to equal the unusual expense which we were put to for fuel.[72]

---

[69] Sandra Kuntz Ficker, "La mayor empresa privada del Porfiriato: el Ferrocarril Central Mexicano (1880–1907)," in Carlos Marichal and Mario Cerutti, eds., *Historia de las grandes empresas de México* (México, D. F.: FCE/Universidad Autónoma de Nuevo León, 1997), 39–63; Sandra Kuntz Ficker, "Economic Backwardness and Firm Strategy: An American Railroad Corporation in Nineteenth-Century Mexico," *Hispanic American Historical Review* 80, no. 2 (2000): 267–98.

[70] Mexican Central Railway Co. Limited, *Annual Report of the Board of Directors of the Mexican Central Railway Co. Limited to the Stockholders for the Year Ending* (Boston: Geo. H. Ellis, Printer, 1880–1908). For other railroad companies, like Tehuantepec, crossties were the largest expenditure. See Teresa Miriam Van Hoy, *A Social History of Mexico's Railroads: Peons, Prisoners, and Priests* (Rowman & Littlefield, 2008), 90–1.

[71] "The Mexican Central R.R. General Manager Robinson Gives His Views Regarding the Road," *The Two Republics*, February 7, 1885. Robinson resigned in 1885, replaced by Edward W. Jackson. See Mexican Central Railway Co. Limited, *Annual Report of the Board of Directors of the Mexican Central Railway Co. Limited to the Stockholders for the Year Ending* (Boston: Geo. H. Ellis, Printer, 1886), 11–12.

[72] "The Mexican Central R.R. General Manager Robinson Gives His Views Regarding the Road."

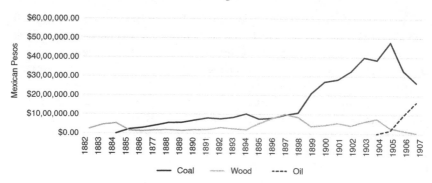

Figure 2.4 Mexican Central Railway expenses by Fuel, 1882–1907.
Source: Mexican Central Railway Co. Limited, *Annual Report of the Board of Directors of the Mexican Central Railway Co. Limited to the Stockholders for the Year Ending*, 1880–1907.

The second cost-cutting strategy involved diversifying the company's energy mix and gradually moving from fuelwood to coal and eventually oil (Figure 2.4). The Central burned fuelwood exclusively during its early years. Once a connection with the US railway system was established at El Paso in 1884, the company also began burning coal. For the company's executives and managers, used to the increasingly coal-based US system, coal was the logical option.[73] It promised to be cheaper than fuelwood and more readily available. Initially, the company imported most coal from the United States but soon acquired some from the increasingly productive Coahuila coal fields. The company also began investing in coal prospecting in Mexico, hoping that local sources would further lower the price. Wood and coal remained the only energy sources until the introduction in 1904 of fuel oil, whose consumption would surpass the other two over the following years.

What was the Central's impact on Mexico's forests? A very rough estimate suggests that between 1882 and 1907 about 1,101 km² of forest (one-third of the US state of Rhode Island) was harvested to fuel the Central's locomotives, 240 km² of this in the 1880s alone.[74]

---

[73] On the USA, see Michael Williams, *Deforesting the Earth: From Prehistory to Global Crisis* (Chicago: University of Chicago Press, 2010), 297.

[74] See Mexican Central Railway Co. Limited, *Annual Report of the Board of Directors of the Mexican Central Railway Co. Limited to the Stockholders for the Year Ending* (Boston: Geo. H. Ellis, Printer, 1880–1908). I calculate this based on several conversions and assumptions. We know how much the

The Central's fuel requirements caused substantial deforestation, but more on the scale of, say, the textile industry than silver mining. The Central's fuelwood consumption fluctuated between 1882 and 1904, largely in response to wood and coal prices, and then began a steady decline after 1904, when the company shifted to oil.

The Central's demand for wood went beyond fuelwood; it included ties and wooden planks for train stations and bridges. Ties took a heavy toll on forests. From 1880 to 1907, the company used 16,179,238 crossties on its tracks. Although some were imported, most came from Mexico's pine, oak, and fir forests. Since the majority were made of softwood, crossties in Mexico lasted about 2 years, meaning that every year hundreds of thousands needed replacement. The duration increased once companies began creosoting crossties in the late nineteenth and early twentieth centuries. Introducing iron and then steel ties also reduced wood consumption. Assuming a rough conversion of 50,000 ties per km^2 of forest, the Central used 323.5 km^2 of forest for crossties between 1880 and 1907, a third of it in the 1880s.[75] Consider this in terms of trees. One single tree typically yielded two ties.[76] Thus, the Central was responsible for cutting three million trees for crossties in the 1880s alone.[77]

Using the Central's data, a few preliminary remarks can be made on the environmental impact of Mexico's railroads. First, railroads did aggravate Mexico's deforestation crisis in the late nineteenth century, but they were less important than contemporaries (and many historians) imagined, certainly compared with silver mining. Railroad-caused deforestation followed decades of forest clearance to feed steam engines at mines,

Central spent on fuelwood annually between 1882 and 1907, which allows us to approximate how many metric tons of wood the company's locomotives consumed. Assuming a temperate forest in Mexico yielded on average 600 metric tons of wood annually, we can convert wood consumption into forest area. The company paid 5–7 dollars per cord of wood in the 1880s. At the time, the exchange rate was about 1 peso per 75 cents of US dollar, so 7 US dollars = 9.34 Mexican pesos per cord. One cord of wood = 640 kg; 1 metric ton of wood = 1.6 cords. Thus, in the 1880s the company paid about *15 Mexican pesos for 1 metric ton of wood*, a very high price. The price of wood for the company comes from "The Mexican Central R.R. General Manager Robinson Gives His Views Regarding the Road"; the exchange rate from Fernando Rosenzweig, "Las exportaciones mexicanas de 1817 a 1911," *Historia Mexicana* 9, no. 3 (1960): 377–413; the conversion of cords to kgs. from "Circulares del presente año a 1914" (November, 1910), Fomento, Bosques, Caja 13, Exp. 21, AGN.

[75] For converting ties to forest area, see Williams, *Deforesting the Earth*, 338–9.

[76] "La tala de bosques," *La Voz de México*, January 11, 1905.

[77] The 1880s total was 5,799,290 crossties. See Mexican Central Railway Co. Limited, *Annual Report of the Board of Directors of the Mexican Central Railway Co. Limited to the Stockholders for the Year Ending* (Boston: Geo. H. Ellis, Printer, 1880–1890).

factories, iron and glassworks, haciendas, and myriad workshops, which themselves compounded "traditional" causes of deforestation like agricultural expansion and population growth. However, railroad wood consumption was highly visible, from the denuded areas close to the tracks, to the massive number of crossties, to the huge piles of fuelwood stacked along the lines. Railroads also made it economically viable to transport bulky, low-cost items such as grain, lumber, nonprecious metals, and export commodities long distances for the first time in Mexico's history. This likely spurred forest clearance in areas previously spared, both because land was now needed to grow things other than trees and because virtually all these activities required wood and fuelwood.[78] Cumulatively, railroads' direct and indirect impacts may have represented 3,000–5,000 km^2 of deforestation in Mexico from 1870 to 1890.

"Islands of Scarcity"

In 1882, Mexico's deforestation crisis spurred a journalistic debate between John Bigelow and Matías Romero, two high-profile figures in US elite and diplomatic circles. Bigelow was a prominent politician and writer with a long career serving various US governments and an influential public voice, especially in New York, where he spent much of his life. Romero served as Mexico's minister to the USA, repeatedly representing his country abroad. He successfully established a close liaison with important US figures over the years, from Lincoln to financiers like Jay Gould.[79] After a brief visit to Mexico, Bigelow published a piece criticizing the country in *Harper's Magazine*, tinged with typical nineteenth-century Anglo-American condescension towards and deep-seated skepticism over the benefits of American capital investment in Mexico.[80] Romero, an effective propagandist and staunch advocate of promoting Mexico's "material development" (*mejoras materiales*) through foreign investment, responded with a lengthy article. Romero was particularly interested in dispelling the notion that Mexico suffered from "scarcity of fuel" or that it was grappling with a "fuel famine," as the British chief engineer of the Mexican National

---

[78] It may have led to some forest regrowth elsewhere, since railroads made regional economic specialization possible. Food could now be transported over long distances, so some regions likely found it cheaper to import food than grow it, alleviating pressure on local forests.

[79] An overview of Romero's early years in the USA is Robert Ryal Miller, "Matias Romero: Mexican Minister to the United States during the Juarez-Maximilian Era," *The Hispanic American Historical Review* 45, no. 2 (1965): 228–45.

[80] John Bigelow, "The Railway Invasion of Mexico," *Harper's Magazine*, October 1882.

Railway reported.[81] Were such a perception to spread among US investors, American capital investment in Mexico could be endangered.

Romero, who knew most of Mexico from first-hand experience and government records, recognized that "after four hundred years of constant consumption the forests in close proximity to the towns have been destroyed and fuel begins now to be scarce and to command a comparatively high price." Increasing fuel consumption by railroads, factories, and other industries – Romero explained – had worsened deforestation, leading the Mexican government to appoint a committee (which included Romero) to organize coal surveys in Mexico. For many government officials, replacing fuelwood with coal would alleviate pressure on Mexico's forests. But after accepting that a fuel problem existed in parts of Mexico, Romero criticized Bigelow for assuming that the price of Mexico City's fuelwood represented prices elsewhere; not only were Mexico City fuel prices the highest in Mexico, but they had doubled in the past few years following railroad construction. He assured North American readers (and investors) that "[t]here are now large forests in Mexico that are yet untouched, and where wood is worth nothing."[82] No doubt Romero was referring to Mexico's tropical rainforests; he added that he had "often seen many poor people living near such places using, for cooking their food, woods of the most expensive kind, such as ebony, rosewood, mahogany cedar, etc.," all found in Mexico's tropical regions. Romero maintained that once railroads penetrated those areas and Mexico's coalfields began producing, the country's fuel problem would disappear.[83]

Romero was essentially correct. The colonial period and the nineteenth century had indeed witnessed intense forest clearance, especially near mining and urban centers. It was also true that steam engines and an expanding railroad network worsened the situation. In fact, while Romero did not say so in his pamphlet, by the 1880s, all the great mining centers of Mexico, Zacatecas, Guanajuato, San Luís Potosí, Chihuahua, and Real de Catorce, and many cities, faced a severe wood shortage. Factories, ironworks, and railroad companies constantly worried about fuel scarcity. Still, Romero understood that describing this situation as a generalized "fuel famine" was an exaggeration; rather, parts of Mexico suffered from acute levels of fuel "malnutrition."

Put more simply, Mexico's deforestation crisis in the 1880s was regional. The situation can be visualized as a series of (big) "islands of scarcity"[84]

[81] Matías Romero, *Railways in Mexico* (Washington, DC: W.H. Moore, 1882), 15–17.
[82] Romero, *Railways in Mexico*, 17.   [83] Ibid.   [84] Sieferle, *The Subterranean Forest*, 26, 59.

strewn across a country otherwise characterized by large swaths of forests and woodlands. Some of these islands were so big and close they formed great tree-poor archipelagos. The principal of these occupied the central highlands and north-central Mexico, flanked by the largely forested spines of the two Sierra Madres in the north, the conifer forests of Michoacán and western Mexico in the middle, and the dry and humid tropical lowland forests along the Atlantic and Pacific coasts and in the south. By the late nineteenth century, dense forests in this vast "island of scarcity" gave way to fragmented or residual woodland. In some parts, forests were replaced by a treeless, barren landscape.

Wood shortages across this territory were undoubtedly aggravated by "the transportation problem." With wood being bulky and of relatively low value, transporting it before railroads was prohibitively expensive after short distances. Any settlement not located close to water transport could only draw wood from within a radius of 15–30 kilometers (sometimes less in mountainous areas). In 1861, a Real del Monte employee described nearby woods as "very dense, so that a person cannot walk through them" but explained that there would be "a great many difficulties to overcome as the roads are in a very bad condition." He deemed the forest, just 12 km away, "too far" for mules.[85] Even when railroad networks emerged, many settlements remained far from the nearest line. With wood abundant in not very distant areas, many people and industries still lived in "islands of scarcity."[86]

"Transcendental Damages"

Mexico's deforestation crisis was a grave problem for Romero and other members of Mexico's political and economic elite. Forest loss meant even higher fuel prices and threatened Mexico's well-being in myriad ways. For nineteenth-century Mexicans, forests "purified the air" by absorbing "carbonic gas" (CO_2); moderated local temperature by reducing the intensity of sunlight; preserved soil moisture and stabilized it; dried out marshes and swamps and other miasma-producing areas;[87] regulated runoff during the

[85] "Real del Monte Mine Business Correspondence" (1860–3), José Villegas Collection on Mining. MSS 758. Special Collections & Archives, UC San Diego.

[86] Sieferle, *The Subterranean Forest*, 59–60. Sieferle argues that "in terms of energy wood was scarce if the energy investment in transportation was higher than the energy yield to the consumer." Mexicans fully understood this connection. See Ricardo Ramírez, *La condición legal de los bosques y su conservación* (México: Imprenta Particular de la Sociedad Agrícola Mexicana, 1900), 4–5.

[87] Miasmatic theory, in Latin America dating back to the colonial period, claimed that poisonous vapors caused disease. Stagnant water, decaying matter, and filth generated vapors. By drying out

rainy season; fostered cloud formation and attracted rain; and provided critical construction material and fuel.[88] Concerns over deforestation and initial efforts to mitigate it reflected a desire not to preserve untouched wilderness but to conserve a critical resource.[89] Theirs was a "wise use" approach like the one forester Gifford Pinchot developed years later in the USA (there was no John Muir in nineteenth-century Mexico). As Fomento's *oficial mayor* (undersecretary) Manuel Fernández Leal argued, without forests industries and agriculture withered. The government had to "avoid the transcendental damages" (*trascendentales perjuicios*) already evident and prevent future generations from accusing them of "shortsightedness and lack of culture."[90]

Not even Mexico's poets adopted a romantic view of forests.[91] When Manuel Gutiérrez Nájera, one of the most celebrated poets in nineteenth-century Mexico, protested that Mexicans were waging war on trees, he did not appeal to their sublime or sacred nature.[92] Rather, Gutiérrez Nájera adopted utilitarian language that emphasized the benefits trees and forests provided to the nation. Forests were like "armies" providing the nation with selfless service, from fueling industries to attracting rainfall. Their soldiers were being picked off by greedy, improvident "dealers" (*negociantes*) and other enemies, who "persecuted trees even in their last refuges and trenches." Mexico's forests had been decimated "like a battalion at the end of battle."

Where did this utilitarian view of forests come from? As a relatively deforested country heavily logged for centuries, Mexico had no intellectual tradition celebrating wilderness and sublime nature. Spanish colonial views, developed in a similarly tree-poor landscape, left a legacy in Mexico of technocratic forest ordinances aimed at securing fuel and timber supplies for industry, war, and hearth. This Spanish American disposition

---

swamps and purifying the air, forests kept miasmas at bay. On miasmatic theory in Latin America, see Marcos Cueto and Steven Palmer, *Medicine and Public Health in Latin America: A History* (New York: Cambridge University Press, 2014), 35–6.

[88] "Circular de la Secretaría de Fomento sobre la devastación de bosques y arbolados en el territorio mexicano," (1880), San Ángel, Montes, exp. 90, AHDF.

[89] For an example of this attitude, "Director de aguas participa que se está talando el bosque del Desierto de los Leones" (1881), Aguas del Desierto, 1878–1915, exp.30, AHDF.

[90] "Circular de la Secretaría de Fomento sobre la devastación de bosques y arbolados en el territorio mexicano."

[91] Occasionally, some elites, like Mariano Bárcena, held views on nature resembling US transcendentalists. See Mariano Bárcena, *Armonías de la naturaleza. Discurso pronunciado por Mariano Bárcena en la velada literaria que tuvo lugar en la ciudad de Puebla en la noche del 19 de enero de 1880* (Mexico City: Filomeno Mata, 1880).

[92] Manuel Gutiérrez Nájera, "Los bosques," *El Nacional: Periódico de Literatura, Ciencias, Artes, Industria, Agricultura, Minería y Comercio*, November 25, 1880.

merged in the nineteenth century with key tenets of German and French forestry.[93] Of the two, the French version emphasizing the benefits that forests provided and concerns over the detrimental effects of forest clearance, especially dangerous runoff and aridification, appealed to Mexico's Francophile and French-speaking elite.

For nineteenth-century modernizing elites, wood scarcity threatened to stall Mexico's incipient industrialization and economic recovery after 1870. Due to what one observer called its "economic influence," forest loss became a recurrent source of anxiety.[94] The biggest consumers – railroads, mines, and factories – voiced their concerns and demanded action. One anonymous Mexican industrialist complained that there were "no few industries that languish due to the excessive cost of fuel" and called for the government to lower coal tariffs.[95] Warnings about the economic impact of high fuel prices and wood scarcity became commonplace in the 1870s and 1880s, appearing repeatedly on the pages of newspapers and periodical publications. Parts of the country such as the Bajío, with its few rivers and scarce fuelwood sources, seemed destined to a future of limited industrial growth.[96] Foreign observers often sang a similar tune. One predicted: "in a country so destitute of water and fuel, it is difficult to see how there ever can be" much manufacturing.[97]

Wood scarcity also threatened cities, especially the urban poor. Mexico City, the seat of Mexico's political and economic power, was in particularly bad shape; in the late 1870s, fuelwood became so costly that some resorted to cutting trees along city avenues.[98] In 1881, a newspaper editorial decried the "plague" of fuel scarcity and sought to bring government attention to its effect on the poor. The price of fuelwood had tripled, the editors observed. The rich, however, could stockpile fuelwood when prices were low and weather shortages. But the urban poor, said the editors, were vulnerable to daily fluctuations in price. For those already living hand to mouth, high fuel costs could push them into destitution and hunger. Of all

[93] For examples, see Miguel Balbontin, "Los bosques," *Boletín de la Sociedad Mexicana de Geografía y Estadística*, 3, no. 1 (1873): 144–52; "Una cuestión de actualidad. La tala de bosques," *La Libertad*, April 25, 1878.

[94] Gabriel Hinojosa, *Memoria sobre la utilidad de los bosques y perjuicios causados por su destrucción dedicada al gobierno del estado de Michoacán* (Morelia: Viuda e hijos de Ortíz, 1873), 22–4; "Leña," *El Siglo Diez y Nueve*, February 9, 1878.

[95] Anónimo, *Datos y reflexiones sobre la industria mexicana: publicación de un industrial.* (México: Imprenta de Ignacio Escalante, 1885), 3.

[96] Busto, *Estadística de la República Mexicana*, vol. 3, 11.   [97] Wells, *A Study of Mexico*, 132.

[98] "Tala de árboles," *El Siglo Diez y Nueve*, June 8, 1878; "Carbón vegetal," *El Nacional: Periódico de Literatura, Ciencias, Artes, Industria, Agricultura, Minería y Comercio*, August 20, 1881.

the different types of shortages, that of fuel "was the most terrible, the least bearable one." "[W]hen meat becomes expensive," they explained, "the poor replace it with maize, [and] nutritious plants; when the aqueducts run dry, they resort to artesian wells; when wheat is scarce, they use maize; but when fuelwood and charcoal become expensive like today, they cannot find a replacement, [and] suffer horribly." "The chain breaks at its weakest link," declared the editorial, warning of possible social unrest.[99]

The poor who supplied urban areas with fuel also suffered. In the mountains surrounding Mexico City, the capital's historical source of fuel, local authorities began arresting people caught cutting trees without permits, presumably to sell to urban residents. Murky colonial titles and their vague boundaries only worsened confusion over who had what rights.[100] Although conflicts over forest rights had a long history in the mountains surrounding Mexico City, they tended to increase with fuel scarcity.

As if the economic and social woes of deforestation were not enough, forest loss was also associated with drought.[101] Particularly concerning was the urban water supply. The largest urban concentration and seat of national government, Mexico City, once again took center stage in the discussion. At the time, Mexico City obtained water from three main sources: the old Chapultepec aqueduct (pre-Columbian but reconstructed during the colonial period), artesian wells, and Desierto de los Leones and

---

[99] "Una plaga para los pobres. La carestía del carbón," *El Monitor Republicano*, July 29, 1881; "Crónica diaria. Carencia de combustible," *La Patria*, July 26, 1882; "Lo que la clase pobre está sufriendo con la carestía del combustible," *La Oposición Radical*, August 2, 1882.

[100] "Aprehensión de varios vecinos por corte de madera" (1877), San Ángel, Gobierno, exp. 78, AHDF; "El auxiliar de La Magdalena se queja de varios abusos que se cometen en el monte por los vecinos de San Nicolás" (marzo 1881), San Ángel, Montes, exp. 94, AHDF.

[101] Scholars call this perspective desiccationism, widely held by many in the USA, Europe, and its colonial empires. See Georgina H. Endfield and David J. Nash, "Drought, Desiccation and Discourse: Missionary Correspondence and Nineteenth-Century Climate Change in Central Southern Africa," *The Geographical Journal* 168, no. 1 (2002): 33–47; Richard H. Grove, "A Historical Review of Early Institutional and Conservationist Responses to Fears of Artificially Induced Global Climate Change: The Deforestation-Desiccation Discourse 1500–1860," *Chemosphere* 29, no. 5 (1994): 1001–13; Vasant K. Saberwal, "Science and the Desiccationist Discourse of the 20th Century," *Environment and History* 4, no. 3 (1998): 309–43. Desiccationism also had a long history in Mexico. See José Antonio Alzate Ramírez, *Gacetas de literatura de México*, vol. 2 (Puebla: Reimpresas en la Oficina del Hospital de San Pedro, 1831), 169. Not all Mexicans supported desiccationism – again, see Alzate Ramírez. Andrew Mathews interprets Mexican desiccationism as justification for expanding government control over forests: "Mexican Forest History: Ideologies of State Building and Resource Use," *Journal of Sustainable Forestry* 15, no. 1 (2002): 17–28. An overview of desiccationism among nineteenth-century Mexican elites is Juan Urquiza, "Miguel Ángel de Quevedo and the Forest Hydrological Conservation Project of National Watersheds in the First Half of the Twentieth Century, 1900–1940," *Historia Caribe* 10, no. 26 (January 2015): 211–55.

Santa Fé, both located next to each other in the mountains west of Mexico City. Mountain water was reputed to be the purest and most crystalline in the valley and theoretically belonged to the city. For years, however, forests at the headwaters were logged mercilessly to make Mexico City's fuelwood and charcoal.[102]

In the late 1870s, disputes over the Desierto forest came to a head around fears that Mexico City was running out of water. According to the liberal newspaper *El Monitor Republicano*, "[f]or some time it has been noticeable the great scarcity of water in the city; in the streets that are not far from downtown, entire weeks have passed during which the residents lacked the indispensable liquid." Acknowledging other probable factors behind the crisis, including mountain settlements diverting too much water and defective and leaky aqueducts, the editors signaled excessive logging as the main cause, which "imped[ed] the attraction and the absorption" of rainfall.[103] President Porfirio Díaz, then serving his first term in office, intervened, instructing the governor of the State of Mexico (which had jurisdiction over part of the forest) to take mitigating measures. The objective, he said, was to avoid "the grave ills that would afflict the capital if deforestation reduced its water supply from the west, which is already insufficient . . . "[104] At the same time, the municipality overseeing the rest of the Desierto forest declared a total logging ban, threatening any transgressor with heavy fines and arrest.[105] Had it been the water supply for towns in remote parts of the country, Mexican elites and officials likely would have acted with less urgency. Desierto de los Leones was declared Mexico's first national park in 1917 partly to protect this key water source for Mexico City.[106]

[102] Opportunists included a British citizen, Juan Burnard. Burnard, it seems, took advantage of the civil war and French invasion to flout municipal cutting orders. "La escasez de agua," *El Monitor Republicano*, November 13, 1877; "Aguas del Desierto de los Leones" (1878–1915), Aguas del Desierto, 1878–1915, exp. 24-56, AHDF.

[103] "La escasez de agua."

[104] "Tala de bosques," *La Gaceta Médica de México*, August 1, 1877. In 1876, the government of Miguel Lerdo de Tejada apparently expropriated the Desierto forest as a source of drinking water for Mexico City, but it is unclear whether this was enforced. See Agustín Tornel Olvera, *Desierto de Los Leones* (México: Talleres de la Dirección de Estudios Geográficos y Climatológicos, 1922), 47.

[105] "Extracto relativo a la prohibición del desmonte de los pueblos de San Nicolás, La Magdalena, Hacienda de La Cañada y San Bernabé" (1877), San Ángel, Montes, exp. 75, AHDF.

[106] On the history of Mexico City's water supply and the Desierto forest in the nineteenth and early twentieth centuries: Inmaculada Simón Ruiz, "Conflictos ambientales y conflictos ambientalistas en el México porfiriano," *Estudios Demográficos y Urbanos* 25, no. 2 (2010): 363–94. Agustín Tornel Olvera, an advocate for declaring the Desierto a national park, stressed protecting forests to attract rainfall. See Tornel Olvera, *Desierto de los Leones*, 38.

If forest loss led to reduced rainfall, it followed that deforestation also put food production at risk. Most farmers and peasants in late nineteenth-century Mexico practiced rain-fed agriculture.[107] Every region in the country (excepting the humid tropical lowlands) repeatedly suffered drought during the nineteenth century. Given drought's catastrophic potential (famine or even starvation), Mexican peasants sought to mitigate its potential causes. This included deforestation. Some clearly considered forests essential for agriculture as they attracted rains and improved public health by purifying air.[108] Peasant desiccationist views may have served as a cultural taboo, discouraging forest clearance and ensuring long-term availability of fuel. Desiccationism may have been one of few shared views between elite and non-elites in nineteenth-century Mexico. Regardless, peasants sometimes had no choice but to clear forests if they wanted to grow more food.[109]

Nineteenth-century Mexicans also worried about deforestation's effect on public health. For agronomist Gabriel Hinojosa, stagnant marshes and swamps produced miasmatic diseases. Forests cleansed these "swampy vapors" (*emanaciones pantanosas*) before they reached human populations. Even settlements near stagnant water would be spared from disease if a forest separated them and "intercepted" miasmas.[110] For that reason, areas like the port of Veracruz, historically affected by diseases including malaria and yellow fever, panicked when logging for railroad ties began in the early 1870s.[111] A few decades later, prominent natural historian and polymath Mariano Bárcena echoed this opinion when he described forests as "hygienic machines." Championing forests as instruments of public health had obvious implications. Bárcena and others embraced the idea that any effective policy against disease should involve planting trees, reforesting cleared areas, creating urban parks, and conserving forests.[112]

---

[107] Teresa Rojas Rabicla, ed., *La agricultura en tierras mexicanas desde sus orígenes hasta nuestros días* (México, D. F.: Consejo Nacional para la Cultura y las Artes: Grijalbo, 1991), 224.

[108] "Varios vecinos de San Bartolo quejándose del pago de un censo y talamiento del monte ordenados por el regidor López y abusos del auxiliar, todo en copias pues los orginales obran en la Prefectura."

[109] While later conservationists such as Miguel Ángel de Quevedo sometimes singled out peasants for Mexico's deforestation, most nineteenth-century observers pointed to industrial consumers. On Quevedo's views, see Christopher R. Boyer, "Revolución y paternalismo ecológico: Miguel Ángel de Quevedo y la política forestal en México, 1926–1940," *Historia Mexicana* 57, no. 1 (2007): 91–138. Fomento itself blamed mining, industry, and railroads, among other culprits, for deforestation in 1880. See "Circular de la Secretaría de Fomento sobre la devastación de bosques y arbolados en el territorio mexicano."

[110] Hinojosa, *Memoria sobre la utilidad de los bosques*, 11.

[111] "Montes y arboledas," *La Voz de México*, September 11, 1873.

[112] Mariano Bárcena, *Selvicultura: breves consideraciones sobre explotación y formación de los bosques* (México: Oficina Tip. de la Secretaría de Fomento, 1892), 42–52.

A Two-Pronged Approach

Proposed solutions to deforestation in the late nineteenth century abounded. Plans fell into two main types: management and substitution. The *Ministerio de Fomento, Colonización, Industria y Comercio* (hereon referred to simply as Fomento) was charged with articulating both approaches. Fomento was created on April 22, 1853, under General Santa Anna's last administration.[113] Lucas Alamán suggested creating a ministry to foster national industry through protectionist policies. (Ironically, Fomento became instrumental in attracting foreign investment during the Porfiriato.) Although Fomento's responsibilities changed substantially over time, in general terms they included expediting development of Mexico's infrastructure and promoting more efficient exploitation of its resources. Fomento played a key role in building Mexico's railway network. The agency also collected, analyzed, and published statistical and scientific data on Mexico through its numerous *anales* and *memorias* and promoted development of new crops and industries. Fomento's efforts were unmistakably utilitarian, including funding of scientific expeditions. The agency was the cornerstone of Mexico's modernizing project during the second half of the nineteenth century.[114]

Forest management essentially called for enacting legislation to protect forests and implementing silviculture or scientific forestry.[115] Independent Mexico's first forestry code was published in 1861, followed by revisions in 1884. Between these dates, Fomento dispatched many memoranda and decrees concerning forest use issues, along with amendments to the 1861 code.[116] By 1900, Fomento had put in place a relatively

---

[113] Porfirio Díaz headed Fomento for some time during Manuel González's presidency (1880–4).

[114] On Fomento, see Casey Marina Lurtz, "Developing the Mexican Countryside: The Department of Fomento's Social Project of Modernization," *Business History Review* 90, no. 3 (2016): 431–55; Claudia Morales Escobar, "Los proyectos geográficos de la Secretaría de Fomento, del Porfiriato a la Revolución," in José Moncada and Patricia Gómez, eds., *El quehacer geográfico: instituciones y personajes (1876–1964)* (México, D. F.: UNAM, Instituto de Geografía, 2009), 34.

[115] Manuel Payno, "Selvicultura," *Boletín de la Sociedad de Geografía y Estadística de la República Mexicana*, Segunda época, 2 (1870): 77–85.

[116] Cámara de Senadores, *Dictamen de la Comisión de Hacienda de la Cámara de Senadores sobre terrenos baldíos y corte de madera en la República.* (México: I. Paz, 1878); "Conservación de Bosques" (1880), San Ángel, Tierras/Montes, exp. 90, AHDF; Secretaría de Fomento, Colonización, Industria, y Comercio, *Reglamento a que debe sujetarse el corte de maderas en bosques y terrenos nacionales.* (San Juan Bautista: Tip. "Juventud tabasqueña" de F. Ghigliazza, 1882); "Circular de la Secretaría de Fomento. Sobre conservación de los montes," in *Manuel Dublán y José María Lozano, Legislación mexicana, o, colección completa de las disposiciones legislativas expedidas desde la Independencia de la República*, vol. XVI (México: Impr. y Lit. de Eduardo Dublán y Compañía, 1887), 312–13; "Circular de la Secretaría de Fomento. Reglas para el corte de árboles en terrenos nacionales," vol. XIX (México: Tip. de E. Dublán y Compañía, 1888), 32–3; Aniceto Villamar, Silvestre Moreno Cora,

comprehensive legal framework for forest conservation, but enforcement remained elusive for some time.[117]

Silviculture required collecting statistics on forests and applying related plans to exploit forests rationally and ensure a sustained long-term yield. While Fomento collected some statistics over the years, systematic compilation followed the creation of a small forestry service in the first decade of the twentieth century. In 1893, the agency made Arbor Day a national holiday to ensure that state governments would annually plant trees and reforest cut areas under their jurisdiction.[118] Then, in 1899, Fomento effected a logging ban in Hidalgo's El Chico forest, declaring it a reserve.[119] Virtually no one at Fomento advocated a national parks system like the Yellowstone model. The idea of a forest reserve appealed to the agency's technocrats because the status could be rescinded and the forest put back into service once recovered.

Substitution involved replacing wood with another fuel. According to Santiago Ramírez, one of Mexico's most prominent nineteenth-century mining engineers, forestry laws that prevented industry, railroads, and consumers from overexploiting forests were pointless without an alternative fuel.[120] One option involved the establishment of eucalyptus plantations across the country. Like California, South Africa, and other parts of

---

and Mexico, *Las leyes federales vigentes sobre tierras, bosques, aguas, ejidos, colonización y el gran registro de la propiedad: colección ordenada y anotada* (México: Herrero Hermanos, 1910); "Instrucciones para el corte de madera en los montes municipales" (n.d.), Fomento, Bosques, caja 86 exp. 12, AGN. On forest legislation in the late nineteenth century, see Lane Simonian, *Defending the Land of the Jaguar: A History of Conservation in Mexico* (Austin: University of Texas Press, 1995), chapter 3, and Marvin D. Crocker, "The Evolution of Mexican Forest Policy and Its Influence upon Forest Resources" (PhD Dissertation, Oregon State University, 1973), chapter 1.

[117] Herman W. Konrad, "Tropical Forest Policy and Practice During the Mexican Porfiriato, 1876–1910," in Harold K. Steen and Richard P. Tucker, eds., *Changing Tropical Forests: Historical Perspectives on Today's Challenges in Central and South America* (Durham: Duke University Press, 1992).

[118] "Se remite a los gobernadores de los Estados esqueletos para que ministren las noticias a que se refieren dichos esqueletos sobre plantación de árboles" (1896), Fomento, Bosques, caja 3, exp. 1, AGN.

[119] Fernando Vargas and Susana Escobar, *Áreas naturales protegidas de México con decretos federales (1899–2000)* (México, D. F.: Instituto Nacional de Ecología-SEMARNAP, 2000), 393. El Chico's official designation was "forest reserve" (*monte vedado*). The decree left open the possibility of revoking protection once forests had regenerated. This represented an important difference from the US national park model and subsequent permanent designations in Mexico. El Chico provided fuel and timber to nearby silver mines for decades. The March 26, 1894 law upon which the decree was based explicitly authorized the federal government to *temporarily* set aside "vacant land" for conservation or reforestation. See Ramírez, *La condición legal de los bosques y su conservación*, 1900, 16.

[120] Santiago Ramírez, *Noticia histórica de la riqueza minera de México y de su actual estado de explotación* (México: Oficina Tip. de la Secretaría de Fomento, 1884), 148.

the world, nineteenth-century Mexicans eagerly introduced eucalyptus not only for its alleged "hygienic" properties but also because it grew rapidly in a variety of environments, making it a valuable source of timber and fuel in tree-poor areas.[121] Mariano Bárcena recommended various eucalyptus species for reforesting the Valley of Mexico as early as 1870.[122] Others suggested planting eucalyptus near wood-scarce cities like Morelia, claiming that this would prevent the government from regulating forests on private property.[123] By the late 1870s, the Real del Monte mining district had planted over 30,000 eucalyptus trees to mitigate its fuel problems.[124]

Far more attractive and popular was the idea of replacing wood with coal. During the second half of the nineteenth century, dozens of articles, pamphlets, books, and official memos agreed: Mexico could only truly solve deforestation if coal became cheap and widely available. Numerous voices called for the government to adopt measures like organizing surveys to locate Mexican coal deposits; offering tax incentives and subsidies to entrepreneurs; negotiating low tariffs with railroads to import cheap coal; and enacting a new code that facilitated coal prospecting and exploitation.[125]

In sum, Mexico's intellectual and political elite articulated two closely related approaches to forest protection: management and substitution. Management followed scientific forestry, mostly derived from the German and French tradition and colonial forest laws. Substitution required replacing wood with other fuels, particularly coal, although additional options like fast-growing eucalyptus were also considered. Management required a strong state and institutions capable of enforcing regulations, but until the 1880s the Mexican state remained weak. With the Porfirian state's consolidation in the 1890s, enforcement became more feasible.[126] This prompted renewed focus on management among conservationists in Mexico

---

[121] Eucalyptus trees were reputedly effective at draining swamps. On eucalyptus in South Africa, see Rune Flikke, "South African Eucalypts: Health, Trees, and Atmospheres in the Colonial Contact Zone," *Geoforum* 76 (2016): 20–7. On eucalyptus in nineteenth-century California, see Ian Tyrrell, "Peripheral Visions: Californian-Australian Environmental Contacts, c. 1850s–1910," *Journal of World History* 8, no. 2 (1997): 275–302.

[122] Mariano Bárcena, "Dictámen sobre la repoblación vegetal del Valle de México," *La Naturaleza*, 1, 6 (1870): 245–51.

[123] Eduardo Ruíz, "El eucalyptus," *Eco de Ambos Mundos. El Diario de la Política*, August 9, 1876.

[124] Santiago Ramírez, "La conservación de bosques," *El Explorador Minero*, May 5, 1877.

[125] There are numerous examples. Three will suffice here: Juvenal, "Boletín del Monitor. La exposición municipal. El carbón de piedra," *El Monitor Republicano*, November 11, 1873; Mariano Bárcena, "Los criaderos de carbón," *El Minero Mexicano*, March 3, 1881; "El carbón mineral," *El Telégrafo*, March 3, 1882.

[126] Named after dictator Porfirio Díaz, who ruled Mexico between 1876 and 1911. The Porfiriato witnessed rapid economic growth, massive foreign investment, political stability, and the development of industry and a modern railroad network.

City after 1900. In the meantime, substitution became Fomento's preferred solution, perhaps because it seemed easiest to implement. All one had to do was find coal.

Conclusion

From an energy perspective, Mexico's industrial development in the second half of the nineteenth century faced similar constraints to other land-based forms of production like agriculture. Although new technologies, including the steam engine, allowed people to transform chemical energy into mechanical energy, it continued to come from the solar radiation stored in trees, not fossil fuels. Early industrialization also relied on ancient technologies like waterwheels. Beyond grinding flour or sawing wood, waterwheels powered mass production of cloth, textiles, and nails. By using water to power machinery, factory owners continued to depend on the sun to drive the local hydrological cycle regulating water-flow. Mexico's early industrialization was embedded in the environment.

Embedded industrialization eventually created an energy and environmental bottleneck. Mechanized manufacturing, mining, and transportation used the products of photosynthesis and the hydrological cycle on which Mexico's largely agrarian economy and society depended.[127] To complicate matters, steam-powered mechanization developed in areas whose forests were already largely exhausted from over 300 years of mining, manufacturing, agricultural expansion, and household consumption in the central highlands and central-northern plateau. Most rivers in this region suffered severe limitations to industrial growth and further mechanization: they were short, they dried out for part of the year, and their waters were largely allocated to users willing to litigate any newcomer to death. From the perspective of a society anxious to industrialize in order to ward off new territorial threats from foreign powers and join the ranks of "civilized" nations, this industrial energy and environmental trap presented an existential threat and demanded an answer. That answer was coal.

---

[127] For an analysis that emphasizes the importance of environmental constraints during early industrialization, see Kenneth Pomeranz, "Political Economy and Ecology on the Eve of Industrialization: Europe, China, and the Global Conjuncture," *The American Historical Review* 107, no. 2 (2002): 425–46.

CHAPTER 3

Searching for Rocks

With coal almost any feat is possible or easy; without it we are thrown
back into the laborious poverty of earlier times.

William Stanley Jevons, *The Coal Question*

In February 1872 a group of Mexican prospectors surveyed an area in the
mountains of Puebla state, central Mexico, rumored to conceal vast coal
deposits. After being received by the mayor of Tecomatlán, the area's
largest town, the prospectors convinced him and a number of local men
to take part in the survey. The men even agreed to work without compen-
sation for the first few months, expecting the town would soon strike it
rich. But funds quickly dried out. The prospectors managed to secure
another investor and work continued, eventually yielding some 10 tons of
coal. Then came transporting it to consumption centers. The prospectors
built ten wheeled carts, each capable of carrying 1 ton, only to realize that
local "roads" were mule pack trails. They decided to build a new road from
scratch, advancing 2–3 km per day. It took one full month to reach Izúcar
de Matamoros, only 80 kilometers away. People in Matamoros and other
nearby towns welcomed the procession of coal-laden carts with tolling bells
and music.[1]

The reception in Puebla City was less enthusiastic. Several individuals
who had previously opposed rail line construction through Puebla spread
word that the coal was worthless and couldn't fuel machinery. Some
merchants who profited from high transportation costs asserted that their
own mule trains would be threatened by cheap transportation. Others
claimed that coal threatened charcoal merchants. Whatever their reasons,
those who spoke out against coal in Puebla succeeded in dissuading sales.
The coal prospectors eventually transported the coal another 160 kilometers
to Mexico City where, with good local connections, they could market it.

---

[1] Félix Maillefert, "La mina de Acatlán," *El Correo del Comercio*, March 7, 1873.

The Tecomatlán venture illustrates the great lengths to which people interested in commodifying coal in Mexico went to acquire it. It also shows the difficulty of its extraction and transport, which limited coal's proliferation between the late nineteenth and early twentieth centuries. The question remains: why did Mexicans covet coal? To start, coal-based industrialization held ideological power. Mexican state officials and entrepreneurs believed coal was essential to securing the country's prosperity. Coal underpinned the industrial success of countries like Great Britain and the USA, in turn affording them enviable geopolitical power. Coal also promised to solve Mexico's "fuel problem" – its lack of cheap, abundant energy. This particularly concerned the country's central highlands, where most people and economic activity were concentrated, and fuel scarcity and deforestation loomed large. Industrialization based on wood and waterpower faced limitations given the country's unfavorable hydrological conditions and the deforestation associated with large-scale fuelwood exploitation. Coal fuel would reduce the need for waterpower and decelerate deforestation while accelerating industrial expansion.

Did coal meet these expectations? What role did coal play in Mexico's transition to fossil fuels? Unlike European and US coal, Mexican coal never became a household fuel, nor did it form the bedrock of Mexican industry. Instead, coal acted as an energy bridge between the nineteenth century's ecologically embedded, wood-and-water-based industrialization and the twentieth century's oil-powered industrial model. What limited coal did circulate in the latter part of the nineteenth century helped sustain key emerging industrial sectors like steel, smelting, railroads, and electricity generation, especially from 1890 to 1910. In turn, coal's fortune in Mexico depended on these sectors. The Mexican Revolution of 1910–20 devastated the fledgling coal industry, but heavy industry secured a role for coal in twentieth-century Mexico as a niche industrial energy source. By fostering key infrastructure, especially railroads, and supporting crucial industrial sectors, coal shaped views and expectations about fossil fuels and played an important role in kick-starting Mexico's fossil-fuel dependency.

Coal before 1880

As viceroy of New Spain, the Marquis of Branciforte ordered a kingdom-wide coal survey in 1794, probably the first in Spanish America.[2] The

---

[2] Julio Sánchez Gómez, "La lenta penetración de la máquina de vapor en la minería del ámbito hispano."

decision seemed spurred by a recent report on coal from creole savant José Antonio de Alzate. Alzate found evidence in old chronicles that Franciscan friars in the New Mexico province burned coal for domestic purposes when lacking fuelwood. The viceroy ordered the *Tribunal de Minería*, the institution behind Mexico City's miners' guild, and delegations across the kingdom to search for coal. Not much came of this effort save a conviction that coal could only be found in the provinces of Texas and New Mexico, over 2,000 km from Mexico City. As the distinguished director of Mexico City's School of Mines, Fausto de Elhuyar, explained in 1806, "coal is not located close to the most important mines and would be very costly to transport it there."[3]

In 1829, Nuevo León's state congress granted one of the first coal mining concessions to Juan Woodbury and Juan Cameron to mine the state's coal and iron. The concession was later renewed when Woodbury and Cameron failed to import the necessary equipment to begin operations.[4] It is unclear precisely where their concession was situated, but reports published after 1880 indicated that the state's only sizable coal deposits were located in the northwest. Despite extra time allotted to the enterprise, Woodbury and Cameron's project apparently failed.

Mexico's perpetual political turmoil, its foreign wars, and the loss of half its territory to the USA over the next two decades stalled further efforts to locate or mine Mexican coal. Incidentally, Mexico's first coaling station was likely a product of American land grabbing. In 1854, the Pacific Mail Steamship Company transported California gold rushers from Nicaragua and Panama to San Francisco. The company operated one coal station in the port of Acapulco.[5] The company incurred great expenses (over 30,000 pesos annually) to keep its Acapulco station supplied with coal, transporting it all the way from England or the US Atlantic states. Looking at the San Francisco–Central America connection, US investors saw a profit opportunity in supplying Acapulco and other Pacific ports with coal from the coastal states of Colima, Michoacán, and Guerrero. With coal fetching M$24 per ton and an annual potential market for thousands of tons,

---

[3] Ibid.

[4] Woodbury and Cameron were likely British or American. "Concesión a los ciudadanos Juan Lucio Wodbury y Juan Cameron para la explotación de minas de fierro y carbón de piedra" (October 4, 1829), Fondo: Capital del Estado; Sección: Reglamentos, decretos y circulares; Colección: Impresos II; Volumen: 6; Exp: 4, AHM.

[5] On another US coaling station in Baja California in the 1860s, see Peter A. Shulman, *Coal and Empire: The Birth of Energy Security in Industrial America* (Baltimore: Johns Hopkins University Press, 2015), 126, 144.

there was reason for optimism.[6] When proponents mentioned potentially inexhaustible fuel for future railroads, ironworks, and Mexican industries – as well as catching up with coal-rich nations like the USA and England – the Santa Anna government acquiesced. As the company's New York-based owners put it, the most prosperous and advanced nations were those where coal production and its "thousand powerful and beneficial ramifications" were greatest.[7]

While negotiating with the Mexican Pacific, the Santa Anna government resorted to more extravagant strategies to acquire coal. In the Mesilla treaty, Mexico ceded 76,000 square kilometers of its territory to the USA. Before the treaty went into effect in 1854, Mexico began negotiating a major coal purchase from American merchant "José Gerner." The agreement stipulated that 358,000 pesos would be deducted from the US indemnity to Mexico for acquiring the Mesilla. Mexico would receive 16,000 tons of the "finest Liverpool or Pittsburgh" coal for its "warships" (which likely existed only in the minds of Mexican officials). Of this, 6,000 tons would go to Veracruz, Tampico, and Isla del Carmen on the Atlantic coast. The remaining 10,000 tons would go to the Pacific ports of San Blas, Mazatlán, Huatulco, and Acapulco. The agreement was signed in July 1854 and stipulated that Mexico would receive coal over the next 13 months. An audit the following year found that despite Mexico paying the entire sum only 13 days after signing, less than half the 16,000 tons had been delivered to Mexican ports. The auditors, however, allowed for the possibility that deliveries went unnoticed when Santa Anna's administration collapsed, for one last time, in August 1855.[8]

As Santa Anna's government crumbled and Mexico further polarized along liberal–conservative lines – leading to civil war 2 years later – the country managed to send a delegation to the Universal Exposition in Paris in 1855. Coal (*charbon de terre*) was among the "natural riches" the delegation presented.[9] Coal, they lamented, was "unfortunately rare in Mexico and the coal beds we have found are located in mountainous places where exploitation would be extremely costly in the absence of means of transportation." Perhaps hoping to lure European investment in Mexican coal mining, the delegation emphasized the allegedly excellent quality of Mexican coal and the country's

[6] Mexican Pacific Coal and Iron Mining and Land Company, *Prospecto de la compañía denominada Mexican Pacific Coal and Iron Mining and Land Company* (Nueva York: Imprenta de Hallet, 1856).
[7] Ibid., 8.
[8] "Estracto [sic] el espediente instruido sobre el contrato de comprar en el estrangero [sic] 16,000 toneladas de carbón de piedra para el servicio de la Marina Nacional,'" *El Republicano*, January 11, 1855. Santa Anna was president of Mexico eleven times between 1833 and 1855.
[9] *Catalogue des produits naturels, industriels et artistiques exposés dans la Section Mexicaine, à l'Exposition Universelle de 1855* (Paris: Typographie de Firmin Didot Frères, 1855).

"considerable deposits." The delegation hypothesized that, once Mexico's coal was profitably exploited, "[Mexico's] iron industry and silver mines will acquire an importance that will be felt around the world."[10]

The prediction fell flat – by the 1860s, Mexico's coal industry and market had little to show for itself.[11] A similar pattern marked the next two decades: boosters promised that Mexico would benefit greatly from importing coal or exploiting domestic deposits. They would then obtain a government concession, but ultimately fail to deliver and disappear from the historical record. This pattern closely resembled Mexico's history of failed railroad concessions.[12]

In the meantime, better and more reliable information about Mexico's coal wealth started being published. During the ephemeral reign of Maximilian of Hapsburg (1864–7), German prospector Jakob Küchler published one of the first geological descriptions of coalfields in the northern state of Coahuila.[13] Küchler explored the Sabinas and Salinas valleys in the state's northeast. He noted that the area was scarcely populated, likely due to invasions of "barbarian Indians" (Apaches and Comanches).[14] Silver and precious metals received all the attention by authors writing about Mexico, Küchler complained, when coal is "the most valuable and important mineral for the future of this country."[15] His report identified coal seams running from the Sabinas valley and adjacent Piedras Negras (Black Rocks) across the Rio Grande to Laredo, Texas, some 120 km northeast.[16] Broken into a series of pockets by mountains and

---

[10] Ibid., 5.

[11] By the decade's end, Mexico claimed some small-scale operations. In Sonora, miners extracted small quantities of anthracite coal close to the capital Hermosillo, Mexico's only location for this type of coal. Production suffered frequent interruptions and labor was scarce due to attacks by nomadic indigenous people. See "Sonora," *El Siglo Diez y Nueve*, August 19, 1869.

[12] Often, failure to build railroads and import coal coincided since both belonged to the same concession. Rights to build a railroad line typically included rights to import coal sans customs duties. See Santiago Méndez, *Nociones prácticas sobre caminos de fierro* (México: Imprenta de Andrade y Escalante, 1864), 249.

[13] Jacobo Kuchler, *Valles de Sabinas y Salinas: reconocimiento y descripción de los Valles de Sabinas y Salinas en el departamento de Coahuila, con las haciendas del Nacimiento, San Juan, Soledad, Álamo, Encinas, Hermanas y Rancho de la Mota* (México: Imprenta Imperial, 1866).

[14] Commercial coal production became possible only when Coahuila's nomadic indigenous people were pushed aside or exterminated, which took place between 1860 and 1880. See Mario Cerutti, *Burguesía y capitalismo en Monterrey, 1850–1910* (Monterrey: Fondo Editorial de NL, 2006), 27–9. A similar story of indigenous displacement for oil extraction occurred in Veracruz several decades later. See Myrna Santiago, *The Ecology of Oil: Environment, Labor, and the Mexican Revolution, 1900–1938* (Cambridge; New York: Cambridge University Press, 2006), chapters 2 and 4.

[15] Kuchler, *Valles de Sabinas y Salinas*, 15.

[16] The Laredo area coalfields were identified a few years earlier by a US-Mexican boundary survey. See William H. Emory, *Report on the United States and Mexican Boundary Survey* (Washington, DC: C. Wendell, printer, 1857), 68.

typically arranged in two horizontal layers separated by clays and other soils, these would prove the most extensive and significant deposits in all of Mexico.

In the following decade, prospectors began surveying central Mexico in earnest. In 1873, mine owners in Puebla commissioned British engineer Patrick Murphy to investigate local coal deposits. Murphy's report extolled coal's importance to modern civilization and a country's industrial prosperity. Echoing Küchler, Murphy declared coal to be more valuable than gold or silver because of its overall effect on other economic activities. Had the Creator excluded Mexico when bestowing this wealth on the world's nations, Murphy wondered? Certainly not. Murphy insisted that half-hearted surveys misled people into believing Mexico lacked coal. Now that Mexico had begun to industrialize, determining how much coal it had was essential. Murphy also argued that coal was "an indispensable necessity" given Mexico's heavily overexploited forests. Fortunately, he continued, the patriotic efforts of others had already shown that Mexico possessed "coal deposits of enormous importance."[17]

Not all news was good news. Despite his optimism, Murphy was one of the first surveyors to mention problematic transportation costs. Central Mexico's rugged terrain presented huge obstacles for delivering coal to market. Noticing water freight's negligible cost, Murphy considered using local rivers to transport the coal. He quickly realized, however, that canalizing rivers in the relatively flat northeastern USA or England posed different challenges than in mountainous central Mexico. Still, Murphy remained confident that commercial coal mining in the region was feasible. Murphy's report and samples from Puebla's coal mines shown at fairs in Puebla and Mexico City caused a flurry of commentary on coal and cheap energy's role in national "progress."[18]

By the late 1870s, foundries were being built on Mexico's Pacific coast for easy access to British coal and iron. This strategy avoided fuelwood scarcity, high prices, and transportation problems afflicting places like Durango, site of Mexico's largest iron ore deposits. On the Pacific, English iron cost M$25 and coal around M$10. Such prices allowed foundries in places like Mazatlán to produce cast iron at half the price of Durango.[19]

[17] Patricio Murphy, "Informe acerca de las minas de ulla ubicadas en Tecomatlán, distrito de Acatlán, estado de Puebla, dado por el Sr. D. Patricio Murphy, ingeniero de minas," *El Minero Mexicano*, October 9, 1873, 4–5.

[18] See Juvenal, "La exposición municipal. El carbón de piedra," *El Monitor Republicano*, 11 November, 1873; Ochoa, "Hulla mexicana," *El Minero Mexicano*, April 2, 1874.

[19] *Anales del Ministerio de Fomento de la República Mexicana* (México: Imprenta de Francisco Díaz de León, 1877), vol. 3, 159–60.

Around the same time, investors established the Compañía Explotadora de Criaderos de Carbón de Piedra de la República Mexicana. The first and perhaps only well-capitalized Mexican coal mining venture before 1880, the company advertised coal as the "principal agent of industry among civilized nations" without which "the progress of civilization would stop."[20] To back its efforts and convince investors to buy stocks, the company turned to Antonio del Castillo, respected mining engineer and founder of geology in Mexico. Castillo surveyed the company's coal lands in the Veracruz Huasteca, a mountainous tropical rainforest in the state's northwest that would become famous after 1900 for its enormous oil gushers. His enthusiastic report stressed the size of coal beds (about 12 km²), their good quality, and their proximity to the Pánuco River for transportation. Castillo estimated that the company could market coal at M$10 per ton in Veracruz, where imported coal sold for M$14 per ton. Considering this report is the company's only appearance in the historical record, it appears not even Castillo's endorsement made it prosper.

The Mainspring of Industrial Civilization

Most of these reports drew intellectual inspiration from Europe and the USA. In 1865, the British economist William Stanley Jevons published *The Coal Question: An Enquiry Concerning the Progress of the Nation, and the Probable Exhaustion of Our Coal Mines*. Enormously influential, the book claimed that coal was the bedrock of British wealth and industrial civilization. It also argued that coal was a finite resource. Unlike many contemporaries, Jevons did not attribute Britain being the world's leading industrial power to intellectual superiority. Other nations had their poets, philosophers, and inventors, and Jevons argued that until recently all of Britain's "arts" had been imported from continental Europe. Britain's success lay – he put wonderfully – in "the union of certain happy mental qualities with [the country's] peculiar material resources." By "material resources," Jevons meant coal. Coal permitted the economic progress that underwrote the growth of cities where intellectual and cultural progress flourished.[21] Jevons thus connected cultural and economic achievements to a country's resource base. The "arts and inventions" Britain contributed to modern civilization were powered by its coalfields.

---

[20] *Compañia explotadora de criaderos de carbón de piedra de la República Mexicana* (México: Imprenta de F. Díaz de León, 1876), 3.

[21] Allen MacDuffie, *Victorian Literature, Energy, and the Ecological Imagination* (Cambridge, England: Cambridge University Press, 2014), 50.

Britain, per Jevons, was not coal's only beneficiary. As energy for mechanical power, coal underpinned nineteenth-century technological prowess everywhere. It was the "all powerful" rock that made steam and iron possible. "With coal," Jevons insisted, "almost any feat is possible or easy; without it we are thrown back into the laborious poverty of early times." Although named the Iron Age, the nineteenth century was truly "the Age of Coal." In sum, Jevons concluded, coal was "the mainspring of modern material civilization."[22]

Jevons also posited a less popular Malthusian critique of progress itself when he argued for material limits to industrial growth.[23] Jevons adapted Malthus's notion of "natural" limits to progress to insist that Britain faced not cultural or political constraints "to go on rising" but material ones, specifically its finite coal reserves: "Here is a definite cause why we cannot always advance."[24]

A distinguished exponent of the idea that coal made industrialization possible, Jevons represented just one link in a long intellectual chain stretching back to the Industrial Revolution's origins. In fact, presenting coal as the basis of modern civilization was commonplace for decades on both sides of the North Atlantic. American chemistry professor Thomas Cooper observed in the early nineteenth century that "[i]n this country every suggestion that brings forward the importance of coal to the public view is of the moment: we know little of its value in Pennsylvania as yet. All the superior wealth, power and energy of Great Britain is founded on her

---

[22] Jevons, *The Coal Question*, 1–2. Present-day scholarship largely supports Jevons's views on coal's industrial significance. See Barbara Freese, *Coal: A Human History* (Cambridge: Perseus, 2003); Maury Klein, *The Genesis of Industrial America, 1870–1920* (Cambridge: Cambridge University Press, 2007); Timothy Mitchell, *Carbon Democracy: Political Power in the Age of Oil* (New York: Verso, 2011); Sidney Pollard, *Peaceful Conquest: The Industrialization of Europe, 1760–1970* (Oxford, New York: Oxford University Press, 1981); Kenneth Pomeranz, *The Great Divergence: China, Europe, and the Making of the Modern World Economy* (Princeton: Princeton University Press, 2000); E. A. Wrigley, *Energy and the English Industrial Revolution* (Cambridge, UK: Cambridge University Press, 2010). Not everybody is convinced. For a skeptical perspective, see Gregory Clark, "Coal and the Industrial Revolution, 1700–1869," *European Review of Economic History* 11, no.1 (2007): 39–72.

[23] Malthus sought to refute Enlightenment notions of human perfectibility and social evolution by emphasizing limits to progress, resource scarcity, and population growth. Thomas R. Malthus, *An Essay on the Principle of Population* (Oxford: Oxford University Press, 2008). For an environmental analysis of Malthus's ideas, see John Barry, *Environment and Social Theory* (New York: Routledge, 2007), 61–3. For a characterization of Malthus as a theorist of the energy limits of the old organic economy, see Wrigley, *Energy and the English Industrial Revolution*, 10–13.

[24] Jevons' views contrasted with geologists' and other natural scientists' conviction about supposedly inexhaustible natural resources. On the debate over coal supplies and natural resource scarcity during the period, see Nuno Luis Madureira, "The Anxiety of Abundance: William Stanley Jevons and Coal Scarcity in the Nineteenth Century," *Environment and History* 18 (2012): 395–421.

coal mining." Fifty years later, Ralph Waldo Emerson referred to every coal basket as "power and civilization." Emerson called coal a "black diamond" and "portable climate" that made "Canada as warm as Calcutta" and carried itself by "rail and by boat" wherever "industrial power" was needed.[25]

By 1880, Mexico's intelligentsia widely accepted these ideas, imbuing them with unique preoccupations and priorities. Echoing Jevons, Mexican statistician Emiliano Busto claimed that coal and iron were "the heart and soul" of modern civilization and key to future advancement. Busto highlighted iron and coal as nature's two most important commodities. From the humblest needle to the largest buildings, iron was present in largely everything humans created. Thanks to coal-fueled steam power, iron machines could do the work of countless laborers. But unlike humans, the iron machine never tired, made mistakes, got distracted, cheated, or lied. It did not speak but "seemed to think." Iron could undertake the roughest jobs as a saw, drill, or hammer. Iron could also handle the most delicate fabric with caution and skill. Under "man's" orders, it could weave, warp, cut, scrape, and sew, all without question or complaint. It was the perfect worker.[26]

Per Busto, iron was the body and coal-produced steam, the soul. Together they made a "sacred monster" that erased distance to "unite all the peoples of the world." Iron, that "second humanity," allowed humans to achieve immortality, mastering time and space, or nature. With coal and iron, humans overcame the limits of life, fulfilling the biblical command to multiply and dominate the world. Machines, the "Prometheus of progress," redeemed workers from drudgery, allowing more and more "workers of labor" to join the ranks of the "workers of the spirit." In a prediction curiously redolent of Marxist utopia, Busto claimed that iron and coal-produced steam would emancipate humanity and the life of the spirit would reign supreme.

Busto not only waxed lyrical about coal and iron's spiritual benefits; he explicitly linked them to national progress and power. For him, it was clear that the nations steering humanity's destiny were endowed with enormous deposits of both. It was also evident that any nation lacking these "elements of civilization" would be left behind, doomed to perpetually serve the "iron nations." Adopting popular Spencerian or social-Darwinist language,

[25] Christopher F. Jones, *Routes of Power: Energy and Modern America* (Cambridge: Harvard University Press, 2014), 27; Freese, *Coal*, 10.
[26] Busto, *Estadística de la República Mexicana*, vol. 2, 22–7.

Busto saw nations as superorganisms engaged in a perennial struggle to survive and argued that "southern" nations that refused to accept and adopt iron and coal would face extinction.[27]

Adopting coal and iron was also portrayed as an act of virility. Busto saw a clear relationship between coal-powered material progress and manliness. In a somewhat circular logic, Busto asserted that the world's most "active" or virile nations employed their iron and coal deposits, which in turn made them powerful and . . . well, more virile. By contrast, weak nations wasted the natural bounty lying untouched beneath their feet. Trapped in what Busto called the "poetry of imagination" and incapable of controlling their passions (both "feminine" attributes), these nations had not yet entered a "virile epoch." Was Mexico one of those feminized nations? Perhaps, but Busto hoped Mexico would finally embark on a path to progress by exploiting its iron and coal deposits. Only they would prevent the country from being blown away by the century's "wind of progress."[28]

For Busto and many Mexican contemporaries, iron and coal would render nature and geography irrelevant. Nineteenth-century Mexicans often viewed the country's rugged topography as recalcitrant, a stubborn obstacle to national development (although the older, Humboldt-inspired vision of Mexico as a cornucopia of natural resources still held currency). With coal, masculine domination of nature would become reality. Deserts would bloom, cities would rise, reservoirs for irrigation and power would be built, tunnels for railroads would bore through mountains. Even remote places would be linked to markets, the ultimate economic dream. Wherever iron and coal existed, industrial civilization would flourish – and wealth would follow.[29]

Fomento Takes the Lead

It was within this intellectual environment that in 1881 Fomento appointed several Mexican mining engineers to locate coal in Mexico.[30] The agency believed that coal was key to unlocking Mexico's industrial potential. Coal would finally solve Mexico's "fuel problem," made acutely worse in the nineteenth century's second half by emerging industrialization and new railroads. Coal would provide cheap and abundant energy, bolstering pro-duction and commerce while simultaneously diminishing transportation

[27] Ibid.   [28] Ibid.   [29] Ibid.
[30] On coalfield commissions, see S. Adalberto de Cardona and Trinidad Sanchez, *México y sus capitales; reseña histórica del país desde los tiempos más remotos hasta el presente; en la cual también se trata de sus riquezas naturales* (México: Tip. de J. Aguilar Vera y Cía. (Sociedad en Comandita), 1900), 97–103.

costs. Crucially, the ministry also believed that coal could solve Mexico's deforestation, which they feared had worsened over the past years. If left unchecked, it would have disastrous consequences. Replacing wood with coal would drastically reduce wood consumption, thus averting uncontrolled deforestation. In short, coal was indispensable to save "industry, the government, and public hygiene from the crisis that threatens them … "[31]

Overseeing these scientific commissions was Santiago Ramírez, his generation's most important mining engineer. Ramírez was born in Mexico City in 1836 to a family with a long mining tradition: his maternal grandfather was one of the first graduates from the *Real Seminario de Minería*, the School of Mines founded by Fausto de Elhuyar in the late eighteenth century. Its early collaborators included Alexander von Humboldt. Another ancestor was a wealthy miner in Pachuca in the late colonial period. Ramírez began his studies at the *Colegio de Minería* (the Republican successor to the Seminario) in 1858 at age 22. He graduated as a mining engineer in 1864 and joined the faculty that same year. He taught mineralogy until the *Colegio*'s closure in 1867.[32] Throughout the 1870s, Ramírez worked for a number of private companies, establishing a reputation as one of Mexico's best mining engineers and coal experts. He established himself among Mexico City's intelligentsia and joined several societies, including the *Sociedad Mexicana de Geografía y Estadística*, the *Sociedad Mexicana de Historia Natural*, and the *Sociedad Científica "Antonio Alzate."* Ramírez actively contributed to mining and engineering periodicals as well, publishing frequently in the *Explorador Minero* and *El Minero Mexicano*, where he wrote on coal and forest conservation, among other issues.[33]

---

[31] These views were widespread in Europe, the USA, and Latin America at the time. The notion of using coal and fossil fuels to address both expensive energy and deforestation was also not specific to Mexico. Many nineteenth-century Cubans, for example, believed the same. See Reinaldo Funes Monzote, *From Rainforest to Cane Field in Cuba*: An Environmental History since 1492 (Chapel Hill: University of North Carolina Press, 2008), 138–52. Germans did, too. See Sieferle, *The Subterranean Forest*: Energy Systems and the Industrial Revolution (Cambridge: The White Horse Press, 2001), 160–70.

[32] On the colonial and nineteenth-century history of the School of Mines, see María Ramos and Juan Saldaña, "Del Colegio de Minería de México a la Escuela Nacional de Ingenieros," *Quipu* 13, no. 1 (January–April 2000): 105–26.

[33] On Ramírez's life, see Lucero Morelos Rodríguez, *La geología mexicana en el siglo XIX: una revisión histórica de la obra de Antonio del Castillo, Santiago Ramírez y Mariano Bárcena* (Morelia; México, D. F.: Secretaría de Cultura del Estado de Michoacán; Plaza y Valdés, 2012), 72–93; José Alfredo Uribe Salas and María Teresa Cortés Zavala, "Andrés del Río, Antonio del Castillo y José G. Aguilera en el desarrollo de la ciencia mexicana del siglo XIX," *Revista de Indias* LXVI, no. 237 (2006): 491–518.

Fomento sent Ramírez and his team to various central Mexican states – Puebla, Veracruz, Tlaxcala, Hidalgo, and Oaxaca – as well as to the Huasteca, a region Antonio del Castillo had explored some years earlier on behalf of the Compañía Explotadora. Thanks to reports like Küchler's, Mexican officials already knew large coal deposits existed along the US border in the states of Coahuila and Sonora. As such, they focused their efforts on central Mexico, where the largest population and manufacturing centers were located.[34]

Like Patrick Murphy years before, Fomento's engineers were optimistic about (and tended to exaggerate) the potential for commercial exploitation of Mexico's coal deposits. Those in Puebla and Hidalgo seemed particularly promising. As always, there was one major obstacle: lack of cheap, reliable, and fast transport to carry coal to consumption centers. One of the reports calculated that, without a railroad line, drivers with packs of 10 or so donkeys carrying 100 kg bundles of coal would have to travel 4 days on dirt paths in the rugged Puebla mountains just to reach the nearest town. From there to the city of Puebla (another day), drivers would transport the coal on oxcart. Once in the city, the cargo could be loaded onto locomotives for distribution elsewhere. By that point, the cost had become too high. After adding the drivers' salaries, animal feed, and extraction costs, a ton of coal in the city of Puebla would fetch some M$19 (M$17 if mules were used instead of donkeys).[35] Mining represented a mere 62 cents, 3 percent of this sum, while transportation represented 97 percent of the total cost. By comparison, the reports calculated that a rail connection from the mine to the city of Puebla would drive the price down to M$4–5.[36] If government agencies and industrialists wanted cheap coal in central Mexico, they would have to look for it elsewhere.[37]

In 1882, Fomento began publishing the reports on Mexico's coal deposits, most of which Ramírez authored.[38] The reports gave a clear idea of many deposits' geography and main characteristics. Much to the

---

[34] See the various coal reports in Secretaría de Fomento, Colonización, Industria y Comercio, *Anales del Ministerio de Fomento de la República Mexicana* VII (México, 1882), but especially 8–10.

[35] Ibid., 83–4. The same report put 2 tons of wood (roughly equal to 1 ton of coal's energy content) in Puebla at M$6.68, about a third the price of coal. The price of 2 tons of fuelwood in Mexico City, however, was M$18, only slightly cheaper than Puebla's coal after rail transportation cost.

[36] Ibid., 79–82.

[37] On the period's coal and wood prices, see Sandra Kuntz Ficker, *Empresa extranjera y mercado interno: el Ferrocarril Central Mexicano, 1880–1907* (México, D. F.: Colegio de México, 1995), 223–8.

[38] Santiago Ramírez, "El poder calorífico de los combustibles minerales por el Ingeniero de Minas Santiago Ramírez," *Anales del Ministerio de Fomento de la República Mexicana* VII (1882): 129–35; "Estudio de unos ejemplares de carbón mineral procedentes del distrito de Tlaxiaco en el estado de Oaxaca que por disposición de la Secretaría de Fomento practicó el que esto subscribe," Ibid.,

disappointment of the federal government and elites in central Mexico, the reports confirmed that Mexico's largest coal seams sat in the north, especially Coahuila and Sonora. Although states like Oaxaca and Puebla contained some sizable deposits, they were largely located in difficult-to-access mountain regions. They underlined that without railroads connecting to urban centers, extraction would not be profitable. Again, rugged topography and lack of navigable rivers foiled plans to mine coal. The commissions also collected many samples, allowing engineers to classify coal deposits in Mexico (crucial to investors).[39]

Fomento's reports made it clear to state officials that Mexico needed a modern legal framework for facilitating and regulating coal extraction. Heated debate broke out between those who argued that coal deposits ultimately belonged to the nation (following the colonial *Ordenanzas de Minería*) and advocates of private property rights. To a point, the controversy was rooted in confusion over the composition of coal and other fossil fuels. For some experts, and seemingly for most lay people, coal's organic

108–13; "Informe que el ingeniero de minas Santiago Ramirez rinde á la Secretaria de Fomento, como resultado de su exploración á los distritos de Matamoros Izúcar, Chiautla y Acatlán en el estado de Puebla, y del estudio de sus criaderos de carbón mineral," Ibid., 7–95; "Informe que rinde a la Secretaría de Fomento el ingeniero de minas que subscribe, sobre su exploración en la municipalidad de Tlaquiltenango, perteneciente al distrito de Tetecala del estado de Morelos para el reconocimiento de unos supuestos criaderos de carbón," Ibid., 114–28; "Informe sobre la exploración hecha en el cantón de Jalapa, con el objeto de examinar sus terrenos carboníferos, presentado a la Secretaría de Fomento por el ingeniero de minas que suscribe," Ibid., 306–32; "Informe sobre la exploración hecha en los terrenos de Tulitic, en la jurisdicción del distrito de Alatriste, perteneciente al estado de Puebla, con el objeto de estudiar sus yacimientos de carbón," Ibid., 524–37; "Informe sobre la exploración hecha en los yacimientos carboníferos del distrito de Huetano, en el estado de Michoacán, que presenta a la Secretaría de Fomento el ingeniero de minas que subscribe," Ibid., 178–91; "Informe sobre los criaderos de carbon mineral que se encuentran en el estado de Tlaxcala. Presentado a la Secretaría de Fomento por el ingeniero de minas Santiago Ramírez," Ibid., 99–107; "Informe sobre los depósitos carboníferos del cerro de El Tambor en el distrito de Huauchinango, rendido a la Secretaría de Fomento por el ingeniero de minas que suscribe," Ibid., 688–699; "Observaciones a la consulta del Sr. Lic. D. Crispiniano del Castillo hechas por el ingeniero de minas Santiago Ramírez," Ibid., 147–63; *Noticia histórica de la riqueza minera de México y de su actual estado de explotación* (México, D. F.: Of. Tip. de la Sría. de Fomento, 1884); Miguel Bustamante, "Informe sobre los criaderos carboníferos de las Huastecas," *Anales del Ministerio de Fomento de la República Mexicana* VII (1882): 538–47; Manuel Urquiza, "Exploración del distrito de Coalcoman, estado de Michoacán, por el ingeniero de minas Manuel Urquiza," Ibid., 195–261. A synthesis of this work appeared 2 years later: Santiago Ramírez, *Noticia histórica de la riqueza minera de México y de su actual estado de explotacion* (Mexico: Oficina Tip. de la Secretaría de Fomento, 1884).

39 Experts classify coal into groups depending on characteristics such as carbon, ash, and moisture content. Most coals tend to fall into one of four categories: lignites, semi-bituminous, bituminous, and anthracites. Lignites have the lower carbon content; anthracites, the highest. Most coal deposits in Mexico are semi-bituminous and bituminous; anthracite is mostly restricted to the state of Sonora. On coal classifications, see Claus Diessel, *Coal-Bearing Depositional Systems* (Berlin: Springer-Verlag, 2012), 74.

origin meant it was not mineral. Critics of this point then argued that nonorganic, geological processes had formed coal, qualifying it as a mineral.[40] As such, coal fell under the jurisdiction of the colonial tradition of state ownership.[41]

The matter was settled in 1884, when the federal government enacted a new mining code. The code's authors were interested in creating appropriate conditions for Mexico's industrialization and believed adopting fossil fuels as the industrial energy base was key to this. Forest conservation coincided with their goal.[42] The new code recognized coal as a mineral (under colonial law) but gave private owners full property rights to surface and subsoil mineral wealth. Thus, the Mexican state relinquished its ownership of subsoil commodities like coal and oil and declared that private landowners could exploit those deposits without government authorization. The code also sought to foster coal and iron mining by exempting both from taxes for 50 years.[43] The code marked a fundamental shift towards creating a market for and regulating the extraction of fossil fuels in

[40] Coal is a fossil fuel, composed of the remains of once-living organisms dating back between 500 and 100 million years, during the Paleozoic and Mesozoic eras, when swamps and shallow seas covered large parts of the Earth. These ecosystems supported abundant vegetation or biomass, which accumulated in layers at the bottom of waterbodies after it died. Oxygen-poor conditions prevented decomposers from breaking down this matter. Over geologic periods of time, enormous pressure and heat turned this detritus into today's fossil fuels. Upper layers that remained closer to the surface underwent little decomposition, becoming coal deposits. Under higher pressure and heat, matter buried at a deeper level – between 2 and 4.5 km – broke into smaller carbon molecules, becoming crude oil. Finally, below 4.5 km, extreme conditions transformed accumulated biomass into natural gas. Fossil fuels are enormously compact energy, essentially "buried sunlight." Although they may continue forming, they are nonrenewable for human purposes. It took approximately 1000 years to produce the amount of fossil fuels that the world uses today in *1 day*. See Richard Wright and Dorothy F. Boorse, *Environmental Science: Toward a Sustainable Future* (Boston: Benjamin Cummings, 2010), 356–7.

[41] Mariano Bárcena, "El proyecto de Código de Minería. Dictamen del representante de los estados de Jalisco y México," *El Minero Mexicano*, October 30, 1884; Juvenal, "Un importante fallo de la Corte. El carbón de piedra," *El Monitor Republicano*, August 3, 1882; Manuel Lizardi, "Opinión que al Sr. ingeniero D. Francisco Glennie presenta en consulta el Licenciado Manuel Lizardi," *Anales del Ministerio de Fomento de la República Mexicana* VII (1882): 164; Santiago Ramírez, "El dominio radical de los criaderos de carbón. Estudio minero-legal por el ingeniero de minas Santiago Ramírez," 136–47; "Observaciones a la consulta del Sr. lic. D. Crispiniano del Castillo hechas por el ingeniero de minas Santiago Ramírez"; "La previa indenmización en los denuncios de minas," *El Minero Mexicano* 4, núm. 2, July 20, 1882.

[42] As Mariano Bárcena explained, "the abundance of this fuel in Mexico will not only save our forests, but it will foster the development of mining and many industries in the country": Mariano Bárcena, "El proyecto de Código de Minería," 435.

[43] Scholars have also interpreted the 1884 mining code as an attempt to attract foreign investment. See Juan Carlos Moreno-Brid and Jaime Ros, *Development and Growth in the Mexican Economy: A Historical Perspective* (Oxford: Oxford University Press, 2009), 54–5.

Mexico. It remained the main legal framework for the coal and oil industries until the Constitution of 1917 was enacted.[44]

The reports had practical effects, too. Thanks in part to the information they provided to investors, by 1884 coal was being mined across Mexico in small quantities, and Coahuila was producing 50,000–100,000 tons annually, a considerable amount for Mexico.[45]

Black Stones

Unlike deposits located in Mexico's largely inaccessible mountainous terrain, most Coahuila coal was located in two main easily accessible regions: Sabinas and Piedras Negras. Sabinas, the largest, sat some 130 km southwest of the US border and covered a total area of around 10,000 km². The Piedras Negras ("Black Stones") field, bordering Texas, extends over some 2,000 km². In total, Coahuila fields contained about 1.2 billion tons of recoverable coal, virtually all different grades of bituminous coal.[46]

C.P. Huntington, one of the Big Four of American railroads, started Coahuila's first commercial operation with the Sabinas Coal Mines. Production began in 1884 and yielded some 100,000 tons of bituminous coal in the first 1 or 2 years. While such an amount was nothing to dismiss in the 1880s, output would probably have been higher had the company's operations not been routinely paralyzed for months at a time by a legal dispute with Irish Mexican entrepreneur Patricio Milmo. The actual owner of the land where the mine was located, Milmo wanted the company

---

[44] *Código de Minería de la República Mexicana* (México: Imprenta y Litografía de I. Paz, 1885), 47. The "Título I. de las minas y de la propiedad minera," article 10.1, states that "Son de la exclusiva propiedad del dueño del suelo, quien por lo mismo, sin necesidad de denuncio ni de adjudicación especial, podrá explotar y aprovechar: I. Los criaderos de las diversas variedad de carbón de piedra." [...] IV. Las sales que existan en la superficie, las aguas puras y saladas, superficiales o subterráneas; el petróleo y los manantiales gaseosos o de aguas termales y medicinales." Article 196 states that "[d]urante el término de cincuenta años, contados desde la fecha de esta ley, estarán exceptuadas de toda contribución directa las minas de carbón de piedra en todas sus variedades, de hierro y de azogue, así como los productos de ellas."

[45] Production in Coahuila began on a modest scale as early as 1881, a year before most of Fomento's reports. The reports likely attracted more investors. By 1884, it was well known in the USA that Coahuila was the place to invest in Mexican coal mining. See Joseph Nimmo, *Commerce between the United States and Mexico: A Report in Reply to a Resolution of the House of Representatives of January 31, 1884* (Washington: G.P.O., 1884), 18, 78; see especially Appendix No. 20 "Statement in regard to the coal fields of Mexico by Mr. Alexander D. Anderson."

[46] On the geography and geology of Coahuila coal, see Rodolfo Corona-Esquivel et al., "Geología, estructura y composición de los principales yacimientos de carbón mineral en México," *Boletín de la Sociedad Geológica Mexicana* 58, núm. 1 (2006): 141–60. Sonora and Oaxaca reserves, Mexico's second and third largest, amount to approximately 85 and 30 million tons, respectively.

to pay him a higher fee per measure of coal. After years of legal battles, the company finally yielded. Sabinas Coal reorganized in 1887 into the Coahuila Coal Company. By the turn of the twentieth century, these companies were also producing coke in some 120 beehive coke ovens.[47] C. P. Huntington owned the controlling interest in all of them. Thus, the companies operated in close connection with the Mexican International Railroad, of which Huntington was also the principal stockholder.[48]

In 1899, New York capitalists organized the Mexican Coal & Coke Co., which would become a major producer. Production began in 1900 at the Las Esperanzas coalfields, an outcrop south of the Sabinas River.[49] The company faced several initial challenges. Mexican labor was scarce and mostly inexperienced in coal mining. Workers were ranchers and farmers, accustomed to what the company's general manager called "the intermittent working life of the farm or ranch." Unbeknownst to company management, these workers would become a transnational and highly mobile workforce that moved bilaterally across the border between Coahuila and Texas.[50] To secure more stable labor, the company hired White American, African American, Chinese, Japanese, and Italian workers. Few stayed long due to brutal working conditions and poor pay, preferring coalfields in the USA. Those who did, the company complained, were prone to heavy drinking, particularly white American miners – "once they [got] the mescal habit," few "recover[ed] from it."[51] Such claims conveniently shifted the responsibility for labor conflicts, workplace accidents, and low productivity from dismal working conditions to the miners' behavior and habits.

The local environment also presented obstacles. The almost complete lack of trees made importing timber inevitable. This problem was exacerbated in the Sabinas region by soft soils above the coal layers, which required heavy and expensive timbering.[52] Water for steam generation and drinking was scarce and mineral-laden, leaving a crust on boilers after

[47] Marvin D. Bernstein, *Mexican Mining Industry, 1890–1950: A Study of the Interaction of Politics, Economics, and Technology* (New York: SUNY Press, 1964), 35. Two other companies were formed in the following years, the Alamo Coal Co. in 1888 and the Fuente Coal Co. in 1894; the latter would exploit the fields adjacent to Piedras Negras (Ciudad Porfirio Díaz at the time).

[48] Frederick E. Saward, *The Coal Trade: A Compendium of Valuable Information Relative to Coal Production, Prices, Transportation, Etc. at Home and Abroad*, with Many Facts Worthy of Preservation for Future Reference (New York: The Coal Trade Journal, 1904), 115–17.

[49] Edwin Ludlow, "The Coal Fields of Las Esperanzas, Coahuila, Mexico," *Transactions of the American Institute of Mining, Metallurgical, and Petroleum Engineers* 32 (1902): 140–56.

[50] Roberto R. Calderón, *Mexican Coal Mining Labor in Texas and Coahuila, 1880–1930* (College Station: Texas A&M University Press, 2000).

[51] Ludlow, "The Coal Fields of Las Esperanzas, Coahuila, Mexico."

[52] Ezequiel Ordóñez, "Coal in Coahuila," *Mining and Scientific Press* 96 (March 14, 1908): 363.

evaporating and making the water unpalatable. Due to its physical composition, the company washed the extracted coal to remove the "bone" (ash)
before it could be used in smelters, adding another cumbersome step to the
production process. The geological formation of Coahuila's coal beds made
industrial-scale extraction difficult, since faults broke them into discontinuous pockets of highly uneven width separated by coal-less terrain.[53]

Despite these problems, Mexican Coal & Coke produced about
1,200 tons of coal daily and employed 3,000 miners by 1902. It also boasted
over 200 beehive ovens to manufacture coke. Its main costumers were
railroads, including Huntington's Mexican International, which both
burned and shipped Coal & Coke's fuel. The Mexican Central, smelters,
and steam-users across the country were also clients, although northern
Mexico was the company's best market. In central and southern Mexico,
the company manager admitted, "we meet a strong competition from West
Virginia coal, coming by water to Tampico and Veracruz."[54]

Coahuila typically met about half of Mexico's coal demand (see Figure 3.1).
Domestic production surpassed imports only after 1909. Several factors
explain this. One, ironically, was the coalfields' location. On one hand, its
location made Coahuila coal accessible and exploitable on an industrial scale.
On the other, it meant that Coahuila's main market was the border US states
and northern Mexico. Shipping Coahuila coal to central and southern
Mexico, where it competed with imports, was much less profitable.[55] As one

---

[53] International Bureau of the American Republics, *Mexico: A Geographical Sketch, with Special Reference to Economic Conditions and Prospects of Future Development* (Washington: Government Printing Office, 1900), 194.

[54] See Ludlow, "The Coal Fields of Las Esperanzas, Coahuila, Mexico." Other companies appeared before 1910. The largest were the Compañía Carbonífera del Norte, Compañía Carbonífera de La Rosita, Compañía Carbonífera de la Agujita, Compañía Carbonífera de Lampacitas, Compañía Carbonífera de San Blas, Compañía Carbonífera de Ciudad Porfírio Díaz, and the Compañía Carbonífera de Rio Grande. See Ezequiel Ordóñez, "Coal in Coahuila," *Mining and Scientific Press* 96 (March 14, 1908): 363–4. A complete list of coal companies in Coahuila in 1910 appears In J. R. Southworth, *The Official Directory of Mines & Estates of Mexico: General Description of the Mining Properties of the Republic of Mexico: In Which Is Included a List of Haciendas and Ranches in Those States and Territories Where It Has Been Possible to Obtain Reliable Data* (Mexico, D. F.: Published by John R. Southworth, F.R.G.S., 1910), 86–8.

[55] As John Birkinbine observed, "the fuel requirements of Mexico are more than double the output of the Coahuila fields, and domestic coal and coke compete with foreign fuel at the capital and other • centers of consumption on the main plateau. [. . .] Fuel is, therefore, an important problem ... " Seeking to address this problem (and profit), Birkinbine tried to make Oaxaca produce coal on an industrial scale, but failed. See John Birkinbine, *Industrial Progress of Mexico*, 15. Frederick Saward, editor of *The Coal Trade Journal*, noted increasing demand for coal and coke in Mexico in 1904. Saward linked growing domestic consumption to industrial development in mining, smelting, and manufacturing, along with dwindling wood supplies. According to Saward, Mexico's demand was more uniform than in the USA. With less severe winters and most coal going to factories, Mexico's consumption was relatively constant throughout the year. He believed this characteristic granted it

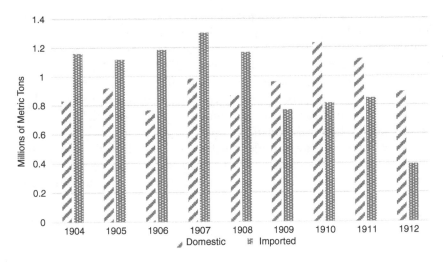

Figure 3.1 Domestic and imported coal in Mexico, 1904–12. Source: Compañía Fundidora de Fierro y Acero de Monterrey, S.A., *Reportes anuales*, 1921, 10.

later observer put it, "[t]he market for Coahuila coal was approximately within an area bounded by imaginary lines touching the cities of Monterrey, Saltillo, San Luis Potosi, Aguascalientes, Durango, and Chihuahua ... "[56]

Central Mexico's consumers often found coal cheaper to import from England or the USA; Coahuila's coalfields were located 1,500 kilometers from Mexico City, while the port of Veracruz was just 400 kilometers away.[57] Most imported coal came from the USA, especially Virginia, Pennsylvania, and Alabama, followed by Great Britain, Germany, and Australia. The USA also supplied most of Mexico's coke before the 1910 Revolution, with annual shipments of some 250,000 tons. Coke, a high-

a more stable labor force. In spite of these favorable conditions, Saward acknowledged that domestic consumption frequently exceeded production. See Frederick E. Saward, *The Coal Trade*, 1904, 116.

[56] John R. Bradley, *Fuel and Power in Latin America* (Washington, DC: United States Government Printing Office, 1931), 118.

[57] "La hulla en México," *El Economista Mexicano*, January 2, 1892, 262. In 1892, Coahuila coal earned M$17 per ton in Mexico City. Imported coal from Colorado and New Mexico earned M$13 in Chihuahua city, while US coal in Veracruz fetched M$13, which probably rose to M$14–15 in Mexico City after freight costs.

quality fuel made by heating coal at an elevated temperature (a process known as pyrolysis), was integral to steel manufacturing.[58]

Politics and crony capitalism also kept Coahuila coal prices high in central Mexico, at least before 1900. In 1890, the daily *El Tiempo* and Mexican writer and politician Francisco Bulnes accused both the Mexican Central Railway and one Mr. Arce of inflating coal prices. The Central's trunk line linked Mexico City to Ciudad Juárez, connecting in Coahuila with C.P. Huntington's Mexican International line. Mr. Arce apparently reached an agreement with the Central to slap Coahuila's coal with high tariffs. As the only line directly connecting northern Mexico to Mexico City, the Central was definitely positioned to do so. Apparently, the high tariff also protected Mr. Arce's monopoly profits as Mexico City's sole importer of coal and prevented Mexican coal from competing with American coal imported into Mexico City, in which the US-owned Central had a stake.[59]

Whether the reasons were environmental, economic, or political, after three decades of commercial coal mining in Mexico, total output remained minuscule compared with the USA and Great Britain. Even Spain, then a minor player in the global coal trade, mined more than twice as much coal as Mexico (Table 3.1).

Table 3.1 *Comparative coal production (millions of metric tons)*

Year	United States	Great Britain	Spain	Mexico[a]
1895	177	194	1.7	0.3
1900	243	228	2.5	0.4
1905	351	239	3.2	0.9
1910	445	264	3.5	1.4

[a] The figures have been rounded up.
Adapted from W. W. Leach, et. al., *The Coal Resources of the World*, vol. 1, 1913, *XIX*; INEGI, *Estadísticas Históricas de México*, vol. 1, 1994, 542–3.

---

[58] Bradley, *Fuel and Power in Latin America*, 1931, 118; Saward, *The Coal Trade*, 1904, 95, 115–17 suggests that 72 percent of the 52 percent of the coal Mexico imported in 1902 came from the USA. This means that 37 percent of all coal consumed in Mexico in 1902 was US coal.

[59] "Minas de carbón," *El Tiempo*, January 25, 1890, 2. In turn, Huntington seemed to deliberately make coal from his newly exploited Piedras Negras fields uncompetitive by elevating Mexican railroad's freight tariffs. In this way, imports into Mexico from the Southern Pacific Railroad, of which Huntington was president, were unaffected.

Figure 3.2 Coal production in Mexico, 1891–1996. Sources: B. R. Mitchell, *International Historical Statistics*, 311–12; INEGI, *Estadísticas históricas de México*, pp. 542–3; Departamento de Minas, *El carbón mineral en México*, 1921, 9.[60]

In spite of such failures, from 1884 onward, Coahuila produced *almost all* the coal mined in Mexico. Output increased steadily until the Mexican Revolution, more than tripling between 1901 and 1911 (Figure 3.2). Production plummeted during the revolutionary years before recovering during the 1920s. After a Depression-era slump, coal began a slow but steady ascent until about 1970. The 1970s and early 1980s brought deindustrialization in the north and severe economic difficulties, both of which spelled trouble for coal. From the mid-1980s onward, however, Coahuila's coal reinvented itself as a major source of electricity in northern Mexico. Production soared and continues growing into the twenty-first century, although it has never represented more than a small percentage of total national electricity generation (about 5–7 percent).

The Expansive Phase, 1884–1910

The history of Mexico's coal consumption, both domestic and imported, went through two major phases: expansion and relative decline. The first

---

[60] The 2,449,976 metric tons for 1910 quoted in *El carbón mineral en México* is almost certainly too high. Most other sources roughly coincide on pre-1910 data and range between 1.4 and 2 million tons for 1910. Historical figures for coal production in Mexico are notoriously unreliable.

phase, from 1884 to 1910, was characterized by coal's close connection to railroads, electricity, and major public works like the Grand Canal in the Valley of Mexico. Coal's heyday in Mexico came at the end of this period, when coal powered the largest smelters the country had ever seen and Latin America's first steel factory (Figure 3.3).

While other railroad lines in nineteenth-century Mexico transported and consumed coal, the Mexican International Railroad developed a particularly codependent relationship with it. In 1881, C. P. Huntington obtained a government concession to build a line from Piedras Negras to Durango City, and from there to Zacatecas, Guanajuato, and Mexico City. The plan was to also extend one line from Durango to a Pacific port – Mazatlán was an option – and build another running from San Luis Potosí to either Tampico or Veracruz. The oceanic and southern links were never built. The trunk line to Durango began construction in 1883, starting from Piedras Negras, adjacent to the Southern Pacific Railroad's terminal point, and moving southwest. By 1884, it reached Monclova, the heart of Coahuila's coal country. The line arrived in Torreón, Coahuila's capital, in 1888, connecting to the Central's trunk line (Ciudad Juárez–Mexico City). By 1892, the line reached Durango, culminating in 980 km of track. In the 1890s, a branch connected the International's main line with the city of Monterrey, all but ensuring that coal played an important role in its industrialization. The railroad "provided an outlet for the extensive coal deposits of Coahuila, and it contributed to upbuilding Mexico's iron smelting industry."[61] Mexican coal owed much of its distribution and success to the International.

The International and Coahuila's coal fields grew hand in hand. As the company informed stockholders in 1892, its lines "run through the only good coal fields in the Republic."[62] Such a position benefitted the company in at least three ways. Seeking cheap and reliable fuel supplies, energy-intensive industries like smelters, ironworks, and Latin America's first modern steel operation were established along the company's tracks. Coal also became the line's main cargo and revenue source. From 1893 to 1908, coal represented between 40 and 50 percent of the company's total annual freight tonnage. Additionally, coal fueled the company's locomotives. The company, in turn, was instrumental to developing Coahuila's

---

[61] Fred Wilbur Powell, *The Railroads of Mexico* (Boston: Stratford, 1921), 138. The International joined the National Railways of Mexico, organized in 1908. The federal government acquired majority stakeholder status of Mexico's most important lines. The International ceased being a separate company in 1910.

[62] Mexican International Railroad Company, *Annual Reports* (New York: John C. Rankin Co., Printers, 1892–1910), 1892, 7.

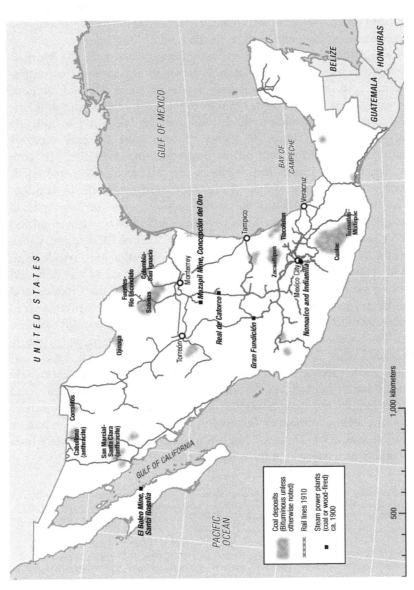

Figure 3.3 Mexico's coal deposits, rail lines, and selected steam-powered plants, early twentieth century.

coal industry.[63] Thanks to the International, Coahuila's coal could reach northern Mexican markets. The International also supplied coal to single large consumers through direct lines, such as the feeder line connecting Coahuila's coal to a huge smelter operated by the Spanish-German concern Peñoles Mining Company in 1899, in the state of Durango.[64]

By the 1890s other major railroad lines began using coal. The Mexican Railway, which ran from the port of Veracruz to Mexico City, consumed imported coal, mostly British and American. The Central accessed American coal at the end of its main line in El Paso, Texas, and domestic coal through its connection to the International in Torreón, Coahuila. By 1908, the Central consumed 60,000 metric tons of coal monthly (720,000 tons annually), half of this imported from the USA.[65] By contrast, regional lines and those without reliable access to imported or domestic coal stuck to wood, the cheaper and more easily obtained option.

The transition to coal was not always smooth, even for large railroad companies with means. Some firms went back and forth between wood and coal for some time, like the Mexican National Railroad Company, which operated its main line from Nuevo Laredo (across the Rio Grande from Laredo, Texas) to Mexico City. The company's railroad, which connected Mexico's most important northeastern cities with the Bajío's mining and agricultural zones and the central highlands, was theoretically positioned to purchase as much American coal as needed. The problem was not coal, but silver. The company paid for coal imports with American gold, which greatly appreciated when Mexican silver lost about half its value in 1893. Coal became more expensive than wood, forcing the company to exclusively burn the latter. In 1898, the National switched back to coal when wood supplies simply ran out, at considerable cost. Expensive fuel remained a constant drain on company finances, typically representing up to half its operating costs as late as 1907.[66] High-priced coal afflicted other major lines until oil became available in the early twentieth century.[67]

[63] A Mexico City newspaper described Huntington as the "pioneer" who opened Coahuila's coal for large-scale exploitation. "Explotación de petróleo," *El Municipio Libre*, March 5, 1899.

[64] On Peñoles, see *The Mexican Yearbook* (London: McCorquodale & Co. Ltd., 1908), 489–90; Bernstein, *Mexican Mining Industry, 1890–1950*, 67–8.

[65] Percy F. Martin, *Mexico of the Twentieth Century*, vol. 1 (New York: Dodd, Mead, 1908), 265.

[66] Mexican National Railroad Company, *Annual Reports*, 15 vols., 1887–1898; Mexican National Railroad Company/National Railroad Company of Mexico, *Annual Reports*, 1899–1907, *passim*. The Mexican National became the National Railroad Company in 1902, which was subsumed into the government-controlled National Railways of Mexico in 1909.

[67] Arturo Grunstein, "¿Competencia o monopolio? Regulación y desarrollo ferrocarrilero en México, 1885–1911," in *Ferrocarriles y vida económica en México (1850–1950)* (Toluca: El Colegio Mexiquense, 1996), 167–221.

In the late nineteenth century, Mexico City's tramway system began using steam-powered locomotives alongside animal-hauled transportation.[68] By 1899, steam cars covered about 15 percent of the company's 247-km network.[69] It remains unclear what these machines consumed, but some coal was likely, given imported coal's availability in Mexico City at the time. In 1900, amidst rapidly expanding demand (the company sold 25,000,000 trips the year before), the company invested in electric-powered cars.[70] The cars operated in the city's downtown area, and some main suburban lines linked to important towns in the valley. Electricity came from burning coal at the Indianilla thermoelectric plant in Mexico City, owned by the tramway company. In 1900, 20 percent of the company's cars used electricity, while the rest continued using animal traction,[71] a ratio that suggests the company replaced some of its steam locomotives with electric ones. The trend towards electrifying Mexico City's urban transport continued apace during the 1900s,[72] although hydroelectricity began displacing coal by the decade's second half (see later).

Other cities like Puebla, Guadalajara, and Veracruz soon followed suit, with a similar business model wherein electric industry and tramways systems were owned and operated by the same companies. In 1906, for example, the Puebla Electric Light Company was acquired by the Puebla Tramway Light and Power Company, another Canadian enterprise.[73] In most cities across the country, either coal or water generated electricity for

[68] Until 1898, the Compañía de Ferrocarriles del Distrito Federal owned the system; that year, Canadian and British investors took over and formed the Mexico Electric Company, based in London. In 1906, the Toronto-based Mexico Tramways Company leased the system from the Mexico Electric Company, running it until 1922.

[69] "La Secretaría de Comunicaciones y Obras Públicas pide datos relativos al desarrollo y situación que guardan actualmente los tranvías y líneas urbanas establecidas en el D.F." (1899), Secretaría de Gobierno del D.F., Estadísticas, caja 1, exp. 15, AHDF. Curiously, the "Reglamento de ferrocarriles urbanos del Distrito Federal" (Code for the Federal District's Urban Railroads) enacted in 1877 stipulated that "all urban railroads will always use animal traction." The code changed after the press, line owners, and Fomento pointed to US and European trends to replace animals with steam engines in urban tramways, arguing the clause would soon prove obsolete. The new version read "For the time being . . ." See Secretaría de Fomento, Colonización e Industria, *Anales del Ministerio de Fomento de la República Mexicana*, vol. I (México: Impr. de F. Díaz de León, 1877), 101–2.

[70] There were 35 of them, 18 feet long, each powered by two 35-horsepower electric motors. See Rafael R. Arizpe, *Estadística de las aplicaciones de la electricidad en la República Mexicana.* (Mexico, 1900), 146–7.

[71] "Datos relativos al desarrollo y situación que guardan actualmente los tranvías y líneas urbanas establecidas en el Distrito Federal" (1900), Secretaría de Gobierno del D.F., Estadísticas, caja 1, exp. 15, AHDF; Rafael R. Arizpe, *Estadística de las aplicaciones de la electricidad*, 130–51.

[72] By 1911, 90 percent of the system was electric-powered. See Mexico Tramways Company, *Director's Report and Accounts* (Toronto, 1911). In 1908, Mexico Tramways acquired controlling stock in the Mexican Light & Power Company to secure reliable electricity for its network.

[73] *The Mexican Yearbook*, 1908, 515.

tramways during these first years of electrification. One exception was the tramway system in the port city of Veracruz, which obtained electricity from Mexico's first oil-fueled power plant (opened in 1908), which used local oil supplies and German-manufactured diesel engines.[74] By the decade's end, electric tramways were so ingrained in the daily lives of Mexico's urban residents that many of them took their final trip to the cemetery by tram.[75]

Like other new industries, the nascent electric sector used coal power. The origins of Mexico's electric industry are found in private businesses like mines and textile factories that produced electricity for self-consumption and then sold extra energy to nearby towns and cities.[76] Soon, city councils began subsidizing electric utilities through generous tax exemptions to build electric street lighting.[77] By the late 1880s, there were eleven privately owned facilities producing electricity for public consumption. Ten of these were thermoelectric plants and only one was hydroelectric. All thermoelectric plants burned coal when they could (and wood when they couldn't). Another seventeen smaller thermoelectric facilities supplied only private customers, including factories and households. Coming into the twentieth century, 89 percent of Mexico's 235 electric plants for illumination were thermoelectric. Many were coal-based.[78]

Two of the country's largest coal-fired thermoelectric plants were located in Mexico City, the Indianilla and Nonoalco plants (Figure 3.4). Both were built in 1898 by Berlin-based company Siemens and Halske. Although company management, later known as the Mexican Electric Company, was in London, a German engineer oversaw Mexico City operations. The Nonoalco plant featured state-of-the-art German boilers, steam engines, and dynamos, with a total initial capacity of about

---

[74] Ibid., 514.

[75] "Conditions of Electric Railway Operation in Mexico City," *Electric Railway Journal* 33, no. 18 (June 1909): 812–20.

[76] The strong connection between mining and electricity persisted in states like Chihuahua with a long history of mining. See "Contrato celebrado entre el Sr. Enrique C. Creel, gobernador constitucional del Estado libre y soberano de Chihuahua y los señores Alberto Terrazas e ingeniero Manuel Gameros para el establecimiento de haciendas metalúrgicas, instalaciones de fuerza motriz y construcción de tranvías o ferrocarriles industriales en el distrito de Iturbide" (1909), Porfiriato y Terracismo; Presidencia; Contratos y Convenios; Chihuahua; caja 33, exp. 19, AHMCH.

[77] A typical contract is "Expediente formado en virtud de establecer en esta ciudad el alumbrado público" (1885), Porfiriato y Terracismo; Tesorería; Reportes y mejoras públicas; Chihuahua, caja 17B15, exp. 13, AHMCH.

[78] Arizpe, *Estadística de las aplicaciones de la electricidad*, 101, 106, 123–4, 130–51. See Gustavo Garza, *El proceso de industrialización en la ciudad de México, 1821–1970* (México, D. F.: El Colegio de México, 1985),166–9. Garza's estimate for thermoelectric production in 1899 is lower than Arizpe's. Garza claims that coal-fired plants produced 61 percent of all electricity generated, while hydroelectric plants produced the other 39 percent.

Figure 3.4 Nonoalco power station, ca. 1900. Coal is visible in the bottom left image. Source: *México Ilustrado*, 1903, 152.

2,400 horsepower, which rapidly expanded to 7,200 horsepower in 1903. Through 232 km of underground and aerial cables, the plant powered over 1,100 streetlights. It was also the largest supplier for private consumers.[79]

The Mexican Electric Company pioneered using electricity for motive power in Mexico City. A few years after beginning operations, the company dominated the market. With a range of almost 10 kilometers, the company's main plant powered factories and workshops citywide. New coal-fired motors – substantially cheaper than steam engines – allowed many workshops and small factories to mechanize production. The company also sold these motors to individual customers.[80]

---

[79] Arizpe, *Estadísticas de las aplicaciones de la electricidad*, 130–51; Rafael Arizpe, *El alumbrado público en la ciudad de México; estudio histórico seguido de algunos datos técnicos acerca de las principales instalaciones destinadas á ese servicio municipal* (Mexico: Tip. y Lit. "La Europea" de J. Aguilar Vera y Ca. (Sociedad en Comandita), 1900), 93; Ernesto Galarza, *La industria eléctrica en México*. (México: Fondo de Cultura económica, 1941), 50. In the 1920s, when local demand for electricity soared, the company multiplied Nonoalco's generating capacity to a huge 40,000 horsepower.

[80] J. R. Southworth, *Mexico ilustrado, Distrito Federal, su descripción, gobierno, historia, comercio e industrias, la biografía del Sr. general d. Porfirio Díaz, en español e inglés.* (Liverpool: Blake & Mackenzie, 1903), 152–3. Mexico City featured two other smaller thermoelectric plants. The first belonged to the Compañía de Gas y Luz Eléctrica, a business operating since the 1860s, when it was the first to introduce hydrogen gas for artificial illumination to Mexico City's streets. The Compañía de Gas's coal-fired plant generated 1,200 horsepower. The Compañía Nacional de Luz

Although thermoelectricity remained dominant as a motive power source in Mexico, hydroelectricity quickly gained importance. In central Mexico, hydroelectricity became especially significant after 1905, when Puebla's famous Necaxa plant began supplying Mexico City.[81] Siemens and Halske (owners of Nonoalco) also controlled Necaxa, located 170 kilometers away from Mexico City. Necaxa was Mexico's most important hydroelectric plant and one of the largest in the world at the time. Other small hydroelectric plants generated power for individual factories in the Valley of Mexico, like the San Ildefonso textile mill (which also sold unused power to Mexico City), in the valley's northwest; the San Rafael Paper Mill, in the foothills of the Iztaccíhuatl volcano and at the time the largest paper factory in Latin America; and the Miraflores factory, which established the first hydroelectric plant in the region in 1889.[82]

Before 1910, coal also played an important role in public works projects, like draining the Valley of Mexico. After centuries of failed, interrupted, and partially successful attempts, the ancient lake system that originally surrounded Mexico City had shrunk considerably by the late nineteenth century. Porfirio Díaz made the project the centerpiece of his government's public works agenda. A new plan called for building a massive canal to drain lake water into a nearby river system that in turn drained into the Gulf of Mexico. Initially granted to an American company, the project was reassigned to Weetman Pearson, a British subject with considerable experience in public works and good connections to the Porfirian administration.[83]

Eléctrica was smallest, producing 750 horsepower. See Arizpe, *Estadística de las aplicaciones de la electricidad*, 113.

[81] Hydroelectricity already dominated in states like Puebla and Veracruz.

[82] Arizpe, *Estadística de las aplicaciones de la electricidad*, 130–51. The San Rafael Paper Company derived a large part of its energy from oil by the 1910s. Around 1900, however, it relied mostly on hydroelectricity, with a generating capacity of 4,000 horsepower. On this specific case, see Chapter 4. The Compañía Explotadora de las Fuerzas Hidroeléctricas de San Ildefonso in Monte Alto, Tlalnepantla, produced 1,100 horsepower for the San Ildefonso textile mill and planned to sell 4,395 horsepower to Mexico City. The company used waters from the river Monte Alto and Tlalnepantla. La Hormiga factory in San Ángel produced 10,000 horsepower via its hydroelectric plant. The Santa Teresa mill, also in San Ángel, used hydroelectricity as well, with 15,000 horsepower at its disposal. La Abeja textile factory had its own hydroelectric plant producing 1,000 horsepower. The Miraflores textile mill, located in Amecameca, used water from the San Rafael river to generate 2,000 horsepower.

[83] On the history of drainage and building the Grand Canal, see Priscilla Connolly, *El contratista de don Porfirio: obras públicas, deuda y desarrollo desigual* (México, D. F.: Fondo de Cultura Económica, 1997); Manuel Perló Cohen, *El paradigma porfiriano: Historia del desagüe del Valle de México* (México, D. F.: Programa Universitario de Estudios Sobre la Ciudad, Instituto de Investigaciones Sociales: M.A. Porrúa Grupo Editorial, 1999); Emily Wakild, "Naturalizing Modernity: Urban

Pearson, who would play a key role in Mexico's oil boom a few years later, successfully completed the canal (opened in 1901) largely using huge, coal-powered dredges.[84] As historian Patricia Connolly explains, "the big innovation was mechanical dredgers, manned exclusively by skilled workers imported from Britain."[85] A man could dig about five cubic meters of soil on soft terrain per day.[86] Pearson's coal-powered dredges could move up to 104 cubic meters *per hour*, or 1,250 cubic meters during a 12-hour shift – 6,000 times the amount of soil a laborer could handle daily. The dredges moved over 6,500,000 cubic meters of soil from 1891 to 1895, consuming about 6,000 tons of coal annually.[87]

Although flooding never ceased, the disappearance of the lakes had long-term consequences for Mexico City residents and the valley's environment: it enabled urban sprawl to expand into the lakebed, caused giant, days-long dust storms, and eradicated various avian and freshwater fauna and flora.[88]

Despite its awesome power and people's fascination with it, coal never became king in Mexico in the way it did in the USA, Britain, and Germany. Within Latin America, countries like Chile found coal more profitable and easily exploited than Mexico ever did.[89] There is little doubt that persistent high prices prevented coal's universal adoption and kept fuelwood competitive until the turn of the twentieth century.[90] Of course, prices varied substantially by region and over time. Around 1900, 1 metric ton of coal cost M$18 in southern Chihuahua and 1 metric ton of wood not even a peso. In central Zacatecas, however, coal cost M$13 per ton and wood M$7, making wood more expensive than coal, since roughly 2 tons of good, dry wood provided the same energy content as 1 ton of coal. Southern Chihuahua sat close to the still vast forests of the Sierra Madre Occidental, so wood remained the best option from a cost

Parks, Public Gardens and Drainage Projects in Porfirian Mexico City," *Mexican Studies/Estudios Mexicanos* 23, no. 1 (2007): 101–23.

[84] Pearson and Son, Ltd., "Drainage of the Valley of Mexico. Grand Canal" (1890–1896), Records of Pearson and Son, Ltd., Reel 153, Box No. 16–17, Mexican Canal, Nettie Lee Benson Latin American Collection Microforms. Pearson made part of his substantial fortune thanks to coal-powered machines, and then invested his capital in developing another fossil fuel: Veracruz oil.

[85] Priscilla Connolly, "Pearson and Public Works Construction in Mexico,1890–1910," *Business History* 41, no. 4 (1999): 48–71. Human laborers dug about a third of the project.

[86] *Memoria histórica, técnica y administrativa de las obras del desagüe del Valle de México, 1449–1900*, vol. 1 (México: Tip. de la Oficina Impresora de Estampillas, 1902), 441.

[87] Pearson and Son, Ltd., "Drainage of the Valley of Mexico. Grand Canal."

[88] Matthew Vitz, *A City on a Lake: Urban Political Ecology and the Growth of Mexico City* (Durham: Duke University Press, 2018), chapter 5.

[89] On Chile's coal history, see Luis Ortega, "The First Four Decades of the Chilean Coal Mining Industry, 1840–1879," *Journal of Latin American Studies* 14, no. 1 (1982): 1–32.

[90] Kuntz Ficker, *Empresa extranjera y mercado interno*, 225–7.

perspective.[91] In similar places across Mexico, wood remained the fuel of choice. In Zacatecas, the matter was less clear. On the one hand, large portions of the state had become treeless landscape after centuries of silver mining. On the other, Zacatecas was crossed by major railroad lines carrying both wood and coal, and the price of both fuels remained close enough between 1890 and 1910 to make other criteria relevant.

The case of Mexico City's water system illustrates the complexities involved in favoring wood or coal in places where the price gap was narrow. In the 1880s, city authorities installed steam engines at the Chapultepec water distribution plant. This site collected potable water from the canals and aqueducts descending from nearby mountains and pumped it across the city. In 1894, the city granted Manuel Olaguíbel the concession to provide the engines with fuelwood, which he acquired in the Desierto de los Leones.[92] That year, Olaguíbel charged the city M$9.50 per ton of wood.[93] City authorities continued to renew Olaguíbel's contract over the years.

In 1901, one Enrique Bornemann offered to supply the city with coal at lower cost than Olaguíbel's wood. Bornemann also proposed covering the cost for adapting the boilers to burn coal.[94] City officials rejected Bornemann's bid, arguing that Olaguíbel had provided excellent service for years. The small savings derived from burning coal, they added, would be offset by the substantial technical problems of using it to fire the boilers. Since coal burned at a higher temperature, authorities feared the extra heat would wear the boilers and pipes faster. This could result in more recurrent breakdowns, a shorter lifespan for parts, and higher repair costs. Olaguíbel's proposal to reduce wood prices sealed the deal.[95]

---

[91] And those forests fueled most of the steam engines used in the industries of Chihuahua City, although coal and even gasoline were making inroads. See "Cuestionarios referentes a los estable-cimientos industriales que existen en esta ciudad" (1903), Porfiriato y Terracismo; Censos, estadísticas y filiaciones; Chihuahua, caja 56, exp. 10, AHMCH; "Censos de la Dirección General de Estadísticas Industriales" (1904), Porfiriato y Terracismo; Secretaría; Censos, estadísticas y filiaciones; Chihuahua; caja 59, exp. 38, AHMCH.

[92] "Disposición que hace el señor Manuel E. Olaguíbel para la explotación del monte del Desierto" (1894), Aguas del Desierto, 1878–1915, exp. 46, AHDF. The wood could be either fir (*oyamel*) or pine (*pino*). A ton of fir was one-third cheaper than one of pine. See "Proposición que hace el Sr. Manuel Olaguíbel para la explotación del monte del Desierto de los Leones" (1894), AHDF, Aguas del Desierto, 1878–1915, exp. 24–56, exp. 46.

[93] "Aguas del Desierto" (1894), Aguas del Desierto, 1878–1915, exp. 24–56, AHDF.

[94] "Enrique Bornemann, por la Compañía Pan-Americana de Combustible, propone la venta de carbón de piedra para las bombas de Chapultepec" (1901), Aguas en general, 1901–15, tomo 8, núm. 42, exp. 570, AHDF. To burnish his credentials, Bornemann claimed that his company was already supplying coal to the Central Mexican Railroad, a "great smelter" in Monterrey, and Mexico City's main power plant.

[95] "Manuel E. Olaguíbel presenta proposiciones para el abastecimiento de combustible para las bombas de Chapultepec" (1902), Ayuntamiento, Aguas en general, vol. 42, exp. 602, AHDF.

Then, in 1906, rising wood prices prompted city authorities to abandon some of their misgivings about coal. Olaguíbel himself began importing coal into Mexico City. He also expanded his operations, now supplying the Secretary of Public Works with both coal and wood. Initially, Olaguíbel had been permitted to use any coal he wanted, but by 1908 the federal government obliged him to give preference to domestic coal, only purchasing foreign fuel when domestic supplies were insufficient. This clause reflected not only the federal government's nationalist impulse to foster Coahuila's coal industry, but also price. In 1908, domestic coal sold in Mexico City for M$22.50 per metric ton, while the English and US products cost M$29 and M$26 per ton, respectively. Moreover, while domestic coal prices kept a downward trend, wood prices increased. In 1909, the city paid Olaguíbel M$17 per metric ton of wood and M$21.50 for domestic coal. Given the previously mentioned wood-to-coal ratio, wood had become almost 60 percent more expensive than coal in Mexico City. A coal transition was clearly underway for Mexico City's water system.

Monterrey and Coal's Heyday

While other parts of Mexico vacillated between wood and coal, the choice was obvious for the city of Monterrey. Monterrey's industrialization began in earnest around 1890, later than central Mexico's. But once it did, the city's industrial capacity exploded, rapidly surpassing other areas. By 1910, it was Mexico's second most important industrial center after Mexico City. Coal fueled much of this spectacular growth. Located relatively close to Coahuila's coal fields, about 300 km away, Monterrey's industries readily adopted coal at the onset of industrialization. Additionally, Monterrey imported foreign coke from the port of Tampico, some 500 km southeast. These unique conditions meant that Monterrey was the only city in Mexico where coal fully powered industrialization. Monterrey's coal-based industrialization may have been exceptional not only for Mexico but for Latin America as a whole.[96] Still, Monterrey's transition to coal was

---

[96] "Una industria nueva," *El Economista Mexicano*, February 15, 1902; "Producción carbonífera," *El Economista Mexicano*, May 10, 1902. Being near Tampico, a major port, meant Monterrey could also import coal at relatively low prices. By 1911, the city's (and Latin America's) largest steel mill imported one-third of its coal. See "La Compañía Fundidora de Fierro y Acero de Monterrey," *El Economista Mexicano*, August 17, 1912. Coal reliance had its problems. Despite the relative proximity of Coahuila's coalmines, Monterrey's industries sometimes faced fuel shortages. See "El carbón de Coahuila," *El Economista Mexicano*, December 22, 1906; "El carbón en México," *El Economista Mexicano*, August 22,

anything but smooth and stayed restricted to industry – households in particular stayed away from the pungent fuel. Monterrey's coal transition also proved short-lived. Almost as soon as it was complete, new sources of energy renewed perennial hopes of energy abundance and inexhaustibility.

Monterrey's diverse industrial base included an array of consumer goods manufacturers. There were fully mechanized breweries whose beer began displacing former favorites like pulque; a glass bottle factory that manufactured millions; and textile factories that spun thread and wove cloth, among others. But the city's main businesses were heavy industry. In addition to a number of smelters and metal factories, in 1901 the city acquired the Compañía Fundidora de Fierro y Acero de Monterrey, S.A., the first and largest steel factory in Latin America.

Fundidora typified Monterrey's dependence on and difficulties with coal. It was founded on May 5, 1900 by Antonio Basagoiti, Eugenio Kelly, Vicente Ferrara, and León Signoret.[97] These men were all foreign born (with the exception of Ferrara), held interest in a variety of Mexican industries, and boasted connections with Mexico's economic and political elite.[98] Their ambitious plan was to build a factory capable of producing 100,000 tons of pig iron (from which steel can be manufactured) annually, a far cry from Mexico's small foundries, which together produced a few thousand tons in a good year. Two main obstacles stood out: obtaining large, reliable supplies of iron ore, coal, and coke, and marketing 100,000 tons of pig iron in a country with little "market depth" for such a product at the time.[99] Securing coal would prove the most challenging.[100]

1914. Monterrey's industrialization has received substantial attention from historians. See Aurora Gómez Galvarriato, "El primer impulso industrializador de México: el caso de Fundidora Monterrey" (BA Thesis, México, D. F., ITAM, 1990); Carlos Marichal and Mario Cerutti, *Historia de las grande empresas en México, 1850–1930* (Monterrey: Universidad Autónoma de Nuevo León ; Fondo de Cultura Económica, 1997); Stephen H. Haber, *Industry and Underdevelopment: The Industrialization of Mexico, 1890–1940* (Stanford: Stanford University Press, 1989); Alex Saragoza, *The Monterrey Elite and the Mexican State, 1880–1940* (Austin: University of Texas Press, 1988). On Latin America's lack of coal, see Shawn William Miller, *An Environmental History of Latin America* (New York: Cambridge University Press, 2007), 156–9.

[97] Compañía Fundidora de Fierro y Acero de Monterrey, S.A., *Informe anual* (Monterrey, N. L., 1948), 6.

[98] Kelly was a New York banker and son-in-law of Patricio Milmo, who had litigated with Huntington over coalfields years before. Basagoiti was a Basque immigrant who became a successful and wealthy Mexico City businessman. Signoret was a French émigré from Barcelonnette who also became wealthy in Porfirian Mexico.

[99] Compañía Fundidora, *Informe anual*, 1948, 6. In 1903, Mexico consumed 178,852 metric tons of iron and steel, only 5.5 percent domestically made.

[100] Economic historians have debated the question of industrial overcapacity and Porfirian Mexico's consumer markets for years. The best-known proponent of excess industrial capacity is Haber, *Industry and Underdevelopment*. Aurora Gómez Galvarriato has questioned Haber's explanation

Despite the obstacles, Fundidora's founders were optimistic and confident in their abilities. They chose to build in Monterrey because the city was, as they put it, in the middle of a circle with a radius of less than 300 km that included Coahuila's coal and some of the richest iron deposits in northeastern Mexico. Another consideration was Monterrey's good rail connection to the regions from which these essential materials came, a feature they hoped would make cheap transportation possible.[101]

But proximity to coalfields was not enough. The company moved to acquire or lease coal-bearing land in Coahuila to avoid depending on Mexico's few coal-mining firms.[102] Starting in 1901 and over the next two decades, Fundidora would invest $1,500,000 pesos in securing land and coal surveying, sometimes by way of the company's annual profits.[103] In 1905, it seemed the company's decision was about to pay off when initial assessments suggested that 200 million tons of high-quality coal were located in one of the company's leased properties, but the claim turned out to be a wild overestimate.[104] Similar misjudgments recurred in the following years. Along with securing its own coal, Fundidora sought to minimize reliance on coke, essential for making pig iron.[105] Since company executives considered dependence on US coke "extremely dangerous for the future of the company," they built a battery of coke-making ovens at the steel plant itself.[106] The plan was clear: mine coal from Fundidora's own properties in Coahuila – and, later, a few minor coal fields in Nuevo León, Monterrey's home state – transport it by rail, and turn it into coke in the company's ovens in Monterrey.

Alas, things did not go quite as planned. By 1909, Fundidora was still buying much of its coal and coke supplies from other companies: about half from Coahuila and half from the USA.[107] This all came at great

using Fundidora and Monterrey in "El desempeño de la Fundidora de Hierro y Acero de Monterrey durante el Porfiriato: acerca de los obstáculos a la industrialización en México," in *Historia de las grandes empresas en México, 1850–1930* (México: UANL/FCE, 1997), 201–43. Gómez Galvarriato emphasizes unreliable coal supplies as a main issue. Edward Beatty offers a critique of Haber's argument in *Technology and the Search for Progress in Modern Mexico* (Berkeley: University of California Press), 2015, 165–6.

[101] Compañía Fundidora, *Informe anual*, 1902, 36–37.   [102] Ibid., 38.

[103] Compañía Fundidora, *Informe anual*, 1919, 407.

[104] Compañía Fundidora, *Informe anual*, 1902, 134.

[105] Pig iron is the intermediate product that, by adding steel scrap, more limestone, and oxygen, can be turned into steel differing in malleability, durability, and strength. Coke provides fuel and acts as a reducing agent when mixed with iron ore and limestone in blast furnaces.

[106] Compañía Fundidora, *Informe anual*, 1902, 66–7.

[107] Typical providers were companies operating in the Laredo coal region. See "Venta de carbón-Rio Grande Coal Company" (March 1, 1909), Contratos, expediente 6, Rio Grande Coal Company, AHFM.

expense: in 1907, fuel costs represented 48 percent of the firm's operating expenses, declining to 25 percent in 1909.[108] Reliable coal supplies eluded Fundidora for years, and the company was often unable to operate normally due to fuel shortages.[109] The coke project delivered more mixed results. Given that Fundidora was unable to become self-sufficient in coal, coke autarky proved impossible. The company was, however, capable of turning purchased coal into coke in its own ovens.[110] Coke was typically more expensive than coal by weight and could suffer damage when stored for long periods, so Fundidora at least managed to exert more control on its supply and save some money on coke.

For Fundidora, energy self-sufficiency proved a moving target, so the company minimized costs by increasing consumption of Mexican coal and coke, both cheaper than their imported counterparts.[111] That said, when able, Fundidora privileged the foreign product for its higher quality. This was especially true for coke because Coahuila's variety had higher ash content and more volatile compounds than American coke, and Fundidora's executives developed what its president described as an "invincible repugnance" for it.[112] To overcome this hostility, Mexican coke companies adapted production practices to meet Fundidora's needs and began carefully washing their product to ensure a maximum ash content of 12 to 13 percent.[113] The steelmaker was, after all, one of Mexico's biggest coke buyers.[114] Coal normally presented much less hassle, since it was largely used for steam generation (Figure 3.5) and coal gas production.[115]

Fundidora's consumption of Coahuila's coal and coke rose between 1909 and 1912, clearly replicating Mexico's trend towards using domestic sources.[116] After a decade of struggle and poor decisions, the company's future began looking up, with production reaching 71,337 metric tons of

---

[108] Compañía Fundidora, *Informe anual,* 1909, 206.

[109] See Compañía Fundidora, *Informe anual,* 1904, 75; 1905, 132; 1907, 141. See also Gómez Galvarriato, "El desempeño de la Fundidora de Hierro y Acero de Monterrey durante el Porfiriato."

[110] Typically, about 1.3 tons of coal are needed to produce 1 ton of coke.

[111] In 1908, Fundidora paid M$8.75 per ton of Coahuila coal. See Compañía Fundidora, *Informe anual,* 1908, 5.

[112] Ibid., 6. Coke quality directly affected steel quality, so this attitude made sense.

[113] A higher ash content could damage the extremely expensive blast furnaces.

[114] In 1910, Fundidora consumed 8 and 17 percent of Mexico's coal and coke production, respectively. That year's domestic coal amounted to 1,304,111 tons; the figure for domestic coke was 220,201 tons. For Mexico's coke production, see Compañía Fundidora, *Informe anual,* 1922, X.

[115] Coal gas was used to fire reheating and open-hearth furnaces as well as soaking pits (insulated chambers that heat up and keep ingots at a uniform temperature).

[116] In 1911, all the firm's coal and 70 percent of its coke came from Coahuila. See Compañía Fundidora, *Informe anual,* 1911, 238; 1921, X. While in 1907 Mexico's economy depended on foreign fossil-fuel imports (coal and oil) for 50–75 percent of its requirements, by 1929 the figure had declined to

Figure 3.5 Coal-fired boilers in Fundidora Monterrey. The coal is visible on the left. Workers had to shovel it into the burners. Source: *Fundidora Monterrey, Reporte anual,* 1921, 572. Courtesy of Fototeca Nuevo León - CONARTE - Fondo Fundidora.

iron and steel, an all-time high. Coal production also soared in 1910 and 1911. Continued growth seemed all but assured. Then the Revolution began, and all hell broke loose.

(Relative) Decline: 1910–50

Mexican coal's best year yet, 1911, marked the beginning of a catastrophic decade and a long-term downturn. The Mexican Revolution broke out in November of 1910, went through a relatively calm period from mid-1911 to early 1913, and resurged in 1914 with devastating ferocity. A brutal civil war raged until 1917, when the conflict's armed phase began to subside. Fights, violence, and political instability continued throughout the 1920s, but

25 percent. See Sandra Kuntz Ficker, *El comercio exterior de México en la era del capitalismo liberal, 1870–1929* (México, D. F.: El Colegio de México), 880–1.

never on the same scale.[117] During the Revolution, coal was both agent and casualty. Coal fueled many of the locomotives transporting troops for several armies. Coal sustained military industrial processes (including iron and steel production) and powered electric plants nationwide. But coal was also one of the war's biggest economic targets, precisely because of its military importance. Various factions fought over Coahuila's coal fields and sometimes destroyed coal mining infrastructure to sabotage the enemy. Unemployed northern miners joined and died for revolutionary forces in large numbers.[118] General disruption of trade and industrial production, above all destruction of track and diversion of railroads, dealt a heavy blow to Mexico's coal industry. Although coal use persisted in Mexico and production rose in absolute terms in the twentieth century's second half, the Revolution initiated coal's clear decline in relation to other energy sources, from which it never recovered. It was almost as if coal were too closely associated with the old Porfirian regime. When the Revolution swept away the Porfiriato, coal went with it.[119]

Consider Fundidora again. The goal of meeting all its coal needs with its own properties finally crashed in 1913, when Fundidora's main coal operation, the Compañía Carbonífera del Norte, went bankrupt.[120] Although Fundidora's coal enterprises had struggled since their inception, the Revolution dealt the final blow. After 1913, Fundidora had no other option but to keep purchasing most of its coal in either Coahuila or the United States. Looking back at its coal ventures over the previous 20 years, in 1919 the firm concluded that the whole endeavor had been a "disastrous ordeal."[121]

In 1914 and 1915, Fundidora took an even riskier approach to solving its fuel problems by replacing coal (but not coke) altogether with oil. The company had been purchasing fuel oil from Weetman Pearson's firm El

[117] The best general account of the Mexican Revolution continues to be Alan Knight, *The Mexican Revolution. Volume 1: Porfirians, Liberals, and Peasants; Volume 2: Counter-Revolution and Reconstruction* (Cambridge; New York: Cambridge University Press, 1986).

[118] Knight, *The Mexican Revolution*, vol. 2, 44; Calderón, *Mexican Coal Mining Labor in Texas and Coahuila, 1880–1930*, 90–2. By 1913, Coahuila's coal and coke production came to a standstill and property losses amounted to millions of dollars. Revolutionary forces targeted mostly coal mines owned by Mexican capitalists and tried to avoid damaging those of foreign companies. The experience of Mexico's coal miners in the Revolution paralleled that of their European counterparts decimated in the battlefields during World War I. See Bruce Pobodnik, *Global Energy Shifts: Fostering Sustainability in a Turbulent Age* (Philadelphia: Temple University Press, 2008), 96.

[119] Not all of the old regime was destroyed, as some scholars show. See Mark Wasserman, *Persistent Oligarchs: Elites and Politics in Chihuahua, Mexico, 1910–1940* (Durham: Duke University Press, 1993).

[120] Compañía Fundidora, *Informe anual*, 1914, 301–2.

[121] Compañía Fundidora, *Informe anual*, 1919, 407.

Águila since January 1910, amounting to some 10,000 barrels that year, which Fundidora employed to power one of its workshops.[122] But oil was not yet a tempting replacement for coal. That same year, the company acquired coal at a much cheaper price.[123] With coal production soaring, the plant's oil purchase went down to a few thousand barrels the following year. Once the revolutionary storm began disrupting the coal industry, Fundidora's oil consumption quickly rose. In 1912, Fundidora signed a 6-year agreement with El Águila for fuel oil to power all its steam engines and replace coal gas in its furnaces and soaking pits. The steelworks then installed a system for storing and distributing 50,000 barrels of oil.[124] The driving force behind the decision was Mexico's extraordinary oil boom, which had been raging for the past couple of years on the Gulf coast. Fundidora's board viewed the boom as an assurance that oil supplies would hold steady in the future. It also helped that by 1912 oil became cheaper than coal.[125] For Fundidora, interest in the coal industry was reduced to coke consumption.

Although the firm did phase out coal for steam and coal gas, it continued to purchase most of its coke elsewhere.[126] Hopes that coke supplies would become more reliable fell short of expectations; the company's blast furnace stopped working more than once due to insufficient coke.[127] The

---

[122] "Contrato de compraventa de gasóleo o combustóleo" (January 1910), Contratos, expediente 10, Compañía Mexicana de Petróleo El Águila, S.A., AHFM.

[123] In 1910, Fundidora paid M$ 9.70 per metric ton of coal and about M$42–43 per ton of oil delivered in Monterrey. Assuming an energy conversion of 1.5–2 tons of coal per ton of oil, oil was two to three times more expensive than coal that year.

[124] "Contrato de compraventa de petróleo combustible" (August 1912), Contratos, expediente 31, Compañía Mexicana de Petróleo El Águila, S.A., AHFM.

[125] The contract stated that Fundidora would receive 40,000 barrels of oil monthly (480,000 barrels annually). Cost per ton was set at M$1.07 per barrel. Since 6.2 barrels of oil make 1 ton and railroads charged M$7.34 pesos for transporting oil to Monterrey, Fundidora paid M$13.9 per ton of oil delivered in Monterrey. This made the ton of oil cheaper than the equivalent 1.5 tons of coal by 1 or 2 pesos. An engineer from El Águila sent to Fundidora to evaluate the project estimated that the steelworks would save up to 100,000 dollars with the shift.

[126] "Contrato de compraventa de 12,000 toneladas de coke entre la Cía. Carbonífera de Sabinas, S. A. y la Cía." (April 1917), Contratos, expediente 44, Compañía Carbonífera de Sabinas, S.A., AHFM; "Contrato de Compraventa de Carbón" (December 1917), Contratos, expediente 55, Compañía Carbonífera de Sabinas, S.A., AHFM; "Contrato de compraventa de coke con Mexican Coal and Coke Co." (June 30, 1917), Contratos, expediente 46, Mexican Coal and Coke Co., AHFM; "Contrato de compraventa de carbón" (February 20, 1918), Contratos, expediente 56, Compañía Carbonífera de Sabinas, S.A., AHFM; "Contrato de compraventa de carbón" (May 10, 1918), Contratos, expediente 62, Compañía Carbonífera de Sabinas, S.A., AHFM; "Contrato de compraventa de carbón" (June 17, 1919), Contratos, expediente 76, Compañía Carbonífera de Sabinas, S.A., AHFM; "Compraventa de coke" (August 1921), Contratos, expediente 98, Compañía de Combustible "Agujita," AHFM; "Contrato de compraventa de coke" (October 31, 1931), Contratos, expediente 101, Compañía Carbonífera de Sabinas, S.A., AHFM.

[127] Compañía Fundidora, *Informe anual* (Monterrey, N.L., 1918), 367.

company also sought to avoid dependence on a single supplier – echoing its former coal policy – and tried acquiring oil from El Águila's rival, Huasteca Petroleum,[128] owned by Henry Clay Pierce. Moreover, in 1925, the company toyed with the idea of reusing coke production's gaseous by-products from a coal property it owned to replace oil used in boilers, furnaces, and electricity generation. The company cited rising oil prices and the industry's volatility and speculative tendencies in rethinking its commitment to oil.[129]

While Fundidora struggled to adapt to the new post-Revolution energy landscape, coal kept losing ground nationwide. Although production recovered to prerevolutionary times by 1925, it grew slowly for decades until 1950, with several slumps along the way. Coal faced both intrinsic and extrinsic challenges to its proliferation. To start, coal never managed to become a household fuel in Mexico – though not for lack of trying. As late as 1935, coal companies sought to convince Mexican households to consume coal using the old argument that it would help forest preservation, but to no avail.[130] Mexicans rejected the acrid fuel and continued burning charcoal when possible, using oil and gas stoves when not. As electricity gradually entered ever more homes, the energy that generated it was water or oil, not coal.[131]

Even for those who favored it, like ironworks and railroads, coal remained expensive. This was partly because production remained limited, itself the result of several factors. First, coal was relatively scarce in Mexico, and what large-scale coal mining existed was concentrated in Coahuila. With coal and coke consumption restricted to a few industries, coal production had little incentive to grow. It also failed to become competitive, dominated as it was by a handful of players who kept prices to their liking. Greater competition might have secured cheaper prices and more successful penetration into nonindustrial markets. Making matters worse, coal mines perennially battled labor scarcity. Conditions in mines were harsh, the work dangerous, and the locations remote, attracting relatively few workers.[132] The absence of a strong and large coal working class in

[128] "Contrato de compraventa de petróleo combustible" (February 27, 1916), Contratos, expediente 40, Sr. Esteban E. Fierros, AHFM.

[129] Compañía Fundidora, *Informe anual* (Monterrey, N. L., 1925), 693–711.

[130] "Introducción de carbón mineral lignita en la República para proteger los bosques de la patria" (May 2, 1935), Fondo: Monterrey Contemporáneo; Sección: Correspondencia; Colección: Civil; Volumen: 631: Exp. 6, AHM.

[131] With some exceptions in the country's north.

[132] Explosions, like the one that killed seventy miners in one Compañía Carbonífera de Coahuila mine in 1910, were common. See "Catástrofe minera," *El Heraldo. Semanario*, October 9, 1910.

Mexico led to low unionization rates, and, in turn, poor working conditions persisted.[133]

For all of these reasons, coal remained a niche fuel after the Revolution rather than Mexico's basis for industrialization and urban growth, as it was in the USA and Europe. Nonetheless, coal helped develop key infrastructure, especially railroads, a modern smelting and steel industry, and many of Mexico's first electric plants. Additionally, coal "locked in" certain industrial sectors' need for higher and cheaper energy inputs. A firm like Fundidora, which would not have existed without coal, could not simply go back to fuelwood if it wanted to grow – imperative for a firm operating in an industrializing, capitalist country. Its only path forward was to adopt a more abundant, cheaper fuel with higher energy density than coal, like oil or natural gas. Similar logic pervaded other sectors of Mexico's economy. Ironically, in its failure to provide abundant energy, coal shaped future expectations, desires, and decisions for many Mexicans regarding energy sources.

Conclusion

According to environmental historian Shawn Miller, "most of Latin America's nations had no known coal reserves, and for those few that did, the reserves were small, of poor quality, or inconveniently located. In fact, there was little call for coal. Much of the region would continue to rely on firewood for both residential and industrial fuel needs."[134] Miller's assessment holds substantial truth. Coal never became the cornerstone of Latin American industrialization, as it did in parts of the USA and Europe. Mexico exemplifies this. The country lacked large supplies of good-quality coal – the USA had violently seized the vast coal resources of Texas, New Mexico, and Colorado in 1848. The few deposits it did have lay in the distant north, forcing central Mexico's industrial establishments and railroads to transport domestic coal cross-country or import it. These conditions kept coal expensive during the late nineteenth and early twentieth centuries, limiting its effect on the country's economy and society.

---

[133] Without powerful coal unions to disrupt a strategic industrial and military energy source, Mexico never developed the type of large, militant, combative coal labor movement that was instrumental in Europe and the USA in nationwide labor reforms and promoting a modern welfare state. See Mitchell, *Carbon Democracy*; Pobodnik, *Global Energy Shifts*. The labor rights Mexican workers did gain resulted from the Mexican Revolution and the militancy of oil, railroad, and electric workers' unions. By the time these became strong and well organized in the 1930s, 1940s, and 1950s, they faced a powerful Mexican state that had already coopted much of Mexico's labor movement.

[134] Miller, *An Environmental History of Latin America*, 156–7.

But Mexican coal also highlights false assumptions in Miller's claim. There was intense demand for coal in Mexico, and it played a more important role than Miller assumes. Not only were people in Mexico convinced that coal was necessary for industrial progress – and the best way to protect overexploited forests; they went to great lengths to secure its supply. By focusing on Latin America's lack of rich coal deposits, Miller overlooks coal's role in meeting some countries' energy needs, particularly in their industrial heartlands.

As a concentrated, dense energy source, coal facilitated Mexico's industrial, demographic, and urban growth between 1880 and 1910. Without coal – from the north and abroad – the pace and timing of Mexico's industrialization would have been very different. The combined economic and environmental limits to water- and-wood-based industrialization were fast approaching by the last decades of the nineteenth century. Coal helped circumvent these limits.

None of this would have happened without the close interplay between coal and railroads, energy and transportation. Coahuila's coal deposits required rail links to bring coal to markets. Once railroads arrived, they became coal's largest consumers, and remained so for decades. Output increased to meet railroads' energy needs. Coal-fueled freight lines then transported growing supplies to mines and railroad yards of industrializing cities like Monterrey and Mexico City. Railroads showed firms across Mexico that coal could be used as a reliable energy source. The interdependence of railroads and fossil fuels would be repeated with the ascendance of oil.

Perhaps more importantly, coal gave industry – and the state – a taste of the power of fossil fuels. Railroads, iron and steel works, and power plants could now transcend the energy confines of wood and waterpower. While coal never became king in Mexico, it did turn Mexican transportation system and industry on to the productive (and perilous) potential of fossil fuels. But if not coal, then what?

CHAPTER 4

The Other Revolution

Oil creates the illusion of a completely changed life, life without work, life for free.

Ryszard Kapuściński, *Shah of Shahs*

On March 18, 1938, Mexico's president Lázaro Cárdenas delivered a radio speech to the nation announcing the expropriation of the oil industry.[1] Cárdenas accused foreign oil companies of disobeying the law and orchestrating a "silent and skilled campaign" to damage Mexico's economy. Cárdenas explained that expropriation was the government's only recourse. Any measure that left the industry in foreign hands would open the possibility of firms attempting to disrupt oil production. Scarce oil, Cárdenas stated ominously, would affect important sectors like transportation and "cause, in brief time, a crisis not only incompatible with our progress, but with domestic peace." An oil shortage would "paralyze banking [and] most commercial activity; public works for the common good would become impossible, and the existence of the government itself would be in great danger, because once the state lost its economic power, it would lose its political power and chaos would ensue."[2]

Expropriation was the culmination of a politics of resource nationalism that began during the Mexican Revolution.[3] It had profound international and domestic implications, which historians have documented well.[4] Expropriation was also culturally significant, marking the moment when

---

[1] The speech was written by General Francisco J. Múgica, Cárdenas's close associate and cabinet member.

[2] *El petróleo de México. Recopilación de documentos oficiales del conflicto de orden económico de la industria petrolera* (México, D. F.: Gobierno de México [Talleres de la Editorial "Cultura"], 1940), 861–4.

[3] Alan Knight, *Repensar la Revolución Mexicana*, vol. II (México, D. F.: El Colegio de México, 2014), 191. However, as Knight emphasizes, expropriation itself resulted from unforeseen circumstances, not long-term planning.

[4] Jonathan C. Brown and Alan Knight, eds., *The Mexican Petroleum Industry in the Twentieth Century* (Austin: University of Texas Press, 1992).

oil became an essential part of Mexico's national identity.[5] From the perspective of Mexico's oil transition, however, expropriation was less path-breaking. As this chapter shows, Mexico's oil transition began far earlier than 1938. By the time of nationalization, Mexico was consuming 76 percent of its oil production. Mexico's political class clearly understood oil's value, as Cárdenas's speech makes evident. Indeed, the success of expropriation depended to no small degree on the fact that Mexico itself was already its own biggest oil market. Had expropriation been attempted a few decades earlier, when most oil was exported, it might very well have failed.

Expropriation did not alter upward trends in domestic oil use. While the years following expropriation suffered technical problems and international boycott campaigns that affected Mexico's newly nationalized industry, these issues barely dented domestic consumption, which nearly doubled by 1950. Cárdenas and the oil industry's nationalization deserve credit for many key changes in twentieth-century Mexico. The shift to oil is not one of them.

This chapter examines this energy revolution from the late nineteenth century to the 1950s. Between approximately 1900 and 1950, oil became the foundation of Mexico's new energy regime. Factories, railroads, and electrical plants adopted oil as their main fuel. Gasoline-powered vehicles emerged onto the scene, initially as an elite luxurious pastime before quickly becoming essential to short-distance transport of people and goods. Oil spilled from factories and locomotives to other areas, eventually powering almost every aspect of Mexico's economy and society. Oil also became the key force behind environmental change during most of the twentieth century. The transition to petroleum established the conditions for the dramatic transformations of Mexico's environment, economy, and society after 1950.

The chapter is divided into three sections. The first traces petroleum's early history in Mexico. Throughout pre-Columbian times and the colonial and early independent periods, indigenous peoples used oil in medicine, for illumination, and to waterproof houses and canoes. By the second half of the nineteenth century, kerosene (oil) became an increasingly important illuminant as well as an industrial lubricant.[6] The second

---

[5] Omar Fabián González Salinas, "El discurso patriótico y el aparato propagandístico que sustentaron a la expropiación petrolera durante el cardenismo," *Estudios de Historia Moderna y Contemporánea de México* 52 (July 1, 2016): 88–107.

[6] Some authors analyze the pre-1900 period but present it largely as a series of failures to strike oil. Others minimize the significance of oil-derived products like kerosene and industrial lubricants. See, for instance, José Domingo Lavín, *Petróleo: pasado, presente y futuro de una industria mexicana* (México: Edición y Distribución Ibero Americana de Publicaciones, 1950), 12–45. A pioneering work underlining the importance of petroleum as an industrial input pre-1900 is Brown and Knight, eds., *The Mexican Petroleum Industry in the Twentieth Century*, chapter 1.

section examines how, after 1900, oil became primarily a fuel source.[7] Oil began replacing coal as the main energy source for industrial production, transport, and electricity generation. Finally, the third section examines oil's consolidation as the country's energy base in the postrevolutionary period.[8]

Before the Oil Boom

Like many cultures worldwide, Mexico's pre-Columbian indigenous peoples knew about oil.[9] Oil was found in seepages and bitumen pools along Mexico's Gulf Coast.[10] The Nahuatl-speaking peoples in central

---

[7] One of the major works on Mexico's oil history, Jonathan C. Brown, *Oil and Revolution in Mexico* (Berkeley: University of California Press, 1993), says little about oil's impact as an energy source within Mexico. Brown's is a business history of the industry relying heavily on company records. Myrna Santiago, *The Ecology of Oil: Environment, Labor, and the Mexican Revolution, 1900–1938* (Cambridge: Cambridge University Press) offers an excellent analysis of oil production's environmental impact in Mexico but is less concerned with oil's role in Mexico's domestic economy and environmental impact in *consumption* centers. An overview of the historiography on Latin America's oil industry emphasizing the lack of attention to consumption is Marcelo Bucheli, "Major Trends in the Historiography of the Latin American Oil Industry," *The Business History Review* 84, no. 2 (2010): 339–62. One of the few authors examining the history of oil consumption in Mexico is Uthoff López, "La industria del petróleo en México, 1911–1938," *América Latina en la Historia Económica* no. 33 (2010): 7–30.

[8] Most literature on the oil transition focuses on Europe and the USA. Good examples are Alfred W. Crosby, *Children of the Sun: A History of Humanity's Unappeasable Appetite for Energy* (New York: Norton, 2006); Marina Fischer-Kowalski and Helmut Haberl, *Socioecological Transitions and Global Change: Trajectories of Social Metabolism and Land Use* (Cheltenham: Edward Elgar, 2007); Astrid Kander, Paolo Malanima, and Paul Warde, *Power to the People: Energy in Europe over the Last Five Centuries* (Princeton: Princeton University Press, 2013); Martin V. Melosi, *Coping with Abundance: Energy and Environment in Industrial America* (Philadelphia: Temple University Press, 1985); David E. Nye, *Consuming Power: A Social History of American Energies* (Cambridge, Mass: MIT Press, 1999); Vaclav Smil, *Energy in World History*, Essays in World History (Boulder: Westview Press, 1994).

[9] Smil, *Energy in World History*, 167–8; Brian Black, *Crude Reality: Petroleum in World History* (Lanham: Rowman & Littlefield Publishers, 2012), chapter 1. Mesopotamians used bitumen as early as 3000 BCE in medicines, waterproofing, and construction. The Bible includes several references to pitch, including the construction of the Tower of Babel, for which bricks and "slime" (pitch) were used. The ancient Chinese began refining oil for heating homes and burning lamps around 2000 BCE. Egyptians used oil to preserve mummies. In Medieval Europe, Muslims introduced distilled oil for illumination to Spain around the twelfth century.

[10] Crude oil is a complex substance, formed tens or hundreds of millions of years ago when dead plants and other organic materials such as zooplankton settled at the bottom of lakes, oceans, and rivers. Over vast timespans, sediment layers buried these organisms. As pressure and heat increased, the carbohydrates these organisms once created were transformed into hydrocarbons. Depending on the amount of pressure and heat, hydrocarbons adopted a solid (coal), gaseous (natural gas), or liquid (oil) form. See "Oil," in Cutler J. Cleveland and Christopher G. Morris, *Handbook of Energy, Volume II* (Burlington: Elsevier Science, 2013). "Petroleum" usually refers to both oil and natural gas. Oil has great energy density, normally 50 percent higher than bituminous coal. The amount of carbon required to form oil was enormous. The average US Gallon (3.8 liters) of gasoline (distilled

Mexico called the substance *tzaucpopochtli*, a combination of the noun *tzauc*, "glue," and the adjective *popochtli*, "aromatic." Oil, then, was "aromatic glue."[11] The existence of a precise word for oil suggests how familiar it was to central Mexico's indigenous peoples. The term became the basis for *chapopote*, the Hispanicized word for oil used in Mexico since the colonial period and still common today. Mexica and other Mesoamerican peoples like the Huastecs and Totonacs of Veracruz employed oil for many purposes. Oil was common in medicine for respiratory ailments, as a poultice, in ointments to fight some skin diseases, and to preserve teeth. Oil also had important religious functions. Across Mexico's central highlands and tropical lowlands, indigenous peoples burned oil as incense on altars and in temples.[12] Beyond religious and medicinal practices, oil served more ordinary purposes like mortar in buildings, caulking boats and canoes, and illuminating torches.[13]

After conquest, colonial society continued using petroleum from pools and seepages. Spaniards called this substance *brea* or *pez* (pitch)[14] before incorporating *chapopote* into their vocabulary. In his encyclopedic work *Historia general de las cosas de Nueva España*, Franciscan missionary Fray Bernardino de Sahagún wrote that Indians collected *chapuputli* from beaches along the Gulf of Mexico to sell in Mexico City's *tianguis* (markets). "*Chapuputli*," wrote Sahagún,

> is a type of bitumen that comes from the sea and it is similar to the *pez* from Castilla, which easily disintegrates and which is brought to land by the sea's currents [...] It floats like a thick and wide cloak, and [local Indians] collect it from the shore. This chapuputli has a strong smell, is appreciated by women, and when it is thrown into the fire, its scent spreads everywhere.[15]

from crude oil) formed from about 90 metric tons of ancient organic marine matter (mostly phytoplankton). On this, see Jeffrey S. Dukes, "Burning Buried Sunshine: Human Consumption of Ancient Solar Energy," *Climatic Change* 61, no. 1–2 (2003): 31–44.

[11] The English words "oil" and "petroleum" derive respectively from the Latin words "oleum" (olive oil) and "petroleum," a combination of "petra" (rock) and "oleum." One of the first written appearances of petroleum comes from *De Natura Fossilium* (1556) by the German mineralogist Georg Bauer, best known by the Latinized Georgius Agricola. Georgius Agricola, *De Natura Fossilium* (Mineola, NY: Dover Publications, 2004 [1543]), book IV.

[12] Ramón Mena, *El libro del petróleo en México* (México: Porrúa Hermanos, 1915), 7–8.

[13] José Vázquez Schiaffino and Joaquín Santaella, *Informes sobre la cuestión petrolera* (México, D. F.: Imprenta de la Cámara de Diputados, 1919), 18.

[14] Soft asphalt or bitumen.

[15] Fray Bernardino de Sahagún, *Historia general de las cosas de Nueva España* (Cambridge: Cambridge University Press, 2011 [1830]), vol. 3, 63–4.

Starting in the mid-sixteenth century, clergymen began selling oil to the faithful in the Valley of Mexico. It came from two bitumen ponds located in the collegiate church of the Villa de Guadalupe, site of Mexico's most important shrine. Until the mid-nineteenth century, churchgoers sought this *agua milagrosa* (miraculous water) to cure skin diseases and rheumatism, and to burn in front of the image of the Virgin of Guadalupe. Apparently, the Pocito Chapel, today a celebrated example of baroque architecture, was built at the site of one well, leading early twentieth-century Mexican artist and writer Dr. Atl to colorfully describe the history of Mexico's oil during the colonial and early independent periods as the "Guadalupe period."[16]

This link between oil and religion was not unusual. Bitumen pools and natural gas seepages became religious sites in many parts of the world, including Mesopotamia, ancient Persia, and ancient Greece, which featured the famous Delphi Oracle. As in other preindustrial societies, New Spain viewed oil as sacred and therapeutic as well as a source of water-proofing and illumination.[17] Despite its widespread and diverse use among preindustrial peoples, there is no evidence in the historical record that any pre-nineteenth-century society used oil as an energy source.

Spanish legal understanding of oil as a state asset had an enduring legacy for independent Mexico's oil history. In 1783, Spanish monarch Charles IV issued the *Ordenanzas de Minería*, the first law regulating exploitation of oil deposits in Spanish America by listing what minerals and substances belonged to the king.[18] It granted subjects the right to claim silver, gold, copper, lead, tin, mercury, calaminar stone (zinc ore), bismuth, salt mines, and deposits containing "bitumen or juices from the earth." This legal framework remained law until 1884, when the Mexican state issued a new mining code.[19] Colonial oil legislation continued influencing lawmakers after 1884, however, as evinced by the 1917 Constitution (discussed later).

---

[16] Dr. Atl, *Petróleo en el Valle de Méjico: una Golden Line en la altiplanicie de Anáhuac* (México: Polis, 1938). On the Villa de Guadalupe's bitumen pools, which Atl calls "mineral springs," see Manuel Orozco y Berra, *Memoria para la carta hidrográfica del Valle de México formada por acuerdo de la Sociedad Mexicana de Geografía y Estadística* (México: Imprenta de A. Boix, 1864), 156–72.

[17] There were military uses, too. The Byzantine Empire's famous "Greek fire," used in naval battles, had distilled oil as its basic ingredient. See Cutler J. Cleveland and Christopher G. Morris, *Dictionary of Energy* (Amsterdam: Elsevier, 2006), 204.

[18] Article 22 from *Reales ordenanzas para la dirección, régimen y gobierno del importante cuerpo de la minería de Nueva España, y de su Real Tribunal General* (Madrid, 1783), 75.

[19] Vázquez Schiaffino and Santaella, *Informes sobre la cuestión petrolera*, 17–18; Mena, *El libro del petróleo en México*, 53–60.

This document once again subordinated individual oil subsoil rights, this time replacing royal with state ownership.

The period between the end of Spanish rule and the middle of the nineteenth century saw little oil exploration. But in the late 1850s, a number of entrepreneurs sought to determine the location, quality, and quantity of Mexican oil deposits. Some tried their luck in the swamps of Tabasco 2 years before oil began flowing along the banks of Oil Creek, Pennsylvania. Others turned to the Villa de Guadalupe, just 3 kilometers north of Mexico City. A group of investors tried exploiting and commercializing local bitumen, but lack of capital and expertise, along with rudimentary extractive technology, marred these efforts. Soon after, imported kerosene from the USA appeared in Mexico City markets for the first time.[20] In 1862, renowned engineer Antonio del Castillo led another attempt to collect oil in the Villa de Guadalupe, with modest success.[21] Extracted oil was distilled into kerosene for illumination, not in Mexico City but on the Veracruz premises of Casa Ritter y Cía., an investor in the project.[22]

The following years saw growing interest in oil among Mexican state officials. In 1864, during the Second Mexican Empire (1864–7), Fomento granted the first permit to extract petroleum in a place called Chapacao in the municipality of Pánuco, Veracruz. The next year, Fomento issued another permit to one Don Ildefonso López, who tried his luck as an oilman in his own hacienda, San José de las Rusias, in the state of Tamaulipas. More oil grants soon followed, mostly in the states of Puebla, Tamaulipas, Veracruz, and Tabasco, without much success.[23]

---

[20] Kerosene, a contraction of the Greek *keroselaion* or "wax-oil" coined by Canadian geologist Abraham Gesner in 1846, comes from distilling crude oil. Also known as paraffin. Alec Groysman, "History of Crude Oil and Petroleum Products," in *Corrosion in Systems for Storage and Transportation of Petroleum Products and Biofuels: Identification, Monitoring and Solutions* (Dordrecht: Springer Netherlands, 2014), 224.

[21] Del Castillo was Santiago Ramírez's mentor in Mexico City's School of Engineering. As Chapter 3 describes, Ramírez eventually became one of nineteenth-century Mexico's most prominent mining engineers and fossil fuel experts and wrote a number of influential reports on Mexico's coal and oil deposits in the 1880s.

[22] Dr. Atl, *Petróleo en el Valle de Méjico*, 11–13. Gerali and Rigguzi consider Castillo's efforts in the Villa de Guadalupe as largely irrelevant to the history of oil exploration in Mexico and dismiss them as mere "chemical experiments." See Francesco Gerali and Paolo Riguzzi, "Los inicios de la actividad petrolera en México, 1863–1874: una nueva cronología y elementos de balance," *Boletín Archivo Histórico de Petróleos Mexicanos* 13 (June 2013): 63–87.

[23] "Sobre el denuncio de varios criaderos de betún mineral hecho por Don Manuel Ortega y García en Puebla" (1865), Fomento, Minas y Petróleo, caja 73, legajo 95, exp 2006, AGN; "Sobre el denuncio que de un manantial de petróleo en terrenos de la Mesa de San Diego, Puebla, hizo Don José Antonio Suárez" (1865), Fomento, Minas y Petróleo, caja 73, legajo 95, exp 2005, AGN; "Sobre la oposición que Don Amado S. Pedro y Socios hacen al denuncio de un criadero de substancia

Perhaps hoping to foster competition and important discoveries, in 1865 the Mexican government issued a decree limiting the total area of a coal and oil grant to 1 km² and began to more or less systematically publish its oil grants. The most important of these came in 1868, when a self-exiled Confederate American of Irish descent known as Dr. Autrey discovered the Cubas *chapopoteras*, later known as Furbero (after English oil prospector Percy Furber), in northern Veracruz. The next year, Mexican investors organized the Compañía Exploradora del Golfo Mexicano in Mexico City to extract the oil. The company managed to produce 6–8 hectoliters daily for some time before shutting down. Dr. Autrey took over the grant, installing Mexico's first refining venture (really an oversized *alambique*, the ancient distilling technology of two vessels connected by a tube) and distilled 16,000 liters of kerosene, which he sold locally or brought by mule to the town of Tuxpan.[24]

By the 1870s, kerosene had become relatively common in some parts of Mexico. That the Mexico City council considered replacing turpentine with oil for public illumination in 1877 suggests as much.[25] At the same time, Mexico's press began publishing on experiments employing petroleum as fuel. *El Minero Mexicano*, for instance, described the attempt by the

betuminosa hizo Don Ildefonso Lopez" (1865), Fomento, Minas y Petróleo, caja 73, legajo 95, exp 2001, AGN; "Sobre el privilegio pedido por Don Manuel Vilchis para explotar una mina de petróleo" (1865), Fomento, Minas y Petróleo, caja 73, legajo 95, exp 2002, AGN. See also Joaquín Santaella, *La industria petrolera en México, conferencia sustentada en la Sociedad Mexicana de Geografía y Estadística* (México: Poder Ejecutivo Federal, Departamento de Aprovisionamientos Generales, Dirección de Talleres Gráficos, 1919), 5–16.

[24] Santaella, *La industria petrolera en México*, 5–16. Some enthusiasts suggested building railroad lines to commercialize oil being extracted from Northern Veracruz. See Manuel F. Soto, "Ferrocarril y comunicación interoceánica por el centro de la República Mexicana," *Boletín de la Sociedad Mexicana de Geografía y Estadística*, 2, 1 (1869): 505–12. Deposits in southern Veracruz also generated excitement. In 1868, US Consul R. C. M. Hoyt in Minatitlán sent an official report to the State Department:

> Petroleum is sufficiently abundant in this district to supply the world. Indications of its locality exist everywhere, and, in many places, it comes to the surface and forms small lakes and springs to such an extent that it can be dipped up in large quantities. In fact, the whole of this side of the Isthmus [of Tehuantepec] is a vast lake of petroleum, in my estimation; and from the explorations I have made I believe it can be found almost anywhere. Its richness has been tested by some of the best chemists in the United States. Professor Percy, of New York, has made an analysis of some of this petroleum taken from the surface, (or, rather, from one of the springs).

See Alexander D. Anderson, *Mexico from the Material Stand-Point: A Review of Its Mineral, Agricultural, Forest, and Marine Wealth, Its Manufactures, Commerce, Railways, Isthmian Routes, and Finances with a Description of Its Highlands and Attractions* (New York: A. Brentano & Co., 1884), 45.

[25] "Proposiciones para que la Comisión de Alumbrado proponga las bases para sustitución por petróleo del alumbrado de trementina" (1877), Alumbrado, 1872–1877, 352, exp. 436, AHDF.

chief engineer of the American navy to use oil over coal to power a steam engine. The engineer demonstrated that petroleum's calorific content was double that of anthracite coal. The publication extolled petroleum's superior qualities over coal: petroleum was compact, easier to transport, and had a higher energy density; it also accurately predicted that petroleum would ultimately replace coal in steamships.[26] The last years of the decade witnessed renewed efforts to commercialize Mexican oil. An American ship captain managed to raise some capital from a group of Boston investors. With this money he purchased drilling equipment, which he transported through the Veracruz rainforest. Soon after establishing a small refinery on the margins of the Tuxpan River, the venture ran out of money. Disheartened, the captain committed suicide.[27]

After two decades, commercial efforts had failed but state officials and (potential) investors had acquired considerable knowledge of Mexico's oil and asphalt surface deposits. From the 1860s, the Sociedad Mexicana de Geografía y Estadística, the Sociedad Mexicana de Historia Natural, and the Secretaría de Fomento published reports on bitumen pools and seepages in Veracruz, Tamaulipas, Chiapas, Tabasco, Jalisco, and the Valley of Mexico. The reports contained some bad news. It seemed that most deposits in the central highlands were commercially unviable. In 1879, Santiago Ramírez confirmed this for the Valley of Mexico when he concluded that the deposits in the Villa de Guadalupe, with an estimated area of over 1000 square meters, could not be exploited profitably, dashing any hopes of securing a large oil source next to Mexico's largest urban center. Luckily, the area between the Tuxpan and Pánuco Rivers was well endowed with petroleum surface deposits. But it also became evident, as Ramírez himself pointed out, that if the country wanted to attract investment there, a new law permitting much larger oil grants would have to be enacted, following the example of Pennsylvania's oil fields.[28]

A series of business failures also made it increasingly evident that the oil business required large capital investments and technical expertise. Take the 1882 venture by oil and coal company La Exploradora. Organized in Puebla, the company haphazardly tried exploiting various oil deposits

---

[26] "Empleo del petróleo para reemplazar el carbón de piedra en las máquinas de vapor," *El Minero Mexicano*, May 14, 1874.

[27] Ezequiel Ordoñez, *El petróleo en México: bosquejo histórico* (México: Empresa Editorial de Ingeniería y Arquitectura, 1932), 36–8.

[28] Mexican law limited the size to 1 km on each side. Santiago Ramírez, *Noticia histórica de la riqueza minera de México y de su actual estado de explotación* (México, D. F.: Oficina Tipográfica de la Secretaría de Fomento, 1884), 206–13. See also Santaella, *La industria petrolera en México*, 5–16.

throughout Veracruz.[29] Similarly, in 1883, Tabasco's governor Simeón Sarlat organized a firm with 1 million pesos in capital to exploit oil deposits in Macuspana, in the southern part of the state. Despite the substantial initial investment, the company proved unsuccessful, even though a nearby site would strike major oil in the early 1900s. Even a seasoned investor like British businessman Cecil Rhodes proved incapable of success. Rhodes organized the Mexican Petroleum and Liquid Fuel Company to prospect for oil in Papantla, Veracruz.

After Rhodes's failure, investors grew pessimistic.[30] Hoping to attract large capital for mining, including oil and coal, the new 1884 Mining Code declared that surface owners also owned petroleum deposits. This broke with the colonial tradition of state ownership of subsoil resources and opened the door for huge capital investments in the early 1900s.[31] A federal decree 3 years later exempted oil production and coal mines from any federal, state, or municipal taxes.

At the close of the nineteenth century, Waters-Pierce, a subsidiary of Standard Oil under US magnate Henry Clay Pierce, successfully developed a market for petroleum-based products.[32] Especially profitable were large consumption centers like Mexico City or Monterrey, which started using oil for public lighting.[33] Pierce imported millions of gallons of US kerosene and oil lubricants for Mexico's manufacturing and farming machinery. Pierce also introduced US crude, which he distilled in his Tampico refinery.[34] At the same time, the Mexican government became more active in oil development. Alongside granting permits for oil exploration and extraction, Fomento now began supervising and inspecting oil operations. The Porfirian government also sought to use the 1893 Industrias Nuevas law to promote the oil

[29] Ramírez, *Noticia histórica de la riqueza minera de México*, 214–17.

[30] P. Harvey Middleton, *Industrial Mexico; 1919 Facts and Figures* (New York: Dodd, Mead and Co., 1919), 48–54.

[31] *Código de Minería de la República Mexicana*, 5–6. On the 1884 Mining Code, see Eduardo Martínez Baca, *Reseña histórica de la legislación minera en México* (México: Oficina Tip. de la Secretaría de Fomento, 1901), 53–62; Mena, *El libro del petróleo en México*, 53–60; Schiaffino and Santaella, *Informes sobre la cuestión petrolera*, 18.

[32] On Pierce, see Brown, *Oil and Revolution in Mexico*, 14–16.

[33] "Alumbrado de petróleo" (November 14, 1892), Fondo: Monterrey Contemporáneo; Sección: Actas; Colección: Actas de Cabildo; Volumen: 999; Exp. 1892/053, AHM.

[34] "Exportación de productos americanos con destino a México," *El Economista Mexicano*, June 23, 1888. On the history of Waters-Pierce in Mexico, see Brown, *Oil and Revolution in Mexico*, 16–25. By the late nineteenth century, kerosene was the most widely used illumination source in Mexico. See Ordóñez, *El petróleo en México*, 51. In 1896 and 1897, Mexico imported 52,503,328 liters of crude oil and 5,556,133 of US refined oil. See Matías Romero, *Geographical and Statistical Notes on Mexico* (New York and London: G.P. Putnam's Sons, 1898), 185.

industry.[35] Fomento signed its first contract with an oil extraction company in Mexico in 1898. The contract obliged the venture to admit two students from Mexican schools (*escuelas nacionales*) to study the oil industry with the aim of creating a cadre of Mexican oil experts. Fomento also required the firm to provide all relevant information on extraction, production, and commercialization, and to sell oil to the government at a 10 percent discount. A 1901 presidential decree on oil exploration, production, and commercialization in Mexico reinforced Fomento's role as overseer.[36]

By 1900, all attempts to exploit oil on a commercial scale had proved unsuccessful or unable to develop beyond modest production levels. Lack of appropriate technology, adequate expertise, a robust local consumer market, and an efficient transport system to bring oil to consumption sites doomed these efforts. Despite these issues, consumption of imported kerosene and oil lubricants was firmly established in most urban and industrializing areas of the country by the century's end. This period also saw the creation of a clear legal framework openly promoting investment in oil ventures by giving developers complete ownership over subsoil resources. The federal government helped lay the groundwork for a future oil industry by consistently publishing government reports on oil deposits, which provided critical information to future prospectors. All the elements for Mexico's oil age were in place. The only thing missing was the oil.

"Mines of Liquid Gold"

Between 1901 and 1921, Mexico experienced an oil boom of epic proportions.[37] By the end of this period, a veritable ocean of oil – "mines of liquid gold" –[38] made Mexico the second-largest petroleum producer in the world behind the USA (Figure 4.1). The entire boom took place along Mexico's gulf coast. The geography of Mexican oil production and a limited domestic market meant that most of this oil was initially exported. Within a few years, a complex infrastructure of derricks, storage deposits, pipelines, tank railroad cars, and

---

[35] The law exempted companies from paying taxes and import dues on machinery and technology for 10 years. On Industrias Nuevas, see Edward Beatty, *Institutions and Investment: The Political Basis of Industrialization in Mexico before 1911* (Stanford: Stanford University Press, 2001), chapter 6.

[36] Mena, *El libro del petróleo en México*, 61–133.

[37] In those 21 years, Mexico's oil production grew 18,695 times; US production, by comparison, grew about 7 times. See Secretaría de Industria, Comercio y Trabajo, *México, sus recursos naturales, su situación actual: homenaje al Brasil en ocasión del primer centenario de su independencia, 1822–1922.* (México: Editorial "Cultura," 1922), 180.

[38] This comes from Middleton, *Industrial Mexico; 1919 Facts and Figures*, 39, 50.

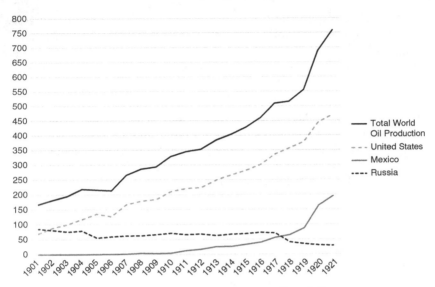

Figure 4.1 World oil production in millions of barrels,[39] 1901–1921.
Sources: Charles Bowles, *The Petroleum Industry*, 1921, 48; *Boletín del Petróleo*, 13, no. 4, 1922, 325.

new port facilities developed on the Gulf, ensuring oil flow from fields to hungry markets abroad.

Since the 1884 Mining Code, subsoil resources belonged to landowners or leasers (the *superficiario*). At the turn of the twentieth century, foreign oil prospectors (mostly American and British) bought or leased vast tracts of land in the Huasteca, Tamaulipas, and northern Veracruz. Most of this activity was concentrated in the region between the Tamesí River, in southern Tamaulipas, and the Tuxpan River, in northern Veracruz.[40] Slumbering towns turned into bustling cities and ports, oil derricks dotted

[39] Oil's universal measure is 42 American gallons (a barrel). This equals 158 liters and 990 milliliters per barrel. Each barrel weighs 15 kilos (192 grams). Standardization of the barrel goes back to 1482, when the English monarch Edward IV decreed 42 gallons to be the legal measure for a barrel of herring. This unit was adopted for a number of commodities, including oil, in the second half of the nineteenth century.

[40] During the oil boom of the early twentieth century, large-scale petroleum production was concentrated in the following regions: A) The Ebano district, some 40 miles west of Tampico and largely controlled by Doheny's Mexican Petroleum Company; B) The Pánuco region, in Veracruz; C) The Huasteca, featuring the famous oil fields Juan Casiano, Cerro Azul, Dos Bocas, and Potrero del Llano; D) The Tuxpan region, in Veracruz, location of the Furbero oil deposit; E) The Tehuantepec-Tabasco area, centered in Minatitlán, where Sir Weetman Pearson had a refinery. See Middleton, *Industrial Mexico; 1919 Facts and Figures*, 53–4.

the tropical landscape, and a road system linked the region's largest population centers, including Ciudad Victoria, Pánuco, Tuxpan, and Tampico.[41]

Two figures, American Edward L. Doheny and British Sir Weetman Pearson, dominated the oil boom.[42] Doheny, a Wisconsin-born businessman of Irish descent who made a fortune exploiting oil in Los Angeles, came to Mexico in 1899.[43] His objective: to extract oil in Mexico to fuel locomotives of the *Ferrocarril Central Mexicano*, an idea suggested to him by the company's president, A. Robinson.[44] According to Doheny's later testimony, Robinson told him that "Mexico was without any substantial fuel supply, the coal being of indifferent quality, and that his railroad company was obliged to get its coal from Alabama … "[45] Doheny's investment was therefore intended to supply Mexico's railroads with fuel oil.

The Díaz government welcomed Doheny's project, providing him with assistance and tax breaks. Díaz viewed oil primarily as a fuel to tackle Mexico's energy problems rather than an illumination source. According to Doheny, Díaz explained to him when they met that "the development of petroleum that could be used for fuel would save the public domain from being denuded of the immense quantities of timber that were being continually cut off for use on railways and for other purposes, and that it would augment the supply of native fuel and save the money which was being sent out of the country for foreign coal."[46] After obtaining Díaz's blessing, Doheny drilled for 3 years with modest success in the haciendas of Tulillo and Chapacao, Tamaulipas. He acquired these and other plots

---

[41] Ordóñez, *El petróleo en México*, 45.

[42] On Doheny, see Martin R. Ansell, *Oil Baron of the Southwest: Edward L. Doheny and the Development of the Petroleum Industry in California and Mexico* (Columbus: Ohio State University Press, 1998). On Pearson, see Brown, "The Structure of the Foreign-Owned Petroleum Industry in Mexico, 1880–1938," in *The Mexican Petroleum Industry in the Twentieth Century*; Lisa Bud-Frierman, Andrew Godley, and Judith Wale, "Weetman Pearson in Mexico and the Emergence of a British Oil Major, 1901–1919," *The Business History Review* 84, no. 2 (2010): 275–300; Connolly, *El contratista de don Porfirio: obras públicas, deuda y desarrollo desigual* (México, D. F.: Fondo de Cultura Económica, 1997).

[43] This was not Doheny's first visit to Mexico. He had prospected for gold and silver in 1887, unsuccessfully. See US Congress, Senate, Committee on Foreign Relations, *Investigation of Mexican Affairs: Preliminary Report and Hearings of the Committee on Foreign Relations*, vol. 1 (Washington, DC: 66th Congress, 1920), 207–9.

[44] Robinson and Doheny had known each other for years. Robinson was vice-president of the Atchison, Topeka and Santa Fe railroad, which bought oil for locomotives from Doheny's California fields. US Congress, Senate, Committee on Foreign Relations, *Investigation of Mexican Affairs*, vol. 1, 207–9.

[45] Ibid., 209.   [46] Ibid., 212.

from local landowners and by despoiling Huastec indigenous communities, whose members often helped company geologists locate oil seepages in the dense tropical rainforest.[47] The wells were only a few kilometers away from El Ébano railroad station – property of the *Ferrocarril Central* – and about 55 kilometers northwest of Tampico.

Doheny informed Robinson when his first well started producing in 1901. Robinson reneged on their agreement, apparently because the Central's executives believed Doheny's oil was too heavy to fuel locomotives.[48] (The opposite was true: in general, Mexico's oil was high in asphalt and low in illuminating grades, making for good fuel.)[49] Over the next 4 years, Doheny could not sell oil to railroads; with no other outlet, he decided to market his heavy crude as asphalt. His company alone paved about half of Mexico City and large portions of Guadalajara, Morelia, Tampico, Veracruz, Puebla, Durango, and Chihuahua.[50]

Doheny organized the Mexican Petroleum Company to pursue his Mexican oil venture. After 4 years of unsuccessful attempts, and with Doheny on the brink of bankruptcy, the company struck oil in April 1904 in El Ébano (named after its local ebony forests). El Ébano became Mexico's largest commercial oil field up to that point, though many more would follow.[51] El Ébano was also the site of Mexico's first massive oil spill. When large-scale extraction began in El Ébano, there was no place to store the oil. A huge reservoir was built nearby, but heavy rain caused the reservoir to collapse and millions of liters of oil flowed into a nearby lagoon, covering it with an iridescent slick. Thousands of birds and other animals died, suffocated by oil.[52]

---

[47] Myrna Santiago, "Culture Clash: Foreign Oil and Indigenous People in Northern Veracruz, Mexico, 1900–1921," *Journal of American History* 99, no. 1 (2012): 62–71.

[48] A different explanation claims that Henry Clay Pierce, who became the Central's president, did not want a competitor to his own oil interests. See *The Mexican Yearbook*, 1920, 293.

[49] Fernando Urbina, *La cuestión del petróleo en México, considerada desde el punto de vista geológico, económico e industrial, especialmente en lo que se refiere a la intervención gubernamental en la producción petrolera* (México: Porrúa Hermanos, Editores, 1915), 31. Mexican oil's chemical composition also meant that kerosene, used for illumination, continued to be largely imported from the USA.

[50] US Congress, Senate, Committee on Foreign Relations, *Investigation of Mexican Affairs: Preliminary Report and Hearings of the Committee on Foreign Relations*, vol. 1, 215–16. The Mexican Petroleum Co. founded the distillery "Compañía Mexicana de Asfalto y Construcciones." After getting its first contract with Mexico City authorities, the company supplied asphalt to cities across the country. See Brown and Knight, *The Mexican Petroleum Industry in the Twentieth Century*, 4.

[51] From 1904 to 1928, Doheny's Mexican Petroleum Co. produced about 448,555,000 barrels of oil, or 27.5 percent of total Mexican production during that period. In 1925, Standard Oil of Indiana bought out the company. See Ordóñez, *El petróleo en México*.

[52] Ordóñez, *El petróleo en México*. On the environmental effects of oil extraction in Mexico during the oil boom, see Santiago, *The Ecology of Oil*, chapter 3.

While El Ébano's remaining wildlife continued suffering the aftermath of the spill, Doheny's business boomed. Mexican Petroleum finally arranged a contract with the Mexican Central Railway. By 1905 – about the same time US railroads began consuming fuel oil on a vast scale – [53] Doheny's firm delivered 6,000 barrels to the Central daily, which apparently cut fuel costs by half compared with coal.[54] Two years later, almost 30 percent of the Central's 470 locomotives were burning fuel oil, and the company spent considerable sums on oil containers along its main line and special tank cars to carry fuel from the Gulf Coast to its reservoirs.[55] Doheny's Mexican venture illustrates the close connection between the history of petroleum in the USA and Mexico. Doheny financed his operations in Mexico with capital accumulated from the 1890s oil boom he initiated in Los Angeles. In turn, Doheny's success in Mexico depended on the fact that even before he set foot in Mexico, the country already had an established oil market based on US imports. After Doheny's success, oil in the two countries would only become more intertwined, with US capital pouring into Mexico for investment in the nascent oil industry. The export of a big part of Mexican oil production before 1921 to supply the US market only deepened this connection.

British capital also played a vital role in Mexico's oil boom via Sir Weetman Pearson. After spending years as a Mexican government contractor in a number of infrastructure projects, Pearson acquired land in northern and southeastern Veracruz in 1901 to prospect for oil. As with Doheny, Pearson initially sought to supply locomotives with fuel, though Pearson's locomotives belonged to his own company, the Tehuantepec Railway.[56] He soon branched out and, by 1905, Pearson's interests produced a small but constant flow of oil products like kerosene, industrial lubricants, and fuel oil for the Mexican market.[57] This production brought

---

[53] Anglo-Mexican Petroleum Products Company, Ltd., *Mexican Fuel Oil* (London: Anglo-Mexican Petroleum Products Co., Ltd., 1914), 76–80.

[54] Middleton, *Industrial Mexico; 1919 Facts and Figures*, 40; US Congress, Senate, Committee on Foreign Relations, *Investigation of Mexican Affairs: Preliminary Report and Hearings of the Committee on Foreign Relations*, vol. 1, 236. Oil's price was already lower than that of coal in parts of Mexico; additionally, an estimate claims that one worker was required to handle engine oil, whereas over twenty were needed for different stages of railroad coal consumption. See Percy F. Martin, *Mexico of the Twentieth Century*, vol. 1 (New York: Dodd, Mead, 1908), 265.

[55] Martin, *Mexico of the Twentieth Century*, vol. 1, 265.

[56] Manuel Flores, *Apuntes sobre el petróleo mexicano, por el Dr. Manuel Flores, dedicados a los señores miembros del XXVI Congreso Federal.* (n.p., 1913), 12; Luis Greaven, "Uso del aceite mineral en el ferrocarril nacional de Tehuantepec en México," *Boletín de la Secretaría de Fomento*, 2nda época, año V, no. I–III (August 1905): 10–32.

[57] Brown, *Oil and Revolution in Mexico*, 6–8.

Pearson into direct conflict with Waters-Pierce Oil. The "Great Oil War" between the two lowered prices in Mexico, which, in turn, fostered domestic consumption.[58]

After years of losses, Pearson's company, now El Águila, struck oil – the largest gusher worldwide at the time – in July 1908 in a place called Dos Bocas. Within 20 minutes of breaking the surface, the well blew the derrick to smithereens, sent the drill and heavy iron casing airborne, and created a crater over 300 meters across. The well caught fire and an inferno raged for 2 months before it was capped. Over 750,000 cubic meters of earth were blown into the air, and the explosion's roar was heard across kilometers.[59] Two years later, in December 1910, the famous Potrero del Llano No. 4 began spewing 100,000 barrels daily into the Tuxpan River, fouling its waters and beaches, killing fisheries, and destroying oyster beds. The layer of oil on the water was so thick that balls of crude formed around the blades of boat oars, impeding river transportation.[60] The gusher was capped 5 months later. Potrero del Llano produced 100 million barrels over its 8-year lifespan. Pearson, along with Doheny, would control the Mexican oil industry for many years.[61]

The gushers – and to a certain degree Mexico's early oil industry – depended on geology. Mexico's coastal oil-producing region at the time stretched over 150 km and some 50 km inland from Tampico in the north to Tuxpan in the south, covering a few hundred square kilometers at most. By comparison, the producing area in the early twentieth-century USA spread over 13,000 km². Mexican oil came from a few pools accumulated in enormous underground reservoirs from a vast area. The reservoirs were under intense water pressure and produced giant gushers when struck. Mexico's relatively few wells (200 in 1920) were thus incredibly productive, yielding on average over 2,000 barrels daily, but after a few years they tended to flood with saltwater. By contrast, US oil was scattered over a large, discontinuous area in widely separated fields under moderate gas pressure. More than 250,000 wells pumped this liquid wealth, producing on average five barrels daily.[62]

[58] Brown and Knight, *The Mexican Petroleum Industry in the Twentieth Century*, 7.

[59] Charles E. Bowles, *The Petroleum Industry* (Kansas City: Schooley Stationery & Printing Co., 1921), 40–1.

[60] *The Mexican Year Book: The Standard Authority on Mexico, 1920–21* (Los Angeles: Mexican Year Book Publishing Co., 1922), 295–6.

[61] Bud-Frierman, Godley, and Wale, "Weetman Pearson in Mexico and the Emergence of a British Oil Major, 1901–1919."

[62] Bowles, *The Petroleum Industry*, 34–6.

These differing geological conditions created unique outcomes. Mexico's wells lived fast and died young, producing huge volumes of oil wastefully over a few years. Industry control largely fell to a few extremely well-capitalized (mostly foreign) players with access to sophisticated and expensive technology to exploit and market this oil. Meanwhile, a more stable US industry yielded moderate productivity under somewhat more diversified ownership almost entirely in the hands of domestic capitalists.[63]

The Emergence of a Domestic Market

Mexico initially exported most of its boom production, since the country's economy could not absorb tens of millions of barrels overnight. That does not mean, as some scholars assume, that Mexico's domestic oil market was negligible before 1921 or that oil companies and Mexican consumers lacked interest in developing it. On the contrary, during the oil boom, Mexican oil became an important fuel for domestic transportation, manufacturing, and electricity generation. The first two decades of the twentieth century not only witnessed Mexico's emergence as a major oil producing-country, but also marked the beginning of the country's energy transition to oil as the basis of its society and economy. Domestic oil consumption would decline slightly in the 1920s and early 1930s (following waning oil production during those years) but resume its upward trend in the 1930s. From then on, most of Mexico's oil was consumed within its borders (Figure 4.2).

Large-scale oil production inspired significant enthusiasm among Mexico's industrialists and railroad owners from the beginning. They believed petroleum could solve Mexico's energy problems.[64] For decades, Mexican manufacturers complained about the lack of abundant, reliable, and cheap fuel to power increased production without breaking the bank. The fuel problem made economies of scale difficult to achieve, thereby rendering industry less competitive both domestically and abroad. Fully aware of experiments to use oil as fuel in places like the USA and Russia, industrialists considered oil to be coal's most promising replacement.

---

[63] Ibid., 37–8, 71. In 1918, foreigners controlled 97 percent of Mexico's oil industry, compared with 4 percent in the USA. The average investment per company in Mexico was $10,000,000, marking a high entry barrier. Twenty-seven companies operated in Mexico that year, but two, El Águila and Huasteca, represented most production. In the USA, the thirty-two top companies produced about 58 percent of its oil in 1918.

[64] "El petróleo empleado como combustible. Importantes experimentos," *El Economista Mexicano*, January 4, 1902.

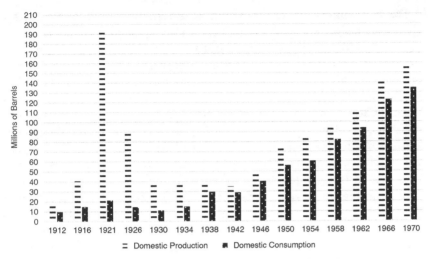

Figure 4.2 Mexico's Domestic Production and Consumption of Oil, 1912–70.
Sources: *Boletín del Petróleo*, vol. 7, June 1919, 612–13; *Boletín del Petróleo*, vol. 13, 1922, 90; Luz María Uhthoff "La industria del petróleo en México, 1911–1938: del auge exportador al abastecimiento del mercado interno. Una aproximación a su estudio." América Latina en la Historia Económica, no. 33 (2010): 5–30; Miguel Manterola, *La industria del petróleo en México*, 1938; *Mañana*, May 12, 1951; INEGI, *Estadísticas históricas de México*, 1986, 455; *Anuario estadístisco de Pemex*, 1977, 30.

As the editors of the daily *El Economista Mexicano* stated: "Interest in oil production in Mexico has reached many manufacturing establishments in the Republic, as it has railroad owners, who realize the immense value oil could have as a fuel, as long as it can be produced in sufficient quantities to replace coal."[65] Another *Economista* editorial emphasized that fuel was key to Mexico's continued industrialization. "For Mexico," the editorial argued, "the discovery of oil deposits and their rapid development are of special importance, because until we can find an abundant reserve of fuel, we will not be able to solve our industrial problem."[66] Others, however, expressed skepticism that Mexico's oil deposits were as abundant as publicized and could be exploited on a large scale for long enough to warrant adopting oil.[67]

[65] "Carbón y petróleo," *El Economista Mexicano*, March 1, 1902.
[66] "El problema industrial y las exploraciones petrolíferas," *El Economista Mexicano*, March 8, 1902.
[67] Martin, *Mexico of the Twentieth Century*, vol. 2, 270.

The following years put those worries to rest. Between 1907 and 1911, Mexican petroleum production skyrocketed from 1,000,000 to 14,000,000 barrels, a 1,300 percent increase. About 10 percent of this output entered the domestic market.[68] As was the case with coal several decades earlier, railroads quickly ranked among the largest oil consumers. In 1909, El Águila and the Mexican National Railway (from Nuevo Laredo to Mexico City) signed a contract for 360,000 barrels of oil annually to power locomotives.[69] This was a significant achievement for El Águila considering that the Mexican National had been one of Mexico's most reliable coal consumers. But company executives were cautious. If El Águila failed to provide the agreed amount, the contract specified, they would bear the cost of retrofitting the locomotive engines back to burning coal and pay the difference in fuel expenses. El Águila and other oil companies proved to be reliable suppliers. Mexico's oil production continued its vertiginous ascent, and other railroads quickly came onboard.

This included the newly nationalized National Railways of Mexico.[70] By 1911, the company's lines consumed some 730,000 barrels of fuel oil annually.[71] The executive board rejoiced: "The benefits which we expected to derive from the substitution of oil for coal as fuel," the board reported to the company's shareholders, "have been fully borne out by the year's results." Particularly gratifying were lower fuel costs. The system's northern half remained wedded to coal for some time given its proximity to coal fields compared with oil fields on the Gulf.[72] By 1912, all major Mexican railway lines had increased their use of fuel oil, consuming over 4,000,000 barrels annually.[73] For perspective, over 800,000 metric tons of coal or wood from

---

[68] Manuel Flores, *Apuntes sobre el petróleo mexicano*, 8–17.

[69] "Contract between S. Pearson & Son Limited and the Mexican Railway Company Limited for the Sale and Purchase of Fuel Oil" (1909), Caja 1796, exp. 50885, AHPEMEX.

[70] As mentioned, the Central Railway, now part of the government-controlled company, had bought Doheny's oil since 1905. The National Railways of Mexico, formed by the Mexican federal government in 1908, included almost all large railroad companies then operating in Mexico. On nationalization, see Arturo Grunstein, "¿Competencia o monopolio? Regulación y desarrollo ferrocarrilero en México, 1885–1911," in *Ferrocarriles y vida económica en México (1850–1950)* (Toluca: El Colegio Mexiquense, 1996), 167–221.

[71] *Annual Report of Ferrocarriles Nacionales de México (National Railways of Mexico)* (Mexico City, New York, 1911), 22.

[72] *Annual Report of Ferrocarriles Nacionales de México (National Railways of Mexico)* (Mexico City/New York, 1912), 23–4.

[73] The monthly breakdown: a) F.C. Nacional and Central (Líneas Nacionales), 180,000 barrels; b) F. C. Interocéanico and Veracruz-Istmo, 75,000 barrels; d) F.C. Nacional de Tehuantepec, 30,000 barrels; e) F.C. Mexicano (still privately owned), 50,000 barrels. The total: 335,000 barrels a month. See Flores, *Apuntes sobre el petróleo mexicano*, 21. Railroads also consumed large amounts of lubricating oil. See "Estimated Railroad Car Oil Business Per Month, El Águila" (1909), caja 2981, exp. 77324, AHP.

Table 4.1 *Railroad
consumption of fuel oil
in Mexico, 1916–22*

Year	Barrels of Oil
1916	2,294,325
1917	2,803,396
1918	3,555,756
1919	3,805,050
1920	4,539,505
1922	5,500,000

Source: Cámara de
Senadores, *El petróleo: la más
grande riqueza nacional,*
1923, 282.

a forest somewhat smaller than Rhode Island would have been required to
provide similar energy inputs.[74] While the Mexican Revolution's bloodiest
years (1913–16) disrupted this trend, purchases increased soon thereafter,
surpassing 1912 numbers by the decade's end (Table 4.1).

Railroads had powerful reasons to shift to oil. Unlike coal, oil could be
stored in tanks along the tracks and transferred into locomotive fuel storage
units by simple gravity. Few if any workers were needed for this process;
those who did participate tended to perform isolated tasks, an attractive
proposition for company managers considering the militancy and effect-
iveness of coal and railroad union organizers.[75] Fuel oil was also cheaper to
handle. While coal cost on average M$5 cents to load 1 ton onto a train,
loading 1 ton of oil cost just M$0.35 cents.[76] Coal loading in parts of

---

[74] I base my estimates on Anglo-Mexican Petroleum Products Co., Ltd., *Petróleo Combustible
Mexicano* (Mexico, D. F.: Compañía Mexicana de Petróleo El Aguila, S.A., 1914), 91–2.

[75] The connection between oil use and potentially fewer workers was clear for contemporaries. See
Flores, *Apuntes sobre el petróleo mexicano*, 22, and Carlos Díaz Dufoo, *La cuestión del petróleo*
(México: Eusebio Gómez de la Puente, Editor, 1921), 42–3. On union activity and strikes in
Coahuila's coal industry, see Roberto R. Calderón, *Mexican Coal Mining Labor in Texas and
Coahuila, 1880–1930* (College Station: Texas A&M University Press, 2000), chapter 5. For an
analysis of railroad workers' labor militancy in early twentieth-century Mexico, see Esther
Shabot Askenazi, "La Gran Liga de Empleados de Ferrocarril y la huelga de 1908," *Estudios
Políticos* 5, no. 18–19 (2019): 205–43. On the link between adopting oil and corporate desires to
dampen labor militancy in the USA and Europe, see Bruce Podobnik, *Global Energy Shifts: Fostering
Sustainability in a Turbulent Age* (Philadelphia: Temple University Press, 2008), chapter 3.

[76] Anglo-Mexican Petroleum Products Company, Ltd., *Mexican Fuel Oil* (London: Anglo-Mexican
Petroleum Products Co., Ltd., 1914), 58–9.

Mexico had been mechanized using coaling towers to funnel it into cars, but workers needed to shovel it onto the tower conveyor. Additionally, Mexican oil's calorific value was between 30 to 65 percent higher than coal kilogram for kilogram and occupied less storage.[77] By burning one unit of oil, locomotives gained one and a half times the energy for less space, allowing trains to transport other valuable cargo. As railroad oil consumption rose, imported coal use dropped from 1,300,000 metric tons in 1907 to 390,000 in 1912.[78]

Along with becoming critical consumers in the early years of Mexico's oil industry, railroads were instrumental in spreading the new fuel to other sectors of the Mexican economy. Roughly a decade after commercial production began, oil companies were selling crude, fuel oil, gasoline, and lubricants to businesses, factories, and a variety of commercial establishments nationwide, including the upscale department store El Palacio de Hierro (The Iron Palace). Even coal companies became costumers.[79] Petroleum firms developed a dense commercial network and established hundreds of storage sites for distribution, all dependent on railroads.[80] In the early days, companies transported petroleum in barrels to consumption centers. Then, most firms adopted tank cars, which made deliveries cheaper and simpler (Figure 4.3). Before construction of oil pipelines, Mexico's railroad network transported oil from coastal production sites to consumption centers inland. Within cities, animal-hauled tanks and later trucks carried oil to individual customers.

The flow of oil and oil-derived products within Mexico was occasionally disrupted during the Revolution when railroads were seized, tracks destroyed, or bridges blown up. El Águila, for example, failed to deliver oil to several clients, who sued for breach of contract. Other times, sales faltered because firms could not pay for deliveries, which in turn led El Águila to pursue legal action.[81] In 1915, probably the Revolution's most violent year, only 109 of El Águila's 169 sales and distribution offices delivered annual sales reports to the company's Mexico City headquarters.[82] Likely, there was nothing good to report from these war-ravaged areas. But in contrast to

[77] Ibid., 19–22.
[78] Flores, *Apuntes sobre el petróleo mexicano*, 21. Flores estimated that replacing imported coal with domestic oil saved railroad companies about M$4,800,000 annually.
[79] "El Águila's Lubricating Oil and Gasoline Contracts in Mexico" (1911), caja 3127, exp. 80295, AHP; "Gasoline Sales, El Águila" (1911), caja 3127, exp. 80282, AHP; "Contracts for Lubricating Oil" (1914), caja 3126, exp. 80279, AHP.
[80] Anglo-Mexican Petroleum Products Co., Ltd., *Petróleo combustible mexicano* (Mexico, D. F.: Compañía Mexicana de Petróleo El Águila, S.A., 1914), 11.
[81] "Contratos de petróleo pendientes de modificación de El Águila" (1916), caja 3089, exp. 79513, AHP.
[82] "Oil Sales and Advertisement Expenses by El Águila" (1914–1915), caja 478, exp. 13570, AHP.

Figure 4.3 Railroad oil-tank car. These 15-ton cars were used to transport oil from
production sites to consumption centers like Mexico City.
Source: Anglo-Mexican Petroleum Products Company, Ltd., *Mexican Fuel Oil,*
1914, 21.

the Revolution's devastating effects on Mexican coal, wartime oil production surged. This was in part due to a thriving export market, which
boomed as World War I combatant nations shifted their navies and armies
to oil. Mexico's own consumption also doubled between 1912 and 1921.
Railroads typically consumed around a third of the domestic oil production during these years. Mexico's war was fought to a substantial degree
through oil-powered railroads,[83] which transported troops and war materials. Mexico's incipient oil revolution literally powered the country's social

---

[83] At the height of Mexico's war in 1914, El Águila sold more than 60 percent of its oil in Mexico,
railroads being the company's biggest costumers. "Reporte de consumo de petróleo crudo perteneciente a esta compañía El Águila, julio-octubre 1914" (November 1914), caja 2005, exp. 54426, AHP.
The trend continued throughout the revolutionary period; see "Fuel Oil for Mexican Railway, El
Águila" (1917), caja 3126, exp. 80266, AHP; "Informes de ventas para la mesa directiva de El Águila"
(1917), caja 482, exp. 13690, AHP. In 1918, railroads used 26 percent of Mexico's oil domestic
consumption. See *Boletín del Petróleo,* vol. 7, 6 (México, D. F., June 1919), 601.

revolution, making the Mexican Revolution one of history's first oil-fueled wars.

Mexican factories, mines, smelting operations, and a number of power plants also adopted oil. Perhaps 75 percent of all industrial establishments now used some amount of petroleum and petroleum derivatives. Industrial consumption may have reached 200,000 barrels monthly in 1912.[84] By 1920, El Águila alone sold 800,000 barrels of oil monthly to various industries and businesses, over 70 percent as fuel.[85] Even industries well-endowed with fuelwood and hydroelectricity began consuming oil, like the San Rafael Paper Mill, founded in 1892 by Tomás Braniff.[86] By the first decade of the twentieth century, the company was the largest paper mill in Latin America, producing over 1,000 metric tons of paper per month.[87] For many, the factory, nestled within a conifer forest at the foothills of the imposing Iztaccíhuatl volcano in the Valley of Mexico's southeast, epitomized modernity, technological sophistication, and human capacity to transform nature. Particularly remarkable for one observer was the way factory machinery transformed a tree into a paper product within 3 hours. Left alone, nature's bounty was wasted. By turning nature into a commodity, San Rafael humanized it and gave it value.[88]

Abundant energy made this process possible. Before oil, rich water and forest resources supplied San Rafael with relatively cheap water-power, hydroelectricity, and fuelwood.[89] As output grew and productive capacity expanded, however, the firm required greater energy

---

[84] Flores, *Apuntes sobre el petróleo mexicano*, 21–2.

[85] "Balance del movimiento general de petróleo habido en esta compañía El Águila en el mes de febrero de 1920" (March 9, 1920), caja 2014, exp. 54622, AHP. The list of consumers included all major firms operating in Mexico at the time. "Domestic Fuel Oil Sales, 'El Águila'" (1921), caja 1826, exp. 51792, AHP.

[86] In 1913, Tomás Braniff, son of famous Porfirian businessman Thomas Braniff, stepped down as company president. Braniff senior was a New York native of Irish descent who had arrived in Mexico in 1865 to partake in constructing the Veracruz–Mexico City railroad line. Over the following decades, Braniff built a business empire and became one of the Porfirian elite's most prominent members. He and José Sánchez founded the San Rafael Paper Mill. On the Braniff dynasty, see María del Carmen Collado, *La burguesía mexicana: el emporio Braniff y su participación política, 1865–1920* (Siglo XXI, 1987).

[87] "Nota de producción y salida de papel en el mez de marzo de 1910" (April 1910), AHPSR.

[88] "Fábricas de Papel San Rafael y Anexas," *El Mundo Ilustrado, 1894–1914*, May 25, 1913, Cartas, vol. 347, AHPSR.

[89] José de la Macorra, "Carta dirigida del Sr. de la Macorra al Lic. Pedro Martínez López" (September 20, 1905), AHPSR; "Señor General, Don Porfírio Díaz, Presidente de la República" (April 1897), Cartas, vol. 347, AHPSR; "Garantía del contrato de compra de concesión de aguas del río Tlalmanalco" (1913), AHPSR; "Balance de l'actif et du passif au 31 de Decembre 1914" (December 31, 1914), AHPSR. The Secretaría de Fomento had granted San Rafael's most important water concessions to the waters of the Tlalmanalco River.

inputs.[90] San Rafael met its growing needs with oil. In 1909, El Águila began an aggressive campaign to develop Mexico's market for fuel oil. As the most industrialized region and Mexico's largest market, the Valley of Mexico was an obvious target. El Águila looked to sell fuel oil to manufacturing operations of all sizes but prioritized large companies like San Rafael, with whom they negotiated a sale in 1909. El Águila delivered this oil through narrow-gauge tank cars from their storage site in the Peralvillo neighborhood, northwest of downtown Mexico City. Soon, the paper mill was consuming 3,000 barrels monthly.[91] To store the oil, San Rafael built enormous steel tanks on its own premises. The mill then burned it in special boilers to generate steam power for machinery.

Energy and technological changes were linked to radical popular mobilizations. The decades-long privatization of lands in the central highlands orchestrated by Porfirian liberal elites combined with the mechanization of industry and food production to limit work opportunities for rural Mexicans. Privatizations concentrated large swaths of communal cultivable land and forests in the hands of the powerful and well-connected at the expense of communities that had once accessed them. In Morelos, sugar estates mechanized refining and replaced human and animal labor. In Chalco, the introduction of railroad lines enabled wealthy investors to expand estates, drain the nearby lake upon which *chinampa* cultivators depended, and introduce mechanical planters, threshers, and harvesters. Next door, huge industrial establishments with fully mechanized production like San Rafael created few permanent jobs and hired workers from other regions. The increasing reliance of San Rafael and other industries on oil energy cut into the labor of many charcoal makers, fuelwood cutters, and muleteers who transported the fuel to factories. Agro-industrial capitalism, railroads, market expansion, and mechanization (increasingly powered by oil) combined with population growth to erode the autonomy and livelihoods of countless communities. No wonder that with the outbreak of revolution, many fought to regain land, water, and forests – all sources of what might be described as energy autonomy.[92]

---

[90] In 1900, San Rafael opened El Progreso Industrial, another paper mill in the Valley of Mexico's northeast. See "Acta de la primera asamblea general de 'El Progreso Industrial, Fábrica de Papel'" (May 1899), AHPSR.

[91] "Fuel Oil for San Rafael Mills" (May 1909), caja 2626, exp. 69980, AHP.

[92] John Tutino, *The Mexican Heartland: How Communities Shaped Capitalism, a Nation, and World History, 1500–2000* (Princeton: Princeton University Press, 2017), chapter 9.

Unfortunately for these communities, the northern Constitutionalist revolutionary faction, which hitched their national project to oil-fueled capitalist development, carried the day. They achieved this through US aid in the form of arm supplies; high demand among World War I combatant nations for oil; and control over oil-producing regions in the Gulf of Mexico, which both generated oil export revenues and powered war mobilization and industrial production. After defeating Villa's populist insurgency in the battlefield, the Constitutionalists would go on to form an exceedingly lasting new political regime largely based upon an oil-centric energy regime. It would rule Mexico for the rest of the twentieth century. While communities fighting for land did not win, their demands shaped postrevolutionary politics for decades to come.[93]

Mexico's domestic consumption soared during the Revolution's final years, oscillating after 1916 between 10 and 21 million barrels annually. Over 90 percent of this fuel powered extraction and processing of oil itself, locomotives, factories, power plants, and, increasingly, cars and trucks.[94] All in all, between 1901 and 1921, Mexico produced 730,000,000 barrels of oil. Around 15 percent of this sum, 110 million barrels, remained in the country.[95]

The oil energy bonanza allowed Mexico to forgo importing some 20,500,000 tons of coal or relying on its own coal industry, which would have not been up to the task anyway (it took the industry 30 years – from 1890 to 1921 – to produce the equivalent amount). Oil consumption thus cut directly into coal's market. Not everybody was happy. A government report from 1920 or 1921 argued that "the country, that is, the government and workers, have lost with the substitution of coal by oil."[96] While Mexican capital existed in the coal industry and the nation's domestic market, the oil sector was controlled by foreigners, who sent most of its production abroad. This also applied to the oil industry's fabulous profits, since companies kept the lion's share. Coal wealth, on the contrary, was dispersed among the countless Mexican workers who extracted, loaded, unloaded, and handled it. Even imported coal, the document maintained,

---

[93] Ibid., Chapter 10 and personal communication.
[94] Díaz Dufoo, *La cuestión del petróleo*, 47, 92. For oil distilled in Mexican refineries (both exported and domestically consumed), 64 percent became fuel, some 15 percent gasoline, only 2 percent kerosene, and the rest became lubricants and other derived products.
[95] José Jofré González argues that from 1910 to 1920, oil became Mexico's largest "modern" (read fossil) energy source, with twice as much tonnage as coal. See Jofré González, "Patrones de consumo aparente de energías modernas en América Latina, 1890–2003" (PhD Dissertation, Universitat de Barcelona, 2012), 69.
[96] "Carbón de piedra y petróleo" (1920), caja 763, exp. 19667, AHP.

generated more jobs and paid more custom duties than oil exports. For the authors, oil was cheaper than coal mainly because it employed far fewer workers. Put simply, oil hurt Mexico's working class.

Others reasoned that abundant oil protected Mexico's forests from increasing demand. General Salvador Alvarado, Yucatan's revolutionary military governor from 1915 to 1918, enacted policies designed to foster oil consumption in the peninsula to protect its forests. Alvarado surmised that, since forests supposedly attracted rain, replacing wood with oil would ultimately benefit agriculture, Yucatan's main source of wealth.[97] The connection between deforestation and rainfall is less direct than Alvarado imagined. But he was right to believe that increased oil consumption would reduce, in relative terms, fuelwood in Yucatan's energy mix (and Mexico's, for that matter). The energy in 1 ton of oil is (very roughly) equivalent to 3 tons of wood. At 600 tons of wood per square kilometer, one would need to harvest the yield from 75,000 km^2 of forest (an area larger than the state of Chiapas) to equal the calorific value of Mexico's oil consumption from 1900 to 1921.[98] While reliable data for nationwide forest cover in the early twentieth century is lacking, some contemporary estimates suggested between 175,000 and 260,000 square kilometers (9–13 percent of Mexico's total area).[99] Even if this figure is too low, it is clear that, by 1921, Mexico would have struggled to power its economy with its forests.

On the other hand, reduced fuelwood use may have been partially offset by economic growth and increased activity of certain oil-powered sectors. With the exception of the Revolution's most destructive years, railroad cargo tonnage of timber and other forest products rose during the first quarter of the twentieth century, which almost certainly contributed to increased deforestation.[100] Oil energy was also important to industrial growth during the revolutionary years, much of which had required wood and timber for various stages of production.[101] And, of course,

---

[97] Salvador Alvarado, "Para traer petróleo al Estado [de Yucatán] en grandes cantidades. La medidad reportará grandes beneficios" (1915), caja 2988, exp. 77480, AHP.

[98] Gustavo Ortega, *Los recursos petrolíferos mexicanos y su actual explotación* (México, D. F.: Talleres Gráficos de la Nación, 1925), 11, 32, 44.

[99] *The Mexican Yearbook*, 1920, 249. Typically, these figures excluded or underestimated Mexico's area under tropical rainforests, which was then extensive. The *Mexican Yearbook* clearly only considered Mexico's temperate forests. See 250.

[100] From 571,959 tons in 1909 to 788,363 tons in 1925. See *Ferrocarriles Nacionales de México, Annual Report*, 1909–25.

[101] Stephen Haber and his collaborators have addressed the paradox of economic growth during the Mexican Revolution. See Stephen Haber, Armando Razo, and Noel Maurer, "Economic Growth Amidst Political Instability: Evidence from Revolutionary Mexico," n.d. These authors suggest

a narrow focus on wood energy substituted by oil ignores the thousands of hectares destroyed and environmental devastation caused by oil production.[102]

In 1921, Porfirian intellectual Carlos Díaz Dufoo published a book on the "oil question" in which he examined Mexico's post-Revolution oil industry. The pamphlet defended foreign oil companies, arguing that they benefited Mexico. The book questioned the nationalist narrative that companies exploited and wasted Mexico's oil. Instead, Díaz Dufoo depicted them as beacons of progress and symbols of human capacity to subdue nature. He also insisted that extracting and commercializing oil required vast capitals and technical expertise, which Mexico lacked. What Díaz Dufoo called the "aggressive and sullen nationalism" (*agresivo y huraño*) of postrevolutionary Mexico would only damage the nation's oil industry with its hostile policies.[103] More importantly, Díaz Dufoo claimed, oil "revolutionized" Mexico's industry and transportation by providing "unexpected amount[s] of energy." He also predicted that oil would solve Mexico's "fuel problem." Since Mexican industry and railroads had overexploited forest for years and coal never lived up to its promise, only oil could provide the "colossal mechanical energy" needed to continue industrializing. Dufoo correctly anticipated that oil's influence on Mexico's economy and society would only grow over the next decades.

When Dufoo published his book in 1921, Mexican oil production had reached its peak. Amidst revolution, counterrevolution, and civil war, oil companies developed an impressive oil infrastructure. Mexico featured 4,000 kilometers of oil pipelines, the longest system behind the country's 20,000-kilometer railroad network.[104] Massive oil tanks were dispersed across the country with the capacity to store over 50,000,000 barrels from 227 productive oil fields.[105] By the end of

that, with exception of the most violent years (1914–17), revolutionary and postrevolutionary Mexican governments guaranteed the property rights of large industrial firms. These companies, in return, generated needed tax revenues. Since virtually all these companies originated during the Porfiriato, this actually preserved the old Porfirian economic elite and sustained economic growth during the period.

[102] "El Presidente Municipal de Pánuco, Veracruz, Leodegario Gea pide se prohíba la incineración de petróleo en presas de compañías por haberse perdido casi la totalidad de siembras de maíz" (1918), Departamento del Petróleo, caja 032, exp. 7, AGN.

[103] Díaz Dufoo, *La cuestión del petróleo*, 111.

[104] Cámara de Senadores, *El petróleo: la más grande riqueza nacional* (México, D. F.: Cámara de Senadores, Sección de Estadística y Anales de Jurisprudencia, 1923) 267. Díaz Dufoo suggested a figure of 15,000 km of pipelines, but that seems implausible. See *La cuestión del petróleo*, 97.

[105] Secretaría de Industria, Comercio y Trabajo, *México, sus recursos naturales*, 182–3.

the Revolution's armed phase, oil was by far Mexico's most important and heavily capitalized industry.[106]

Redirecting the Flow

Mexico's oil production declined precipitously after 1921. Some cite Venezuelan oil's global rise to prominence for this decline. Per this argument, foreign oil companies stopped investing in Mexico's waning oil fields in favor of Venezuela, where production costs were lower.[107] A more recent analysis suggests a simpler explanation: Mexico's main oil fields simply ran out.[108]

Whatever the reasons, output plummeted throughout the 1920s, stabilizing in the early 1930s. Not until the 1970s, using offshore drilling technology developed after World War II, would the industry production surpass 1921 figures.[109] Though in 1924 Mexico was still the world's second largest exporter of petroleum, its share dropped from 25 to 14 percent of total global production (Table 4.2). Most went to the USA (73 percent), with a substantial 12 percent exported to other Latin American countries. Decline in Mexico's oil production affected exports far more than domestic consumption, which only experienced a moderate drop in the 1920s and largely recovered by the 1930s. As exports continued falling, Mexico's oil consumption doubled between 1934 and 1938. Oil shares bound for domestic market continued growing in the following years, reaching over 80 percent by 1942.

A key factor that allowed domestic oil consumption to expand after the oil boom was Mexico's increasing numbers of cars, trucks, and tractors. Elites imported the first motor vehicles around 1895.[110] They viewed driving, like their European counterparts, as a leisure or sport rather than

---

[106] Díaz Dufoo calculated that in 1921 the oil industry of Mexico was worth close to M$700,000,000; Díaz Dufoo, *La cuestión del petróleo*, 103.

[107] Lorenzo Meyer, *Mexico and the United States in the Oil Controversy, 1917–1942* (Austin, University of Texas Press, 1977), 8–12. An analysis of the differences between oil government policies in twentieth-century Mexico and Venezuela is in María del Mar Rubio, "Contabilidad nacional medioambiental para productores de petróleo. Estimaciones para México y Venezuela (1901–1985)," *Investigaciones Históricas de Historia Económica*, núm. 8 (2007): 141–65. Rubio contends that Mexican authorities viewed petroleum as cheap energy for domestic industry. Venezuela, by contrast, assumed an export-oriented strategy whereby oil sales financed national development.

[108] Stephen Haber, Noel Maurer, and Armando Razo, "When the Law Does Not Matter: The Rise and Decline of the Mexican Oil Industry," *The Journal of Economic History* 63, no. 1 (2003): 1–32.

[109] Ibid.

[110] J. Brian Freeman, "El despertar del camión de carga en México," in *Automotores y transporte público. Un acercamiento desde los estudios históricos, Ilse Angélica Álvarez Palma, Ed.* (Toluca: El Colegio Mexiquense, 2017), 121–43.

Table 4.2 *Global oil output in 1924*

Country	Number of Barrels	Percentage of Total
USA	714,000,000	70.4
Mexico	139,678,000	13.7
Russia	45,162,000	4.4
Persia	31,845,000	3.1
Dutch East Indies	21,000,000	2.0
Rumania	13,296,000	1.3
Venezuela	9,500,000	0.9

Source: Ortega, *Los recursos petrolíferos mexicanos y su actual explotación,* 1925, 34.

Table 4.3 *Mexico's oil consumption by sector,* *1922*

Sector	Number of Barrels
Industry	1,862,068
Railroads	5,500,000
Cars, Trucks, and Tractors	9,439,655

Source: El petróleo: la más grande riqueza nacional, 1923, 282.

transportation. Excepting the odd electric and steam-powered unit, most vehicles featured gasoline-fueled internal combustion engines. A few thousand more fossil fuel vehicles were introduced in the early twentieth century but remained rare outside cities, especially Mexico City, and the oil region, where company trucks transported heavy machinery around oil fields. Yet by the early 1920s, the number of motor vehicles in Mexico had increased to the point that they became oil's largest consumers (Table 4.3).

During the first two decades of the twentieth century, motor traffic remained a quintessentially urban phenomenon and even a curiosity in some cities as late as 1916.[111] Mexico City was the unquestionable center of automobilism in the country, with more motor vehicles than all other

---

[111] "Relación de toda clase de vehículos que actualmente se hallan en uso en Monterrey" (1916), Industria, Comercio y Trabajo, caja 1, exp. 4, AENL. By the late 1920s, a city of 45,000 inhabitants like Chihuahua City still had only around 1,000 motor vehicles registered, a mere 2.2 percent of the total population. See "Lista de propietarios de automóviles y camiones registrados en la ciudad"

urban areas combined.[112] It was there that the first system of buses for public transportation emerged.[113] The influx of people fleeing the Mexican Revolution rendered the existing tramway service insufficient, so around 1915, a few privately owned taxis began operations to complement it. Then, in 1916, tramway workers struck for better conditions, paralyzing urban transport. Some truck owners with entrepreneurial spirit quickly organized impromptu bus services. They added a makeshift wooden chassis to old Ford trucks or cars, which provided lateral seats for eight passengers, and covered these with canvas tarps to protect from the rain. The public nicknamed these buses "Julias," with numerous examples soon circulating. This novel bus system lacked regulations and schedules. A piece of cardboard on the windshield named the bus destination while an assistant yelled out stops to passengers. Drivers changed their route at a whim if it promised more customers, simply forcing passengers already onboard to get off. Sometimes, drivers picked up clients at specific addresses, functioning like taxis. A sought-after clientele was construction workers in working-class neighborhoods commuting to posh, up-and-coming neighborhoods like Roma. It was an "improvised and anarchic" system.[114] But it was relatively cheap, charging individuals 10 cents of a peso per ride at a time when average worker salaries in Mexico City fetched 40 cents daily.[115]

While at first buses mimicked tramway routes, they soon organized separate routes, directly threatening the tramways' grip on Mexico City's urban transportation. In the 1920s, a full-blown price war between bus and tram operators erupted with occasional physical violence. Tramways began a slow retreat, bleeding customers to buses year after year. By 1942, buses were transporting over 160 million passengers in Mexico City, and this grew into a 50 million-peso industry, effectively replacing tramways as the main transportation form for urban residents.[116] This shift marked the transition to a fossil-fueled public transit system, a system replicated across cities

---

(1928) Reconstrucción; Secretaría; Censos, estadísticas y filiaciones; Chihuahua, caja 65, exp. 24, AHMCH.

[112] *Dun's Review*, vol. 18, 1, 1911, 49–50. Thirty years later, nothing had changed. In 1938, Mexico City claimed 39 percent of the country's private cars, 28 percent of taxis, 22 percent of trucks, 21 percent of buses, and 44 percent of motorbikes. See Moisés T. de la Peña, *El servicio de autobuses en el Distrito Federal* (México, D. F., 1943), 116.

[113] De la Peña, *El servicio de autobuses en el Distrito Federal.*   [114] Ibid., 14–15.

[115] Javier L. Arnaut, "Mexican Real Wages before the Revolution: A Reappraisal," *Iberoamericana – Nordic Journal of Latin American and Caribbean Studies* 47, no. 1 (2018): 45–62. Information for the middle years of the Revolution is missing; the 40-cent average refers to 1911.

[116] De la Peña, *El servicio de autobuses en el Distrito Federal*, 37–41, 118–21.

Table 4.4 *Number of oil and muscle-powered vehicles in Mexico, 1925–60.*[117]

Year	Oil-Powered Vehicles	Muscle-Powered Vehicles
1925	54,367	9,916
1930	71,945	5,542
1935	96,126	4,485
1940	149,455	5,414
1945	188,981	11,758
1950	308,206	13,958
1955	561,133	8,127
1960	827,017	12,754

Adapted from: INEGI, *Estadísticas históricas de México*, tomo 2, 3a edición, 1994, 694.

nationwide.[118] A similar process of technological substitution took place outside urban areas, with freight trucks largely supplanting trains by mid-century. In the 1950s, trucks surpassed trains in terms of total cargo tonnage transported annually.[119]

From the 1920s to the 1950s, the number of fossil-fueled vehicles in Mexico doubled every decade, reaching half a million by the early 1950s. In addition to tramways and freight trains, this explosion sounded the death knell for another long-standing transportation mode: animal-hauled vehicles, which marched into insignificance during this period (Table 4.4).

Mexico's motor traffic takeover required a simultaneous roadbuilding spree. In 1921, most of Mexico's roads were dirt and gravel paths made for people and animals.[120] The few paved roads that existed traced their origins to the late nineteenth-century bicycle craze, which soon faded.[121] In the years before the Revolution, elite car culture began taking over these thoroughfares. After 1920, road construction became a fundamental strategy for postrevolutionary regimes to legitimize power and burnish their

---

[117] The chart excludes tractors, of which there were over 20,000 in 1950. While they overestimate the number of tractors, a good analysis of the "tractorization" of rural Mexico after 1940 is Palacios and Ocampo, "Los tractores agrícolas de México," Revista Mexicana de Ciencias Agrícolas, 4 (2012), 812–24.

[118] Mexico City tramways ran mostly on electricity, over half of which was water-generated.

[119] J. Brian Freeman, "El despertar del camión de carga en México," 121–43.

[120] Michael K. Bess, *Routes of Compromise: Building Roads and Shaping the Nation in Mexico, 1917–1952* (Lincoln: University of Nebraska Press, 2017), 1.

[121] According to writer Salvador Novo, by the 1920s, only "rich kids" (*niños bien*) rode bikes in Mexico City. See Salvador Novo, *El joven* (México, D. F.: UNAM, 2012 [1923]).

modern credentials. Paved roads became synonymous with progress, their absence associated with backwardness. Veracruz governor Ángel Carvajal declared roadbuilding one of his administration's top priorities, since modern highways "enable the economic development of our people and their spiritual growth."[122] Different levels and agencies of the Mexican state, from local to national government, funded and subsidized this new infrastructure. More importantly, Mexico's modern roads were largely bankrolled by a gasoline tax.[123] Put simply, oil paid for the petroleum-based roads upon which gasoline-powered vehicles drove. Between 1930 and 1960, Mexico's road system exploded from about 1,400 km to 45,000 km, an over 3,000 percent increase.[124]

With their proliferation, oil-powered motor vehicles began transforming various aspects of Mexican life and culture, from film and literature to different social practices and even sexual mores. Unlike some avant-garde European writers, Mexican modernist writers viewed cars with either trepidation or outright hostility. One famous author decried them as apocalyptic machines that left behind "carbon flatulence."[125] The ubiquity of automobiles also disappointed foreign authors, who flocked to post-Revolution Mexico seeking the primitive, authentic, and picturesque. Later literary figures like Mexico City's chronicler Salvador Novo adopted a different perspective, celebrating a new urban culture shaped by motor vehicles and a modern, mechanized cityscape.[126] Automobiles stood at the center of Mexico's most important silent film of the era, *The Grey Car* (*El automóvil gris*, 1919). A film with ambitions of documentary realism, it depicted a band of thieves disguised as federal soldiers who robbed mansions of wealthy Mexicans.[127] These thieves moved around by car, a symbol of status and wealth, instead of on foot or horse, like typical bandits before. Young couples found in cars a new private space beyond supervision to engage in unauthorized sexual behavior. As one car

---

[122] *Informe de labores del ciudadano Gobernador Constitucional del Estado de Veracruz, 1949–1950* (Jalapa: 1950), 87.

[123] In later years governments used public debt and various partnerships with private enterprise to fund roads. See Bess, *Routes of Compromise*, chapter 4.

[124] INEGI, *Estadísticas históricas de México*, vol. 2, 3a edición, 1994, 692.

[125] J. Brian Freeman, "Los Hijos de Ford: Mexico in the Automobile Age, 1900–1930," in *Technology and Culture in Twentieth Century Mexico* (Tuscaloosa: University of Alabama Press, 2013), 214–32.

[126] Ibid.

[127] Paul A. Schroeder Rodríguez, *Latin American Cinema: A Comparative History* (Berkeley: University of California Press, 2016), 37–39.

magazine put it, "a lot of things can happen inside of cars when gasoline is abundant."[128]

Motorism and new roads also promoted mass tourism. People traveled the country in their cars, which, ironically, fostered an appreciation of nature. It was only in the context of widespread automobilism that Mexico created its national park system,[129] most of which consisted of protected areas located close to urban centers and accessible by car.[130] Motorism also gave urbanites and foreign tourists ready access to indigenous, "traditional" cultures in formerly remote areas.[131] As poet Salvador Novo wrote tongue-in-cheek in his 1934 poem *Del pasado remoto*,

It's necessary to develop tourism. / When the México-Laredo highway is finished / many more Lions and Rotaries will come / to toast in Xochimilco to the prosperity of Mexico, / which is closer for them than Egypt, relatively speaking, / and also has the Monte Albán ruins.[132]

Some effects of Mexico's new motorized age were less sexy. The environmental impact of fossil-fueled vehicles and the oil-based network of roads that crisscrossed Mexico by mid-century was profound. Not only did road construction involve turning vast volumes of soil and paving them with an impermeable surface, but roads gave oil-powered vehicles access to previously inaccessible areas, promoting greater exploitation of Mexico's environments. Take forests. Trucks allowed loggers and charcoal makers to penetrate forests formerly out of reach or economically unexploitable with animal-powered transportation (Figure 4.4). Motor vehicles also led to the decline of certain animal species in Mexico; hunters could now access relatively remote areas in large numbers, make a kill, and transport the carcass out with

[128] *El Automóvil en México: Revista Mensual Automovilística*, núm. 29, May 1921.
[129] The first parks, El Chico and Desierto de los Leones, dated back to the late nineteenth and early twentieth centuries, respectively. From 1935 to 1941, the autonomous Departamento Forestal y de Caza y Pesca (Forest, Game, and Fishing Department) created forty-seven parks. In the 1940s, the department was subsumed under the Department of Agriculture. From 1941 to 1955, only two more parks were created. Although the national park system covered some 10,000 km², these were mostly "paper" parks, since insufficient funds were assigned to enforce their protected status. Parks largely protected scenic and "patriotic" landscapes. See Alfonso Loera Borja and Roberto Villaseñor Angeles, *El problema forestal de México* (México: Impresora Periodística Comercial S. de R.L., 1958). On Mexico's national park program after the Revolution, see Emily Wakild, *Revolutionary Parks: Conservation, Social Justice, and Mexico's National Parks, 1910–1940* (Tucson: University of Arizona Press, 2011).
[130] Some publications touted automobilism and access to rural nature as medical treatment for "urban" maladies like anxiety. See *El Automóvil en México: Revista Mensual Automovilística*, 29, May 1921.
[131] Freeman, "Los Hijos de Ford: Mexico in the Automobile Age, 1900–1930."
[132] Salvador Novo, *Salvador Novo* (México, D. F.: UNAM, 2009).

Figure 4.4 Truck transporting charcoal from the mountains between Mexico City and Toluca, 1921. Source: *El automóvil en México*, February 1921, 26, 8.

ease.[133] Cars posed risks not just to fauna. Urban air pollution from automobiles became noticeable by the 1950s, especially in Mexico City, although the first medical assessments of its detrimental health impacts would have to wait a few more years.[134]

Equally far-reaching, motor traffic and asphalt roads remade cities and promoted urban growth. Mexican cities were soon planned (or improvised) around cars, featuring gas stations and other forms of automobile infrastructure (Figure 4.5). Although his specific urban plan for Mexico City was never implemented, Carlos Contreras's vision of a city reorganized around broad avenues and suburban growth predicated on car ownership was.[135] In fact, the phenomenal expansion of Mexico City and several other Mexican cities after mid-century was largely driven by fossil-fueled vehicles. The rise in motor vehicles forced authorities to invest in road infrastructure to alleviate increased traffic congestion. As more vehicles

[133] Charles Sheldon, "The Big Game of Chihuahua, Mexico, 1898–1902," in *Hunting and Conservation: The Book of the Boone and Crockett Club* (New Haven: Yale University Press, 1925), 141–2.

[134] Dr. Miguel Bustamante, "Nuevos problemas de salud pública," *Gaceta Média de México*, July 1, 1966. Cars did not only kill urban residents through exhaust. Traffic accidents rose from the 1940s onward and by the 1970s were among the top seven causes of mortality in Mexico. See Hugo Vilchis and Pedro Iturrioz, "Los accidentes de tránsito: una problemática actual," *Salud Pública de México* (1986) 28, no. 5: 537–42.

[135] Carlos Contreras, *El plano regulador del Distrito Federal* (México, D.F.: The Author, 1933).

Figure 4.5 Filling the tank in Mexico City, ca. 1930. Source: Fototeca INAH.

circulated, those roads would again become congested, prompting another round of expansion. In the 1940s, Mexico City began building a series of circuits around the city to ease traffic,[136] but before long these also became clogged. Many similar temporary solutions were implemented during the following decades, consolidating the automobile and its associated network of roads, bridges, passes, and freeways in Mexican cities.

From Hydroelectricity to Thermoelectricity

While oil-powered technologies took Mexico's transportation by storm in the decades following 1920, waterpower slowed oil's takeover of the national power grid. Unlike rivers in Europe and the USA, most of Mexico's waterways were useless for transporting anything but small boats. They were short and usually ran their course over brief distances and steep gradients, all of which made them suitable for electricity generation once hydropower technology became widely available in Mexico after 1900. Coal dominated

---

[136] De la Peña, *El servicio de autobuses en el Distrito Federal*, 140.

electricity generation until the construction of large hydroelectric plants in central Mexico in the early 1900s. It took almost 40 years for another fossil fuel – oil – to surpass water as a power source in Mexico nationwide.

From a regional perspective, things remained more varied. By the 1920s, Mexico was divided into areas dominated by hydroelectricity and thermal power plants, respectively. In thermal-controlled zones, oil supplanted coal with the exception of parts of the north, like coal-producing Coahuila, and northwestern states closer to coal fields than to Gulf oil or with easier access to imported coal. In water-dependent areas, like most of the central highlands and western Mexico, oil-fired plants became the preferred backup option for hydroelectricity.[137]

Hydroelectric plants, like waterwheels, suffered seasonal water scarcity due to Mexico's variations in waterflow and recurrent drought. Constructing enormous dams helped alleviate the challenge – at the expense of peasants displaced from their land – but drought could still have devastating effects on power generation. In 1921, drought ravaged large parts of central Mexico, including the mountainous area featuring the giant Necaxa dam, still the largest in the world.[138] Necaxa was owned and operated by the Canadian-based Mexican Light and Power, by far Mexico's largest electric utility during the first half of the twentieth century. It provided power to Mexico City, the Pachuca and other important mining districts like El Oro, and various towns in central Mexico. The drought was severe, depleting Necaxa's water reservoir and frequently disrupting service. The Mexico City press reported on the situation constantly, often making dire predictions of a future of scarcity and deprivation.[139] One of them bemoaned that electricity shortages made Mexico City a "cursed place."[140] The power company's oil-fired plants worked at full capacity to offset this. Such events consolidated oil-fired thermal power plants over time in regions previously dominated by hydroelectricity. In the case of

---

[137] In areas dominated by hydroelectricity, oil also served as a lubricant. Falling water produced the electricity, but the machinery depended on a film of oil. Moreover, long-distance transmission became possible only with new "oil switches," which kept high-potential transformers in an "oil bath" to prevent them from igniting. See Robert Joseph MacHugh, *Modern Mexico* (New York: Dodd, 1914), 133–5.

[138] Ibid., 192.

[139] "Todo este año, la ciudad estará envuelta en las tinieblas," *El Demócrata*, March 28, 1921, Fondo Expropriación, caja 2354, exp. 64264, AHP; "Mexican Light and Power. The Handicap of Water Shortage," *The Financier*, April 20, 1921, Fondo Expropriación, caja 2356, exp. 64336, AHP; "Dentro de diez días la situación será muy angustiosa. Si no se proporcionan cien tanques de petróleo a la compañía, ésta se verá precisada a suspender los servicios de luz, agua y tranvías," *El Demócrata*, June 8, 1921, Fondo Expropriación, caja 2356, exp. 64336, AHP.

[140] "Primavera triste," *El Excélsior*, April 20 1921, Fondo Expropriación, caja 2354, exp. 64264, AHP.

Table 4.5 *Mexican Light and Power
Company: generating capacity in kW, 1921–60*

Year	Hydroelectric	Thermoelectric
1921	174,950	18,300
1925	177,760	18,000
1930	210,337	36,826
1935	210,337	36,826
1940	223,650	32,240
1945	223,650	55,000
1950	267,595	110,900
1955	313,195	176,900
1960	313,000	354,000

Source: Annual Reports.

Mexican Light and Power, thermal capacity grew quickly after 1940 and overtook hydroelectricity in the late 1950s (Table 4.5).

Certain trends in Mexico's power industry became clearly identifiable by the late 1920s and early 1930s. Industry, rather than households, drove Mexico's increasing electrification. North of Mexico City, in mining's historic heart, mineral extraction and processing spearheaded this. Old silver mining districts like Real del Monte boomed with the electrification of operations; the district became Mexico's largest producer and a major world producer, representing 11 percent of global supply in 1926. Electricity also boosted mining of nonprecious metals, especially zinc and lead. Mining companies and processing plants became essential clients for electric utilities, consuming vast amounts of power on a stable and long-term basis.[141] While hydroelectricity met much of this surging demand, thermal plants in the arid north rose to the challenge, making mining key to consolidating fossil fuel–fired plants in the region. In the northeast, the oil industry was also rapidly electrifying its own operations while supplying electric utilities with oil, including Mexico's largest oil-fired thermal plant in Tampico. Meanwhile, central and western Mexico's electrification piggybacked off mining and textile industries, the latter dominating states like Puebla, parts of Veracruz, and Jalisco. Over 75 percent of this power came from hydroelectric plants.[142]

---

[141] José Herrera y Lasso and Luis N. Morones, *La fuerza motriz en México* (México: Secretaría de Industria, Comercio y Trabajo, 1927), 103–13.

[142] Ibid., 133–5. Mining and textiles consumed 39 percent of all electricity in 1931. See Comisión Nacional de Irrigación, *La industria eléctrica en México: estudios estadísticos preliminares* (México: Editorial Cultura, 1931), 17.

A second trend was the growing complexity of Mexico's power grid and the federal government's transformation into the ultimate arbiter of the country's electrification process. Originally, states and municipalities granted concessions for power generation. As power lines crossed state lines and grids became more intricate, the federal government took over. Power generation oversight and regulation and use of electricity regardless of energy source became the purview of the national government in 1926 under a new national electric code.[143] Federal control over power generation mattered; the Mexican government increasingly turned to oil-fired thermal plants to solve power shortages, particularly those caused by recurrent drought.[144]

Few places witnessed oil-generated electricity become so important and so clearly serve the interests of big industrial firms more than Monterrey.[145] With a population of almost 140,000 around 1930, Monterrey was Mexico's second most important industrial hub.[146] Over 250 large industrial establishments, from steelworks to metal refineries, silver and lead smelters, breweries, glassmakers, cotton and textile mills, food processing plants, and cement factories called the city home.[147] Virtually all these manufacturers employed electricity in their productive process, half of which came from the Compañía de Tranvías, Luz y Fuerza Motriz, which switched from coal to fuel oil and natural gas.[148] Industrial firms themselves produced the rest with their own private plants, mostly burning either oil or coal. The power company depended heavily on industrial consumption, since only two customers – the mighty Cementos Monterrey and Vidriera Monterrery, Mexico's largest glassmaker – absorbed over a quarter of total generation. The company charged lower rates the more power a customer used, clearly favoring large, industrial consumers.[149] This policy also pushed industrial firms to evolve economies

---

[143] Herrera y Lasso and Morones, *La fuerza motriz en México*, 173–6. The new code completed a process begun when the Constitution of 1917 declared all water courses and bodies to be national property, effectively turning hydroelectricity into a federal concession.

[144] Emilio Rodríguez Mata, *Generación y distribución de energía eléctrica en México, período 1939–1949* (México, D. F.: Banco de México, 1952), 36.

[145] "Egresos de los departamentos de luz, fuerza y calefacción de la Cía. de Tranvías, Luz y Fuerza Motriz de Monterrey, S.A." (1933), Energía eléctrica, caja 7, exp. 1, AENL.

[146] "Población del estado por municipio y sexo" (1930), Correspondencia de alcaldes, estadística, Monterrey.1930.77 FSII, AENL. The first was Mexico City.

[147] Barry Dibble, "Uso de energía en Monterrey, N.L. y mercado probable para la energía hidroeléctrica del proyecto de Don Martín" (1928), caja 512, exp. 4838, AHA.

[148] Ibid. Coal was slightly cheaper than oil in Monterrey, but as Dibble put it, "the expense of handling it places it at a disadvantage with oil."

[149] Ibid. Thirty-six percent of the city's power company customers were large industries in 1928.

of scale (more consumption proved less expensive). Oil-generated electricity rewarded industrial growth, which demanded more electricity, and so on. One of the ways this growth happened was by allowing electrified factories to operate 24 hours a day year-round, something that would have been virtually impossible to achieve using water or animal muscle.

After reaching its historic peak nationally around 1934 with 64 percent of total capacity, hydroelectricity began losing share to thermal. Three years later, it sat around 59 percent, where it remained for a few years.[150] The trend towards fossil fuel–generated electricity received a major boost with the expansion of Mexico' pipeline network. The earlier export-oriented bent of Mexico's oil industry meant that for years, most pipelines were located in the Gulf and connected oil fields with ports rather than inland cities and towns. Railroad car tanks transported oil for thermal power plants to the interior, making the cost of generating electricity higher than for hydroelectric plants.[151] With the development of a pipeline network and refining capacity in the interior in the 1930s and 1940s, power generation began shifting to oil as the main energy source.[152]

Common people sometimes greeted expanding oil infrastructure with outright hostility. Especially unwelcome were oil refineries like that in Azcapotzalco, north of Mexico City, which connected to Tampico's oil fields through a new pipeline and distributed oil to all of central Mexico. Shortly after its construction, local inhabitants protested against the "bad odors" (*malos olores*) that arose nightly in the area. They initially suspected water shortage in the sewage system, but it became clear that hydrogen

---

[150] Rolfo Ortega, "Aspecto general del problema en la industria eléctrica en el país," *Revista Industrial*, June 1934. Secretaría de la Economía Nacional/Dirección General de Estadística, "Catálogo de empresas y plantas generadoras de energía eléctrica" (1937), Fondo Expropriación, caja 3808, exp. 91739, AHP.

[151] Ernesto Galarza, *La industria eléctrica en México* (México, D. F.: Fondo de Cultura Económica, 1941), 49–51.

[152] A watershed was the completion of a direct 490-km pipeline connecting Tampico's oil fields and Mexico City's Azcapotzalco refinery in 1932. See "El Águila, S.A., Cía. Mexicana de Petróleo. Tanques de operación en Azcapotzalco" (1933), Secretaría de Industria, Comercio y Trabajo, Departamento del Petróleo, caja 1127, exps. 1, 2, 3, 6, 8, AGN. The Atzcapotzalco refinery distilled 11,000 barrels per day (bpd), representing 10.7 percent of Mexico's installed capacity. By 1950, Atzcapotzalco refined 29 percent of the country's oil, making it Mexico's second largest refinery. Another 155-km pipeline connected San Pedro Roma, Tamaulipas, and Monterrey in 1936. By then, a pipeline connected Mexico's two most important industrial centers to oil. By 1940, 1,509 km of pipeline connected production and consumption sites across Mexico. By 1970, there were 10,574 km of pipelines. Like the earlier railroad boom, the years between 1930 and 1970 saw the consolidation of a system of pipelines connecting much of the country to oil. By 1970, 83.6 percent of all oil was distributed to different parts of the country by pipelines. See Gustavo Garza, *El proceso de industrialización en la ciudad de México, 1821–1970* (México, D. F.: El Colegio de México, 1985), 390–402.

sulfide and carbon disulfide in fumes emitted by the oil refinery (property of El Águila) were to blame. The pestilence, described as smelling like "firecrackers" and "rotten eggs," afflicted entire neighborhoods, largely working-class. Resident and chemist Francisco Escamilla Arce filed a complaint with the Department of Public Health (*Salubridad Pública*) suggesting that El Águila burn the gases instead of simply releasing them into the atmosphere. The agency ignored Escamilla, despite possessing the power to shut down industries that threatened people's health. Confronted with official indifference, Escamilla moved to another part of the city, while the neighbors organized a mass protest against El Águila and its refinery, all to no avail.[153]

Two developments marked the mid-century. First, Mexico had enormously expanded its electricity-generating capacity, from about 390,000 kW in 1926 to 1,400,000 kW in 1951, an almost 260 percent increase.[154] Expansion was strategic: providing access to electricity became a way of cementing political support for the postrevolutionary regime.[155] Second, such growth resulted from new, mostly oil-fired thermal power plants (along with some natural gas and coal plants). These now produced half of Mexico's electricity (Figure 4.6).[156] The country's increasing

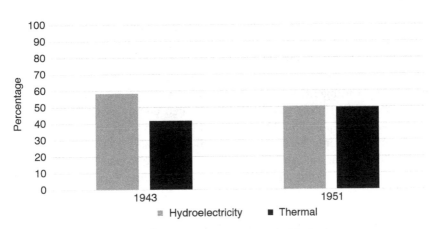

Figure 4.6 Percentage of power-generating capacity in Mexico by energy source. Adapted from Lara Beautell, *La industria de energía eléctrica*, 51.

[153] "Una calamidad para los vecinos de Atzcapotzalco" (1933), Caja 4521, exp. 105326, AHP.
[154] Cristóbal Lara Beautell, *La industria de energía eléctrica* (México: Fondo de Cultura Económica, 1953), 42.
[155] "Asuntos varios" (1935), Fondo Lázaro Cárdenas, caja 562, exp. 502.1, AGN.
[156] Mata, *Generación y distribución de energía eléctrica en México*.

electrification, especially in its cities, had important ramifications. For one, electric systems became essential for urban growth. A city of millions covering an area of hundreds of square kilometers could hardly operate with aqueducts. Modern water systems depended on electric pumps. Electricity removed key obstacles to modern urban growth.[157] Increasingly, this flow of electricity depended on the flow of oil.

Conclusion

From a national perspective, Mexico's transition to oil happened in three phases. Mexican oil started out as kerosene lighting and an industrial lubricant. From the 1860s to the late nineteenth century, these two oil-distilled products became staple commodities across Mexico. Households, cities, and factories adopted kerosene as their preferred illuminant, displacing time-honored practices like using turpentine. Oil-based lubricants also penetrated Mexican industrial establishments, railway lines, and agricultural production during this period. A second phase emerged between 1901 and 1921 with a dramatic shift in Mexico's status as a net importer of oil products to the world's second largest oil producer. Crucially, petroleum also made inroads in manufacturing, modern transportation, and electricity generation, especially in Mexico's main industrializing and urban regions. A third and final phase, from the early 1920s to the mid-century, marked the consolidation of an oil-powered nation.

From a local perspective of individual users, Mexico's oil transition was a messier, contingent, and less linear process. In places like Monterrey, many industries shifted to oil for most of their energy by the 1920s. Even large coal consumers like the Fundidora Monterrey steelworks embraced oil, leaving coal only for its use as coke in furnaces.[158] The firm consumed such an enormous amount of oil annually – up to 480,000 barrels[159] – that it even tried supplying part of its own consumption (unsuccessfully).[160] Fundidora adopted oil believing it met three critical requirements: reliability, low cost on a long-term basis, and abundance. But shortly after making the switch, company's executives began expressing doubts about the size of

---

[157] Galarza, *La industria eléctrica en México*, 17.
[158] Compañía Fundidora, *Informe Anual* (Monterrey, N.L., 1922–8).
[159] Fundidora Monterrey, "Contrato de compraventa de petróleo combustible" (October 20, 1928), Contratos, expediente 108, Compañía Mexicana de Petróleo El Águila, S.A., AHFM.
[160] "Cía. Fundidora de Fierro y Acero de Monterrey, S.A. Concesión de derechos para explorar y explotar petróleo en las haciendas de El Álamo y Encinas, Coahuila" (1926), Departamento del Petróleo, caja 143, exp. 1, AGN.

Mexico's oil reserves and frustration over price swings attributed to excessive speculation. As such, Fundidora's energy mix included oil, natural gas, and coal, whose individual shares in the company's energy budget rose or declined with the times. Other Monterrey industrialists occasionally returned to coal and even briefly to fuelwood or sought to increase natural gas consumption between the 1920s and 1940s during periods of particularly unstable oil prices, among other reasons.[161]

Sometimes, these energy choices were shaped by decisions beyond any individual company's control, including international politics. Some Monterrey firms had been purchasing natural gas from a Mexican company since 1934. Service, however, was frequently unreliable, causing costly stoppages in certain key productive processes, which meant that overall consumption remained limited. Monterrey industrialists tried buying natural gas from a Texas-based company, but the Railroad Commission of Texas opposed the deal, claiming it was "inimical to the interests of the state to export its natural resources." Then, in 1945, the US Department of State and Department of Commerce backed the sale to Monterrey's industries as part of their Good Neighbor Policy, declaring that Monterrey should receive the fuel "as an act of equity and reciprocity for the services that Mexico had provided during the war, when the country had put its natural resources at the disposal of the Allies without consideration over their diminution."[162] In this sense, the oil transition never followed a linear process of eliminating previous fuels, like coal, or permanently privileging oil over other fossil fuels, like natural gas. Rather, the transition negotiated a shifting energy landscape shaped by political, technological, and economic changes.

Mexico's oil transition was also incomplete. By mid-century, oil had failed to replace charcoal and wood, domestic fuels with a long history in Mexico, in households. National policies had promoted oil first and foremost as an industrial and transportation fuel. But when state agencies sought to foster oil consumption in Mexican households, consumer preferences and habits resisted. In the late 1920s, the Secretary of Industry, Commerce, and Labor contacted El Águila about the possibility of using gasoil for cooking and heating, looking to make it "a popular fuel."[163] The oil company replied that they, and Pierce Oil, had promoted gasoil among Mexican households without much success. "The poor classes," El Águila

---

[161] "Use of Power in Monterrey, N.L., and Probable Market for Hydroelectric Energy from Don Martín Project" (1928), Energía eléctrica, caja 4, exp. 3, AENL.
[162] Compañía Fundidora, *Informe anual* (Monterrey, N.L., 1944–6).
[163] "Use of Gasoil as Fuel for Domestic Use" (1929), caja 3901, exp. 93859, AHP.

argued, "can burn charcoal or wood without the need of costly devices."
This suggests that part of consumer reluctance to adopt new fuels at home
was rooted in a sense of autonomy and control over the energy sources they
depended on. The poor retained far more independence by burning wood
to cook their meals or heat their homes, given how simple wood-fired
cooking and heating was to implement and repair in-house. Using oil, on
the contrary, implied relying on an energy source that came from far away
and required buying expensive, imported, and patented technology. This
sense of autonomy had also animated the radical popular insurgency in the
central highlands during the Mexican Revolution, which pitted many
communities against capitalist industrial and agricultural development
based on labor-saving mechanization (increasingly fueled by oil) and the
privatization of land, forests, and water.

Despite these obstacles, oil had clear advantages as an energy source: its
liquid nature, high energy density, relatively cheap cost, and great abundance made it very appealing to industries, railroads, power companies,
and, obviously, motor-vehicle owners. For large firms, the fact that oil
needed only a few workers to be transported, dispatched, and consumed
made it more favorable than coal, which required a large workforce that
could leverage their influence when negotiating better working conditions.
The postrevolutionary state also paved the way for the oil transition. The
national government's decision to invest millions of pesos into building oil
infrastructure, including pipelines, oil-powered thermal plants, and a road
system for oil-based technologies like motor vehicles, was instrumental to
making oil widely available in Mexico. In turn, postrevolutionary governments relied on oil revenues to fund the state and its program of rapid
import–substitution–industrialization, which began in earnest in the
1940s. The political legitimacy of Mexico's new regime and the country's
shift to oil as the basis of its economy and society thus became intimately
linked. Initially pitched as a key industrial energy source, oil's influence
extended over time into every facet of Mexican society.

By 1950, Mexico was consuming about 77 percent of its oil production –
almost 56 million barrels. Since the late 1930s, Mexico had been one of the
world's largest oil consumers, behind only the USA, Russia, England,
France, Canada, Germany, Japan, and Argentina.[164] Domestic consumption in number of barrels had nearly doubled since the expropriation of the

---

[164] José Sotero Noriega, *Influencia de los hidrocarburos en la industrialización de México* (Banco de
México, 1944), 197. The USA was by far the largest consumer in the world at 1 billion barrels
annually.

Mexican oil industry in 1938, when the country consumed over 70 percent of total production. The influx of oil represented a massive energy boon for Mexico. Mexico would have needed to harvest the annual yield of over 38,000 km² of forest – a forest as large as the entire state of Yucatan – to match the energy it consumed as oil in 1950.[165] At that rate, the country would have exhausted all of its forests in less than a decade. Mexico now depended on an underground sea of energy.[166] Oil had become Mexico's lifeblood.

---

[165] Conversion of oil consumption into forest area in 1950: 55,921,000 barrels = 7,660,411 metric tons of oil = 22,981,233 metric tons of wood (at 1 ton of oil per 3 tons of fuelwood) = 38,302 km² (assuming 600 metric tons of wood per km²). For conversion factors, see FAO, "Conversion Factors and Energy Equivalents," accessed July 26, 2019, www.unece.org/forests/mis/energy/guide.html.

[166] Sieferle described Europe's coal deposits as a "subterranean forest." Sieferle, *The Subterranean Forest*.

CHAPTER 5

1950s: Fossil-Fueled Society

> Anyone who believes exponential growth can go on forever in a finite world is either a madman or an economist.
>
> attributed to Kenneth Boulding

By the mid-twentieth century, fossil fuels powered virtually every aspect of Mexican society. Fossil energy, especially oil and natural gas, fueled most sectors of the economy. Transport systems relied on fossil energy. Motor vehicles with internal combustion engines drove down fossil fuel–derived roads. Ships depended entirely on fuel oil. Kerosene-propelled aircrafts carried a growing number of passengers. Industrial manufacturing burned fossil fuels to produce heat, carry out mechanical work, and distribute goods across the country. Over half of the country's electricity came from thermal power plants burning fossil energy. Additionally, the Mexican food system was undergoing a series of dramatic changes, later known as the Green Revolution, using fossil-fueled agricultural machinery, electricity-powered irrigation, and oil fuel and feedstock for chemical fertilizer and other synthetic inputs.

The direct and indirect effects of this new energy regime proved nothing short of revolutionary. Cars and roads reshaped Mexico's culture, class and gender divisions, and the way people experienced the nation's territory and environments. Mexican cities were experiencing a period of accelerated physical and demographic growth, in part powered by fossil energy. The country was rapidly transitioning from rural to urban and from agrarian to industrial. Mexico's population achieved one of the highest rates of growth worldwide, along with unprecedented rates of economic growth in the nation's history. Mexico's fossil fuel energy revolution supported all these changes to various degrees. The effects of these changes rippled throughout the twentieth century and continue to impact Mexico today.

While many in Mexico at the time celebrated these profound shifts as "progress," others began to raise concerns about less welcome developments. Observers criticized increasing economic and cultural disparity between cities like Mexico City and Monterrey and the rest of Mexico – as well as between the haves and the have-nots. Also troublesome was the growing wealth gap between a rapidly industrializing north and an agrarian south, a process exacerbated by the differing access these regions had to fossil fuels. Those areas in the country that transitioned more fully to fossil fuels were becoming wealthier, aggravating the relative poverty of those largely stuck in the old solar energy regime, who continued relying on customary energy sources, like water, wood, or muscle. Mexico's fossil-fueled regions were leaping forward and leaving others behind. People also began expressing anxiety over air pollution, especially in Mexico City, and rapid environmental damage caused by fossil-fueled technologies, principally deforestation. But those voices remained a minority among the chorus of optimism and enthusiasm for the new society emerging on the foundation of fossil fuels.

"The Lifeblood of Mexico's Economy"

On a Sunday morning, July 30, 1950, Mexico's president Miguel Alemán inaugurated the Salamanca oil refinery.[1] Accompanied by Pemex director Antonio Bermúdez, Guanajuato's state governor, and an entourage of locals, government officials, and reporters, Alemán toured the refinery for over 2 hours. He inspected the laboratory that determined octane ratings[2] of various fuels, the power plant with diesel-powered generators, and the Dubbs thermal cracking plant that separated crude oil into an endless array of fuels and products, among other facilities. Pictures were taken, hands were shaken, and lofty words were exchanged about a prosperous, oil-soaked future. The visit concluded over 2 years of building at 134 million pesos (almost 11 million dollars), paid entirely by Pemex. A journalist wrote that a "message of progress and economic liberation" marked the occasion. Echoing official narratives, he claimed that the new refinery represented an "industrial, scientific, and economic" revolution. "Oil," he wrote, "is the lifeblood of Mexico's economy."[3]

The enormous installation sat in the heart of the old agrarian and mining Bajío region, north of Mexico City. Connected by a 440-kilometer-long pipeline to the Poza Rica oil field in Veracruz, the

---

[1] Felipe Morales, "Un potencial de riqueza para todo el país," *Mañana*, August 12, 1950.
[2] A measure of their resistance to detonation.
[3] Morales, "Un potencial de riqueza para todo el país."

Salamanca refinery could process 30,000 barrels of oil daily. Its main objective was to ensure supplies of oil and oil derivatives to north-central Mexico, from Querétaro to San Luís Potosí, as well as Jalisco and Michoacán in western Mexico. The Salamanca refinery illustrates both the centrality oil had already achieved in Mexico and national and state government commitment to expanding its role further.

It also highlights the enormous complexity and interdependence of Mexico's fossil fuel–based energy system. Under the solar energy regime, energy systems largely consisted of autonomous entities deriving energy from local or regional sources (a nearby forest for wood or a hacienda for animal power). By the mid-twentieth century, a colossal and highly sophisticated infrastructure was required to extract and transport fossil fuels over hundreds of kilometers to refining plants for final processing. The boundaries of the energy system had vastly expanded, integrating huge territories under a growing network through which fossil energy flowed and was delivered to consumers (Figure 5.1).[4]

Since the mid-1920s, the share of oil and natural gas in Mexico's energy budget had grown rapidly. By 1955, these two fossil fuels represented over 75 percent of the country's gross energy consumption, up from about 34 percent in 1925 (Figure 5.2).[5] The vast majority of this energy came from oil, though natural gas was making inroads in both industry and households. Meanwhile, coal declined from about a quarter of overall energy consumption in 1925 to a mere 5 percent by 1955. Coal was now almost exclusively used in the form of coke in the steel and iron industry, having lost its position as a dominant fuel for railroads and electricity and steam generation. Even wood and charcoal, the sole providers of heat energy for millennia and a major source of mechanical energy for nineteenth-century steam engines and locomotives, became marginal. In 1955, forests supplied around 6 percent of Mexico's energy, although this figure likely underestimates wood consumption at the time, given it only includes commercial transactions (many families in rural areas harvested their own supply from local forests).

[4] Vaclav Smil, *Energy Transitions: History, Requirements, Prospects* (Santa Barbara: Praeger, 2010), 13. The emergence of a separate "energy" system was itself a historical process indicating the predominant role that inanimate, measurable energy sources acquired. An "energy sector" based on, say, muscle power is hardly conceivable. See Jean-Claude Debeir, Jean-Paul Deléage, and Daniel Hémery, *In the Servitude of Power: Energy and Civilisation through the Ages* (London: Zed Books, 1991), chapter 5.
[5] Gross energy consumption is all energy available at the moment that is incorporated into the economy, including energy to produce, transform, and transport energy itself to consumers. This distinguishes it from net energy consumption, which refers to all energy sources available minus that used for production, transformation, and distribution.

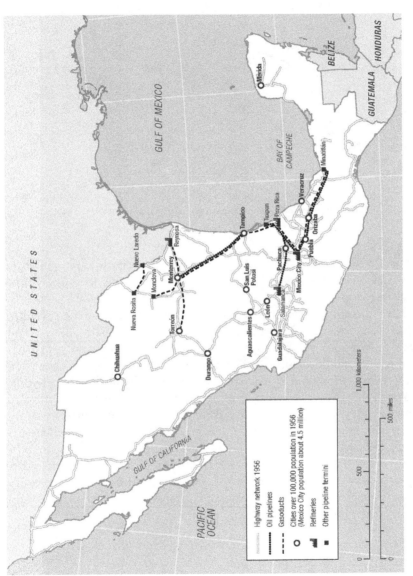

Figure 5.1 Fossil fuel infrastructure in Mexico, 1956.

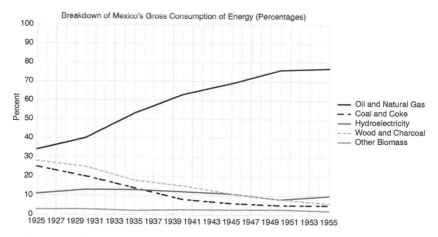

Figure 5.2 Mexico's gross consumption of energy, 1925–55. Source: Secretariat of the Economic Commission for Latin America, *Energy in Latin America*, 1957, 155.

Despite the increase in absolute terms of hydroelectricity after 1925, its share of overall energy consumption rose only slightly until the late 1930s before returning in 1955 to the same figure as 30 years earlier, around 10 percent.

How did this energy profile compare with other countries? Within Latin America, total energy consumption of inanimate sources had been growing for years, almost doubling between 1937 and 1954 from 43.8 to 83.9 million tons of oil equivalent.[6] Almost all this expansion came from various types of commercial energy (fossil fuels and hydroelectricity). Latin America's oil consumption nearly quintupled between 1929 and 1954, growing from 9.4 to 45.1 million tons of oil equivalent and from 55 percent to 76 percent of all commercial energy. By 1954, fossil fuels (oil, natural gas, and coal) provided about 60 percent of Latin America's gross energy consumption. Wood and other plant-based fuels came second at 30 percent. In mid-twentieth-century Latin America, two civilizations coexisted side by side: one fossil-fueled, the other wood-powered.

---

[6] Secretariat of the Economic Commission for Latin America, *Energy in Latin America*, Document E/CN.12/384 Rev. 1 (Geneva: United Nations Dept. of Economic and Social Affairs, 1957), 19. Tons of oil equivalent is a unit amounting to the energy produced by burning 1 metric ton of oil. Any amount from a different energy source can be converted into tons of oil equivalent, allowing standardization and comparisons between various sources.

These regional trends, however, masked enormous differences between countries. First, most growth in Latin America's energy consumption accrued to only five nations: Argentina, Brazil, Mexico, Chile, and Colombia. In 1954, these countries represented over 70 percent of the region's total. Brazil topped the list at around 27 percent, followed by Argentina and Mexico (17 percent each). While fossil fuels became increasingly important across Latin America, wide disparities also existed in the contribution they made to different countries' energy makeup (Table 5.1). In Argentina and Mexico, fossil fuels met around 80 percent of energy requirements, although coal represented a slightly higher share in Argentina (7.9 percent) than in Mexico. In Chile and Colombia, coal played a much more relevant role, while fossil fuel consumption was also high (66 and 56 percent, respectively). Brazil was different: fossil fuels provided only 38 percent of the country's energy needs in 1954, while wood and charcoal supplied a whopping 45 percent and hydroelectricity 18 percent, a figure unmatched in the rest of Latin America.[7]

Per capita fossil fuel consumption also evinced considerable differences across Latin America. In 1956, the average Chilean and Argentine citizen consumed almost double the fossil energy of the average Brazilian and Colombian. Mexicans were somewhere in between. When only oil and

Table 5.1 *Latin America: breakdown of gross consumption of energy (percentages), 1954*

	Oil and Natural Gas	Coal	Hydroelectricity	Biomass
Argentina	72	7.9	1	19.1
Brazil	32.4	5.6	17.1	44.9
Chile	32.7	33.3	17.3	16.7
Colombia	37	18.8	11.3	32.9
Mexico	77.1	5.3	8.8	8.8
Latin America	53.8	7.1	9.5	29.6

Adapted from Secretariat of the Economic Commission for Latin America, *Energy in Latin America*, 1957, 106.

---

[7] Warren Dean, *With Broadax and Firebrand: The Destruction of the Brazilian Atlantic Forest* (Berkeley: University of California Press, 1997), 254. Dean emphasizes the importance of wood and charcoal for mid-twentieth-century Brazil, although his estimate is much higher, at 79 percent of all energy used in 1948.

Table 5.2 *Latin America: gross consumption of energy compared with the rest of the world, 1954*

	Total Energy Consumption[a]	Percentage of Global Energy Consumption	Per Capita Consumption[b]
Commercial Energy			
Latin America	59	2.9	345
Western Europe	560	27.7	1,687
USA	945	46.8	5,819
Other	456	22.6	393
Total Energy			
Latin America	84	3.7	491
Western Europe	592	26.2	1,783
USA	968	42.8	5,961
Other	616	27.3	531

[a] Millions of tons of oil equivalent
[b] Kilograms of oil equivalent
Adapted from Secretariat of the Economic Commission for Latin America, *Energy in Latin America*, 1957, 20.

natural gas were considered, Argentina and Mexico were at the top, while most other countries lagged behind.[8]

Compared with the USA and western Europe, Latin America's energy use remained small. As Table 5.2 shows, in 1954 the USA consumed over eleven times more energy, and western Europe around seven times more, than Latin America's mere 3.7 percent of the world's total energy consumption. At 491 kg of oil equivalent, Latin America's per capita consumption represented around one-quarter that of the average western European resident and one-twelfth of a US citizen.[9] Mexico's energy patterns showed a similar relationship with the USA and western Europe. While Mexico and other Latin American economies transitioned to fossil fuels to a degree that paralleled the USA and western Europe, a fossil fuel–based economy was compatible with relatively modest consumption of energy in both absolute and per capita terms.

[8] Secretariat of the Economic Commission for Latin America, 34. The Peronist state funded construction of gas pipelines and heavily promoted urban consumption of natural gas. See Natalia Milanesio, "The Liberating Flame: Natural Gas Production in Peronist Argentina," *Environmental History* 18 (July 2013): 499–522.
[9] The USA was a global outlier regarding energy use.

Dreaming of Industry

In 1935, Ramón Beteta, a high-ranking Cardenista official, delivered a speech on industrialization. "We have dreamt," he said, "of a Mexico of ejidos and small industrial communities, electrified, with sanitation, in which goods will be produced for the purpose of satisfying the needs of the people; in which machinery will be employed to relieve man from heavy toil, and not for so-called overproduction."[10] When Beteta became Minister of Finance for the Miguel Alemán administration (1946–52), this Gandhian-esque dream of small villages and rural industrialization was replaced by a Nehru-style vision of giant dams and large-scale urban industrialization. Beteta, wrote one scholar, typified "the change that has taken place in official economic philosophy since Cárdenas left office."[11]

Mexico, of course, had been industrializing for 100 years. But by the middle of the twentieth century, the process began developing on an unprecedented scale due to a combination of historical contingencies and new international and domestic conditions. Since 1940, the Mexican national government had committed to a pro-industrialization program to substitute the agrarian reform agenda of President Lázaro Cárdenas (1934–40). War conditions and scarcity of industrial imported products facilitated development of the Mexican initiative. Industry, not the *ejido*, would be Mexico's way out. The national government passed two manufacturing laws (in 1941 and 1946) giving large tax concessions to both new industries and industries "necessary" for Mexico's development. The laws also gave the Secretary of the National Economy, which managed economic development, the ability to make concessions on customs duties to facilitate importing industrial machinery and technology. But it was under the administration of Miguel Alemán that industrialization became the government's main objective.[12]

For Alemán, "the entire country clamored for industrialization."[13] Through industrialization, Mexico would achieve economic independence and be safeguarded from the fluctuations of the global economy. Industry would raise wages, since factory employees typically earned better salaries than agricultural workers. Better incomes among the working class would increase consumption, strengthening the domestic market and, in turn,

---

[10] Quoted in Sanford Alexander Mosk, *Industrial Revolution in Mexico* (Berkeley: University of California Press, 1950), 58.

[11] Ibid., 58.   [12] Ibid., 61–5.

[13] The following analysis relies heavily on Blanca Torres, *Hacia la utopía industrial* (México D. F: El Colegio de México, 2006), 25–44.

allowing further industrial development. Alemán and subsequent administrations believed that government support should focus on industries that transformed Mexico's natural resources into essential products like clothing, food processing, housing, and construction. Additionally, the country should promote industries fundamental for Mexico's economic autonomy, including electricity, chemicals, steel, and oil.

The government focused the plan around private capital and assumed a supportive role. Mexico's national government would secure the viability of key industries, but would otherwise leave private capital to create economic growth and advance industrialization, provided this growth benefitted the whole nation, not just private investors.[14] Foreign investment was welcome insofar as it aligned with national interests and aided rather than drove economic growth. That power would remain in Mexican hands.

Corporatist ideas suffused the industrialization agenda. Mexico's political elites believed the country's different classes should collaborate for the nation's benefit. Industrialists should abide by labor laws, while workers should refrain from making excessive demands. Economic growth and "national abundance" should be the goal, not higher worker salaries that could lead to inflation. The state acted as arbiter between industrialists and labor. In spite of their multiple disagreements with the "bourgeois" and capitalist government, in general, both the Mexican labor movement and left-wing intellectuals believed in the need for rapid industrialization.[15] There was also strong consensus among politicians, industrialists, and workers that the state should protect industry through tariffs, credit, and better infrastructure (especially for fast and cheap transportation of goods), and, crucially, by guaranteeing adequate fuel supplies for both industrial development and agriculture. Its job was to create what the Austrian-American historian of Mexico, Frank Tannenbaum, called the "conditions of economic progress."[16]

---

[14] Overall investment grew 7 percent on average from 1950 to 1962. Public investment increased 5.7 percent and private 8.1 percent annually in real terms. Over 90 percent of private investment was domestic. Enrique Cárdenas, *La política económica en México, 1950–1994* (México, D. F.: FCE, 1996), 31–5.

[15] When differences over industrial wealth distribution inspired labor militancy or defiance of policies, the government typically tried coopting labor leadership or violently suppressing the workers' movement. Consider the 1950s railroad labor movement. See José Luís Reyna, "El conflicto ferrocarrilero: de la inmovilidad a la acción," in *Historia de la Revolución Mexicana, período 1952–1960: El afianzamiento de la estabilidad política* (México, D. F.: El Colegio de México, 1978), 157–214.

[16] Frank Tannenbaum, *Mexico: The Struggle for Peace and Bread*, Borzoi Book (New York: Alfred A. Knopf, 1950), 173.

Agriculture's role in this plan was clear. It would provide industry with an abundance of essential raw materials at cheap prices. It would also produce cheap food for the growing urban working class. Crucially, agricultural exports would help finance acquisition of industrial technologies from abroad. There was a clear shift after 1940 from rural land redistribution to an increase in credit, investment in irrigation, and technical assistance, mainly for large landholdings with enough capital. As the national government came to favor a technocratic approach to addressing Mexico's rural and agricultural problems, most investment went to large irrigation projects and production mechanization concentrated in areas with the right conditions to deliver rapid returns on investment.[17] Maximizing production of profitable export crops or cash crops that could be sold domestically became the priority of Mexico's agricultural policy. Accordingly, private, large-scale industries like cotton, sugar cane, and wheat benefitted the most from government largesse, not Mexico's peasants.

In sum, Mexico's national government after 1940 heavily supported infrastructure projects to facilitate industrial and economic growth. Frequently, the state outsourced its public works program to companies in order to stimulate private industry. In those areas deemed critical to Mexico's economy, the state itself became the main capitalist and investor. It also adopted a series of policies protecting domestic industry against foreign competition, made importing industrial technology accessible to Mexican firms, and adopted an agricultural policy that ensured cheap food for urban workers, inexpensive and abundant raw materials for domestic industries, and sufficient export crops to purchase industrial machinery and capital goods abroad.

These policies worked for some time, some metrics, and some people. Between 1940 and 1970, Mexico's GDP grew at one of the highest rates in the world[18] (Table 5.3). Industry and the service sector became cornerstones of the economy (Table 5.4). By the late 1960s, Mexico – along with Argentina and Brazil, which also favored domestic manufacturing through tariffs, state investment, and government-private sector alliances – boasted manufacturing shares in GDP similar to those of rich countries like the USA and western European nations. Moreover, there was a shift from light

---

[17] On irrigation policy, see Mikael D. Wolfe, *Watering the Revolution: An Environmental and Technological History of Agrarian Reform in Mexico* (Durham: Duke University Press, 2017), chapter 5.

[18] Between 1950 and 1962, Mexico's GDP grew on average 6.2 percent annually, while GDP per capita grew at 3 percent, indicating commercial output outpaced an increase in the population's material welfare. See Cárdenas, *La política económica en México, 1950–1994*, 24–6.

Table 5.3 *Mexico's
GDP, 1895–1970
in millions of pesos
(1970 prices)*

1895	30,837
1900	34,414
1905	43,352
1910	47,054
1921	50,658
1925	56,024
1930	51,473
1935	57,752
1940	69,941
1945	93,779
1950	124,779
1955	167,270
1960	225,448
1965	318,030
1970	444,271

Source: INEGI,
*Estadísticas históricas de
México*, vol. 1, 1994,
401–2.

Table 5.4 *Contribution to Mexico's GDP by economic sector in millions
of pesos, 1945–70 (1970 prices)*

	GDP (Millions of Pesos)	Agriculture[a]	Industry[b]	Services[c]
1945	93,779	11,211	15,746	26,735
1950	124,779	15,968	27,275	32,941
1955	167,270	20,841	37,720	45,747
1960	225,448	23,970	54,553	64,238
1965	318,030	30,222	80,876	92,488
1970	444,271	34,535	121,798	128,628

[a] Includes ranching, forestry, and fishing
[b] Includes mining, oil and coal, electricity, construction, manufacturing, and food
processing
[c] Includes commerce, transportation, communications, government, and tourism
Adapted from INEGI, *Estadísticas históricas de México*, vol. 1, 1990, 320–37.

industry and consumer goods to heavy industry and chemicals. These countries had become "semi-industrialized."[19]

In Mexico, this rapid economic growth and industrialization came to be known as the "economic miracle." While it was perhaps miraculous for some – privileged workers, a growing middle class, and the wealthy – large segments of Mexico's population faced growing precariousness and insecure lives. Income inequality persisted and worsened. Mexico's "postwar carbon democracy" was friendly to capitalist industrialization but unresponsive and sometimes hostile to the needs of the poor and social distribution of wealth.[20] The "miracle" was also inefficient and costly. Starting in the 1940s, Mexico's government implemented a variety of industry protections. As industries consolidated power, they pressured the government to maintain those safeguards at the expense of other sectors. In the long term, most industries never managed to export their products and only survived in a heavily protected domestic market.[21]

Mexican exports came to be dominated by a handful of agricultural products: cotton, coffee, and sugar. Moreover, industry became import-intensive, especially with intermediate and capital goods.[22] Mexico and other Latin American countries were stuck with exporting agricultural products at unstable prices in the global market and importing industrial technology whose prices tended to stabilize or increase, all to further domestic industrialization.

Despite these and other shortcomings, Mexico's *trente glorieuses* were revolutionary. The decades between 1940 and 1970 witnessed Mexico's transformation into a predominantly urban and industrial country; population growth of epic proportions; agriculture's Green Revolution; the electrification of daily life; mass production of motor vehicles and road transport; and accelerated alteration of the country's ecosystems. Fossil fuels powered much of these processes.[23] Fossil energy underwrote the "positive externalities," in the parlance of economists, created by publicly and privately funded infrastructure. Investment in roads, power plants, manufacturing capacity, and irrigation created the conditions for

[19] Victor Bulmer-Thomas, *The Economic History of Latin America since Independence* (New York: Cambridge University Press, 2014), 303.

[20] Matthew Vitz, "'To Save the Forests': Power, Narrative, and Environment in Mexico City's Cooking Fuel Transition," *Mexican Studies/Estudios Mexicanos* 31, no. 1 (2015): 125–55.

[21] Bulmer-Thomas, *The Economic History of Latin America since Independence*, 303–4, 336, 344.

[22] Ibid., 304–5. Mexico was able to partially offset domestic industry's inability to export with tourism.

[23] For analysis of the link between energy and modern economic growth, see David Stern and Astrid Kander, "The Role of Energy in the Industrial Revolution and Modern Economic Growth," *The Energy Journal*, 33, no. 3 (2012): 125–52.

wholesale economic growth.[24] All of these endeavors required abundant, cheap energy. Once in place, this infrastructure required vast amounts of fossil fuels to maintain and function, reinforcing the economy's reliance on fossil energy. Without fossil fuels, Mexico's "miracle" (as well as its misfortunes) would not have occurred.

Urban Nation

Mexico's newfound fossil fuel dependence set off various economic, social, and environmental changes. Mexico became a predominantly urban country. Fossil energy powered several changes that sent Mexico's people flocking to cities until urbanites made up 50 percent of the country's population around 1960, for the first time in Mexican history (Figure 5.3).[25] Fossil energy fueled transportation systems that moved urban residents across progressively longer distances. It also powered the urban growth and suburbanization that characterized Mexican cities after 1940. Thermal plants supplied

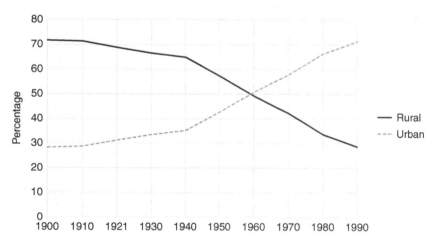

Figure 5.3 Percentage of rural and urban population in Mexico, 1900–90.
Source: INEGI, *Estadísticas históricas de México*, vol. 1, 1994, 41–2.

[24] Cárdenas, *La política económica en México, 1950–1994*, 35–7.
[25] By comparison, in 1956, Latin America as a whole was 65 percent rural and 35 percent urban. Buenos Aires was the largest Latin American city, with 5,744,000 people, followed by Mexico City (4,460,000), Sao Paulo (3,069,000), and Rio (2,895,700 people). See *Agricultural Geography of Latin America*, 1958, 25–30.

over half the electricity used across economic sectors, from factories to apartment buildings and movie theaters. In the meantime, cheap and abundant oil and natural gas concentrated industries in urban areas. Industry employed a growing number of the country's labor force, while Mexico's rural workforce began to decline, partially due to agriculture's mechanization. As the Green Revolution progressed, rural inhabitants migrated *en masse* to Mexico's cities or emigrated to the USA as cheap agricultural laborers. Fossil fuels also powered vehicles and built roads that transported vast quantities of food and raw materials from rural areas to cities. Mexico's cities soon resembled giant metabolic systems sucking ever-greater amounts of energy and materials from ever-expanding rural hinterlands and expelling ever-growing waste.

The numbers convey explosive urbanization during these decades. While Mexican cities grew at a considerable rate of over 1 percent in the twentieth century's first four decades, between 1940 and 1970 Mexico experienced its highest rate of urbanization in the whole century, and almost certainly in its urban history. At almost 3 percent per year on average, expansion was relentless, mostly chaotic, and deeply impactful. Between 1940 and 1970, about 630,000 people moved to Mexico's cities annually – 19 million people over three decades. Twenty-nine new cities emerged in the 1940s alone. In 1950, Mexico claimed a total of 84 urban areas; a decade later, there were 124, and by 1970, 174.[26] In a mere two decades, the number of Mexican cities had more than doubled.

Equally remarkable, the country underwent a population explosion that more than tripled its numbers between 1940 and 1980, from 20 million to almost 70 million. Energy, production, and consumption needs rose correspondingly – a reversal of the catastrophic demographic collapse of the sixteenth century.[27] Much of this growth resulted from better sanitation infrastructure, access to potable water, vaccination campaigns, and the introduction of antibiotics, organized and funded by state health programs.[28] The federal government considered population growth critical for national development and actively promoted it from the 1930s onward. Only in the 1970s did state concerns about overpopulation translate into

---

[26] Gustavo Garza, *La urbanización de México en el siglo XX* (México, D. F.: El Colegio de México, 2003), chapter 3.

[27] I thank John Tutino for this insight.

[28] See Tutino, *The Mexican Heartland: How Communities Shaped Capitalism, a Nation, and World History, 1500–2000* (Princeton: Princeton University Press), 339–48; María Eulalia Mendoza and Eugenia Tapia, "Situación demográfica de México 1910–2010," in CONAPO, *La situación demográfica de México* (México, D. F.: CONAPO, 2010), 11–20.

national policies intent on reducing growth, including the creation of a national population agency.[29] Mass-produced contraceptives like the pill – first developed in Mexico with the knowledge, expertise, and labor of indigenous rural gatherers of barbasco, a wild yam – became available in Mexico, especially in urban areas.[30] High birth rates, lower infant mortality, rural mechanization and displacement caused by the Green Revolution, and few employment opportunities combined to ensure the continuous exodus of rural families into cities.

As cities grew, fossil fuel infrastructure expanded.[31] Oil pipeline construction started in the 1940s during the war as part of an emergency plan to ensure fuel availability. One of the first, finished in 1943, connected the Azcapotzalco refinery (north of Mexico City) to the Nonoalco power plant downtown. Owned by the local power company, Nonoalco was in the process of increasing its generating capacity. In the 1950s, the pace of building urban pipelines accelerated. The pipeline network erected in Mexico City grew particularly fast, in part because Pemex and various federal and local agencies (the Secretaría de la Economía Nacional and the Departamento del Distrito Federal) hastily approved construction permits. Sometimes, pipelines were laid and put into service without authorization and barely any planning. Oil storage sites, many privately owned, also sprang up in different parts of the city without official approval. Since distributing fuel oil was considered a "public service" under article 15 of the Ley del Petróleo, building distribution infrastructure could be easily expedited.[32]

Fossil energy and fossil fuel-based infrastructure enabled rapid urban growth everywhere, but not all cities developed the same economic base. Location influenced what activities dominated. Consider industrial production. By 1970, a third of all Mexican cities had a manufacturing base. This was particularly true of Mexico City, Monterrey, Guadalajara, and cities like León in the Bajío region. In other cities, especially those located along the US border, commerce played a more important role. As roads connected agricultural and mining regions with border towns, these areas

---

[29] "Política demográfica y desarrollo nacional," *El Informador*, September 7, 1977.
[30] Gabriela Soto Laveaga, *Jungle Laboratories: Mexican Peasants, National Projects, and the Making of the Pill* (Durham: Duke University Press, 2009).
[31] "Obras de ampliación en Poza Rica y refinería de Azcapotzalco" (1951–1955), Departamento del Petróleo, caja 933, exp. 4, AGN; "Construcción de la nueva planta de Lechería" (1952), Departamento del Petróleo, caja 18, exp. 1, AGN.
[32] "Oleoducto de la refinería 18 de Marzo a la planta de distrinbución de combustible" (1952), Departamento del Petróleo, caja 933, exp. 4, AGN; "Oleoducto para diesel desde la refinería 18 de Marzo a la distribuidora México" (1952), Departamento del Petróleo, caja 1132, exp. 2, AGN.

became key crossing and shipping points for export commodities headed to US markets. These included Tijuana (which grew at an incredible average rate of 13.4 percent annually between 1940 and 1970), Mexicali (13 percent), and Ciudad Juárez (8.1 percent). Other urban areas like Ciudad Obregón and Culiacán in the northwest along with Orizaba in Veracruz and Mérida in the Yucatan peninsula became hubs for commercial agriculture increasingly reliant on fossil energy.[33]

Whatever their niche, cities across Mexico came to shape progressively larger territories, effectively growing their hinterlands. With rapid road development, including a highway system after 1940 (Table 5.5), roads made it possible for items manufactured in Mexico City or Monterrey to easily reach distant consumers in remote areas. In turn, proliferation of roads and trucks made it economical for cities to consume formerly inaccessible resources. Mexico City, for example, could now burn charcoal and wood from the forests of San Luís Potosí and Tamaulipas, some 500–700 km away.[34] Curiously, the new fossil-fueled transportation system enabled urbanites to consume old energy sources like wood and charcoal. This was particularly true of the urban poor, some of whom

Table 5.5 *Mexico's road system, 1930–60*

Year	Total Length in km
1930	1,426
1935	5,237
1940	9,929
1945	17,404
1950	22,455
1955	32,224
1960	44,892
1965	61,252
1970	71,520
1975	186,218

Source: INEGI, *Estadísticas históricas de México*, vol. 2, 1994, 692.

[33] Gustavo Garza, "Evolución de las ciudades mexicanas en el siglo XX," *Notas. Revista de Información y Análisis*, no. 19 (2002): 7–16.
[34] "La Ciudad de México devora diariamente un bosque," *El Universal*, April 10, 1952.

continued cooking with a charcoal fire. At the same time, another technology came along to undermine wood-based cooking. Pemex, the national oil company, successfully marketed oil and gas for fossil-fueled stoves, which became common in urban areas in the 1950s.[35]

Road expansion also transformed city hinterlands more subtly. When a toll highway (one of the first in Mexico) was completed between Cuernavaca and Mexico City in 1949, real estate and land speculation in Cuernavaca boomed. Many wealthy Mexico City residents moved or bought a second home, while others commuted daily, which profoundly altered the local economy. Elsewhere, new roads enabled former towns to become satellites of central urban areas. For example, Tlalnepantla, a town of pre-Columbian origin in the Valley of Mexico, became an industrial suburb of Mexico City around the mid-twentieth century.[36]

While heightened urban–rural connectivity allowed cities to influence and control larger territories and their resources, it also facilitated mass migration to urban areas. Once again, Mexico City found itself at the center of the phenomenon. The city's population rose from 1.8 million in 1940 to 8.5 million in 1970, an astonishing 372 percent growth. During that time, over four million people abandoned their homes in the countryside to start anew in the capital. New media like radio, TV, and film, which expanded with rural electrification, enticed many to migrate to cities with messages that "evoked an advanced, remunerative, and exciting way of life as an alternative to the static poverty of the countryside." In Mexico City, this perception was not entirely mistaken. By 1960, the average Mexico City family income exceeded the national average by 185 percent.[37] But few migrants found formal employment in the city, thus swelling the ranks of the urban under- and unemployed. Many rural migrants became peddlers, food vendors, or newspapers sellers, or tended parked cars for a small tip (*cuidadores de autos* became ubiquitous in Mexican cities). All were low-paid

---

[35] Consumers could purchase oil stove tanks in stores, which were purple (color-coded) for easy identification. "Use petróleo diáfano," *El Porvenir*, August 18, 1959. Cylinders for butane and propane gas (today omnipresent in Mexico) also became popular among urban consumers and were made by six different firms: three in Mexico City, two in Monterrey, and one in Guadalajara. See United States, *Investment in Mexico, Conditions and Outlook for United States Investors* (Washington: US Govt. Print. Off., 1956), 169. An excellent analysis of this transition is Vitz, "'To Save the Forests'."

[36] Floyd Dotson and Lillian Dotson, "Urban Centralization and Decentralization in Mexico," *Rural Sociology* 21, no. 1 (1950): 41–9.

[37] Jonathan Kandell, *La Capital: The Biography of Mexico City* (New York: Random House, 1988), 485–506.

jobs with no security.[38] Mass migration to cities turned both unemployment and underemployment, formerly an overwhelmingly rural problem, into an urban phenomenon.

Urban inequality consequently soared. By 1960, Mexico City's richest 10 percent controlled 40 percent of the city's wealth. Half of this belonged to the top 3 percent of the population.[39] Such inequality had spatial dimensions: the rich controlled most of the urban landscape. Just 14 percent of the wealthiest households occupied 36 percent of the city's area, while the poorest 36 percent crammed into just 11.5 percent. In wealthier sections of the city, occupants enjoyed fewer than 1 person per room on average, while an average of 3.4 people shared a room in the poorest areas.[40] This divide created a paradox: the more Mexico City grew, the scarcer housing became.

Urban growth predicated on motor vehicles and cheap fossil energy acutely exacerbated urban sprawl and suburbanization. While it took 100 years for Mexico City's area to expand from about 15 km^2 in 1845 to about 117 km^2 in 1940, between 1940 and 1970 the city ballooned to over 700 km^2 (Figure 5.4). Such relentless expansion came at the expense of surrounding *ejidos*, farmland, and forests. Some farmers and peasants tried unsuccessfully to halt rapid urban growth. In Guadalajara, peasants protested the expansion of the city's sewage system into their lands, much to the confusion of city authorities and the press, who accused them of irrationality. But peasants understood all too well that urban services would be followed by land expropriation for urban development.[41]

As Mexican cities grew outward, many middle- and upper-class urbanites abandoned downtown areas for the outskirts, commuting to the city by car. This process of suburbanization and what can be considered "class flight" involved replacing middle-class and wealthy urban residents with rural immigrants who moved into the old urban core. Here, unscrupulous landlords turned colonial and nineteenth-century mansions and buildings that had, until recently, housed shopkeepers and professionals into overcrowded tenements. Some observers decried this shift as a sign of urban decay and blamed immigrants.[42] The new, large urban middle class that emerged after 1940, which included government employees, teachers, small

---

[38] Antonio Canchola, "Relaciones sociales y económicas de la ciudad y el campo en México," *Revista Mexicana de Sociología* 19, no. 1 (1957): 15–23.

[39] Kandell, *La Capital*, 507.

[40] Oscar Lewis, "México desde 1940," *Investigación Económica* 18, no. 70 (1958): 185–256.

[41] "Les pareció mal a los agraristas que fuese instalado un drenaje," *El Informador*, October 20, 1950.

[42] "La desintegración de las grandes ciudades," *Periódico Oficial del Estado de Campeche*, August 3, 1960.

URBAN AREA OF MEXICO CITY, 1940–1990

- -Square Kilometers

Figure 5.4 Growth of Mexico City's urban area, 1940–90.
Source: Conapo, *Escenarios demográficos y urbanos de la Zona Metropolitana de la Ciudad de México, 1990–2010*, 1998, 30–1.

merchants, warehouse clerks, skilled workers, small industrialists, intellectuals, and professionals, settled in new apartment buildings or neighborhoods that were once the abode of the Porfirian elite.[43]

Unprecedented urban growth brought new problems. By the 1950s and 1960s, air pollution became a serious issue. Given the comparatively small role coal played in powering them, Mexican cities were spared the killer fogs of London or Pittsburgh that turned day into night and poisoned urban dwellers to death if atmospheric conditions kept pollution in place too long.[44] But increased motor traffic, thousands of factories concentrated in urban areas, and the urban economy's overall shift to oil and natural gas meant that Mexican cities began suffering poor air quality. A 1959 UNESCO report indicated that 200 tons of "smoke" (air pollutants) was released into Mexico City's air daily. One observer noted, "the haze that hangs over the city is not as aggressive as the smog of Los Angeles or the fog of London, but it grows thicker every year."[45]

---

[43] Oscar Lewis, "México desde 1940," 185–256.

[44] John R. McNeill, "Epilogue: Latin American Environmental History in Global Perspective," in *A Living Past: Environmental Histories of Modern Latin America* (New York: Berghahn Books, 2018), 266–76.

[45] The UNESCO figure and quote come from Lewis Hanke, *Mexico and the Caribbean* (Princeton: Van Nostrand, 1959), 82.

The formerly famous blue skies of Mexico City and other highland urban areas became memories, something only strong winds or rain could momentarily bring back. Such changes made some (a minority, certainly) rethink whether smoke-belching factories and exhaust-spewing motor vehicles were necessarily signs of progress.[46] Others began to wonder if air pollution caused madness.[47] One physician, concerned about the health effects of urban air pollution, lamented that the "automobile, which has changed the life of millions of people, is slowly suffocating the cities that the automobile itself made grow and every day it demands a tribute of blood and suffering."[48] Other medical professionals blamed factories, particularly cement producers, and called for their relocation in the countryside – seemingly unconcerned with the health of rural inhabitants.[49]

Some urban environmental changes were viewed more benevolently. Such was the case of urban encroachment on rivers, celebrated using the language of reclamation.[50] The dramatic annual fluctuations in water volume of many Mexican rivers created real problems for urban growth. The solution almost everywhere was to channel or pipe them. In turn, piping made it easier for cities to use rivers for disposing of untreated industrial and organic waste. Other effects unfolded so slowly that they largely escaped public attention. Take the fact that Mexico City was sinking about 30 cm per year due to accelerating consumption of its underground aquifers, which had for centuries stabilized the spongy soils upon which the city rested.[51]

[46] G. Viniegra and H. Bravo, "Polución atmosférica en la ciudad de México; informe preliminar," *La Prensa Médica Mexicana* 24, no. 2 (1959): 73–80. "Alto grado de contaminación del aire en México, D. F.," *El Informador*, March 24, 1965. As in places like Britain, it took time for people in Mexico to "invent" fossil fuel pollution. In Britain, it was only in the late nineteenth and early twentieth centuries that people began to see coal as a dangerous pollutant, centuries after its widespread adoption. See Peter Thorsheim, *Inventing Pollution: Coal, Smoke, and Culture in Britain since 1800* (Athens: Ohio University Press, 2006), chapter 1.

[47] "Factores que influyen en el desquiciamiento," *El Informador*, June 10, 1966.

[48] Dr. Miguel Bustamante, "Nuevos problemas de salud pública," *Gaceta Médica de México*, July 1, 1966.

[49] "Debe evitarse que las ciudades al crecer alberguen grandes fábricas," *El Informador*, April 18, 1969.

[50] "Terrenos ganados al cauce del Río Santa Catarina," *Periódico Oficial del Estado de Nuevo León*, April 6, 1960; "Obras de canalización del Río Chuvíscar," *Periódico Oficial del Estado de Chihuahua*, December 30, 1961.

[51] Tonatiúh Gutiérrez Olguín, "Los recursos naturales renovables en el desarrollo económico de México," *Investigación Económica*, 22, no. 86 (1962): 231–607. City planners, scientists, and government officials, however, became concerned about it around this time. See Matthew Vitz, *A City on a Lake: Urban Political Ecology and the Growth of Mexico City* (Durham: Duke University Press, 2018), conclusion.

Two Mexicos

In 1941, Berkeley professor Lesley Byrd Simpson published his landmark book *Many Mexicos*, which emphasized the country's great geographic, cultural, and social diversity throughout history.[52] This appraisal, while it certainly captured a fundamental aspect of Mexico's past, was less useful in describing the new fossil-fueled reality emerging precisely at the moment of its publication. The transition to fossil fuels after 1940 exacerbated regional inequality, helping some areas urbanize and industrialize much faster than others. In general, Mexico City and the north (as well as certain parts of western Mexico) benefitted most, while many southern regions were left behind. By the early 1960s, eight northern states plus Mexico City concentrated 63 percent of Mexico's GDP and enjoyed a GDP per capita many times higher than the rest of the country. At the opposite end, the combined economies of Mexico's eight poorest states, all located in the south and parts of the Bajío – one of the richest regions in the Americas 160 years earlier – represented only 25 percent of national GDP, with an income per capita far lower than that of the wealthier states. The poorest state, Oaxaca, had an income per capita ten times smaller than Mexico City and twelve times smaller than Baja California Norte, the country's highest.[53] Mexico's historical diversity was being reduced to a dual reality: rapidly industrializing areas derived the majority of their energy from fossil fuels, while agrarian regions, despite being shaped by urban-industrial economies dependent on fossil energy, remained caught in the solar energy regime.

Few places had profited more from fossil energy since the late nineteenth century than Monterrey. The city not only sat close to Coahuila's coal mines; it could also import foreign coal through the nearby port of Tampico when domestic supplies faltered. Thanks in part to geographic luck, Monterrey became the center of Mexico's heavy industry by the early twentieth century. As mentioned, Fundidora Monterrey, Latin America's first and largest steel factory until the foundation of the Volta Redonda steel mill in Brazil in 1941, called the city home.[54] Over its 80-year history

---

[52] Lesley Byrd Simpson, *Many Mexicos* (Berkeley: University of California Press, 1966).

[53] Gabriel Ortiz, *El desarrollo económico del Valle de México y la zona metropolitana de la Ciudad de México* (México, D. F.: Oficina de Estudios Económicos y Reglamentaciones, 1964), 3. The eight northern states were, in descending order, Baja California Norte, Nuevo León, Sonora, Tamaulipas, Coahuila, Baja California Sur, and Chihuahua. The eight poorest states were, in ascending order, Oaxaca, Hidalgo, Tlaxcala, Michoacán, Guerrero, Tabasco, Querétaro, Zacatecas, and Guanajuato.

[54] On Volta Redonda, see Oliver Dinius, *Brazil's Steel City: Developmentalism, Strategic Power, and Industrial Relations in Volta Redonda, 1941–1964* (Stanford: Stanford University Press, 2010).

(it shut down in 1986), Fundidora, and therefore Monterrey, remained one of Mexico's largest consumers of coal and coke. But Monterrey was also located near Mexico's oil fields in northern and central Veracruz and the Texas natural gas fields. The city's industry and power plants began using oil early in the twentieth century. By the 1920s, many large manufacturing establishments in Monterrey shifted to oil, early by national and even global standards.[55] Natural gas became common in the 1940s in industry and power generation. By mid-century, Monterrey's economy depended almost entirely on the trinity of oil, coal, and natural gas to a degree almost unmatched elsewhere in Mexico.

By the early 1950s, Monterrey had more than 800 industries within its limits, representing a total investment of over 1.5 billion pesos. These firms included Mexico's largest brewery, iron and steel, glass, food processing, furniture, cement, textiles, meat packing, fertilizers, leather goods, clothing, oil refining, and many others. One out of six residents worked in factories, where they earned well above the national average wage. Car ownership, access to electricity, and various industrial consumer goods were common among the general population. Energy consumption per capita ranked among the highest in the country. Monterrey symbolized Mexico's industrial dream, although the dream continued to evade parts of the city with their "stubborn residue of slums, beggars, unschooled children, inadequate water . . ."[56]

To manage the city's industrial economy and ensure its continued growth, a powerful and wealthy group of Monterrey and Mexico City bankers, industrialists, and businessmen founded a technological institute, the ITESM (Instituto Tecnológico de Estudios Superiores de Monterrey) in 1943. The university was patterned after the Massachusetts Institute of Technology and designed to prepare engineers and technical personnel for Monterrey's and Mexico's expanding industrial economy. It offered degrees in civil, mechanical, electrical, and chemical engineering, among others, along with degrees in business, administration, and economics.[57] While ITESM educated a Mexican cadre of professionals in industrial administration and technology, US corporations routinely sent Monterrey personnel to home factories to train. Some US firms, like San Antonio's Southwest Research Institute, carried out industrial research in Monterrey.

---

[55] "Domestic Fuel Oil Sales, El Águila" (1923), caja 2373, exp. 64916, AHP; "Renewal Fuel Oil Contracts, El Águila" (1922), caja 1791, exp.50665, AHP.
[56] Tomme Clark Call, The Mexican Venture: From Political to Industrial Revolution in Mexico (New York: Oxford University Press, 1953), 47.
[57] *Investment in Mexico, Conditions and Outlook for United States Investors, 63.*

The Mexican government, in turn, founded industrial development labs in the city.[58]

While Monterrey and other large cities thrived in the new fossil-fueled industrial era, Mexico City became the indisputable political, economic, and industrial center of the country. Mexico City had been the country's locus of power since pre-Columbian times, but between 1940 and 1970 the city achieved a level of dominance unmatched since the long-gone days of Aztec rule. Crucially, mid-twentieth-century Mexico City drew its economic, political, and cultural power from its ability to concentrate vast volumes of fossil energy.

Mid-twentieth-century Mexico City was by far the largest consumer of energy in the country, much of it in the form of oil and natural gas. The city was served by the Mexican Light and Power Company, Mexico's most important power utility. In 1960, the firm controlled almost a quarter of Mexico's power generating capacity, over half of which relied on fossil fuels, and most of which went to Mexico City's huge industrial base and rapidly growing number of residents.[59] Mexico City was also the indisputable hub of Mexico's oil and natural gas pipeline network and refining capacity. As the center of Mexico's railroad and road networks, Mexico City functioned as the country's main distribution point for crude oil or oil derivatives transported by rail tanks or trucks.

Such energy dominance supported an extraordinary concentration of wealth, industrial productive capacity, services, and population in Mexico City, a kind of national "macrocephaly," according to one observer.[60] Mexico City's transformation into the biggest agglomeration of people, materials, and resources the country had ever seen reflected this accumulation of energy-dense fossil fuels. Mexico City produced most of the nation's industrial manufacturing, peaking in 1960. Occupying merely 0.1 percent of Mexico's land area, in 1960 the Federal District (the city's administrative entity) claimed 31.5 percent of all industrial establishments, and its manufactures' value represented a whopping 44.5 percent of the national total (Table 5.6). By 1960, one out of four Mexican factory workers lived in Mexico City, and almost 40 percent of the city's residents labored in some sort of industrial establishment. As Cornell economic

---

[58] Call, *The Mexican Venture*, 57.

[59] In 1960, Mexican Light's generating capacity was 667 MW of power, while Mexico had 3,057 MW. In that year, the company held 22 percent of the nation's capacity. See The Mexican Light and Power Company, Limited, *Annual Report* (Toronto: The Mexican Light and Power Company, Limited, 1960), 11, and INEGI, *Estadísticas históricas de México*, vol. 1, 1994, 589.

[60] Gutiérrez Olguín, "Los recursos naturales renovables en el desarrollo económico de México," 337.

Table 5.6 *Mexico City's share of Mexico's industrial sector and output, 1940–88*

Year	Mexico City Percentage of National Industrial Establishments	Mexico City Percentage of National Industrial Production
1940	22.3	31.3
1950	22.6	33.1
1960	31.5	44.5
1970	27.6	43.9
1980	28.1	43.3
1988	21.4	32.1

Adapted from Gustavo Garza, "Dinámica industrial de la Ciudad de México, 1940–1988," *Estudios Demográficos*, 1991.

geographer M. Ogden noted as early as 1933, in Mexico City, "labor, capital, raw materials, and power are combined to make [Mexico City] the greatest industrial zone in Mexico."[61]

Besides manufacturing the majority of Mexico's industrial goods, Mexico City and its surrounding region had a virtual production monopoly in several key items. Synthetic fertilizer, an essential commodity for Mexico's Green Revolution, is one example. Established in 1943 with financial support from the country's national development bank, Nacional Financiera, the main plant, Guanos y Fertilizantes de México, was located in the industrial suburb of Tlalnepantla, north of Mexico City. By the mid-1950s, the factory produced about 180,000 metric tons of nitrogen, ammonium sulfate, and superphosphates, which dramatically increased yields of cotton in La Laguna, in the country's north, and sugar cane plantations in places like the state of Morelos. Maize and wheat growers were also important customers.[62] Mexico City also dominated production of electric appliances and equipment. The Industria Eléctrica de México was established in Tlalnepantla in 1945 through a joint venture between Mexico's national government and the US firm Westinghouse Electric Co. Westinghouse supplied technical support and granted patent rights to Eléctrica to sell electric equipment in Mexico, while

[61] M. Ogden Phillips, "Manufacturing in the Federal District, Mexico," *Economic Geography* 9, no. 3 (1933): 279–91.

[62] *Investment in Mexico, Conditions and Outlook for United States Investors, 165.*

Mexican and US private investors supported by Nacional Financiera provided capital (about 85 percent). A board of directors from Mexico's banking and business community controlled the firm. Over time, the factory's 2,000 workers produced many of Mexico's refrigerators, transformers, watt-hour meters, electric irons, radios, air conditioning units, and paints and enamels for electrical equipment.[63]

Concentration of the nation's industrial capacity in Mexico City was paralleled by centralization in consumption of goods and services. The capital claimed half of Mexico's telephones and radio receivers as well as the majority of television sets. Oscar Lewis, the famous anthropologist who studied Mexico's urban poverty, found in a Mexico City tenement "more radios than metates."[64] Low-income families in the city bought new electric appliances in installments, a system that gave families access to new technologies (although by putting them seriously in debt). Mexico City radio commercial stations and television broadcasting companies dominated national programming and exerted unmatched cultural influence over the rest of the country. In the 1950s, newspapers were published in 51 Mexican cities, but only 5 of them, all from Mexico City, circulated over 100,000 copies daily.[65] All major book publishers, including the prestigious Fondo de Cultura Económica, had their headquarters in Mexico City, far and away the country's biggest book market with its large and (mostly) literate population.[66]

In part, acute centralization resulted from government spending, especially on new infrastructure. The new road and highway system, like railroads before it, centered around Mexico City. All three major north–south highways connected Nogales, Juárez, and Nuevo Laredo with Mexico City.[67] It was common for vehicles to drive first to Mexico City in order to reach a different destination. A truck coming from the northeast en route to the Gulf took a detour through Mexico City to connect with a road leading east. When the city received half of all federal spending in the 1950s,[68] much of this was put towards expanding the city's road system and redesigning the capital to accommodate motor traffic. Unsurprisingly,

[63] Mosk, *Industrial Revolution in Mexico*, 177–9. Tlalnepantla also housed auto, truck, and trailer assembly plants for firms like Nash and Hudson. See 187.

[64] Lewis, "México desde 1940." A *metate* is a saddle quern of pre-Hispanic origin.

[65] *Investment in Mexico, Conditions and Outlook for United States Investors*, 70–78.

[66] In 1960, 87 percent of the Federal District's population was considered literate; nationally, 64 percent. See INEGI, *Estadísticas históricas de México*, vol. 1, 1994, 120; Nacional Financiera, S. A., *La economía mexicana en cifras* (México, D. F.: Nacional Financiera, 1965), 227.

[67] *Investment in Mexico, Conditions and Outlook for United States Investors*, 68–73.

[68] Lewis, "México desde 1940."

vehicle ownership skyrocketed. In the late 1950s, Mexico City claimed 38 percent of Mexico's cars, 36 percent of its buses, and 13 percent of its trucks.[69] Moreover, the new air traffic system, which by mid-century had reached over fifty cities nationwide, was also developed with Mexico City at its center.[70] With three times as many international flights entering the country in 1953, many air travelers found that flights, like roads, led to Mexico City.

The convergence of energy, resources, infrastructure, and population (almost 17 percent of the nation's total in 1960) amassed wealth in the nation's capital.[71] By the early 1960s, Mexico City represented 36.5 percent of national GDP. The city alone surpassed the combined GDP of Mexico's nine poorest states by 10 percent. The disparity in 1960 between Mexico City and Oaxaca in income per capita paralleled that between the USA and Costa Rica or between Great Britain and Thailand. Despite its frenetic demographic expansion from 1950 to 1960 – when its population grew annually by an average of 4.8 percent – Mexico City's GDP per capita rose by a remarkable 10 percent annually during the same period. In the meantime, income per capita in adjacent states of Hidalgo and Tlaxcala grew at only 2.4 percent, lower than their demographic growth; these two states, in fact, became poorer. The wealth gap between Mexico City and other parts of the country was the widest it had ever been, and growing.

Mexico City's shift to a fossil fuel–based manufacturing economy and the explosive growth of its surface area led to a precipitous decline in nearby food production. During the 1950s, production of maize, beans, and wheat, basic staples in most Mexican diets, decreased by 14.5 percent in the Federal District. By 1960, agriculture represented a mere 2.8 percent of Mexico City's GDP.[72] Mexico City now imported most of its food from places like nearby Hidalgo and Tlaxcala, which became main suppliers of grain and other basic foods. But Mexico City could also harvest supplies for its expanding population from faraway places and ship them quickly thanks to roads and fossil energy. The city's residents, for example, could now easily consume meat from the distant north. As a result, per capita consumption of all types of meats doubled with respect to the rest of the country.[73] A similar pattern occurred with fish: Mexico City consumed

[69] *Investment in Mexico, Conditions and Outlook for United States Investors*, 70.   [70] Ibid., 73–4.
[71] The following information comes from Ortiz, *El desarrollo económico del Valle de México y la zona metropolitana de la Ciudad de México*, 3–9.
[72] Ibid., 1–21.
[73] United States Tariff Commission, *Agricultural, Pastoral and Forest Industries in Mexico* (Washington, DC: US Govt. Print. Off., 1948), 13.

almost 20 percent of the country's total catch in 1960.[74] Half a century earlier, around 1900, coal-fired dredges had given the *coup de grace* to the Valley of Mexico's lakes and extinguished Mexico City's main source of fish. Now gasoline-powered refrigerated trucks brought fish from distant coasts. Like other cities in industrial countries, Mexico City exported manufactured products to the rest of Mexico in exchange for food (increasingly grown using fossil fuels).

The "Quiet Revolution"

In 1971, a year after receiving a Nobel Peace Prize for his contribution to what was now called the Green Revolution,[75] US agronomist Norman Borlaug looked back at the changes he had facilitated during the previous quarter of a century. He recalled how 1940s Mexico was forced to import half of its wheat and a high percentage of its maize for consumption. At the time, yields for these crops were low while the country's population was growing. Mexico urgently needed to increase food production, so The Rockefeller Foundation, Borlaug's employer, decided "to help Mexico to help itself."[76] After the introduction of new dwarf Mexican wheat varieties, yields began rising; between 1948 and 1970, the national average grew fourfold, from about 750 kg to 3,000 kg per hectare. In 1956, Mexico became self-sufficient in wheat. Borlaug described this achievement as the "Quiet Revolution" and the progenitor of the Green Revolution in India and Pakistan a decade later.[77] While it certainly represented a technical feat, the Quiet Revolution had another, perhaps deeper, meaning.

Before the advent of fossil fuels, Mexican agriculture, like any food production system largely powered by muscle, operated more or less as a closed energy system. It produced by necessity more calories than it consumed – the alternative was starvation.[78] This harsh reality changed with fossil energy's influx into agriculture, a fundamental part of the Green

---

[74] Gutiérrez Olguín, "Los recursos naturales renovables en el desarrollo económico de México," 462–6.

[75] The term "Green Revolution" was first popularized in the late 1960s by William Gaud, administrator of the Agency for International Development (AID).

[76] Norman E. Borlaug, "The Green Revolution: For Bread and Peace," *Bulletin of the Atomic Scientists,* June 1971, 6–48.

[77] Ibid.

[78] According to Rolf Sieferle, the ratio of energy spent to energy yielded in preindustrial agrarian systems must be *at least* 1:5 given that humans only convert about 20 percent of food into mechanical energy (labor). This ratio, which allows the farmer to barely subsist, includes preparation of the fields, processing the food, and transporting it. See Sieferle, *The Subterranean Forest: Energy Systems and the Industrial Revolution* (Cambridge: The White Horse Press, 2001), 15.

Revolution. Abundant and cheap fossil energy in the form of synthetic fertilizer, tractors, electricity for irrigation, and other inputs necessary for implementing new, high-yielding farming methods inverted the former energy ratio. Farmers were now using more calories than they produced. Fossil-fueled agriculture meant that regions undergoing the Green Revolution went from being net producers of energy to energy sinks.

This dramatic transformation had a start date. In 1943, The Rockefeller Foundation sent plant pathologist Jacob George Harrar to Mexico to coordinate their joint undertaking with the Mexican Department of Agriculture. The program's goal was to improve Mexico's agricultural productivity. More specifically, the program aimed to increase yields with less labor in order to meet the food and employment needs of Mexico's industrializing economy. The initiative received support from the highest-ranking officials in the Mexican government, including the president, a commitment that would continue over several successive administrations. True to Mexico's centralizing tendencies, the Office of Special Studies (the program's coordinating center) was established in Mexico City and the main field laboratory was located in Chapingo, 25 miles east. Regional centers in Guanajuato and Morelos followed later.[79] The plan might have targeted Mexico's countryside, but Mexico City would direct it.

Mexican authorities' enthusiasm for the Rockefeller project reflected overlapping interests and goals. After the end of the Cárdenas administration, the national government's commitment to agrarian reform and land distribution dwindled considerably. The focus became rapid urban industrialization. In order to feed Mexico's growing urban and industrial population, officials deemed it necessary to promote large-scale, mechanized, commercial agriculture. The Rockefeller initiative complemented this aspiration since it emphasized technical innovation, not land reform, to achieve increased food production. Additionally, both the Mexican government and the Rockefeller Foundation, with the US government's blessing and support, considered cheap and abundant food in a "developing" country like Mexico critical to fighting the global communist threat. The Green Revolution, one historian observed, "was a child of the Cold War."[80]

---

[79] Jacob George Harrar, *Mexican Agricultural Program: A Review of the First Six Years of Activity under the Joint Auspices of the Mexican Government and the Rockefeller Foundation* (New York: The Rockefeller Foundation, 1950), 1–15.

[80] McNeill, *Something New under the Sun: An Environmental History of the Twentieth-Century World* (New York: W.W. Norton & Company, 2001), 222.

By 1951, the Office of Special Studies had distributed rust-resistant wheat strains to irrigated districts of Mexico's north and northwest, particularly Sonora. While new hybrid seeds were the project's most visible component, improved grain varieties were part of a larger package that included credit, irrigation, and mechanization, along with systematic use of chemical fertilizers, pesticides, and insecticides. "Without fertilizer or without controlled irrigation," one analyst observed, "the new varieties usually yield no more and sometimes less than traditional strains. With them they give substantially higher yields per acre."[81] With the exception of credit, all these other elements required either energy, usually generated with fossil fuels, or petroleum-based products. While Mexico became the birthplace of the Green Revolution partly because it had already transitioned to fossil fuels, the new agricultural regime reinforced Mexico's reliance on fossil energy by cementing a chemically dependent, commercially oriented farming system that relied on machinery and poorly paid seasonal labor.

To ensure the project's success, the Mexican government embarked on an ambitious plan. First, it allocated vast sums of public money to expand land under irrigation. Between 1945 and 1970, irrigated land more than tripled, from 640,746 to 2,063,687 hectares (rain-fed agriculture doubled in area during the same period).[82] By 1970, about 13 percent of Mexico's farmland was irrigated. This required extracting enormous volumes of water from underground aquifers using electric pumps.[83] In the north, the site of most new irrigation districts, much of this electricity came from fossil fuels by the mid-twentieth century. Second, northern Mexico's new irrigation districts required numerous tractors, multi-plows, and other heavy equipment. The Mexican state heavily subsidized diesel fuel, importation and domestic manufacture of tractors, and credit so that farmers could purchase such expensive machinery.[84] As a result, the number of tractors in Mexico skyrocketed after 1950 (Table 5.7).

By 1960, Mexico's rural sector was the most mechanized in Latin America. The majority of its tractors were large (over 40 horsepower),

---

[81] Harry Cleaver, "The Contradictions of the Green Revolution," *The American Economic Review* 62, no. 1/2 (1972): 177–86.

[82] INEGI, *Estadísticas históricas de México*, vol. 1, 1994, 436.

[83] Gutiérrez Olguín estimated that 7,200,000 cubic meters of aquifer water were needed annually to irrigate 800,000 ha; by 1960, 1,689,839 ha were irrigated, so the amount of extracted water that year must have been near 14,000,000–15,000,000 cubic meters. By comparison, Mexico's population of 34,000,000 in 1960 consumed 3,723,000 cubic meters of water. See Gutiérrez Olguín, "Los recursos naturales renovables en el desarrollo económico de México," 324, 340.

[84] Omar Masera Cerutti, *Crisis y mecanización de la agricultura campesina* (México, D. F.: El Colegio de México, 1990), 31.

Table 5.7 *Number of tractors
in Mexico, 1940–80*

Year	Number of Tractors
1940	4,600
1950	22,700
1960	54,500
1970	91,400
1980	154,700

Adapted from Omar Masera
Cerutti, *Crisis y mecanización de la
agricultura campesina*, 1990, 34.

which meant that mechanization met mostly the needs of large landowners with substantial capital means, not small farmers (Figure 5.5). Mechanization of large, commercial agricultural units displaced human labor. Especially affected were temporary agricultural workers, who now found themselves unemployed.[85] Many were forced to migrate to cities, joining the ranks of the urban poor, or the USA as undocumented immigrants or members of the Bracero Program.[86] The fossil-fueled Green Revolution thus led to modern transnational migratory patterns by creating a large class of seasonal laborers seeking work on both sides of the border, often under highly exploitative conditions that exposed these laborers to a cocktail of toxic chemicals.[87]

The final ingredients for Mexico's Green Revolution were chemical inputs like synthetic fertilizers and pesticides.[88] Borlaug himself underlined this when he wrote that "[i]f the high-yielding dwarf wheat and rice varieties are the catalysts that have ignited the Green Revolution,

[85] Ibid., 33–8.
[86] Between 1942 and 1955, about 1.5 million Mexican agricultural laborers went to work in the USA as braceros, most from rural areas. This figure does not include undocumented immigrants. See Oscar Lewis, *Five Families: Mexican Case Studies in the Culture of Poverty* (New York: Basic Books, 1955), 10.
[87] Angus Wright, *The Death of Ramón González: The Modern Agricultural Dilemma* (Austin: The University of Texas Press, 2005).
[88] Though organic local fertilizers (chicken and green manure) were often superior to chemical fertilizers, The Rockefeller Foundation, the Office of Special Studies (later renamed CIMMYT or Centro Internacional para la Mejora del Maíz y el Trigo), and the government pushed peasants to adopt the latter. The government owned the national fertilizer company. See David Clawson and Don Hoy, "Mexico: A Peasant Community that Rejected the 'Green Revolution,'" *The American Journal of Economics and Sociology* 38, no. 4 (1979): 371–87.

Figure 5.5 Fossil-fueled technologies like tractors became common in Mexico under the Green Revolution. Source: Jacob George Harrar, *The Agricultural Program of the Rockefeller Foundation*, 1956.

then chemical fertilizer is the fuel that has powered its forward thrust."[89] Fossil fuels were essential to developing these synthetic inputs, both as fuel for their manufacture and national distribution as well as feedstock or raw material. Starting in the 1950s, Pemex supplied the main plant, Guanos y Fertilizantes de México, the government-owned agency that produced these chemicals, located just outside Mexico City, with natural gas completely free of charge.[90] With such heavy subsidies, Mexico's fertilizer production

---

[89] Borlaug, "The Green Revolution."

[90] World Bank, *The Economic Development of Mexico* (Baltimore: Johns Hopkins University Press, 1953), 76. Fertilizer production, industrial growth, and widespread adoption of gas stoves drove up Mexico's natural gas consumption from the equivalent of 4.4 million barrels of oil in 1939 to 9.3 million in 1950. See ibid., 260.

Figure 5.6 The use of chemical inputs in Mexican agriculture grew rapidly after 1950. Spraying pesticides in an orchard, ca. 1950. Source: Gonzalo Blanco, *Agriculture in Mexico*, 1950, 32.

grew from a mere 11,429 metric tons of both nitrogen and phosphates in 1950 to 252,715 metric tons by 1960 and 1,068,920 metric tons by 1970, an astonishing over 9,000-percent increase in 20 years.[91] Petroleum-based chemical inputs also became common in Mexican agriculture after 1950, not only for wheat and maize, the jewels of the Quiet Revolution, but for products like fruits (Figure 5.6). Once in place, the Green Revolution increased Mexico's self-sufficiency in a variety of crops, albeit temporarily – imports resumed by the 1980s.[92] It also mostly benefitted large, export-oriented agribusinesses at the cost of permanent fossil fuel dependence – a risky gamble – displacement and impoverishment of numerous rural communities and their locally adapted farming practices, and environmental

[91] INEGI, *Estadísticas históricas de México*, vol. 2, 1990, 528. By 1980, production had almost doubled again to 1,819,423 metric tons.
[92] The federal government briefly sought to reestablish food self-sufficiency in the early 1980s through the Mexican Food System (SAM), funded with oil revenues. Once oil prices crashed in 1983, the program folded. See David A. Sonnenfeld, "Mexico's "Green Revolution," 1940–1980: Towards an Environmental History," *Environmental History Review* 16, no. 4 (Winter, 1992): 28–52.

degradation.[93] Other facets of Mexican life would follow similar patterns.[94]

Eating Oil

At the beginning of his novella *Las Batallas en el Desierto* (*Battles in the Desert*), Mexican writer José Emilio Pacheco has his main character, Carlos, reminisce about 1950s Mexico and its unbridled optimism. At the time, many people envisioned a future of

> plenty and universal wellbeing. Clean cities, without injustice, poor people, violence, traffic, or garbage. Each family would have an ultramodern and aerodynamic house [. . .] Nobody would lack anything. Machines would do all the work. The streets would be full of trees and fountains, run by cars that gave no exhaust, made no noise, and never crashed. It would be paradise on earth. Utopia would be conquered at last.[95]

Pacheco ridiculed such aspirations. He benefitted from hindsight, writing in the early 1980s after most of those dreams were dashed. In the 1950s and 1960s, they seemed achievable, partly because the massive influx of cheap, ostensibly limitless fossil energy made anything seem possible.

Even oil steaks. As one newspaper suggested, it was possible that in the near future Mexicans would be eating mouthwatering steaks . . . made of oil. Once scientists harnessed microorganisms to produce edible oil protein, the journalist predicted, a cornucopia of delicious, gourmet, oil-based food would arrive on Mexican tables.[96] Such ideas not only exemplify the period's fossil fuel optimism but illustrate the degree to which oil and fossil fuels dominated Mexican society. Everyday life for a growing number of Mexicans was now organized around high-energy consumption and fossil fuel–based technologies like automobiles and (mostly oil- and-coal-generated) electricity. This

---

[93] Ibid.

[94] Although the Green Revolution largely targeted well-off farmers with credit, there were some half-hearted efforts to reach peasants. These efforts mostly failed, not least because many peasants rejected key parts of the package, with good reason. New hybrids had short stalks to reduce blowdowns. But long stalks fed draft animals. Since peasants could not replace animal power with fossil-fueled machinery, introducing new varieties would have eliminated essential food for animal power. Additionally, many peasants resisted purchasing cash seeds, chemical fertilizer, and insecticides, all of which undermined their autonomy. Still, the government pushed the package to local peasants by making other government benefits dependent on its adoption. See Clawson and Hoy, "Mexico: A Peasant Community that Rejected the 'Green Revolution.'"

[95] José Emilio Pacheco, *Las batallas en el desierto* (México: FCE, 2010), 11.

[96] "Alimentos sintéticos: solución para un mundo hambriento," *Mañana*, March 2, 1968.

high-consumption lifestyle, in turn, began shaping class identity and other forms of social differentiation.

Take food. Fossil energy not only assisted food growers in Mexico's countryside; it was now becoming the main energy source in many Mexican kitchens. Charcoal – long Mexico's dominant cooking fuel – was rapidly being replaced by natural gas. This process accelerated after 1940, particularly in urban areas.[97] The new energy source became a status symbol. By mid-century, charcoal consumption in Mexico City was viewed as an unmistakable sign of poverty.[98] "Traditional" energy sources became associated with backwardness, while gas and electricity character- ized "modern" households. Gas stoves, aluminum items, and electric appliances like blenders, toasters, and refrigerators replaced brick ovens and earthenware pots and bowls. People's diet changed, too. Instead of traditional staples – tortillas, corn gruel, beans, and chile[99] – American- style breakfasts of juice, eggs, toast, and coffee became common, at least for the middle class. Many people began eating "lunch" outside rather than "*comida*" at home and had turkey for Christmas (cooked in a gas oven). Industrially processed food became widely available both for households and as street food (this included milkshakes or hamburgers, hotdogs, and doughnuts). Government-sponsored efforts to increase animal protein popularized processed items like powdered milk.[100]

Perhaps nothing better exemplified how profound these changes were than the mechanization of tortilla production and the commercialization of dehydrated, factory-made maize flour. Tortilla mills originated in the Porfiriato, but workable models only appeared in the 1920s. Early versions in villages without electricity used gas engines, causing people to complain that tortillas tasted like gas. The mills remained a curiosity for years, but with electricity's rapid expansion they became almost ubiquitous; between 1950 and 1970, over 60,000 machines were sold nationwide. Opponents persisted, insisting that mill-produced tortillas tasted like "electricity."

---

[97] Juana Meléndez Torres and Luis Aboites Aguilar, "Para una historia del cambio alimentario en México durante el siglo XX. El arribo del gas y la electricidad a la cocina," *Revista de Historia Iberoamericana* 8, no. 2 (December 25, 2015).

[98] "Es alarmante la escasez de carbón. Las familias humildes sufren lo indecible para adquirir una mínima ración," *El Universal*, January 2, 1947. And ownership of a US-made gas stove, among a poor urban family's "most valuable possessions." See Lewis, *Five Families*, 65.

[99] Sandra Aguilar, "Nutrition and Modernity: Milk Consumption in 1940s and 1950s Mexico," *Radical History Review*, no. 110 (Spring 2011): 36–58.

[100] By 1956, four factories in Mexico City, Jalisco, Querétaro, and Tlaxcala were producing some 500 metric tons of powdered milk annually. See *Investment in Mexico, Conditions and Outlook for United States Investors*, 1956, 160.

Others embraced them, especially poor women, who could spend up to 5 hours daily on their knees grinding maize kernels, turning them into a dough, and cooking them over a *comal* (griddle).[101]

With mechanization came industrial maize flour. The first factory producing dehydrated maize flour opened in 1949 near Monterrey (today's corporate giant Molinos Azteca, better known as Maseca). It was followed the next year by Maíz Industrializado or Minsa, a government-owned company in Tlalnepantla, the industrial suburb of Mexico City mentioned earlier. While mechanization of tortilla-making and industrialization of maize flour perhaps alleviated daily labor for many poor women, these changes had a darker side. Industrialized foods made people dependent on far-away sources and corporations for producing what was historically Mexico's most important dietary item. Such reliance dangerously undermined local autonomy regarding food production. Industrially made maize flour may also have led to the disappearance of many local corn varieties and may have homogenized Mexican foodways more than American processed food.[102]

In the context of cheap, novel energy forms, cultural practices also began to change. Radio, movies, and television – all made possible by widespread electrification – became key sources of entertainment and information for a growing number of Mexicans. Older, non-electricity-based amusements, including bullfighting and popular theater, faded, especially in cities. These developments were politically charged; despite occasional tensions between Mexico's postrevolutionary regime and television companies, their close collaboration was instrumental in legitimizing political rule after 1950. Fossil energy made mass media outlets like television available to "those interested in winning the hearts and minds of citizens." Fossil fuels created new relationships between political power and culture.[103]

No fossil fuel–based technology more profoundly shaped Mexican lives and cultural practices than the automobile. Cars signaled social status and associations with new understandings of freedom, masculinity, and national identity. Automobiles also influenced people's relationship with the environment, often in contradictory ways. On the one hand, cars and roads reinforced notions that progress meant taming and conquering

---

[101] Jeffrey Pilcher, "Mexico's Pepsi Challenge: Traditional Cooking, Mass Consumption, and National Identity," in *Fragments of a Golden Age: The Politics of Culture in Mexico since 1940* (Durham: Duke University Press, 2001), 71–90.

[102] Ibid.

[103] Celeste González de Bustamante and Richard Cole, *Muy Buenas Noches: Mexico, Television, and the Cold War* (Lincoln: University of Nebraska Press, 2013), 24.

Mexico's environment, seen as a historical source of national weakness.[104] On the other, automobiles and roads opened up Mexico's natural wonders to both citizens and tourists alike, leading some to contemplate the environment's fragility and the need to conserve it.

For many, fossil-fueled society looked like Americanization and caused considerable cultural anxiety. They pointed to industrialized food, describing it as the "Coca-Cola-ization" of Mexico. For others, the phenomenon involved a much wider variety of US cultural influences, from "Santa Claus to psychoanalysis."[105] These changes triggered a period of soul-searching among Mexican intellectuals, who became obsessed with discussing the meaning of Mexicanness.[106] It also inspired a new cadre of academics who studied Mexico's challenges as it industrialized and urbanized. A new Instituto de Investigaciones Sociales was founded at UNAM, Mexico's national university, whose new campus in Mexico City's southern outskirts was inaugurated in 1951. Interestingly, UNAM's vast, sprawling new campus of over 7 km² was designed for motor traffic, making Mexico's modern cultural and academic powerhouse a clear reflection of the country's fossil fuel era. Social-science journals like *El Trimestre Económico*, *Investigación Económica*, *Revista Mexicana de Sociología*, and *Problemas Agrícolas e Industriales de México* published work that attracted considerable readership.[107]

A central concern for many of these scholars was what can be anachronistically termed growing energy inequality. While electricity generation in Mexico had increased fourteenfold since 1920, by 1960 less than half of Mexico's total population had access to electricity.[108] Differential access to modern energies exacerbated the wealth divide between both individuals and regions. States like Colima in the west, Tlaxcala in the center, or Quintana Roo in the south barely produced any electricity and had extremely low per capita energy consumption. There was clear overlap between modern energy consumption and wealth. Chiapas, among the poorest states in Mexico with a large population of historically disenfranchised indigenous groups, had the lowest consumption per capita of electric power; the industrial state of Nuevo León (which has Monterrey

---

[104] Ben Curtiss Fulwider, "Driving the Nation: Road Transportation and the Postrevolutionary Mexican State, 1925–1960" (PhD Dissertation, Georgetown University, 2009), 265.

[105] Lewis Hanke, *Mexico and the Caribbean* (Princeton: Van Nostrand, 1959), 88.

[106] The classic work is Octavio Paz, *El Laberinto de la Soledad* (México, D. F.: FCE, 2015 [1950]).

[107] Hanke, *Mexico and the Caribbean*, 92.

[108] See Secretaría de Industria y Comercio, *VII Censo Industrial 1961* (México, D. F., 1965); Meléndez Torres and Aboites Aguilar, "Para una historia del cambio alimentario en México durante el siglo XX."

as its capital city) had the highest.[109] Power companies reinforced the link between modern energy access and an affluent lifestyle in their marketing campaigns by depicting electricity as a new type of domestic servant always at consumers' disposal.[110]

Ironically, the cultural and economic impact of Mexico's energy transition to fossil fuels largely bypassed some of the very people and places that produced them. Coahuila's coal miners had extracted the fuel since the 1880s, but by the mid-twentieth century their standard of living and lifestyle remained largely unchanged. Mining was still extremely dangerous and physically taxing (few aspects were mechanized), pay was insufficient, and their lives still revolved around coal companies. In 1951, Coahuila's coal miners struck for better working conditions and wages and union independence. When coal companies ignored their demands, the miners decided to walk from Coahuila to Mexico City, 1,500 km away, intending to meet President Alemán. Although the miners received popular support along their long march (and financial backing from US coal miners), they were relentlessly attacked by the press, which repeatedly characterized them as communist agitators influenced by foreign interests. Once they reached Mexico City, President Alemán refused to receive them and ordered the miners back to Coahuila on buses.[111] Coahuila's coal miners enjoyed few of the benefits of a fossil-fueled society yet suffered many of its negative effects, including work-induced diseases and polluted environments. This was not unique to Mexico. Coal-mining regions in the USA have historically been among the country's poorest, leading one US historian to describe them as "sacrifice zones."[112]

Forests

The effects of Mexico's fossil-fueled society on its forests were contradictory in the short term, benefitting some forest ecosystems while damaging others. The overall long-term effect was more clearance at an increasingly rapid pace, especially in the decades following the mid-twentieth century. Consider the beneficial influence of fossil fuel dependence. For 100 years, government officials, intellectuals, and scientists in Mexico argued that

---

[109] Gutiérrez Olguín, "Los recursos naturales renovables en el desarrollo económico de México."
[110] The Mexican Light and Power Company, *Annual Report*, 1957.
[111] "Una huelga que no existe," *Impacto*, November 4, 1950; "La caravana de la legalidad," *El Informador*, February 19, 1951; "La caravana del hambre," *El Informador*, March 26, 1951.
[112] Christopher Jones, *Routes of Power: Energy and Modern America* (Cambridge: Harvard University Press, 2014), 12.

shifting to fossil energy sources was the most effective strategy for preserving Mexico's forests. In the nineteenth and well into the twentieth century, forests were widely viewed as climatic engines that regulated rainfall critical for food production and purified "miasmas" or polluted air. During the brief reign of Maximilian of Habsburg (1864–7), the renowned Mexican savant Leopoldo Río de la Loza advised his majesty that "the most direct measure to impede [. . .] total destruction [of the country's forests] would be to adopt coal, both for steam engines and ironworks furnaces, and in any other operation in which coal can be used . . . ."[113] Almost 70 years later, in 1932, then President Pascual Ortiz Rubio visited Tláhuac, an area north of Mexico City that promised to become a source of natural gas for the city. One newspaper touted that natural gas would "free" local forests and woodlands from their "enemy," fuel consumption. Mexico City residents, it claimed, should adopt natural gas for cooking if they wanted to avoid turning their valley into a desert. If they did not, the newspaper prophesied, "their children's wails would reach their tombs, reproaching them for having destroyed a good that could have been made fertile, beautiful, and productive."[114]

The view that increased fossil fuel use was a solid conservation strategy persisted among experts and government officials into the 1950s. In 1958, two Mexican foresters lauded the official government policy to replace charcoal and wood with fossil energy sources in households, which led to substantial reduction in wood consumption. They also suggested that more work needed to be done, noting that the transition to fossil-fueled cooking was most advanced in cities and towns with small population centers, while areas located close to forests lagged behind.[115]

Quantitative data on Mexican forests from the 1950s should be taken with some skepticism, since the country still lacked a systematic national survey.[116]

---

[113] Leopoldo Río de la Loza, *Escritos de Leopoldo Río de la Loza* (México: Imprenta de Ignacio Escalante, 1911), 332. Río de la Loza believed that a "patriotic call" on individuals to follow forest regulations would fall on deaf ears and that constant political turmoil prevented their enforcement.

[114] "Noticias sobre los pozos de gas de Tláhuac" (1932), caja 3722, exp. 90119, AHP.

[115] Alfonso Loera Borja and Roberto Villaseñor Angeles, *El problema forestal de México* (México: Impresora Periodística Comercial S. de R.L., 1958), 12.

[116] In 1952, the Camara Nacional de las Industrias Forestales estimated forest area at 25 million hectares. Forest engineer Alfonso Escudero calculated 31 million hectares, while Ing. Miguel Ruíz Vite estimated 28 million. D. T. Griffiths, from the Misión Forestal de la FAO en México, calculated 26 million in 1954. Ing. Felipe Castro stated 36.5 million hectares. Ing. Rober Villaseñor and the Instituto Mexicano de Recursos Naturales Renovables claimed 33.5 million hectares in 1956. In short, estimates varied from 25 to 36.5 million hectares of forest in the 1950s, between 12–13 percent and 18–19 percent of national territory. See Manuel Hinojosa Ortiz, *Los bosques de México: relato de un despilfarro y una injusticia* (México: Instituto Mexicano de Investigaciones Económicas, 1958), 11. A FAO mission directed by British forest expert Fred Hummal in collaboration with Mexican

Still, several lines of evidence corroborate the foresters' claim. The most reliable evidence suggests that throughout the 1940s and 1950s, fuelwood and charcoal consumption across Mexico did decline, although perhaps less markedly than foresters believed. In Latin America, the Caribbean and large parts of South America (including Chile and Venezuela, both heavy fossil fuel users) also experienced a drop. Brazil, representing half of the continent, defied the trend and saw its per capita consumption of fuelwood surge, suggesting wood's great significance to postwar Brazilian industrialization (Table 5.8).[117] Remarkably, this reduction in fuelwood use occurred despite Mexico's 30 percent population growth between 1941 and 1955.[118] By the late 1950s, Mexico had by far the lowest fuelwood consumption per capita in Latin America at about half that of forest-deprived southeastern South America (Uruguay and Argentina), the second lowest.[119]

The foresters' appraisal of urban and rural wood consumption was also correct. In Mexico City, fuelwood and charcoal consumption diminished by 85 percent from the early 1940s to the mid-1950s. By 1955, only about 100,000 families in the city used wood or charcoal for cooking and heating. In other, smaller cities, about half of households had already replaced wood with fossil fuels, usually natural gas or oil. In many rural areas, fuelwood and charcoal remained dominant or important.[120]

Overall decline in household fuelwood consumption reduced pressure on certain forest ecosystems like conifer forests, which were normally the

---

foresters initiated the first national forest survey in the early 1960s. See Instituto Nacional de Investigaciones Forestales, *Inventario forestal nacional de México, 1961–1964: informe técnico.* (México: Instituto Nacional de Investigaciones Forestales, Organizacion de las Naciones Unidas para la Agricultura y la Alimentación, 1965) and "El inventario forestal," *El Informador,* julio 18, 1962.

[117] The South American data was not disaggregated in the FAO source used here. Venezuela's case may have distorted Colombia's, where fuelwood consumption was among the highest in all of Latin America. See Economic Commission for Latin America (ECLA) and Food and Agriculture Organization of the United Nations (FAO), *Latin America: Timber Trends and Prospects,* Document E/CN.12/624: FAO/LAFC-62/5 (New York: United Nations, 1963), 131.

[118] *Aprovechamiento de los recursos forestales; informes presentados por la Misión Forestal de la Organización de las Naciones Unidas para la Agricultura y la Alimentación.* (México: Banco de México; Departamento de Investigaciones Industriales, 1956) vol. II, 312.

[119] In 1956–9, Mexico's per capita consumption was 0.27 cubic meters. Southeastern South America's was 0.49. See ECLA and FAO, *Latin America Timber Trends and Prospects,* 131.

[120] *Aprovechamiento de los recursos forestales,* vol. II, 309–11. Wood consumption for fuel declined in Mexico City from 700 metric tons per day in the 1941 to 100–125 tons per day in 1955. Yet this amount still required harvesting the yield of a sizable 330 km² of forest. Not only did most urban households adopt fossil fuels for cooking and heating by the 1950s, but those who still burned fuelwood consumed far less than their rural counterparts. For example, while the remaining families using fuelwood in Mexico City by mid-century consumed an average of 3 m³ of it per year, in rural areas (especially cold ones) this figure could rise to 8 m³ per year.

Table 5.8 *Consumption of fuelwood by region in Latin America*

	Per Capita Fuelwood Consumption (Cubic Meters)	
	1948–1951	1956–1959
Mexico	0.35	0.27
Central America	1.04	1.34
The Caribbean Islands	0.71	0.61
Northern South America	1.25	1.15
Southwest South America	0.75	0.51
Brazil	1.07	1.44
Southeast South America	0.55	0.49
Latin America	1.06	0.9

Source: ECLA and FAO, *Latin America: Timber Trends and Prospects*, 1963, 131.

source of about 60 percent of all fuelwood in Mexico.[121] Most of this exploitation occurred in places like Michoacán, Durango, and Chihuahua. Tropical forests were probably less affected by the shift in Mexican household energy use because most wood extracted from those forests went to making furniture or construction. Regardless, the conservation dream of generations of Mexican elites finally became reality; fossil fuel exploitation curbed deforestation. In a country where roughly 80 percent of harvested wood became fuelwood,[122] what people did in their kitchens mattered.

While fossil energy mitigated deforestation in some parts, Mexico's new fossil-fueled, rapidly industrializing society placed other burdens on forests that would play out on a much larger scale. It would take a few decades before the effects of these developments became evident. Only a few mid-twentieth-century observers began to suspect that the same energy sources championed to save forests would power transformations that endangered the country's forests like never before.

This included a shift in wood use. By mid-century, wood use in the production of consumer goods surged.[123] People now purchased wood furniture and trinkets for their homes. Low-income Mexicans satisfied themselves with cheap softwood or plywood products, while middle and upper-middle urbanites wanted furniture and cabinets made of precious

[121] Ibid., 221.   [122] Ibid., 312.
[123] Between 1950 and 1980, nonfuel production of wood tripled, from about 6 million to almost 18 million cubic meters annually. During this time, charcoal production barely increased from 430,000 to 485,000 cubic meters. See INEGI, *Estadísticas históricas de México*, vol. 1 (México: INEGI, 1990), 434–6.

tropical woods. Starting in the 1950s, tropical forests in Mexico were exploited on an unprecedented scale, replicating a global trend. The "great onslaught" on tropical forests had begun.[124] Mexico's tropical forests were not pristine ecosystems. According to one source, there were no untouched tropical forests in Mexico in the mid-century: only exhausted or exploitable, in good condition but not "virgin" (see Figure 5.7). Logging of hardwood species had a long history dating back to the colonial period. The Porfiriato (1876–1911) saw substantial tropical deforestation in

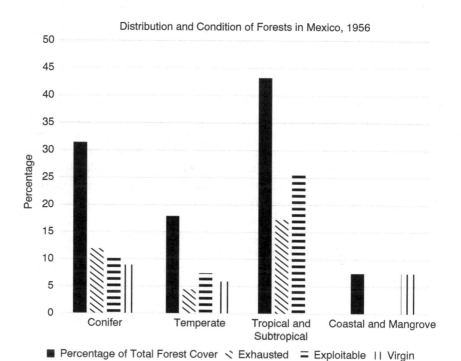

Figure 5.7 Distribution and condition of forests in Mexico, 1956.
Adapted from Instituto Mexicano de Recursos Renovables, *Mesas redondas sobre problemas forestales de México*, 1956, 23.

[124] See Michael Williams, *Deforesting the Earth: From Prehistory to Global Crisis* (Chicago: University of Chicago Press, 2010), chapter 13. Mexican consumers were not the only ones responsible for clearing Mexico's tropical forests. About half of all tropical woods were exported to the USA or Europe.

southeastern Mexico by large timber companies exporting abroad.[125] But tropical wood extraction was now aided by fossil-fueled technologies, including roads, trucks, and tractors used to haul massive hardwoods out of the forest.[126] By the early 1960s, large-scale tropical deforestation was in full swing. A third of the heavily forested state of Campeche in southeastern Mexico, for example, was handed over to timber companies for commercial exploitation.[127] A government-backed policy dubbed "march to the sea" – initiated in the 1940s to colonize the humid tropics with landless peasants from the overcrowded highlands – augmented the rapid clearance of Mexico's tropical forests after 1950.[128]

Another critical development was the industrialization of forests.[129] In the 1940s and 1950s, Mexico's government partnered with private companies to create a series of "industrial units of forest exploitation" (*unidades industriales de explotación forestal*).[130] These *unidades* were government concessions managed by private companies that exploited forests industrially.[131] Their objective was to supply national industry and consumers with commodified forest products. In theory, they would follow silvicultural techniques for sustainable forest harvest. In practice, they did not. Once established, *unidades* covered vast areas (in one case, 600,000 hectares) and the people whose property fell under their

---

[125] Jan de Vos, *Oro verde: la conquista de la selva lacandona por los madereros tabasqueños, 1822–1949* (México, D. F.: Fondo de Cultura Económica, 1996), chapter 7.

[126] Misión Forestal de la Organización de las Naciones Unidas para la Agricultura y la Alimentación, *Aprovechamiento de los recursos forestales* (México, D. F.: Banco de México, S. A., Departamento de Investigaciones Industriales, 1956), vol. I, 48–9.

[127] Instituto Nacional de Investigaciones Forestales, *Inventario forestal nacional de México, 1961–1964*, vols. II–V (México, D. F.: Instituto Nacional de Investigaciones Forestales; Organización de las Naciones Unidas para la Agricultura y la Alimentación (FAO), 1965), 129–31.

[128] President Ávila Camacho made this policy official in 1941 with his "march to the sea" speech, depicting the tropical lowlands as a promised land of great fertility that would relieve congested and eroded lands in central Mexico. Despite the government encouraging peasants and small farmers to emigrate, Ávila Camacho envisioned large-scale, commercial agriculture for Mexico's tropics. See Mosk, *Industrial Revolution in Mexico*, 220. When tropical commercial agriculture ventures failed, newly arrived peasants turned to ranching, causing widespread deforestation. By 2000, Mexico had lost over 90 percent of its tropical rainforests (dry tropical forests fared somewhat better). For a case study of how peasant settlements changed their new home over time, see Leticia Durand and Elena Lazos, "Colonization and Tropical Deforestation in the Sierra Santa Marta, Southern Mexico," *Environmental Conservation* 31, no. 1 (2004): 11–21.

[129] An overview of this process is in Christopher R. Boyer, *Political Landscapes: Forests, Conservation, and Community in Mexico* (Durham: Duke University Press, 2015), chapters 4 and 5.

[130] All information for this paragraph comes from Loera Borja and Villaseñor Angeles, *El problema forestal de México*, 33–7.

[131] Ibid., 33–6, 43. By law, forests in public lands belonged to the nation. Additionally, given that *unidades* were legally declared public utilities (*utilidad pública*), they could infringe on some private property rights.

jurisdiction were forced to lease or sell their timber to the company. The *unidad* was effectively a state-sponsored private monopoly. Since *unidad* contracts could be rescinded and reissued to different concessionaires, *unidades* typically operated on a get-rich-quick mentality with little concern for local forests. The largest concessions were allotted to paper, cellulose, and plywood companies, wood manufacturers, and sawmills. In total, these enterprises controlled some 25,000 km² of forests in the late 1950s.

The impact of these new enterprises was considerable. Their detractors – clearly a minority at the time – believed that existing industrial forest units, with few exceptions, "do not meet their original and useful purpose. They have not been developed and do not operate as a well-organized industry that rationally manages forests and defends them [from overexploitation]."[132] Critics pointed out that the forest industry was enormously profligate, wasting over half of all wood it harvested, destroying forest, and benefitting only a few wealthy families while robbing the nation of an essential asset.[133] Supporters – which included the federal government, most foresters, and industrialists – advocated more forest industrialization, not less. Enrique Beltrán, Mexico's most prominent twentieth-century biologist, believed that industrial forestry could work properly provided the state, foresters, and industrialists collaborated closely. The state would develop adequate forest policy and fund scientific research, the industrialist would provide capital and expertise, and the forester would act as mediator to ensure exploitation followed rational norms.[134] Their most ardent enthusiasts viewed forest industrial units as part of a larger program of state- and expert-led industrialization of natural resource exploitation. From this perspective, only a technocratic approach could ensure that Mexico's natural wealth would be used to its maximum capacity and nature mobilized efficiently for national benefit.[135]

A paradox emerged. As one observer put it: "History teaches us that nothing can satisfy our vast needs. The effect of previous economic and social measures soon ebbs, favorable returns always diminish, works and benefits for the common good become insufficient, not because our impulse to build has stopped, but because, despite our development, one cannot meet a need that always continues to grow."[136]

---

[132] Ortiz, *Los bosques de México*, 39.   [133] Ibid., 51, 61.

[134] Instituto Mexicano de Recursos Renovables, *Mesas redondas sobre problemas forestales de México* (México, D. F.: Ediciones del Instituto Mexicano de Recursos Naturales Renovables, 1956), 241.

[135] Gutiérrez Olguín, "Los recursos naturales renovables en el desarrollo económico de México," 231–607.

[136] Ibid., 538–539.

Conclusion

At the end of *Las Batallas en el Desierto* (*Battles in the Desert*), Carlos, the story's protagonist, offers a devastating observation about 1950s Mexico. "That country is gone. There is no memory of the Mexico from that time. And nobody cares: who could feel nostalgic for that horror?" Pacheco's story was published in 1981, when the Mexican Miracle was showing signs of exhaustion (Mexico's economy almost collapsed the following year) and public cynicism over the country's political regime began to boil. In hindsight, the promise of perennial prosperity that inspired much of the 1950s had faded on a bad wind, leaving "horror" in its wake. But what Pacheco saw was not the end of an era. It was its metamorphosis.

The 1950s marked the consolidation of fossil fuels as the basis of Mexican society. A cycle initiated 70 years earlier by coal-powered railroads had come full circle. Mexico now powered most domestic transportation, manufacturing, and electricity generation with fossil fuels. An increasingly large share of the country's food was produced using various fossil fuel inputs, from chemical feedstock for synthetic fertilizer to fuel for increasing numbers of tractors. Even Mexican households, long the last line of defense against fossil energy's domestic takeover, began shifting to natural gas. Over the following decades, this thermo-industrial revolution would power continued environmental, economic, and social change on an unprecedented scale.

By the 1980s, the consequences of Mexico's energy transition to fossil fuels were coming into increasingly sharper focus. It is true that fossil fuels, especially petroleum, solved Mexico's age-old "fuel problem." After decades of searching for cheap, reliable, and abundant energy, Mexico tapped into its vast stores of liquid and gaseous fossil energy. This energy boon facilitated rapid industrial and economic growth, raising the material welfare of many. But Mexico's dependence on fossil fuels also led to unchecked urban and population growth; rural exodus on a large scale; mechanized production and chronic labor insecurity; a transport system often favoring cars and trucks over mass transit; and massive ecological degradation. Fossil fuels turned many parts of Mexico into vibrant and dynamic hubs. They also set the country on a path to becoming a nation with seemingly intractable social, urban, and environmental problems. Short-term success came at the price of chronic unsustainability.

Such was the Janus-faced nature of Mexico's fossil fuel transition. That was the world industrialists pursued, political elites supported, and Pacheco lamented. That is the world Mexico continues to inhabit.

Amidst all other developments of the twentieth century – the wars and revolutions, the pivotal changes in society, politics, and environment – fossil fuels seeped further and deeper into every corner of Mexican life. They became the foundation upon which so much of Mexico's history in the second half of the twentieth century was built. It only follows that fossil energy underwrote the country's successes as well as its failures.

Conclusion

In the mid-nineteenth century, Mexico lived under the solar energy regime. A combination of animal and human muscle, water, and wood powered the vast majority of human activities, from growing food – itself the main energy source – to extracting, producing, and transporting goods. Only some factories in the flourishing textile industry and silver mines had adopted steam engines, the first to mechanize certain stages of manufacturing, the second to draw water from flooded mines. Steam engines, while few, allowed Mexico's inhabitants for the first time ever to convert heat into work without a human or animal body. This transitional moment was part of Mexico's long, eventful energy and environmental history. This included the sixteenth-century demographic collapse of the indigenous population, the critical role of silver mining, and important developments in the first decades of independent life, especially the loss of energy-rich northern territories to the USA. Mid-nineteenth-century Mexico was born from this history.

Operating under diminished territory and limited energy resources, a slow but resilient process of regional industrialization and mechanization unfolded until the 1880s. Silver production began rising again, partly powered by steam. A revived mining industry, historically the main source of deforestation in Mexico, soon began devouring large swaths of forests. Steam engines also became common in the textile industry, where they complemented unreliable and limited waterpower. By 1880, steam engines were ubiquitous across Mexico, found in modest workshops, bakeries, small factories, sawmills, and dredges. Around the same time, Mexico's railroad network expanded from a few hundred to thousands of kilometers using foreign capital and the full support of the Porfirian state. Combined with habitual consumers of large amounts of fuelwood such as iron foundries and cities, the various and new applications of steam power caused severe deforestation and led to an energy bottleneck in Mexico by the 1880s.

Alarm over the country's "fuel problem" and its potential to stall economic "progress" – as well as the effects of forest loss on farming, climate, and people's health – convinced Mexico's government and industrialists to pursue coal. Fully aware of the role coal had played in the industrialization of Europe and the USA, Fomento (Mexico's development ministry) funded surveys that identified domestic coal deposits. Only those of Coahuila, in the far north, turned out to be both large and accessible enough for commercial exploitation, limiting its market to Mexico's northern half. However, in combination with imports, coal managed to become an important energy source for railroads – by far its largest consumer – which in turn transported coal to smelters, power plants, mines, and industries in cities like Monterrey and Mexico City. By 1910, coal extraction and consumption were growing rapidly in Mexico, just as oil from Veracruz was entering Mexican markets. Then the Mexican Revolution broke out.

Driven by large-scale land privatization and partly by fossil-fueled mechanization that left many with precarious livelihoods and little autonomy, the Revolution severely disrupted the coal industry. By contrast, fuel-hungry World War I combatant nations and Mexico's own railroads and industries would catapult oil into the center of the domestic economy and politics during this time. Exports declined rapidly after 1921, redirecting the flow of Mexico's oil within its own borders. By the 1930s, Mexico was consuming most of its oil production, with industrial hubs and cities at the forefront. The fate of the postrevolutionary state – committed to capitalist industrialization – and oil became closely intertwined. State intervention was critical for the expansion of oil-based infrastructure like roads and, after the expropriation of 1938, oil production and commercialization. In turn, oil wealth supported and legitimized postwar governments. While households and hydroelectricity slowed the transition, by mid-century, Mexico's economy and society largely depended on fossil energy.

Mexico now lived under the fossil fuel energy regime. With the state dedicated to fossil-fueled industrialization, Mexico experienced the largest and longest expansion of the country's commercial economy in its history – its own Great Acceleration.[1] Far-reaching environmental and social changes followed. Mexico – or, rather, parts of it – became an urban and industrial nation supported by a complex system of roads, motorized transportation, thermoelectric plants, pipelines, and refineries. All this

---

[1] John R. McNeill and Peter Engelke, *The Great Acceleration: An Environmental History of the Anthropocene since 1945* (Cambridge: The Belknap Press of Harvard University Press, 2014).

demanded ever-growing infusions of cheap fossil energy. An unprecedented population explosion caused by better sanitation and modern
medicine combined with a fossil energy–based Green Revolution to dis-
place Mexico's rural population, sending millions to cities and the USA. As
mechanized industrial and food production offered few secure jobs,
inequality deepened. Some regions and social classes attached to the fossil
economy increased their prosperity, while others became poorer and led
insecure and precarious lives.

What does Mexico's energy transition to fossil fuels offer our understanding of energy shifts in general and those experienced by other fossil-
fueled societies? While this is somewhat obvious, Mexico illustrates
a nonetheless important fact: there was a fundamental similarity in energy
shifts to fossil energy worldwide. As in Mexico, fossil fuel transitions
globally involved moving away from muscle power and renewables like
wood and water to coal and then oil and natural gas. Shifts also tended to
aggregate and mix energy sources rather than simply replace one with
another. Mid-twentieth-century Mexico was fossil fuel dependent, but it
still consumed fuelwood and hydroelectricity. This broad, global convergence towards fossil energy–based societies happened despite differences in
policy, economic system, and levels of wealth.

That said, the timing, length, speed, and importance of the different
stages varied by region, as did the specific circumstances and factors
shaping them. Consider the role coal played in Mexico's transition.
While coal was king for a century in the USA and Europe, in Mexico it
remained a scarce and expensive commodity whose period of greatest
influence lasted just 20 or 30 years. Coal's most important role was as an
energy bridge between agrarian society and the oil-powered industrial
nation Mexico would later become. This unique dynamic meant that
Mexico experienced a distinct transition whose effects on its environmental, political, and labor conditions both compare and contrast with the
USA and Europe. Mexico did not battle coal pollution like London and
Pittsburgh, or today's Beijing. Pollution came later from gasoline-powered
motor traffic, as it did in Los Angeles and much of California.[2] As in the
USA, Mexico's shift to oil began at the turn of the twentieth century and
was largely complete by the 1940s; Europe would wait until the decades
after World War II before this transition fully materialized.

---

[2] James C. Williams, *Energy and the Making of Modern California* (Akron: University of Akron Press,
1997), 295–7.

The Mexican case also highlights the regional nature of many energy transitions. In Mexico, as in other parts of the world, the transition began locally before spreading until eventually consolidating at the national level. Mexico's transition began in Mexico City and Monterrey and their respective hinterlands. Only after fossil fuels established themselves in cities, industries, and transportation did they spill over to the countryside with the Green Revolution. Why certain regions transitioned first depended on local environmental, geographic, geological, and political conditions. Mexico City and Monterrey shifted in large part due to their location and resources, existing environmental conditions and concerns, and the powerful interests that would see them industrialized like other North Atlantic regions. Monterrey was close to both the US border and Mexico's coal and oil deposits. Mexico City was the center of political power and the country's transportation hub. It also suffered severe local deforestation that needed a quick solution. Had these conditions not existed, it is hard to imagine that the transition would have begun in these two cities. Their fossil economy, in turn, tended to reinforce the privileged positions these regions enjoyed within their nation-states.

Mexico's shift, like others, was not a linear process. It was messy, marked by ups, downs, and periods in which the transition was gradual and slow (sometimes even locally reversed). Nor did it come at the hands of individuals. While specific elites argued for adopting coal and oil, Mexico's shift to fossil fuels was ultimately carried out by industrial interests and a state motivated by "national security" concerns and desires to establish Mexico as a "civilized" or "modern" nation, depending on the century. In Mexico, as in other cases, "fossilization" was a (largely undemocratic) state and industrial policy. In turn, the concentrated energy of fossil fuels expanded state power and increased industry's influence and profits to an unprecedented scale.

While some regions, the state, large industrial interests, and the middle and upper classes won under this new energy regime, many urban poor and rural people were displaced or left out of the high-energy economy. Worse, many lost much of the autonomy historically granted by more localized and decentralized energy systems. In this sense, Mexico's energy transition not only exemplifies shifts elsewhere but also underlines a central theme in the modern environmental history of Mexico: the socially differentiated and unequal effects of environmental change.[3] This scholarship has shown

---

[3] Christopher R. Boyer, *Political Landscapes: Forests, Conservation, and Community in Mexico* (Durham: Duke University Press, 2015) Myrna Santiago, *The Ecology of Oil: Environment, Labor, and the Mexican Revolution, 1900–1938* (Cambridge: Cambridge University Press, 2006); Matthew Vitz, *A City on a Lake: Urban Political Ecology and the Growth of Mexico City* (Durham: Duke

that the benefits of modern environmental change often accrued to a minority, while the rest bore its consequences – displacement, precarious lives, marginality, and exposure to pollution and environmental damage. This implies not only that environmental degradation exacerbates social inequality, but that reducing such inequities might limit negative environmental change. Genuinely solving environmental and energy problems thus requires addressing social and political issues.

Finally, Mexico's case illustrates another trait shared with other energy shifts: the deep connection between a society's energy regime (how it extracts, consumes, and transports energy) and its very makeup. Change the energy regime, and society itself is transformed. The shift to fossil fuels as the basis of Mexican society radically reshaped Mexico's economy, environment, and people. But the change went beyond the material. Proponents of fossil fuels not only argued for robust industry and healthy forests; they argued for the mastery of nature and endless, fossil-fueled growth. These beliefs and aspirations underpinned energy transitions worldwide and, in turn, became orthodoxy naturalized through the fossil economy. They continue to be the focus of policy in Mexico and the global community – even at a time when science and lived experience urgently argue for a transition *away* from fossil fuels to avoid catastrophic climate change.[4]

It is in this regard that the real value of the environmental histories of Mexico – including this book – ultimately lies. They highlight a key aspect of the national project of modernization in its various incarnations, from Porfirian "progress" to twentieth-century "development." These programs and policies achieved short-term success – typically understood as more of everything, be it economic growth or pipelines – at the cost of long-term unsustainability. From irrigation projects in La Laguna, to the industrialization of forests, capitalist urbanization, and the transition to fossil fuels, Mexico's model of a modern, capitalist, industrial nation appears environmentally unviable in the long run, despite some genuine and distinct conservation efforts.[5]

University Press, 2018); Mikael D. Wolfe, *Watering the Revolution: An Environmental and Technological History of Agrarian Reform in Mexico* ((Durham: Duke University Press, 2017).

[4] Climate change will hit Mexico hard. One report ranks Mexico as the 8th most vulnerable country to climate change out of a survey of 67. See Ashim Paun et al., "Fragile Planet: Scoring Climate Risks around the World" (HSBC Global Research, March 2018), 5.

[5] Lane Simonian, *Defending the Land of the Jaguar: A History of Conservation in Mexico* (Austin: University of Texas Press, 1995); Emily Wakild, *Revolutionary Parks: Conservation, Social Justice, and Mexico's National Parks, 1910–1940* (Tucson: University of Arizona Press, 2011).

By 2020, Mexico had lived under a fossil energy regime for roughly 70 years – about the same time it took to shift to fossil fuels. Over that period of time, population growth slowed, economic crises and a recession struck, and since the 1980s Mexico's political elite has implemented a neoliberal set of policies that deregulated the economy, privatized land on a Porfirian scale, and deeply integrated the country into the global economy – again. In the meantime, total carbon dioxide emissions grew unabatedly from 62 to 455 $MtCO_2$ between 1965 and 2019, consistently ranking Mexico among the top 10–15 emitters in the world.[6] There are signs that certain sectors of Mexico's economy are already moving towards renewable energy – although the commitment to a fossil-fueled society and capitalist growth remains as strong as ever – but the path forward is neither obvious nor inevitable. One can only hope it will be different from the past.

[6] BP, *Statistical Review of World Energy*, June 2020. Mexico's cumulative carbon dioxide (CO2) emissions represented 1.2 percent of the global total until 2019, the largest in Latin America and on par with those of Italy, South Africa, and Iran. The USA (25 percent), the European Union (22 percent), and China (12.5 percent) are by far the most important historical contributors to global emissions. See Hannah Ritchie and Max Roser (2020) - "CO_2 and Greenhouse Gas Emissions". *Published online at OurWorldInData.org*. Retrieved from: 'https://ourworldindata.org/co2-and-other-greenhouse-gas-emissions'.

Bibliography

Archives

Archivo del Estado de Nuevo León (AENL), Monterrey
Archivo Eugenio Garza Sada (AEGS), Monterrey
Archivo General del Estado de Veracruz (AHEV), Xalapa
Archivo General de la Nación (AGN), Mexico City
Archivo Histórico del Agua (AHA), Mexico City
Archivo Histórico del Distrito Federal (AHDF), Mexico City
Archivo Histórico de la Fundidora Monterrey (AHFM), Monterrey
Archivo Histórico de Monterrey (AHM), Monterrey
Archivo Histórico de la Papelera San Rafael (AHPSR), State of Mexico
Archivo Histórico de Pemex (AHP), Mexico City
Archivo Histórico Municipal de Chihuahua (AHMCH), Chihuahua City
Bancroft Library, University of California, Berkeley
Biblioteca Manuel Orozco y Berra, Mexico City
Fototeca Nacional INAH, Pachuca
Hemeroteca Nacional de México, Mexico City
Iberoamerikanisches Institut, Berlin
Nettie Lee Benson Library, Latin American Microforms Collection, University of
    Texas, Austin
Special Collections & Archives, UC San Diego, La Jolla

Published Primary Sources

Academia Mexicana de Jurisprudencia y Legislación. *Estudios jurídicos: petróleo y carbón de piedra.* México, D. F.: Librería de la vida, de Ch. Bouret, 1905.
Actas de cabildo del Ayuntamiento Constitucional de México. México: Imprenta de la Escuela Correccional de Artes y Oficios, 1885.
1886.
1887.
1889.
Adalberto de Cardona, S., and Trinidad Sanchez. *México y sus capitales; reseña histórica del país desde los tiempos más remotos hasta el presente; en la cual*

también se trata de sus riquezas naturales. México: Tip. de J. Aguilar Vera y Cía (Sociedad Comanditaria), 1900.

Agricola, Georgius. *De Natura Fossilium.* Mineola, NY: Dover Publications, 2004 [1543].

Aguilera, J. G. "The Carboniferous Deposits of Northern Coahuila." *The Engineering and Mining Journal* 88 (1909): 15.

Alamán, Lucas. *Memoria sobre el estado de la agricultura é industria de la República, que la Dirección de estos ramos presenta al Gobierno Supremo, en cumplimiento del articulo 26 del decreto orgánico de 2 de diciembre de 1842.* México, 1843.

— *Representacion dirigida al exmo. señor Presidente provisional de la República por la Junta General Directiva de la Industria Nacional, sobre la importancia de esta, necesidad de su fomento y medios de dispensarselo.* México: Impr. de J.M. Lara, 1843.

— *Obras de D. Lucas Alamán.* México: V. Agüeros, 1899.

Album de los Ferrocarriles. México: Secretaría de Fomento, 1889.

Almaraz, Ramón. *Memoria de los trabajos ejecutados por la comisión científica de Pachuca en el año de 1864.* México: J.M. Andrade y F. Escalante, 1865.

Almonte, Juan Nepomuceno. *Guía de forasteros y repertorio de conocimientos útiles.* México: Imprenta de Ignacio Cumplido, 1852.

Alzate y Ramírez, José Antonio de. *Gacetas de Literatura de México.* Vol. 2. 3 vols. México: Oficina Tip. de. la Secretaría de Fomento, 1893.

American Automobile Association. *The Pan American Highway.* New York: American Automobile Association, 1953.

American Institute of Mining, Metallurgical, and Petroleum Engineers. *Transactions of the American Institute of Mining, Metallurgical and Petroleum Engineers* 32 (1902).

Anales del Ministerio de Fomento de la República Mexicana. Vol. 1–3. México: Imprenta de Francisco Díaz de León, 1877.

— Vol. 4–5. México: Imprenta de Francisco Díaz de León, 1881.

— Vol. 7. México: Imprenta de Francisco Díaz de León, 1882.

Anderson, Alexander D. *Mexico from the Material Stand-Point. A Review of Its Mineral, Agricultural, Forest, and Marine Wealth, Its Manufactures, Commerce, Railways, Isthmian Routes, and Finances. With a Description of Its Highlands and Attractions.* Washington, DC; New York: A. Brentano & Co.; Brentano Bros., 1884.

Anglo-Mexican Petroleum Products Co. *Mexican Fuel Oil.* London: Anglo-Mexican Petroleum Products Co., Ltd., 1914.

— *Petróleo combustible mexicano.* México, D. F.: Compañía Mexicana de Petróleo El Aguila, S.A., 1914.

Anónimo. *Datos y reflexiones sobre la industria mexicana: publicacion de un industrial.* México: Imprenta de Ignacio Escalante, 1885.

Antuñano, Esteban de. *Ampliacion, aclaración y corección a los principales puntos del manifiesto sobre el algodón.* Puebla: Oficina del Hospital de San Pedro, 1833.

— *Pensamientos para la regneración industrial de México, escritos y publicados por el ciudadano Estevan de Antuñano a beneficio de su patria.* Puebla: Imprenta del Hospital de San Pedro, 1837.

Ventajas políticas, civiles, fabriles y domésticas, que por dar ocupación también a las mugeres en las fábricas de maquinaria moderna que están levantando en México, deben recibirse. s.l.: s.n., 1837.

Economía política en México: apuntes para la historia de la industria mexicana. Puebla: Imprenta Antigua en el Portal de las Flores, 1842.

"Documentos para la historia de la industria algodonera de México, en lo fabril y en lo agrícola, o sea narraciones y cálculos estadísticos sobre ella." *El Siglo Diez y Nueve.* March 28, 1843.

"Noticias estadísticas, artísticas y morales de la fábrica de hilados y tejidos de algodón, nombrada la Constancia Mexicana, movida por rueda hidráulica, de la propiedad de Estevan de Antuñano, situada en los suburbios de Puebla." *El Siglo Diez y Nueve.* March 28, 1843.

"Estado de la industria manufacturera de algodones en Puebla, nacida en dicha ciudad el año de 1835." *El Siglo Diez y Nueve.* March 1843.

Pensamientos para la regeneracion industrial de Mexico, escritos y publicados por el ciudadano. Mexico: M. Porrúa, 1955.

Obras: documentos para la historia de la industrialización en México, 1833–1846. México: Secretaría de Hacienda y Crédito Público, 1979.

Aprovechamiento de los recursos forestales: informes presentados por la misión forestal de la Organización de las Naciones Unidas para la Agricultura y la Alimentación. Vols. II. México, D. F.: Banco de México, Departamento de Investigaciones Industriales, 1956.

Aprovechamiento de los recursos forestales; informes presentados por la misión forestal de la Organización de las Naciones Unidas para la Agricultura y la Alimentación. Mexico: Banco de México, S.A., Departamento de Investigaciones Industriales, 1958.

Arizpe, Rafael R. *Estadistica de las aplicaciones de la electricidad en la Republica Mexicana.* Mexico: Tip. y Lit. "La Europea" de J. Aguilar Vera y Ca. (Sociedad Comanditaria), 1900.

Armenta, Rafael de. "Consumo de leña en las minas de Real del Monte." *Boletín de la Sociedad Mexicana de Geografía y Estadística* II ([1834] 1870): 509.

Arróniz, Marcos. *Manual del viajero en Mejico, ó, compendio de la historia de la Ciudad de Mejico, con la descripcion é historia de sus templos, conventos, edificios publicos; las costumbres de sus habitantes, etc., y con el plan de dicha ciudad.* Paris: Librería de Rosa y Bouret, 1858.

Ávila González, Salvador, et al. *Guía de fuentes documentales para la historia del agua en el Valle de México, 1824–1928: Archivo Histórico del Ayuntamiento de la Ciudad de México.* México, D. F.: CIESAS, 1997.

Bach, Federico, and M. de la Peña. *México y su petróleo. Síntesis histórica.* México, D. F.: Editorial "México Nuevo," 1938.

Balbontin, Miguel. "Los bosques." *Boletín de la Sociedad Mexicana de Geografía y Estadística* 3, 1 (1873): 144–52.

Bárcena, Mariano. "Dictámen sobre la repoblación vegetal del Valle de México." *La Naturaleza* 1, 6 (1870): 245–51.

Armonias de la naturaleza. Discurso pronunciado por Mariano Bárcena en la velada literaria que tuvo lugar en la ciudad de Puebla en la noche del 19 de enero de 1880. Mexico City: Filomeno Mata, 1880.

"Los criaderos de carbón." *El Minero Mexicano*. March 3, 1881.

Los ferrocarriles mexicanos. México: Tip. de F. Mata, 1881.

"El proyecto de Código de Minería. Dictamen del representante de los estados de Jalisco y México." *El Minero Mexicano*. October 30, 1884.

Tratado de geología, elementos aplicables á la agricultura, á la ingeniería y á la industria. México: Oficina Tip. de la Secretaría de Fomento, 1885.

Selvicultura: breves consideraciones sobre explotación y formación de los bosques. México: Oficina Tip. de la Secretaría de Fomento, 1892.

Baz, Gustavo Adolfo, and Eduardo L. Gallo. *Historia del ferrocarril mexicano: riqueza de México en la zona del Golfo á la Mesa Central, bajo su aspecto geológico, agrícola, manufacturero y comercial. Estudios científicos, históricos y estadísticos*. Mexico: Gallo y Compañia, Editores, 1874.

Becher, H. C. R. *A Trip to Mexico: Being Notes of a Journey from Lake Erie to Lake Tezcuco and Back, with an Appendix Containing and Being a Paper about the Ancient Nations and Races Who Inhabited Mexico before and at the Time of the Spanish Conquest, and the Ancient Stone and Other Structures and Ruins of Ancient Cities Found There*. Toronto: Willing and Williamson, 1880.

Beltrán, Enrique. *El hombre y su ambiente; ensayo sobre el Valle de Mexico*. Mexico: Tezontle, 1958.

La batalla forestal: lo hecho, lo no hecho, lo por hacer. México: No publisher identified, 1964.

Los museos de historia natural en México y la Sociedad Mexicana de Historia Natural. México: Museo de Historia Natural de la Ciudad de México, 1971.

La Sociedad Mexicana de Historia Natural en su segunda época (1936–1986). México: Sociedad Mexicana de Historia Natural, 1986.

Best, Alberto. *Noticia sobre las aplicaciones de la electricidad en la República Mexicana*. México: Imprenta de la Secretaría de Fomento, 1889.

Bibliografía del petróleo en Mexico. Monografias bibliograficas mexicanas. Núm. 8. Mexico: Impr. de la Secretaría de Relaciones Exteriores, 1927.

Bigelow, John. "The Railway Invasion of Mexico." *Harper's Magazine*. October 1882.

Birkinbine, John. "Notes on Engineering in Mexico." In *Proceedings of the Engineers' Club of Philadelphia*, Vol. X: 222–240. Philadelphia: Engineers' Club of Philadelphia, 1893.

Industrial Progress of Mexico. Philadelphia, No publisher identified, 1909.

The Iron and Steel Industry of Mexico; an Article Apropos of the Centennial of the Mexican Republic. New York, No publisher identified, 1910.

Blanco, Gonzalo. *Agriculture in Mexico*. American Agriculture Series. Washington, DC: The Pan-American Union, 1950.

Borlaug, Norman E. "The Green Revolution: For Bread and Peace." *Bulletin of the Atomic Scientists*. June 1971, 6–48.

Bowles, Charles E. *The Petroleum Industry*. Kansas City: Schooley Stationery & Printing Co., 1921.

Bowles, Oliver, and A. Taeves. *Cement in Latin America*. Information Circular / United States Department of the Interior, Bureau of Mines; 7360. Washington, DC: US Dept. of the Interior, Bureau of Mines, 1946.

BP. *Statistical Review of World Energy*, June 2020.

Bradley, John R. *Fuel and Power in Latin America*. Washington, D.C.: United States Government Printing Office, 1931.

Breve reseña de las obras del desagüe del Valle de México. México: Tip. de F. Díaz de León.

Bullington, John P. "The Land and Petroleum Laws of Mexico." *The American Journal of International Law* 22, no.1 (1928): 50–69.

Bureau of the American Republics. *Bulletin 91*. Washington, DC: Bureau of the American Republics, 1899.

Burkhart, Juan. "Memoria sobre la explotación de minas en los distritos de Pachuca y Real del Monte de México." *Anales de la Minería Mexicana*. January 1, 1861.

Bustamante, Miguel. "Informe sobre los criaderos carboníferos de las Huastecas." *Anales del Ministerio de Fomento de la República Mexicana VII* (1882), 538–47.

"Nuevos problemas de salud pública." *Gaceta Médica de México*. July 1, 1966.

Busto, Emiliano. *Estadística de la República Mexicana. Resúmen y análisis de los informes rendidos á la Secretaría de Hacienda por los agricultores, mineros, industriales y comerciantes de la República y los agentes de México en el exterior, en respuesta á las circulares de 1° de agosto de 1877*. 3 vols. México: Imprenta de Ignacio Cumplido, 1880.

Calderón de la Barca, Frances. *Life in Mexico*. Berkeley: University of California Press, 1982 [1852].

Call, Tomme. *The Mexican Venture: From Political to Industrial Revolution in Mexico* (Oxford: Oxford University Press, 1953).

Camacho, Sebastián. *Estadística del estado libre y soberano de Veracruz*. Jalapa: Impreso por Blanco y Aburto, en la Oficina del Gobierno, 1831.

Cámara de Senadores. *Dictamen de la Comisión de Hacienda de la Cámara de Senadores sobre terrenos baldíos y corte de madera en la República*. México: I. Paz, 1878.

El patrimonio forestal de México. México: Cámara de Senadores, XLIV Legislatura, 1958.

El petróleo: la más grande riqueza nacional. México, D. F.: Cámara de Senadores, Sección de Estadística y Anales de Jurisprudencia, 1923.

Canchola, Antonio. "Relaciones sociales y económicas de la ciudad y el campo en México." *Revista Mexicana de Sociología* 19, 1 (1957): 15–23.

Carpenter, William W. *Travels and Adventures in Mexico: In the Course of Journeys of Upward of 2500 Miles, Performed on Foot; Giving an Account of the Manners and Customs of the People, and the Agricultural and Mineral Resources of That Country*. New York: Harper & Brothers, Publishers, 1851.

Castillo, Antonio del. *Riqueza mineral de la República*. Mexico: Imprenta de Ignacio Cumplido, 1861.

"Discurso pronunciado por el señor ingeniero de minas Don Antonio del Castillo, presidente de la Sociedad, en la sesión inaugural verificada el día 6 de Septiembre de 1868." *La Naturaleza* 1, no. 1 (1869–70): 1–5.

"Las supuestas minas de carbón de piedra, de plata, cobre, et., en el Valle de México y montañas que lo circundan." *El Minero Mexicano* VII, 6 (1880).

Castro, Casimiro, J. Campillo, L. Auda, and G. Rodríguez. *México y sus alrededores: coleccion de monumentos, trajes y paisajes*. México: Establecimiento Litográfico de Decaen, Editor, Portal del Coliseo Viejo, 1856.

Castro, Lorenzo. *The Republic of Mexico in 1882*. New York: Thompson & Moreau, printers, 1882.

Catalogue des produits naturels, industriels et artistiques exposés dans la section mexicaine, à l'Exposition Universelle de 1855. Paris: Typographie de Firmin Didot Frères, 1855.

CEPAL, ONU. "El transporte en América Latina," 1965.

Cervi, Emilio. *Algo sobre el petróleo mexicano*. México: Imprenta Victoria, 1916.

"Charcoal in Mexico." *Journal of the United States Association of Charcoal Iron Workers* 3, 1 (1882): 8–11.

Chihuahua: Reseña geográfica y estadística. París; México: Librería de la Vda. de C. Bouret, 1909.

Chimalpopoca, A. A. "El presente y el porvenir industrial en México. Proposiciones previas. Estudio presentado por el socio de número, señor ingeniero A.A. Chimalpopoca." *Boletín de la Sociedad Mexicana de Geografía y Estadística IV* (1897): 358–464.

Chism, Richard E. "Iron in Mexico." *The Engineering and Mining Journal* 46, 19 (1888): 891.

The Mining Code of the Republic of Mexico. Mexico: Published by the Translator, 1888.

Encyclopedia of Mexican Mining Law. A Digest of the Mexican Mining Code, with All the Explanatory Circulars and All Subsidiary Laws, Decrees and Enactments. Also, a Glossary of Mining Terms. Mexico: Impr. del Minero Mexicano, 1900.

"Circular de la Secretaría de Fomento sobre conservación de los montes, número 8635." *Legislación Mexicana*, January 1, 1881.

"Coal Trade Notes. Mexico." *Engineering and Mining Journal* 39 (1885): 375.

Cockrell, Thos. J. *The Mexican National Railways Views: Photographs in Black*. New York: Albertype Co., 1891.

Código de Minería de la República Mexicana. México: Imprenta y Litografía de I. Paz, 1884.

Cole, William E. *Steel and Economic Growth in Mexico*. Austin: University of Texas Press, 1967.

Colomo, José, and Gustavo Ortega. *La industria del petróleo en Mexico*. Mexico: Talleres Gráficos de la Nación, 1927.

Comisión Federal de Electricidad. *Empresas y plantas electricas en la República Mexicana*. México: La Comisión, 1950.

Comisión Nacional de Irrigación. *La industria eléctrica en México; estudios estadísticos preliminares.* México, D. F.: Editorial "Cultura," 1931.

Comité de Asesoría Técnica Forestal. *La situación forestal de México es grave; contribución al conocimiento de las causas que la engendran y a la posible solución de sus problemas.* México: Cámara Nacional de las Industrias del Papel, 1958.

Compañía de las Fábricas de Papel de San Rafael y Anexas, S.A. *Asamblea general ordinaria de accionistas celebrada el 4 de Junio de 1914. Informes del consejo de administración y Comisario. Resoluciones de la asamblea.* México: Tipografía y Litografía de Müller Hnos., 1914.

Compañia explotadora de criaderos de carbón de piedra de la República Mexicana. México: Imprenta de F. Díaz de León, 1876.

Compañía Fundidora de Fierro y Acero de Monterrey, S.A. *Informe anual.* Monterrey, N. L.: Cía. Fundidora de Fierro y Acero de Monterrey, S.A., 1901–21, 1922, 1925, 1930, 1944, 1955, 1957, 1959.

Compañía Industrial y Explotadora de Maderas, ed. *Contrato celebrado entre la Secretaría de Fomento, Colonización e Industria y la Compañía Industrial y Explotadora de Maderas, S.A., para la introducción de petróleo crudo libre de derechos de importación a Guaymas (Son.).* México: Impr. de la Cámara de Diputados, 1912.

"Conditions of Electric Railway Operation in Mexico City." *Electric Railway Journal* 33, 18 (1909): 812–20.

Consejo Superior de Gobierno del Distrito Federal. *Memoria del Consejo Superior de Gobierno del Distrito Federal, presentada al Señor Secretario de Estado y del Despacho de Gobernación. Correspondiente al período transcurrido del 1 de Julio de 1903 al 31 de Diciembre de 1904.* Vol. 1. México, D. F.: Talleres de Tipografía, Encuadernación y Rayados de Pablo Rodríguez, 1906.

Contreras, Carlos. *El plano regulador del Distrito Federal.* México, D. F.: The Author, 1933.

Coordinación General de los Servicios Nacionales de Estadística, Geografía e Informática. *Estadística Industrial Anual.* México, D. F.: Coordinación General de los Servicios Nacionales de Estadística, Geografía e Informática, 1964.

Covarrubias, Manuel (ed.). *Guadalajara Jalisco.* Los Angeles: International Data Corp., 1959.

"Cuadro que manifiesta la producción de carbón por compañías durante los años de 1921 y 1922." *Anuario de Estadística Minera,* 1924.

Dahlgren, Charles Bunker. *Historic Mines of Mexico. A Review of the Mines of that Republic for the Past Three Centuries. Comp. from the Works of von Humboldt, Ward, Burkart, Egloffstein, Reports of the United Mexican Mining Association, the Files of the "Minero Mexicano," and Geographical Society of Mexico, and Reports of Various Engineers of Mines and Mining Companies.* New York: Printed for the Author, 1883.

Day, David Talbot. *A Handbook of the Petroleum Industry,* 2 vols. New York: John Wiley & Sons, 1922.

DeGolyer, E. *The Furbero Oil Field, Mexico.* New York: American Institute of Mining Engineers, 1915.

The Significance of Certain Mexican Oil Field Temperatures. Lancaster, PA: Economic Geology Pub. Co., 1918.

Departamento del Petróleo. *Legislación petrolera; leyes, decretos y disposiciones administrativas referentes a la industria del petróleo.* Mexico: Talleres Gráficos de la Nación, n.d.

Díaz Arias, Julián. *La industria eléctrica y la industrialización de México.* México: Editorial América, 1946.

Díaz Dufoo, Carlos. *La cuestion del petróleo.* Mexico: Eusebio Gomez de la Puente, Editor, 1921.

Dicken, Samuel N. "Monterrey and Northeastern Mexico." *Annals of the Association of American Geographers* 29, 2 (1939): 127–58.

Dirección General de Industria. *Memoria sobre el estado de la agricultura é industria de la República, que la Dirección de estos ramos presenta al Gobierno Supremo, en cumplimiento del articulo 26 del Decreto Orgánico de 2 de diciembre de 1842.* México: Imprenta de J.M. Lara, 1843.

Memoria sobre el estado de la agricultura e industria de la República en el año de 1844. México: José M. Lara, 1845.

Directorio general de la República Mexicana. México: Ruhland & Ahlschier, 1903.

Dotson, Floyd, and Lillian Dotson. "Urban Centralization and Decentralization in Mexico." *Rural Sociology* 21, 1 (1950): 41–9.

Down, F. J. *Embracing a Sketch of the Most Thrilling Incidents in the History of Ancient Mexico and Her Wars, the Present State of the Country, and Its Mines; a Full Account of the War between the United States and Mexico.* New York: 128 Nassau-Street, 1850.

Dr. Atl. *Petróleo en el Valle de Méjico: una Golden Line en la altiplanicie de Anahuac.* México: Polis, 1938.

Dumble, E. T. "Cretaceous of Western Texas and Coahuila, Mexico." *Bulletin of the Geological Society of America* 6 (1895): 375–88.

Dun's Review, International Edition. Vol. 18, no. 1, September 1911.

Economic Commission for Latin America (ECLA), and Food and Agriculture Organization of the United Nations (FAO). *Latin America Timber Trends and Prospects.* United Nations. [Document]E/CN.12/624: FAO/LAFC-62/5. New York: United Nations, 1963.

Edmonson, Munro Sterling. *The Mexican Truck Driver.* New Orleans: Middle American Research Institute, Tulane University, 1959.

Electrical World. *The Electric Power Industry: Past, Present and Future.* 1st ed. New York: Electrical World, 1949.

El Automóvil en México: Revista Mensual Automovilística. México, D. F.: Gustavo Alañá, Editor, 1921, 1922.

El carbón mineral en México. Recopilación formada con los informes, artículos, folletos, etc., publicados hasta la fecha sobre la materia. México, D. F.: Dirección de Talleres Gráficos, 1921.

Elízaga, Lorenzo, Luis Ibarra, and Manuel Fernández. *Proyecto de Ley del Petróleo, y exposicón de motivos de la misma que presentan al Ministerio de Fomento los Sres. Lics. Lorenzo Elízaga y Luis Ibarra y El Ing. Manuel Fernández Guerra.* México: Talleres Tipográficos de "El Tiempo," 1905.

Emory, William H. *Report on the United States and Mexican Boundary Survey.* Washington, DC: C. Wendell, printer, 1857.

Estadistica gráfica: progreso de los Estados Unidos Mexicanos. México: Empresa de Ilustraciones, 1896.

Facts and Figures about Mexico and Her Great Railroad: The Mexican Central. Mexico City: Bureau of Information of the Mexican Central Railway Co. Limited, 1897.

FAO. *World Forest Resources.* Rome: FAO, 1957.

Farnham, Thomas Jefferson. *Mexico: Its Geography, Its People, and Its Institutions: With a Map, Containing the Result of the Latest Explorations of Fremont, Wilkes, and Others.* New York: H. Long & Brother, 1846.

Farrugia Manly, Federico. "Memoria sobre la metalurgia práctica del plomo y de la plata en el distrito de Minas de Zimapán, Hidalgo." *La Naturaleza* (January 1871): 323–36.

Ferry, Gabriel. *Vagabond Life in Mexico.* New York, 1856.

Fernández Leal, Manuel. *Memoria de la Secretaría de Fomento, Colonización e Industria de la República Mexicana. Corresponde a los años transcurridos de 1892 a 1896.* México: Oficina Tip. de la Secretaría de Fomento, 1897.

Ferrocarriles Nacionales de México. *Annual Report of Ferrocarriles Nacionales de México (National Railways of Mexico).* Mexico City; New York: Ferrocariles Nacionales de México, 1909–18.

Facts and Figures about Mexico and Its Great Railway System, the National Railways of Mexico. México: Traffic and Industrial Departments of the National Railways of Mexico, 1909.

Figueroa, Pedro Pablo. *Historia de la fundación de la industria del carbón de piedra en Chile: don Jorge Rojas Miranda.* Santiago de Chile: Impr. del Comercio, 1897.

Fleury, Juan. "Informe sobre las minas de carbón de San Felipe y El Hondo, que rinde a la Secretaría de Fomento el ingeniero Inspector de Minas J. Fleury." *Anales del Ministerio de Fomento de la República Mexicana* 11 (n.d.): 40–69.

Flippin, John R. *Sketches from the Mountains of Mexico.* Cincinnati: Standard Publishing Co., 1889.

Flores, Blas M. *Exploración practicada en el desierto de Coahuila y Chihuahua.* México: Oficina Tip. de la Secretaría de Fomento, 1892.

Flores, Manuel. *Apuntes sobre el petróleo mexicano, por el Dr. Manuel Flores, dedicados a los señores miembros del XXVI Congreso Federal.* n.p.: n.p., 1913.

Flores, Teodoro. "Consideraciones generales sobre el uso de motores de gasolina en las minas." *Boletín de la Secretaría de Fomento*, Segunda época, no. II (1905–06): 451–9.

Forbes, Alex C. *A Trip to Mexico; or Recollections of a Ten-Months Ramble in 1849–50.* London: Smith, Elder & Co., 1851.

"Foreign Mining News. Mexico." *The Engineering and Mining Journal* 39, 7 (1885): 112.

The Engineering and Mining Journal 46, 14 (1888): 290–1.

Engineering and Mining Journal 46, 12 (1888): 246–7.

Fox, Conde de. *De México a Necaxa.* México, D. F.: Compañía Impresora Mexicana, 1919.

Fuentes, Carlos. *La región más transparente.* México, D. F.: Debolsillo, 2017.

Galarza, Ernesto. *La Industria eléctrica en México.* México: Fondo de Cultura Ecónomica, 1941.

Galicia, Daniel F. "Mexico's National Parks." *Ecology* 22, 1 (1941): 107–10.

Galloway, Robert Lindsay. *Annals of Coal Mining and the Coal Trade.* London: Colliery Guardian, 1898.

Garay, Antonio. *Memoria de la Dirección de Colonización e Industria, Año de 1849.* México: Imprenta de Vicente G. Torres, 1850.

García Cubas, Antonio. *The Republic of Mexico in 1876. A political and ethnographical division of the population, character, habits, costumes and vocations of its inhabitants.* México: "La Enseñanza" Printing Office, 1876.

Album del Ferrocarril mexicano. Colección de vistas pintadas del natural por Casimiro Castro, y ejecutadas en cromolitografía por A. Sigogne, C. Castro, etc., con una descripción del camino y de las regiones que recorre. México: V. Debray y Co., 1877.

Cuadro geográfico, estadístico, descriptivo é histórico de los Estados Unidos Mexicanos. México: Oficina Tip. de la Secretaría de Fomento, 1884.

Atlas pintoresco e histórico de los Estados Unidos Mexicanos. México: Debray Sucesores, 1885.

Mexico – Its Trade, Industries, and Resources. Mexico: Typographical Office of the Department of Fomento, Colonization, and Industry, 1893.

Geografía e historia del Distrito Federal. Mexico: Antigua Imprenta de E. Murguía, 1894.

El libro de mis recuerdos: narraciones historicas, anecdóticas y de costumbres mexicanas anteriores al actual estado social, ilustradas con más de trescientos fotograbados. Mexico: Imprenta de A. García Cubas, Hermanos Sucesores, 1904.

García Gómez, Guillermo. "Electrificación del norte de los estados de Coahuila y Tamaulipas." *Revista Industrial* 2, 5 (1934), 817–19.

García Rojas, Antonio, "La industria del gas en México." *Boletín de la Sociedad Geológica Mexicana* 24, 1 (1961): 31–41.

García y Alva, Federico. *México y sus progresos. Album-directorio del estado de Sonora. Obra hecha con apoyo del gobierno del estado.* Hermosillo: Impr. Oficial Dirigida por A.B. Monteverde, 1905.

Garfias, Valentin R. *Petroleum Resources of the World.* New York: John Wiley & Sons, Inc., 1923.

Garfias, Valentín R., and M. C. Ehlen. *Tablas y diagramas para petróleo.* México: Departamento Universitario y de Bellas Artes, Dirección de Talleres Gráficos, 1921.

Garloch, Lorene A. "Cotton in the Economy of Mexico." *Economic Geography* 20, 1 (1944): 70–7.

"General Southern Coal and Coke Notes. Mexico." *The Black Diamond* 33, 7 (1904): 394.

Gil, Romero. "Selvicultura. Destrucción de los bosques en el estado de Jalisco. Observaciones sobre los bosques, bel Barón de Humboldt y un profesor de la escuela de minas. Ordenanzas antiguas sobre bosques y necesidad de observarlas." *Boletín de la Sociedad Mexicana de Geografía y Estadística* 1, 2 (1869): 9–14.

Gilliam, Albert M. *Travels over the Table Lands and Cordilleras of Mexico. During the Years 1843 and 44; Including a Description of California and the Biographies of Iturbide and Santa Anna.* Philadelphia: J. W. Moore, 1846.

"Glosario de términos usados en la industria petroleroa y vocabulario inglés-espanól de la misma industria." *Revista Industrial* (July 1933).

González, F., L. Salazar, and A. Grothe. *The Mining Industry of Mexico.* Mexico: Impr. y Fototipia de la Secretaría de Fomento, 1911.

González Roa, Fernando. *El Problema ferrocarrilero y la compañía de los Ferrocarriles Nacionales de México.* México: Impresora de Hacienda, 1917.

Good, John E. *The Coal Industry of Brazil.* USA: US Govt. Print. Off., 1949.

Greaven, Luis. "Uso del aceite mineral en el Ferrocarril Nacional de Tehuantepec en México." *Boletín de la Secretaría de Fomento,* 2nda época, año V, no. I–III (August 1905): 10–32.

"Growth of Coal Mining in the United States." *The Mining World* 22, 18 (1905): 465–6.

Gurza, Jaime. *La política ferrocarrilera del gobierno.* México: Tip. de la Oficina Impresora de Estampillas, 1911.

Gutiérrez Olguín, Tonatiúh. "Los recursos naturales renovables en el desarrollo económico de México." *Investigación Económica* 22, 86 (1962): 231–607.

Hahn, Otto H. "On the Development of Silver Mining in Mexico." *Transactions of the Institution of Mining and Metallurgy* 8 (1900): 232–303.

Hall, W. H. *Across Mexico in 1864–5.* London and Cambridge: Macmillan and Co., 1866.

Hamilton, Leonidas Le Cenci. *Hamilton's Mexican Handbook; a Complete Description of the Republic of Mexico, Its Mineral and Agricultural Resources, Cities, and Towns of Every State, Factories, Trade, Imports and Exports, How Legally to Acquire Property in Mexico, How to Transact Business under Mexican Laws, Railroads and Travelling in the Republic, Tariff Regulations, Duties, Etc.* London: Sampson Low, Marston, Searle, and Rivington, 1884.

Hanke, Lewis. *Mexico and the Caribbean.* Anvil Original. Princeton: Van Nostrand, 1959.

Harrar, Jacob George. *Mexican Agricultural Program: A Review of the First Six Years of Activity under the Joint Auspices of the Mexican Government and the Rockefeller Foundation.* New York: The Rockefeller Foundation, 1950.

The Agricultural Program of the Rockefeller Foundation. New York: The Rockefeller Foundation, 1956.

Hermosa, Jesús. *Manual de geografía y estadística de la República Mejicana.* Paris: Librería de Rosa y Bouret, 1857.

Herrera y Lasso, José. *La fuerza motriz en México.* México, D. F.: Talleres Gráficos de la Nación, 1927.

Herrera y Lasso, José, and Luis N. Morones. *La fuerza motriz en México.* México: Secretaría de Industria, Comercio y Trabajo, 1927.

Hinojosa, Gabriel. *Memoria sobre la utilidad de los bosques y perjuicios causados por su destruccion dedicada al gobierno del estado de Michoacan.* Morelia: Vida e hijos de Ort., 1873.

Hinojosa Ortiz, Manuel. *Los bosques de México: relato de un despilfarro y una injusticia.* México: Instituto Mexicano de Investigaciones Económicas, 1958.

Hogar del agricultor: arquitectura rural, fabricación de carbón de leña, fabricación de cal, el jardín, abonos y guanos, cría de gallinas, cría del pavo común, cría de palomas, la cabra y el carnero, el cerdo, la vaca, la leche y el queso, el caballo, conservación de sustancias alimenticias: legumbres, frutas y carnes. México: F. Vázquez, 1903.

Humboldt, Alexander von. *Ensayo político sobre el reino de la Nueva España.* 4 vols. Paris: Casa de Rosa, gran patio del Palacio Real, 1822.

Tablas geográfico-políticas del reino de la Nueva España en el año de 1803, que manifiestan su superficie, población, agricultura, fábricas, comercio, minas, rentas y fuerza military. México: UNAM, 1993 [1803].

Iglesias, Carlos. "El papel del petróleo en la economía nacional." *Revista Industrial* (March 1933).

INEGI. *Estadísticas históricas de México.* vol. II. (3a edición). INEGI, 1994.

INEGI. *Estadísticas Históricas de México.* vols. 2. Aguascalientes: INEGI, 1996.

INEGI. *Indicadores sociodemográficos de México. (1930–2000).* Aguascalientes: INEGI, 2001.

INEGI and SEMARNAP. *Estadísticas del medio ambiente.* Aguascalientes: INEGI, 1998.

Instituto Mexicano de Recursos Renovables, ed. *Mesas redondas sobre problemas forestales de México.* México: Ediciones del Instituto Mexicano de Recursos Naturales Renovables, 1956.

Instituto Nacional de Investigaciones Forestales. *Inventario forestal nacional de México, 1961–1964.* Vol. II–V. México, D. F.: Instituto Nacional de Investigaciones Forestales; Organizacion de las Naciones Unidas para la Agriculture y la Almentacion (FAO), 1965.

Inventario forestal nacional de México, 1961–1964: informe técnico. México: Instituto Nacional de Investigaciones Forestales, Organizacion de las Naciones Unidas para la Agriculture y la Almentacion, 1965.

International Bureau of the American Republics. *Mexico: A Geographical Sketch, with Special Reference to Economic Conditions and Prospects of Future Development.* Washington, DC: Government Printing Office, 1900.

Kuchler, Jacobo. *Valles de Sabinas y Salinas: Reconocimiento y descripción de los valles de Sabinas y Salinas en el departamento de Coahuila, con las haciendas del*

Nacimiento, San Juan, Soledad, Álamo, Encinas, Hermanas y Rancho de la Mota. México: Imprenta Imperial, 1866.

James, Preston E. "Industrial Development in São Paulo State, Brazil." *Economic Geography* 11, 3 (1935): 258–66.

Jevons, William Stanley. *The Coal Question; an Enquiry Concerning the Progress of the Nation, and the Probable Exhaustion of Our Coal-Mines*. London: Macmillan, 1865.

Jiménez, Luis G. *Los carbones minerales: su origen, leyenda, historia y desarrollo en México*. México: UNAM, 1944.

Kapuściński, Ryszard. *Shah of Shahs*. New York: Vintage Books, 1985.

Lamberg, E. "Inspección de las colonias militares de Chihuahua." In *Boletín de La Sociedad Mexicana de Geografía y Estadística* III: 19–25, 1852.

Lara Beautell, Cristóbal. *La industria de energía eléctrica*. México: Fondo de la Cultura Económica, 1953.

La República Mexicana: estados del norte: Sonora, Chihuahua, Coahuila, Nuevo León, Tamaulipas. Paris; México: Librería de la Vda. de Ch. Bouret, 1910.

La República Mexicana: Nuevo León, Reseña geográfica y estadística. Paris: Librería de la Vda. de C. Bouret, 1910.

Latrobe, Charles Joseph. *The Rambler in Mexico*. New York: Harper & brothers, 1836.

Lavín, José Domingo. *Petróleo: pasado, presente y futuro de una industria mexicana*. México: Edición y Distribución Ibero Americana de Publicaciones, 1950.

Leach, W. W., D. B. Dowling, and William McInnes. *The Coal Resources of the World: An Enquiry Made upon the Initiative of the Executive Committee of the 12th International Congress, Canada, 1913*. Toronto: Morang & Co., Limited, 1913.

Lerdo de Tejada, Miguel. *Cuadro sinóptico de la Republica Mexicana en 1856, formado en vista de los ultimos datos oficiales y otras noticas fidedignas*. México: Imprenta de Ingacio Cumplido, 1856.

Lewis, Oscar. *Five Families: Mexican Case Studies in the Culture of Poverty*. New York: Basic Books, 1955.

"México Desde 1940." *Investigación Económica* 18, 70 (1958): 185–256.

The Children of Sanchez: Autobiography of a Mexican Family. New York: Vintage Books, 1961.

"Ley Forestal." *Periódico Oficial Del Estado de Nayarit*, January 20, 1960.

Livas, Pablo. *El estado de Nuevo León, Su situación económica al aproximarse el centenario de la independencia de México: obra escrita con datos oficiales*. Monterrey, NL: n.p., 1909.

Loera Borja, Alfonso, and Roberto Villaseñor Angeles. *El problema forestal de México*. México: Impresora Periodística Comercial S. de R.L., 1958.

Long, W. Rodney. *Railways of Mexico*. [United States] Bureau of Foreign and Domestic Commerce (Dept. of Commerce) Trade Promotion Series, No. 16. Washington, DC: Govt. Print. Off., 1925.

López de la Parra, Manuel. "Significado y desarrollo actual de los caminos vecinales y en general de las vías de comunicaciones del país." *Investigación Económica* 18, 72 (1958): 675–98.

Loría, Francisco. *Lo que ha sido y debe de ser la política ferrocarrilera de México.* México: Tipografía Económica, 1914.

Ludlow, Edwin. "The Coal Fields of Las Esperanzas, Coahuila, Mexico." *Transactions of the American Institute of Mining, Metallurgical, and Petroleum Engineers* 32 (1902): 140–56.

MacHugh, Robert Joseph. *Modern Mexico.* New York: Dodd, 1914.

Magalhães, J. C. "Lenha e Carvão Vegetal Para o Estado Da Guanabara." *Boletim Carioca de Geografia* 15, 1/2 (1961): 27–60.

Maia, Emilio Joaquim da Silva. *Discurso sobre os males que tem produzido no Brasil, o corte das matas, e sobre os meios de os remediar: lido na sessão publica da Sociedade de Medicina do Rio de Janeiro, em 30 de junho de 1835.* Rio de Janeiro: Na Typographia Fluminense de Brito & Comp., 1835.

Manterola, Miguel. *La industria del petróleo en México.* México: Secretaría de Hacienda y Crédito Público, 1938.

"Máquina de vapor en el mineral de Pasco, Perú." *Gaceta Extraordinaria del Gobierno de México.* April 1817, tomo VIII, núm. 1059.

Martin, Lawrence. *The Standard Guide to Mexico and the Caribbean.* New York: Funk & Wagnalls, 1956.

Martin, Percy F. *Mexico of the Twentieth Century.* Vol. 1–2. New York: Dodd, Mead, 1908.

Martínez Baca, Eduardo. *Reseña histórica de la legislación minera en México.* México: Oficina Tip. de la Secretaría de Fomento, 1901.

Martinez de la Torre, Rafael, and Juan Chynoweth. *Alegato de bien probado que presentó el Lic. Rafael Martínez de la Torre como patrono de la compañía del Mineral del Monte y Pachuca, en el juicio promovido por el Sr. D. Juan Chynoweth, pretendiendo tener derecho a la mina de S. Pedro.* México: Imprenta Literaria, 1867.

Martínez D'Meza, Héctor. "Control de la industria eléctrica. Las plantas generadoras de energía eléctrica." *Revista Industrial* 1, 1 (1933): 159–67.

"Industria eléctrica en México, producción y consumo, 1932–1933." *Revista Industrial* (July 1933).

"La electrificación en los Estados Unidos Mexicanos y en el estado de Sinaloa." *Revista Industrial* (April 1934).

Mason, R. H. *Pictures of Life in Mexico.* London: Smith, Elder and Co., 1852.

Mayer, Brantz. *Mexico as It Was and as It Is.* New York: J. Winchester: New World Press, 1844.

Mexico, Aztec, Spanish and Republican: A Historical, Geographical, Political, Statistical and Social Account of That Country from the Period of the Invasion by the Spaniards to the Present Time: With a View of the Ancient Aztec Empire and Civilization, a Historical Sketch of the Late War, and Notices of New Mexico and California. Hartford: S. Drake and Company, 1850.

McCabe, L. C., and G. D. Clayton. "Air Pollution by Hydrogen Sulfide in Poza Rica, Mexico. An Evaluation of the Incident of Nov. 24, 1950." *Archives of Industrial Hygiene & Occupational Medicine* 6, 3 (1952): 199–213.

Memoria de la Secretaría de Fomento. México: Oficina Tipográfica de la Secretaría de Fomento, 1866, 1870, 1885, 1892, 1896, 1910.

Memoria histórica, técnica y administrativa de las obras del desagüe del Valle de México, 1449–1900. Vol. 1. México: Tip. de la Oficina Impresora de Estampillas, 1902.

Mena, Ramón. *El libro del petróleo en México.* México: Porrúa Hermanos, 1915.

Méndez, Santiago. *Nociones prácticas sobre caminos de fierro.* México: Imprenta de Andrade y Escalante, 1864.

Mexican Central Railway Co. Limited. *Annual Report of the Board of Directors of the Mexican Central Railway Co. Limited to the Stockholders for the Year Ending.* Boston: Geo. H. Ellis, Printer, 1880.

Introductory Report. Boston: Mexican Central Railway Co. Limited, 1881.

Annual Report of the Board of Directors of the Mexican Central Railway Co. Limited to the Stockholders for the Year Ending. Boston: Geo. H. Ellis, Printer, 1881.

Facts and Figures about Mexico and Her Great Railway System, the Mexican Central Railway Company, Ltd. Mexico: Industrial Dept. of the Mexican Central Railway Company, 1906.

Mexican International Railroad Company. *Annual Report of the Mexican International Railroad Company.* New York: John C. Ranking Co., Printers, 1893–1895, 1900–1903, 1905–1910.

Mexican National Railroad Company. *Annual Reports.* 1887–1907.

Mexican Pacific Coal and Iron Mining and Land Company. *Prospecto de la compañia denominada Mexican Pacific Coal and Iron Mining and Land Company.* New York: Imprenta de Hallet, 1856.

Mexican Publishing Company, S.A. *The Mexican Mining Journal.* Mexico City: Mexican Publishing Company, 1907.

México. *Coleccion de leyes, decretos, disposiciones, resoluciones y documentos importantes sobre caminos de fierro.* México: Impr. de F. Díaz de León, 1882.

México, Cincuenta años de Revolución. México, D. F.: Fondo de Cultura Económica, 1960.

"Mexico." *Engineering and Mining Journal* 40, 10 (1885): 169.

"Mexico." *Engineering and Mining Journal* 11, 22 (1885): 375.

"Mexico." *The Engineering and Mining Journal* 48, 4 (1889): 80.

"Mexico Coal." *The Mining World* 22, 18 (1905): 465.

Mexico Tramways Company. *Director's Record and Accounts.* Toronto, 1908. 1911, 1921, 1922.

Fifteenth Annual Report of the Board of Directors. Toronto, 1928.

Middleton, P. Harvey. *Industrial Mexico; 1919 Facts and Figures.* New York: Dodd, Mead and Co., 1919.

Monroy, Don Pedro L. "Observaciones sobre algunos combustibles minerales de México." *La Naturaleza* 1,. 1 (1869): 87–93.

Mosk, Sanford Alexander. *Industrial Revolution in Mexico*. New York: Russell & Russell, 1950.

"Motores de vapor." *Anales de la Minería Mexicana*. January 1, 1861.

Murphy, Patricio. "Informe acerca de las minas de ulla ubicadas en Tecomatlán, Distrito de Acatlán, estado de Puebla, dado por el Sr. D. Patricio Murphy, ingeniero de minas." *El Minero Mexicano*. October 9, 1873.

Informe sobre las minas de ulla ubicadas en Tecomatlán, distrito de Acatlán. México: Imprenta de F. Díaz de León y S. White, 1873.

Nacional Financiera, S.A. *50 Años de Revolución Mexicana en cifras*. México, D. F.: Nacional Financiera, 1963.

La economía mexicana en cifras. México, D. F.: Nacional Financiera, 1965.

National Railways of Mexico. *Facts and Figures about Mexico and Its Great Railway System, the National Railways of Mexico*. México, D. F.: V.M. Gutiérrez, 1911.

Navarro, F. *1er Directorio Estadístico de La República Mexicana*. México, D. F.: Eduardo Dublán y Compañía, Impresores, 1890.

"Necrología de Leopoldo Río de La Loza." *La Naturaleza* 1, 3 (1876): 426.

Negrete, Emilio del Castillo. *Mexico en el siglo XIX, o sea su historia desde 1800 hasta la época presente*. México: Las Escalerillas, 1887.

"Notas estadísticas del Departamento de Querétaro." *Boletín de la Sociedad Mexicana de Geografía y Estadística* 3 (1852): 169–236.

Novo, Salvador. *La vida en México en el período presidencial de Miguel Alemán*. México, D. F.: Consejo Nacional para la Cultura y las Artes, 1994.

La vida en Mexico en el periodo presidencial de Adolfo Ruiz Cortines. II. México, D. F.: Consejo Nacional para la Cultura y las Artes, 1996.

La vida en México en el periodo presidencial de Adolfo López Mateos. México, D. F.: Consejo Nacional para la Cultura y las Artes: Dirección General de Publicaciones, Instituto Nacional de Antropología e Historia, 1998.

Seis siglos de la ciudad de México. México, D. F.: FCE, 2006.

Salvador Novo. México, D. F.:UNAM, 2009.

El joven. México, D. F.: UNAM, 2012 [1923].

Ober, Frederick A. *Mexican Resources: A Guide to and through Mexico*. Boston: Estes and Lauriat, 1884.

Ochoa, Claudio, and Isidro Gondra. "Apuntes para formar la estadística minera de la República Mexicana." *Boletín del Instituto Nacional de Geografía y Estadística de la República Mexicana* 2 (1864): 163–219.

Ordóñez, Ezequiel, and Manuel Rangel. *El Real del Monte*. México: Oficina Tip. de la Secretaría de Fomento, 1899.

"Coal in Coahuila." *Mining and Scientific Press* 96 (1908): 363.

El petróleo en México. Bosquejo histórico. México, D. F.: Empresa Editorial de Ingeniería y Arquitectura, 1932.

Oreamuno, José Rafael. *Industrialization in Latin America, an Outline of Its Development*. Washington, DC: Inter-American Development Commission, 1946.

Orozco y Berra, Manual. *Memoria para la carta hidrográfica del Valle de México formada por acuerdo de la Sociedad Mexicana de Geografía y Estadística.* Mexico: Impr. de A. Boix, 1864.

Ortega, Gustavo. *Los recursos petrolíferos mexicanos y su actual explotacion.* Mexico, D. F.: Talleres Gráficos de la Nación, 1925.

Ortega, Rolfo. "Aspecto general del problema en la industria eléctrica en el país." *Revista Industrial* (June 1934).

Ortiz, Gabriel. *El desarrollo económico del Valle de México y la zona metropolitana de la ciudad de México.* México, D. F.: Secretaría de Recursos Hidráulicos, Oficina de Estudios Económicos y Reglamentaciones, 1964.

Osborne, John. *Guide to the West Indies, Madeira, Mexico, Northern South-America, &c., &c., Comp. from Documents Specially Furnished by the Agents of the Royal Mail Steam Packet Company, the Board of Trade, and Other Authentic Sources.* London: Royal Mail Steam Packet Co., 1845.

Pacheco, José Emilio. *Las batallas en el desierto.* México: Fondo de Cultura Económica, 2010.

Palacios, Daniel. *Tratado práctico de calderas de vapor.* México: Oficina Tip. de la Secretaría de Fomento, 1890.

Pan American Union. *Visit Mexico.* Washington, DC, 1959.

Paredes, Trinidad. *El problema del petróleo en Mexico.* México: publisher not identified, 1933.

Parker, Edward W. "Coal in Mexico." *The Engineering and Mining Journal* 77, 5 (1904): 190.

Payno, Manuel. "Selvicultura." *Boletín de la Sociedad de Geografía y Estadística de la República Mexicana*, Segunda época, 2 (1870): 77–85.

Pechar, John. *Coal and Iron in All Countries of the World: Compiled from Official Sources and with the Assistance of Eminent Living Authorities.* Manchester; London: John Heywood; Simpkin, Marshall & Co., 1878.

Peña, Moisés T. de la. *El servicio de autobuses en el Distrito Federal.* México, D. F.: Talleres Gráficos de la Nación, 1943.

Peñafiel, Antonio. *Cuadro sinóptico informativo de la administración del señor General Don Porfirio Díaz, Presidente de la Republica hasta 1909.* México: Imprenta y Fototipia de la Secretaría de Fomento, 1910.

Estadística industrial 1902. Mexico: Oficina Tip. de la Secretaría de Fomento, 1903.

Pérez Hernández, José María. *Estadística de la República Mejicana. Territorio, población, antigüedades, monumentos, establecimientos públicos, reino vegetal y agricultura, reino animal, reino mineral, industria fabril y manufacturera, artes mecánicas y liberales, comercio, navegacion, gobierno, hacienda y crédito público, ejército, marina, clero, justicia, instruccion pública, colonias militares y civiles.* Guadalajara: Tip. del Gobierno, 1862.

"Petróleo crudo y sus derivados, de producción nacional, exportados por México durante los cinco primeros meses de 1933." *Revista Industrial* (July 1933).

Phillips, M. Ogden. "Manufacturing in the Federal District, Mexico." *Economic Geography* 9, 3 (1933): 279–91.

Ogden Phillips, M. "Manufacturing in the Federal District, Mexico." *Economic Geography* 9, 3 (1933): 279–91.

Officer of the US Army, *Pictorial History of Remarkable Events in America. Embracing a Sketch of the Most Thrilling Incidents in the History of Ancient Mexico and Her Wars; the Present State of the Country and Its Mines; a Full Account of the War between the United States and Mexico; the Lives of Distinguished Chieftains, Including Generals Scott, Taylor. Illustrated with More than Fifty Engravings on Wood and Steel.* New York: 128 Nassau Street, 1850.

"Plantas generadoras de energía eléctrica." *Revista Industrial* (December 1933).

Pombo, Luis. *Mexico: 1876–1892.* México: Imprenta de "El Siglo Diez y Nueve," 1893.

Powell, Fred Wilbur. *The Railroads of Mexico.* Boston: Stratford, 1921.

Powell, J. Richard. *The Mexican Petroleum Industry, 1938–1950.* Berkeley: University of California, 1956.

Prantl, Adolfo, and José L. Grosó. *La ciudad de México, novísima guía universal de la capital de la República Mexicana; directorio clasificado de vecinos, y prontuario de la organizacion y funciones del gobierno federal y oficinas de su dependencia. Obra illustrada con fotograbados de Ulderigo Tabarracci y accompañada de un plano topográfico de la ciudad.* México: J. Buxó, 1901.

"Precios de la gasolina en México en junio de 1933." *Revista Industrial* (July 1933).

Prieto, Guillermo. *Memorias de mis tiempos: 1840 a 1853.* México: Librería de la Vda. de C. Bouret, 1906.

Problemas agrícolas e industriales de México: publicación trimestral. México, 1946–59.

"Producción total de plata y oro en México, desde el arribo de los españoles hasta el año de 1922." *Anuario de Estadística Minera*, 1924.

Quevedo, Miguel Angel de. "Los desastres de la deforestación en el Valle y Ciudad de México." *México Forestal* IV, 7–8 (1926): 67–82.

Ramírez, Ignacio, Gumersindo Mendoza, Luís Malanco, and Ignacio Cornejo. "Bosques y arbolados." *Boletín de la Sociedad Mexicana de Geografía y Estadística, Segunda época* 2 (1870): 14–24.

Ramírez, Ricardo. *La condición legal de los bosques y su conservación.* México: Imprenta Particular de la Sociedad Agrícola Mexicana, 1900.

Ramírez, Santiago. "La conservación de bosques." *El Explorador Minero.* May 5, 1877.

⸻. *Informe que como resultado de su exploración en la Sierra Mojada, rinde al Ministerio de Fomento el ingeniero de minas Santiago Ramirez.* México: Impr. de Francisco Díaz de León, 1880.

⸻. "Informe sobre el mineral del Guadalcázar en el estado de San Luís Potosí." In *Anales del Ministerio de Fomento*, 3: 339–404. México: Imprenta de Francisco Díaz de León, 1880.

⸻. *Opúsculos científicos y literarios.* México: Tip. Literaria de F. Mata, 1880.

⸻. *Estudios sobre el carbón mineral.* México: Imprenta de Francisco Díaz de León, 1882.

Noticia histórica de la riqueza minera de México y de su actual estado de explotacion. México: Oficina Tip. de la Secretaría de Fomento, 1884.

Datos para la historia del Colegio de Minería. Efemérides del Colegio de Minería. México: Impr. del Gobierno Federal, 1890.

Real ordenanza para el gobierno de los montes y arbolados de la jurisdicción de marina. Madrid: Imprenta Real, 1803.

Reales ordenanzas para la dirección, régimen y gobierno del importante cuerpo de la minería de Nueva España, y de su Real Tribunal General. Madrid: Imprenta Real, 1783.

Regil, José María, and Alonso Peón, "Estadística del Departamento de Yucatán." *Boletín de la Sociedad Mexicana de Geografía y Estadística* 3 (1853): 237–336.

Reglamento para la explotación de los bosques y terrenos baldíos y nacionales. México: Secretaria de Comunicaciones y Obras Publicas, 1894.

"Relación de las plantas generadoras de energía eléctrica existentes en el Departamento de Control de la industria eléctrica de la Secretaría de la Economía Nacional." *Revista Industrial* 1, 6 (1933): 203.

Religious Tract Society. *Mexico: The Country, History, and People*. London: The Religious Tract Society, 1863.

"Revista de las actividades petroleras en México, hasta el 30 de Noviembre de 1933." *Revista Industrial* (December 1933).

Reyes, J. Ascensión. *El automóvil gris; novela de los tiempos de la revolución constitucionalista*. San Antonio, TX: Lozano, 1922.

Rivera Cambas, Manuel. *Memoria sobre el mineral de Pachuca*. México: Impr. de. J. M. Andrade y F. Escalante, 1864.

México pintoresco, artístico y monumental: vistas, descripción, anécdotas y episodios de los lugares más notables de la capital y de los estados, aún de las poblaciones cortas, pero de importancia geográfica e histórica. México: Imprenta de la Reforma, 1880.

Río de la Loza, Leopoldo, Joaquín Velázquez, and Felipe Zaldívar. "Dictamen que presentó la Comisión de Ciencias Naturales sobre la muestra de carbón de piedra de la mina situada en el Departamento de San Juan de los Llanos del estado de Puebla." *Boletín de la Sociedad Mexicana de Geografía y Estadística* 3 (1852): 17–18.

Robelo, Cecilio Agustín. *Diccionario de pesas y medidas mexicanas, antiguas y modernas y de su conversión: para uso de los comerciantes y las familias*. Tlalpan, D. F.: CIESAS, 1995.

Robertson, William Parish. *A Visit to Mexico, by the West India Islands, Yucatan and United States: With Observations and Adventures on the Way*. London: Simpkin, Marshall & Company, Stationers' Hall Court, 1853.

Robles Pezuela, Luis. "Decreto adoptando el sistema métrico decimal." In *El Diario del Imperio*, Vols. 202–301, 469. México: El Diario del Imperio, 1865.

Memoria presentada á S.M. el Emperador por el Ministero de Fomento Luis Robles Pezuela de los trabajos ejecutados en su ramo el año de 1865. México: Imprenta de J.M. Andrade y F. Escalante, 1866.

Rodríguez de San Miguel, Juan Nepomuceno. *Manual de providencias economico-politicas para uso de los habitantes del Distrito Federal.* México: Imprenta de Galván, 1834.

Rodríguez Mata, Emilio. *Generación y distribución de energía eléctrica en México, período 1939–1949.* México, D. F.: Banco de México, 1952.

Rojas, Isidro. *Consulta que el ministerio de Fomento, Colonizacion é Industria hace a aquella respetable corporación por acuerdo del Señor Presidente de la República. Pueden declarase denunciables los criaderos de carbón de piedra en todas sus variedades, así como los manantiales de petróleo, existan ó no en terrenos de propiedad particular? Voto razonado del académico Lic. Isidro Rojas.* Mexico: Antigua Casa Editorial "José Maria Mellado," 1905.

Romero, Matías. *Railways in Mexico.* Washington, DC: W.H. Moore, 1882, 15–17. *Geographical and Statistical Notes on Mexico.* New York and London: G.P. Putnam's Sons, 1898.

Rosa, Luis de la. *Memoria sobre el cultivo de maiz en México.* México: Impr. de la Sociedad Literaria, 1846.

Rothwell, Richard Pennefather, Joseph Struthers, David Hale Newland, Edward K. Judd, and Walter Renton Ingalls. *The Mineral Industry, Its Statistics, Technology, and Trade.* New York: The Scientific Publishing Company, 1919.

Rovirosa, José N. *La hidrografía del sudeste de México y sus relaciones con los vientos y las lluvias. Lectura de turno presentada á la Academia de ciencias exactas, fisicas y naturales correspondiente de la Real de Madrid, en la sesión ael 6 de septiembre de 1897.* San Juan Bautista de Tabasco: La Universal, 1899.

Rugendas, Johann Moritz. *Johann Moritz Rugendas in Mexiko: Malerische Reise in den Jahren 1831–1834: Ausstellung des Ibero-Amerikanischen Instituts Preussischer Kulturbesitz in Berlin, 13. Dezember 1984–23. Februar 1985.* Berlin: Ibero-Amerikanisches Institut Preussischer Kulturbesitz, 1984.

Ruxton, George Frederick Augustus. *Adventures in Mexico and the Rocky Mountains.* London: J. Murray, 1847.

Safley, James Clifford. *Mexican Vistas.* San Diego: Union-Tribune Pub. Co., 1952.

Salgado, Daniel. "*La cuestión del consumo de carbón vegetal en el Distrito Federal.*" *Boletín de Economía y Estadística,* no. 27, México, 1935.

Salonio, Antonio María. "Reglamento para la conservación y aumento de bosques." *Boletín de la Sociedad Mexicana de Geografía y Estadística* 2, 1 (1869): 14–20.

Santaella, Joaquín. *La industria petrolera en México, conferencia sustentada en la Sociedad Mexicana de Geografía y Estadistica.* México: Poder Ejecutivo Federal, Departamento de Aprovisionamientos Generales, Dirección de Talleres Gráficos, 1919.

Santamaría, Miguel. *Las chinampas del Distrito Federal: informe rendido al señor Director General de Agricultura.* Mexico: Impr. y Fototípia de la Secretaría de Fomento, 1912.

Sartorius, Carl Christian, and Johann Moritz Rugendas. *Mexico about 1850.* Mexiko. Landschaftsbilder. Stuttgart: Brockhaus, 1961.

Sartorius, Christian. *Mexiko. Landschaftsbilder und Skizzen aus dem Volksleben.* Darmstadt: Gustav Georg Lange Verlag, 1859.

Saward, Frederick Edward. *The Coal Trade: A Compendium of Valuable Information Relative to Coal Production, Prices, Transportation, Etc., at Home and Abroad, with Many Facts Worthy of Preservation for Future Reference.* New York: The Coal Trade Journal, 1874.

Schmidt, Geo A. *Mexiko.* Dietrich Reimer: Berlin, 1921.

Secretaría de Comunicaciones y Obras Públicas. *Memoria.* México: Tipografía de la Dirección General de Telégrafos, 1902.

Reseña histórica y estadística de los ferrocarriles de jurisdiccion federal desde agosto de 1837 hasta diciembre de 1894. Mexico: Tipografía de la Dirección general de Telégrafos Federales, 1905.

Reseña histórica y estadística de los ferrocarriles de Jurisdicción Federal desde 1900 hasta 1906. México: Tipografía de la Dirección General de Telégrafos Federales, 1906.

Documentos para la historia de las carreteras en México. México: Secretaría de Obras Públicas, 1964.

Secretaría de Fomento, Colonización, Industria y Comercio. *Album de los ferrocarriles.* México: Oficina Tipográfica de la Secretaría de Fomento, 1891.

Anales del Ministerio de Fomento de la República Mexicana. Vol. VII.México: Imprenta de F. Díaz de León, 1882.

Anuario estadístico de la República Mexicana. México: Oficina Tip. de la Secretaría de Fomento, 1896, 1897, 1902, 1907.

Boletín de la Secretaría de Fomento. Vol. 1–7. México: Oficina Tipográfica de la Secretaría. de Fomento, 1901.

Vol. 2, 1903.

Boletín de la Dirección General de Estadística. Vol. 1. México, D. F.: Secretaría de Fomento, 1912.

Boletín Minero. Vol. XI. México, D. F.: Direccion de Talleres Gráficos, 1921.

Coleccion de leyes, decretos, disposiciones, resoluciones y documentos importantes sobre caminos de fierro, años de 1824 a 1870. 6 vols. México: Impr. de F. Díaz de León, 1882.

Memoria de la Secretaría de Fomento. México: Oficina Tip. de la Secretaría de Fomento, 1857.

Vol. 5, 1887.

Reglamento a que debe sujetarse el corte de maderas en bosques y terrenos nacionales. San Juan Bautista: Tip. "Juventud tabasqueña" de F. Ghigliazza, 1882.

Secretaría de Industria, Comercio y Trabajo. *Algunos documentos relativos al Primer Congreso Nacional de Industriales.* México: Imprenta "Victoria," 1917.

Anuario de estadística minera. Mexico: Talleres Gráficos de la Nación, 1923.

Boletin del Petróleo, 1916, 1919, 1933, Vol. 8–13, 1922.

Reseña y memorias del primer Congreso Nacional de Industriales, reunido en la Ciudad de México bajo el patrocinio de la Secretaría de Industria, Comercio y Trabajo. México: Departamento de Aprovisionamientos Generales. Dirección de Talleres Gráficos, 1918.

Documentos relacionados con la legislación petrolera mexicana. Vol. 2. Distrito Federal: Talleres Gráficos de la Nación, 1922.

México, sus recursos naturales, su situación actual: homenaje al Brasil en ocasión del primer centenario de su independencia, 1822–1922. México: Editorial "Cultura," 1922.

Monografía sobre el estado actual de la industria en México. México: Talleres Gráficos de la Nación, 1929.

Reglamento del Código Nacional Eléctrico. México, D. F.: Talleres Gráficos F. Sanz y Cía., 1929.

Directorio de manufactureros de la ciudad de México, anticipo al directorio de la república. México: Sría. de Industria Comercio y Trabajo, Depto. de Industrias, 1932.

VII Censo Industrial 1961. México, D. F.: Talleres Gráficos de la Nación, 1965.

Secretaría de la Economía Nacional. *Anuario de Estadística Minera.* México: Secretaría de la Economía Nacional, 1922.

"Costos comparativos y propiedades caloríficas del carbón, del petróleo y del gas, como combustible." *Revista Industrial* 1, 1 (1933): 84.

Primer censo industrial de 1930. Resúmenes generales. Vol. I. México, D. F.: Dirección General de Estadística, 1933.

Secretariat of the Economic Commission for Latin America. *Energy in Latin America.* Document (United Nations); E/CN.12/384 Rev. 1. Geneva: United Nations Dept. of Economic and Social Affairs, 1957.

Septién, Alfonso. *La industrialización de México.* México, D. F.: Academia Mexicana de Jurisprudencia y Legislación, 1952.

Sheldon, Charles. "The Big Game of Chihuahua, Mexico, 1898–1902," in *Hunting and Conservation: The Book of the Boone and Crockett Club.* New Haven: Yale University Press, 1925.

Sierra, Justo, and Augustin Aragón. *Mexico, Its Social Evolution.* Mexico: Ballescá, 1900.

Silva Herzog, Jesús. "La cuestión del petróleo en México." *El Trimestre Económico* 7, no. 25 (1) (1940): 1–74.

Petróleo mexicano, historia de un problema. México, D. F.: Fondo de Cultura Económica, 1941.

Simpson, Lesley Byrd. *Many Mexicos.* Berkeley: University of California Press, 1966.

Sistema métrico-decimal: tablas que establecen la relación que existe entre los valores de las antiguas medidas mexicanas y las del nuevo sistema legal, formadas en el Ministerio de Fomento, conforme a la Ley de 15 de Marzo de 1857. México: Imprenta de J.M. Andrade y F. Escalante, 1857.

Sketches of the War in Northern Mexico. With Pictures of Life, Manners and Scenery. In Two Parts. New York: D. Appleton and Co., 1848.

Skilton, Julius. *Mining Districts of Pachuca, Real del Monte, El Chico and Santa Rosa, State of Hidalgo, Republic of Mexico.* Boston: Tolman & White, 1882.

Smith, Jackson. *The National Lines of Mexico. National Railroad Company of Mexico. Mexican International Railroad. Interoceanic Railway of Mexico.* Chicago: Poole Bros., 1904.

Sociedad Carbonífera y Minera Mexicana. *Estatutos de la Sociedad Carbonífera y Minera Mexicana: Sociedad Anónima.* México: Tip. de "El Gran Libro," de F. Parres, 1889.

Sociedad para el Fomento de la Industria Nacional, Mexico. *Reglamento de una sociedad para el fomento de la industria nacional.* México: Impreso por Ignacio Cumplido, 1839.

Sotero Noriega, José. *Influencia de los hidrocarburos en la industrialización de México.* México, D. F.: Banco de México, 1944.

Soto, Manuel F. "Ferrocarril y comunicación interoceánica por el centro de la República Mexicana." *Boletín de la Sociedad Mexicana de Geografía y Estadística* 2, 1 (1869): 505–12.

Southworth, J. R. *El directorio oficial de la minas y haciendas de Mexico: descripción general de las propiedades mineras y de las haciendas y ranchos de aquellos estados y territorios donde se han podido obtener datos fidedignos de la Republica Mexicana. The Official Directory of Mines & Estates of Mexico: General Description of the Mining Properties of the Republic of Mexico: In Which is Included a List of Haciendas and Ranches in Those States and Territories Where it has Been Possible to Obtain Reliable Data.* Mexico, D. F.: Published by John R. Southworth, F.R.G.S., 1910.

El Estado de Veracruz-Llave. Su historia, agricultura, comercio é industrias, en inglés y español. Liverpool: Blake & Mackenzie, printers, 1900.

Mexico ilustrado, Distrito federal, su descripcion, gobierno, historia, comercio e industrias, la biografia del sr. general d. Porfirio Diaz, en español e ingles. Liverpool: Printed by Blake & Mackenzie, 1903.

Southworth, John R. and Percy G. Holms, *El Directorio Oficial Minero de México: "Las minas de Mexico" y "Directorio minero de Mexico" (Fusionados). Historia, geologia, antigua minera, y descripción general de las propiedades mineras de la República Mexicana. Español e inglés.* Liverpool: Blake & Mackenzie, Ltd.,1908.

Stephens, John L. *Incidents of Travel in Yucatan.* New York: Harper & brothers, 1848.

Strode, Hudson. *Now in Mexico.* New York: Harcourt, Brace and Company, 1947.

Tannenbaum, Frank. *Mexico: The Struggle for Peace and Bread.* Borzoi Book. New York: Alfred A. Knopf, 1950.

Tejada, Miguel Lerdo de. *Cuadro sinóptico de la República Mexicana en 1856.* México: Imprenta de Ignacio Cumplido, 1856.

"The Charcoal Iron Industry of Europe." *United States Association of Charcoal Iron Workers* 3, 1 (1882): 28–31.

"The Coalfields of Mexico." *The Engineering and Mining Journal* 57, 23 (1894): 535.

The Iron Trade Review. Vol. XXXVI. Cleveland: Day & Carter, 1903.

The Mexican Light and Power Company, Limited. *Electric Light and Power in the City of Mexico.* Montreal: The Mexican Electric Light Company, Limited, 1905.

Annual Report. Toronto: The Mexican Light and Power Company, Limited, 1906–1965.

The Mexican Mining Journal 10–11, 1910.

The Mexican Yearbook. London: McCorquodale & Co. Ltd., 1908. 1920.

"Costos comparativos y propiedades caloríficas del carbón, del petróleo y del gas como combustibles." *Revista Industrial* Vol. 1, no. 1 (July 1933).

The Petroleum Review, with Which is Incorporated "Petroleum." Vol. 17. London: The Petroleum Review, 1907.

"The Shipment of Coal in 1893." *The Colliery Guardian* 68 (1894): 441.

Thomas, Kirby. "The Coal Deposits of Mexico and Their Development." *The Black Diamond* 4: 223.

Thompson, Waddy. *Recollections of Mexico.* New York, London: Wiley and Putnam, 1847.

Tornel Olvera, Augustín. *Desierto de Los Leones.* México: Talleres de la Dirección de Estudios Geográficos y Climatológicos, 1922.

Torón Villegas, Luis. *La industria siderúrgica pesada del norte de México y su abastecimiento de materias primas.* México, D. F.: Banco de México, 1963.

Torre, Juan de la. *Bosquejo historico y estadistico de la Ciudad de Morelia, capital del estado de Michoacán de Ocampo.* México: Imprenta de Ignacio Cumplido, 1883.

Historia y descripción del Ferrocarril Central Mexicano. Reseña histórica de esa vía férrea. Noticias sobre sus principales obras de arte. Datos históricos, estadísticos, descriptivos, referentes á los estados, ciudades, pueblos, estaciones, y en general á todos los lugares notables de la línea. Noticias semejantes sobre el Ferrocarril Internacional Mexicano de Torreón á Piedras Negras. México: Imprenta de Ignacio Cumplido, 1888.

Torres Gaytán, Ricardo. *La industria petrolera mexicana: conferencias en conmemoración del XX aniversario de la expropiación.* México, D. F.: UNAM, 1958.

Trentini, Francisco, ed. *El florecimiento de México.* México: Tipografía de Bouligny & Schmidt Sucs., 1906.

United Nations. *An Enquiry into the Iron and Steel Industry of Mexico.* New York: United Nations, 1954.

United States. *Investment in Mexico, Conditions and Outlook for United States Investors.* Washington, DC: US Govt. Print. Off., 1956.

Mexican Industrial Productivity Center (Centro Industrial de Productividad) a Case Study of an Industrial Technical Cooperation Program. Washington, DC: Technical Aids Branch, International Cooperation Administration, 1958.

United States Association of Charcoal Iron Workers. *Journal of the United States Association of Charcoal Iron Workers.* Vol. 3. Harrisburg, 1882.

United States Congress, Senate, Committee on Foreign Relations. *Investigation of Mexican Affairs: Preliminary Report and Hearings of the Committee on Foreign Relations.* Vol. 1. 2 vols. Washington, DC: 66th Congress, 1920.

United States Department of Agriculture, Foreign Agricultural Service, *Mexico's Livestock and Meat Industry.* FAS-M-27. Washington, DC: Foreign Agricultural Service, 1957.

United States Department of Agriculture, Office of Foreign Agricultural Relations, *The Dairy Industry in Mexico.* Foreign Agriculture Circular FD 3-52. Washington, DC: Office of Foreign Agricultural Relations, 1952.

United States Department of Commerce. *World Survey of Agricultural Machinery and Equipment.* Washington, DC: U.S Department of Commerce, 1959.

United States Geological Survey. *Mineral Resources of the United States.* Vol. 25. Washington, DC: Bureau of Mines, 1882.

United States Tariff Commission. *Agricultural, Pastoral and Forest Industries in Mexico.* Washington, DC: US Govt. Print. Off., 1948.

Mining and Manufacturing Industries in Mexico. Washington, DC: United States Tariff Commission, 1946.

Urbina, Fernando. *La cuestion del petróleo en México, considerada desde el punto de vista geológico, económico e industrial, especialmente en lo que se refiere a la intervención gubernamental en la producción petrolera.* México: Porrúa Hermanos, Editores, 1915.

US Dept. of Agriculture, Foreign Agricultural Service, *Agricultural Geography of Latin America.* Washington, D.C.: Foreign Agricultural Service, US Dept. of Agriculture, 1958.

Valle, Juan N. del. *El viajero en México; completa guia de forasteros para 1864; obra util a toda clase de personas.* México: Impr. de Andrade y Escalante, 1864.

El viajero en México, ó sea la capital de la República, encerrada en un libro. México: Tipografía de M. Castro, 1859.

Vavasour, Bernard. *British Petroleum Entrepreneurs in Mexico Photograph Album.* 1910. Graphic.

Vázquez Schiaffino, José, and Joaquín Santaella. *Informes sobre la cuestión petrolera.* México, D. F.: Imprenta de la Cámara de Diputados, 1919.

Velasco, Alfonso Luis. *Geografía y estadística de la República Mexicana.* 23 vols. México: Oficina Tip. de la Secretaría de Fomento, 1889.

Geografía y estadística de la República Mexicana. Coahuila de Zaragoza. Vol. 19. México: Oficina Tip. de la Secretaría de Fomento, 1897.

Villarelo, Juan D. *Algunas regiones petrolíferas de México.* Boletín del Instituto Geológico de México 26. México: Imprenta y Fototípia de la Secretaría de Fomento, 1908.

Villarreal, Arnulfo. *El carbón mineral en México. (Notas para la planeación de la industria básica).* México, D. F.: Edición y Distribución Ibero Americana de Publicaciones, 1954.

Viniegra, G., and H. Bravo. "Polución atmosférica en la ciudad de México; informe preliminar." *La Prensa Médica Mexicana* 24, 2 (1959): 73–80.

Vogt, William. *Los recursos naturales de México*. México: Artes Gráficas del Estado, 1946.

Ward, H. G. *Mexico in 1827*. London: Henry Colburn, 1828.

Weidner, Federico. *El Cerro del Mercado de Durango. Compendio de noticias mineralógicas, orognósticas, históricas, estadísticas y metalúrgicas de dicho cerro y la ferrería de San Francisco*. México: Imprenta de Andrade y Escalante, 1858.

Wells, David A. *A Study of Mexico*. New York: D. Appleton and Company, 1887.

Wislizenus, F. A. *Denkschrift über eine Reise nach Nord-Mexiko, Verbunden mit der Expedition des Obersten Donniphan, in den Jahren 1846 und 1847*. Braunschweig: Druck und Verlag von Friedrick Vieweg und Sohn, 1850.

World Bank. "Appraisal of the Toll Transport Facilities Project: Mexico," Report No. TO-315e. Washington, DC: Department of Technical Operations, 1962.

The Economic Development of Mexico. Baltimore: Johns Hopkins University Press, 1953.

Zaremba, Charles W. *The Merchants' and Tourists' Guide to Mexico*. Chicago: The Althrop Pub. House, 1883.

Zevada, Manuel J. "El costo de producción de la gasolina en México." *Revista Industrial* 1, 1 (1933): 67–9.

Zevada, Manuel J., and Santiago González, eds. *Extracto de la obra en preparación titulada: glosario de la industria petrolera y vocabulario español-inglés e inglés-español de los términos técnicos usados en esta industria*. México: Talleres Gráficos de la Nación, 1930.

Secondary Sources

Agnoletti, Mauro, and Simone Neri Serneri, eds. *The Basic Environmental History*. Cham: Springer, 2014.

Aguilar, Sandra. "Nutrition and Modernity: Milk Consumption in 1940s and 1950s Mexico." *Radical History Review* 110 (2011): 36–58.

Aguirre Anaya, Carmen. "Industria y tecnología: motricidad en los textiles de algodón en el XIX." *Siglo XIX: Cuadernos* 3, 6 (1993): 23–33.

Agustín, José. *Tragicomedia mexicana: la vida en México de 1940 a 1970*. México, D. F.: Planeta, 1990.

Albritton Jonsson, Fredrik. "The Industrial Revolution in the Anthropocene." *The Journal of Modern History* 84, 3 (2012): 679–96.

Alegre, Robert Francis, "Contesting the 'Mexican Miracle': Railway Men and Women and the Struggle for Democracy in Mexico, 1943–1959," PhD Dissertation, Rutgers, 2007.

Allen, Robert C. "Backward into the Future: The Shift to Coal and Implications for the next Energy Transition." *Energy Policy, Special Section: Past and Prospective Energy Transitions – Insights from History* 50 (2012): 17–23.

The British Industrial Revolution in Global Perspective. Cambridge; New York: Cambridge University Press, 2009.

Almanza, Joel, and Andrea Báez. "La construcción en tierra caliente del ferrocarril entre Veracruz y México, 1842–1864." *Historia 2.0* 7 (2014): 86–114.

Almazán Reyes, Marco Aurelio. "Usos, perspectivas y conflictos por los recursos forestales en los pueblos de montaña (Nevado de Toluca) durante el Porfiriato, 1876–1911," Master's Dissertation in Social Anthropology, CIESAS, 2011.

"Montes en transición. Acceso y aprovechamiento forestal en torno al Nevado de Toluca, del Porfiriato a la Posrevolución." *Letras Históricas* 20 (2019): 65–90.

Almeida-Lenero, L., H. Hooghiemstra, A. M. Cleef, and B. van Geel. "Holocene Climatic and Environmental Change from Pollen Records of Lakes Zempoala and Quila, Central Mexican Highlands." *Review of Palaeobotany and Palynology* 136, 1–2 (2005): 63–92.

Altamirano Poe, Ma. Elena. "José María Velasco, científico." *Ciencias/UNAM* 45 (1997): 32–5.

Alvarado, Jesús. "We Welcomed Foreign Fabrics and We Were Left Naked: Cotton Textile Artisans and the First Debates on Free Trade Versus National Industry in Mexico," PhD Thesis, University of Wisconsin-Madison, 2007.

Álvarez de la Borda, Joel. *Crónica del petróleo en México: de 1863 a nuestros días.* México, D. F.: Petróleos Mexicanos, 2006.

"Transportes, negocios y política: La Compañía de Tranvías de México, 1907–1947." In *Las compañías eléctricas extranjeras en México, 1880–1960,* 67–105. Puebla: Benemérita Universidad Autónoma de Puebla, 2010.

"Adolfo Autrey y el petróleo de El Cuguas." *Historias. Revista de la Dirección de Estudios Históricos* 90 (2015): pp. 99–108.

Anderson, Rodney D. *Outcasts in Their Own Land: Mexican Industrial Workers, 1906–1911.* DeKalb: Northern Illinois University Press, 1976.

Andrews, Thomas G. *Killing for Coal: America's Deadliest Labor War.* Cambridge, MA: Harvard University Press, 2008.

Angus, Ian. *Facing the Anthropocene: Fossil Capitalism and the Crisis of the Earth System.* New York: NYU Press, 2016.

Ansell, Martin R. *Oil Baron of the Southwest: Edward L. Doheny and the Development of the Petroleum Industry in California and Mexico.* Columbus: Ohio State University Press, 1998.

Antonio, Escobar Ohmstede. *Desastres agrícolas en México. Catálogo histórico II. Siglo XIX.* México, D. F.: Fondo de Cultura Económica, 2004.

Anuario estadístico de la minería mexicana. México, D. F.: Servicio Geológico Mexicano, 2017.

Araújo, Kathleen. "The Emerging Field of Energy Transitions: Progress, Challenges, and Opportunities." *Energy Research & Social Science* 2014, 112–21.

Low Carbon Energy Transitions: Turning Points in National Policy and Innovation. Oxford: Oxford University Press, 2017.

Arnaut, Javier L. "Mexican Real Wages before the Revolution: A Reappraisal." *Iberoamericana – Nordic Journal of Latin American and Caribbean Studies* 47, 1 (2018): 45–62.

Arreola, Daniel D. "Nineteenth-Century Townscapes of Eastern Mexico." *Geographical Review* 72, 1 (1982): 1–19.

Arrom, Silvia Marina. *The Women of Mexico City, 1790–1857.* Stanford: Stanford University Press, 1985.

Asociación Mexicana de Energía Eólica. *El potencial eólico mexicano: oportunidades y retos en el nuevo sector eléctrico.* México: AMDEE, n.d.

Assadourian, Carlos Sempat. "La bomba de fuego de Newcomen y otros artificios de desagüe: un intento de transferencia de tecnología inglesa a la minería novohispana, 1726–173I." *Historia Mexicana* 50, 3 (2001): 385–457.

Ávalos-Lozano, Antonio, and Miguel Aguilar-Robledo. "Reconstructing the Environmental History of Colonial Mining: The Real del Catorce Mining District, Northeastern New Spain/Mexico, Eighteenth and Nineteenth Centuries," 47–70. In John R. McNeill and George Vrtis, eds. *Mining North America: An Environmental History Since 1522.* Berkeley: University of California Press, 2017.

Ávila García, Patricia. *Agua, cultura y sociedad en México.* Zamora de Hidalgo: El Colegio de Michoacán, 2002.

Aviles-Galán, Miguel Ángel. "A Todo Vapor: Mechanization in Porfirian Mexico. Steam Power and Machine Building, 1862 to 1906," PhD Dissertation, University of British Columbia, 2010.

Azuela, Luz Fernanda. *Tres sociedades científicas en el Porfiriato las disciplinas, las instituciones y las relaciones entre la ciencia y el poder.* México, D. F.: Sociedad Mexicana de Historia de la Ciencia y de la Tecnología, Universidad Tecnológica de Nezahualcóyotl, Universidad Nacional Autónoma de México, Instituto de Geografía, 1996.

Bachelor, Steven Jon. "The Edge of Miracles: Postrevolutionary Mexico City and the Remaking of the Industrial Working Class, 1925–1982," PhD Dissertation, Yale University, 2003.

Bahre, Conrad. "The Impact of Historic Fuelwood Cutting on the Semidesert Woodlands of Southeastern Arizona." *Journal of Forest History* 4 (1985): 175–86.

  A Legacy of Change: Historic Human Impact on Vegetation in the Arizona Borderlands. Tucson: University of Arizona Press, 2016.

Barak, On. "Outsourcing: Energy and Empire in the Age of Coal, 1820–1911." *International Journal of Middle East Studies* 47, 3 (2015): 425–45.

Barbero, María Inés. "Business History in Latin America: A Historiographical Perspective." *Business History Review* 82, 3 (2008): 437, 555–75.

Barca, Stefania. "Enclosing the River: Industrialization and the 'Property Rights' Discourse in the Liri Valley (South of Italy), 1806–1916." *Environment and History* 13, 1 (2007): 3–23.

  "Energy, Property, and the Industrial Revolution Narrative." *Ecological Economics* (2010).

"Laboring the Earth: Transnational Reflections on the Environmental History of Work." *Environmental History* 19 (2014): 3–27.

Bardini, Carlo. "Without Coal in the Age of Steam: A Factor-Endowment Explanation of the Industrial Lag before World War I." *The Journal of Economic History* 57, 3 (1997): 633–52.

Bargalló, Modesto. *La minería y la metalurgia en la América española durante la época colonial.* México, D. F.: Fondo de Cultura Económica, 1955.

Barrett, Ross, and Daniel Worden, eds. *Oil Culture.* Minneapolis: University of Minnesota Press, 2014.

Bartoletto, Silvana, and Mar Rubio. "Energy Transition and CO_2 Emissions in Southern Europe: Italy and Spain (1861–2000)." *Global Environment* 2 (2008): 46–81.

Barton, Greg. *Empire Forestry and the Origins of Environmentalism.* Cambridge: Cambridge University Press, 2002.

Bauer, Arnold J. "Millers and Grinders: Technology and Household Economy in Meso-America." *Agricultural History* 64, 1 (1990): 1–17.

Baynes, Timothy M., and Xuemei Bai. "Reconstructing the Energy History of a City." *Journal of Industrial Ecology* 16, 6 (2012): 862–74.

Bazán, Gerardo. *Transporte y energía: consumo de energía en el sector transporte.* México: Fondo de Cultura Económica, CONACYT, 1992.

Bazant, Jan. *Estudio sobre la productividad de la industria algodonera mexicana en 1843–1845: Lucas Alamán y la revolución industrial en México.* México: Banco Nacional de Comercio Exterior, 1962.

"Evolution of the Textile Industry of Puebla 1544–1845." *Comparative Studies in Society and History* 7, 1 (1964): 56–69.

Beatty, Edward. "Bottles for Beer: The Business of Technological Innovation in Mexico, 1890–1920." *The Business History Review* 83, 2 (2009): 317–48.

Institutions and Investment: The Political Basis of Industrialization in Mexico before 1911. Stanford: Stanford University Press, 2001.

Technology and the Search for Progress in Modern Mexico. Berkeley: University of California Press, 2015.

"Technology in 19th-Century Mexico." *Oxford Research Encyclopedia of Latin American History.* Oxford: Oxford University Press, 2017.

Becerril, Gustavo. "Fuentes para el estudio de los usos y aplicaciones en las manufacturas de la Ciudad de México, a partir de documentos del Archivo Histórico del Distrito Federal, 1900–1902." *Boletín de Monumentos Históricos* 4 (2005).

"Maquinaria para los procesos de manufactura de algodón y lana en fábricas del Valle de México, 1870–1916." *Boletín de Monumentos Históricos* 7 (2006).

"El obrador y fábrica de textiles de San Antonio Abad (1843–1901). Un establecimiento pionero en el Valle de México." *Boletín de Monumentos Históricos* 9 (2007).

"El proceso de construcción de estaciones productoras de energía eléctrica. El caso de las fábricas Santa Teresa y la Hormiga (1896–1907)." *Boletín de Monumentos Históricos* 16 (2009).

"Los materiales de construcción en la arquitectura industrial textil: las fábricas de algodón la colmena y barrón, Siglos XIX y XX." *Boletín de Monumentos Históricos* 23 (2011).

Bernstein, Marvin D. *The Mexican Mining Industry, 1890–1950: A Study of the Interaction of Politics, Economics, and Technology.* New York: SUNY Press, 1964.

Bess, Michael K. *Routes of Compromise: Building Roads and Shaping the Nation in Mexico, 1917–1952.* Lincoln: University of Nebraska Press, 2017.

"On the Course of 'Progress': A Review of Literature on Road Building in Latin America." *Mobility in History* 8, 1, 2018.

"Revolutionary Paths: Road Building, National Identity, and Foreign Power in Mexico, 1917–1938." *Mexican Studies/Estudios Mexicanos* 32, 1 (2018): 56–82.

Birkle, P., V. Torres Rodríguez, and E. González Partida. "The Water Balance for the Basin of the Valley of Mexico and Implications for Future Water Consumption." *Hydrogeology Journal*, 6, 4 (1998): 500–17.

Black, Brian. *Petrolia: The Landscape of America's First Oil Boom.* Baltimore: Johns Hopkins University Press, 2000.

Crude Reality: Petroleum in World History. Lanham: Rowman & Littlefield Publishers, 2012.

"Oil for Living: Petroleum and American Conspicuous Consumption." *Journal of American History* 99, 1 (2012): 40–50.

Blanco Martínez, Mireya, and José Omar Moncada Maya. "El Ministerio de Fomento, Impulsor del estudio y el reconocimiento del territorio mexicano (1877–1898)." *Investigaciones Geográficas. Boletín del Instituto de Geografía* 74 (2011): 74–91.

Blum, Ann Shelby. "Cleaning the Revolutionary Household: Domestic Servants and Public Welfare in Mexico City, 1900–1935." *Journal of Women's History* 15, 4 (2004): 67–90.

Boden, T. A., G. Marland, and R. J. Andres. "Global, Regional, and National Fossil-Fuel CO_2 Emissions." Carbon Dioxide Information Analysis Center, Oak Ridge National Laboratory, US Department of Energy, Oak Ridge, Tennessee, USA, 2011.

Boyer, Christopher R. "Revolución y paternalismo ecológico: Miguel Ángel de Quevedo y la política forestal en México, 1926–1940." *Historia Mexicana* LVII, 1 (2007): 91–138.

ed. *A Land between Waters: Environmental Histories of Modern Mexico.* Tucson: University of Arizona Press, 2012.

"La Segunda Guerra Mundial y la 'crisis de producción' en los bosques mexicanos." *HALAC* II, núm. 1 (2012–2013): 7–23.

Political Landscapes: Forests, Conservation, and Community in Mexico. Durham: Duke University Press Books, 2015.

Boyer, Christopher R., and Emily Wakild. "Social Landscaping in the Forests of Mexico: An Environmental Interpretation of Cardenismo, 1934–1940." *Hispanic American Historical Review* 92, 1 (2012): 73–106.

Boyer, Dominic, and Imre Szeman. "Breaking the Impasse: The Rise of Energy Humanities." *University Affairs* 42 (2014).

Boyer, Richard E. *Urbanization in 19th Century Latin America: Statistics and Sources.* Statistical Abstract of Latin America. Supplement Series; 4. Los Angeles: Latin American Center, University of California, 1973.

"Las ciudades mexicanas: perspectivas de estudio en el siglo XIX." *Historia Mexicana* 22, 2 (1972): 142–59.

Brannstrom, Christian. "Was Brazilian Industrialisation Fueled by Wood? Evaluating the Wood Hypothesis, 1900–1960." *Environment and History* 11, 4 (2005): 395–430.

Bray, David B., and Peter Klepeis. "Deforestation, Forest Transitions, and Institutions for Sustainability in Southeastern Mexico, 1900–2000." *Environment and History* 11, 2 (2005): 195–223.

Bray, David B., Leticia Merino-Perez, and Deborah Barry. *The Community Forests of Mexico: Managing for Sustainable Landscapes.* Austin: University of Texas Press, 2005.

Briones, Oscar, Alberto Búrquez, Angelina Martínez-Yrízar, Numa Pavón, and Yareni Perroni. "Biomasa y productividad en las zonas áridas mexicanas." *Madera y Bosques* 24, 0 (2018).

Briseño, Líllian. *Candil de la calle oscuridad de su casa: la iluminación en la ciudad de México durante el porfiriato.* Mexico, D. F.: Miguel Ángel Porrúa, 2008.

British Petroleum. "Statistical Review of World Energy 2018." British Petroleum, 2018.

Bronstein, Clara. "La introducción de la máquina de vapor en México," Tesis de Maestría, UNAM, 1965.

Brown, Jonathan C. "Why Foreign Oil Companies Shifted Their Production from Mexico to Venezuela during the 1920s." *The American Historical Review* 90, 2 (1985): 362–85.

"The Structure of the Foreign-Owned Petroleum Industry in Mexico, 1880–1938." In *The Mexican Petroleum Industry in the Twentieth Century.* Austin: University of Texas Press, 1992.

Oil and Revolution in Mexico. Berkeley: University of California Press, 1993.

Brown, Jonathan C., and Alan Knight, eds. *The Mexican Petroleum Industry in the Twentieth Century.* Austin: University of Texas Press, 1992.

Bryant, R. L. "Romancing Colonial Forestry: The Discourse of 'Forestry as Progress' in British Burma." *The Geographical Journal* 162, 2 (1996): 169.

Bucheli, Marcelo. "Major Trends in the Historiography of the Latin American Oil Industry." *The Business History Review* 84, 2 (2010): 339–62.

Bud-Frierman, Lisa, Andrew Godley, and Judith Wale. "Weetman Pearson in Mexico and the Emergence of a British Oil Major, 1901–1919." *The Business History Review* 84, 2 (2010): 275–300.

Bullock, Stephen H., and J. Arturo Solis-Magallanes. "Phenology of Canopy Trees of a Tropical Deciduous Forest in Mexico." *Biotropica* 22, 1 (1990): 22–35.

Bulmer-Thomas, V., John H. Coatsworth, and Roberto Cortés Conde. *The Colonial Era and the Short Nineteenth Century*. Cambridge: Cambridge University Press, 2006.

Bulmer-Thomas, Victor. *The Economic History of Latin America since Independence*. New York: Cambridge University Press, 2014.

Bunker, Steven B. *Creating Mexican Consumer Culture in the Age of Porfirio Díaz*. Albuquerque: University of New Mexico Press, 2012.

Burke III, Edmund. "The Big Story: Human History, Energy Regimes, and the Environment." In *The Environment and World History*, 33–53. Berkeley: University of California Press, 2009.

Burke III, Edmund, and Kenneth Pomeranz. *The Environment and World History*. Berkeley: University of California Press, 2009.

Burke, Marshall, Solomon M. Hsiang, and Edward Miguel. "Global Non-Linear Effect of Temperature on Economic Production." *Nature* 527, 7577 (2015): 235–9.

Butler, Edgar W., James B. Pick, and W. James Hettrick. *Mexico and Mexico City in the World Economy*. Boulder, CO: Westview Press, 2001.

Butzer, Karl W. "The Americas before and after 1492: An Introduction to Current Geographical Research." *ANNA Annals of the Association of American Geographers* 82, 3 (1992): 345–68.

Butzer, Karl W., and Elisabeth K. Butzer. "The Natural Vegetation of the Mexican Bajio: Archival Documentation of a 16th-Century Savanna Environment." *Quaternary International* 43144 (1997): 161–72.

Caballero Deloya, Miguel. "La verdadera cosecha maderable en México." *Revista Mexicana de Ciencias Forestales* 1, 1 (2010): 5–16.

Calderón, Roberto R. *Mexican Coal Mining Labor in Texas and Coahuila, 1880–1930*. College Station: Texas A&M University Press, 2000.

Camarena, Mario. *Jornaleros, tejedores y obreros: historia social de los trabajadores textiles de San Angel, 1850–1930*. Col. San Rafael, México, D. F.: Plaza y Valdés Editores, 2001.

"Fábricas, naturaleza y sociedad en San Ángel (1850–1910)." In *Tierra, agua y bosques: historia y medio ambiente en el México central*. México, D. F.: Centre français d'études mexicaines et centraméricaines; Instituto de Investigaciones Dr. José María Luis Mora; Potrerillos Editores: Universidad de Guadalajara, 1996.

Camou-Guerrero, Andrés, Adrián Ghilardi, Tuyeni Mwampampa, et al. "Análisis de la producción de carbón vegetal en la cuenca del lago de Cuitzeo, Michoacán, México: Implicaciones para una producción sustentable." *Investigación Ambiental Ciencia y Política Pública* 6, 2 (2016).

Campbell, Timothy. *Food, Water, and Energy in the Valley of Mexico*. Berkeley: Institute of Urban and Regional Development, University of California, Berkeley, 1982.

Campos Aragón, Leticia. *La electricidad en la ciudad de México y área conurbada: historia, problemas y perspectivas*. México, D. F.: Siglo XXI, 2005.

Candiani, Vera S. *Dreaming of Dry Land: Environmental Transformation in Colonial Mexico City*. Stanford: Stanford University Press, 2014.

Cañizares-Esguerra, Jorge. *Nature, Empire, and Nation: Explorations of the History of Science in the Iberian World*. Stanford: Stanford University Press, 2006.

Canseco, Mercedes. *Energías renovables en América Latina*. Madrid: Fundación Ciudadanía y Valores, 2010.

Canudas, Enrique. *Las venas de plata en la historia de México: síntesis de historia económica, siglo XIX*. Univ. Juárez Autónoma de Tabasco, 2005.

Cárdenas, Enrique. *La industrialización mexicana durante la Gran Depresión*. México, D. F.: Colegio de México, 1987.

La política económica en México, 1950–1994. México, D. F.: Fondo de Cultura Económica, 1996.

Cuándo se originó el atraso económico de México: la economía mexicana en el largo siglo XIX, 1780–1920. Madrid: Biblioteca Nueva: Fundación Ortega y Gasset, 2003.

Carey, Mark. "Latin American Environmental History: Current Trends, Interdisciplinary Insights, and Future Directions." *Environmental History* 14, 2 (2009): 221–52.

Carmagnani, Marcello. *The Other West: Latin America from Invasion to Globalization*. Berkeley: University of California Press, 2011.

Carranza Castellanos, Emilio. *Desarrollo del alumbrado publico en el siglo XX Ciudad de México*. México, D. F.: Fundación Ingeniero Alejo Peralta y Díaz Ceballos, 2000.

Casillas Hernández, Alberto. "El acervo gráfico del Archivo Histórico Fundidora." *Alquimia* 54 (2017): 68–75.

Cerutti, Mario. *Burguesía, capitales e industria en el Norte de México: Monterrey y su ámbito regional (1850–1910)*. Monterrey: Universidad Autónoma de Nuevo León, 1992.

"Empresarios y sociedades empresariales en el norte de México (1870–1920)." *Revista de Historia Industrial* 6 (1994): 95–115.

Burguesía y capitalismo en Monterrey, 1850–1910. Monterrey: Fondo Editorial de NL, 2006.

Cerutti Masera, Omar. *Crisis y mecanización de la agricultura campesina*. México, D. F.: El Colegio de México, 1990.

Challenger, Antony. *Utilización y conservación de los ecosistemas terrestres de México: pasado, presente y futuro*. México, D. F.: CONABIO, 1998.

Chico, Rachel Anne. "Route to the Capital, Route to the Sea: Domestic Travel, Regional Identity and Local Isolation in the Veracruz-Mexico City Corridor, 1812–1876," PhD Dissertation, University of California, Berkeley, 2006.

Christensen, Paul. "History of Energy in Economic Thought," 117–30. In Cutler J. Cleveland, ed., *Encyclopedia of Energy*, New York: Elsevier, 2004.

Christian, David. *Maps of Time: An Introduction to Big History*. Berkeley: University of California Press, 2004.

Cioc, Mark. "The Impact of the Coal Age on the German Environment: A Review of the Historical Literature." *Environment and History* 4, 1 (1998): 105–24.

Cipolla, Carlo M. *The Economic History of World Population*. Baltimore: Penguin Books, 1970.

The Industrial Revolution, 1700–1914. Hassocks, England: Harvester Press, 1976.

Clapp, B. W. *An Environmental History of Britain since the Industrial Revolution*. Hoboken: Taylor and Francis, 2014.

Clark, Brett, Andrew K. Jorgenson, and Daniel Auerbach. "Up in Smoke: The Human Ecology and Political Economy of Coal Consumption." *Organization & Environment* 25, 4 (2012): 452–69.

Clark, Gregory. "Why Isn't the Whole World Developed? Lessons from the Cotton Mills." *The Journal of Economic History* 47, 1 (1987): 141–73.

"Coal and the Industrial Revolution, 1700–1869." *European Review of Economic History* 11, 1 (2007): 39–72.

Clausius, Rudolf. *The Mechanical Theory of Heat, with its Applications to the Steam-Engine and to the Physical Properties of Bodies*. London: John Van Voorst, 1 Paternoster Row, 1867).

Clawson, David, and Don Hoy. "Mexico: A Peasant Community That Rejected the 'Green Revolution'." *The American Journal of Economics and Sociology* 38, 4 (1979): 371–87.

Cleaver, Harry. "The Contradictions of the Green Revolution." *The American Economic Review* 62, 1/2 (1972): 177–86.

Cleveland, Cutler J. *Concise Encyclopedia of History of Energy*. San Diego: Elsevier, 2009.

Coatsworth, John H. "Anotaciones sobre la producción de alimentos durante el Porfiriato." *Historia Mexicana* 26, 2 (1976): 167–87.

"Obstacles to Economic Growth in Nineteenth-Century México." *The American Historical Review* 83, 1 (1978): 80–100.

"The Impact of Railroads on the Economic Development of Mexico, 1877–1910," 1980.

Growth against Development: The Economic Impact of Railroads in Porfirian Mexico. Origins of Modern Mexico. DeKalb: Northern Illinois University Press, 1981.

Los orígenes del atraso: nueve ensayos de historia económica de México en los siglos XVIII y XIX. México, D. F.: Alianza Editorial Mexicana, 1990.

Cole, William Edward. *Steel and Economic Growth in Mexico*. Austin: University of Texas Press, 2014.

Colegio de México. *Estadísticas económicas del porfiriato: fuerza de trabajo y actividad económica por sectores*. México, D. F.: El Colegio de México, 1965.

Collado, María del Carmen. *La burguesía mexicana: el emporio Braniff y su participación política, 1865–1920*. México, D. F.: Siglo XXI, 1987.

Colmenares, Patricio. "Petróleo y crecimiento económico en México, 1938–2006." *Economíaunam* 5, 15 (2007): 53–65.

Comisión Nacional del Agua. *Atlas del agua en México*. México, D. F.: CONAGUA, 2011.

Common, Michael S., and Sigrid Stagl. *Ecological Economics: An Introduction*. Cambridge: Cambridge University Press, 2005.

Connolly, Priscilla. *El contratista de don Porfirio: obras públicas, deuda y desarrollo desigual*. México, D. F.: Fondo de Cultura Económica, 1997.

"Mexico City: Our Common Future?" *Environment and Urbanization* 11, 1 (1999): 53–78.

"Pearson and Public Works Construction in Mexico, 1890–1910." *Business History* 41, 4 (1999): 48–71.

Consejo Nacional de Población. *El poblamiento de México: una visión histórico-demográfica.* México, D. F.: Consejo Nacional de Población, 1993.

Constant, Edward W. "Scientific Theory and Technological Testability: Science, Dynamometers, and Water Turbines in the 19th Century." *Technology and Culture* 24, 2 (1983): 183–98.

Contreras, Camilo. "Geografía del mercado de trabajo en la cuenca carbonífera de Coahuila." *Frontera Norte* 13, no. esp. (2001).

——— "La explotación del carbón en la cuenca carbonífera de Coahuila (1866–1900). La división espacial del trabajo." *Relaciones. Estudios de Historia y Sociedad* XXII, 87 (2001): 177–203.

——— "Fundidora de Monterrey y la Cuenca del Carbón: La formación de un espacio económico a través de las relaciones comerciales interempresariales." In *Procesos y espacios mineros: Fundición y minería en el centro y noreste de México durante el Porfiriato*, 133–53. Tijuana: El Colegio de la Frontera Norte, 2004.

Contreras, Camilo, and Rosalía Chávez. "El Ferrocarril Internacional y su centralidad en el nacimiento de la cuenca carbonífera de Coahuila (1866–1900)." *Mirada Ferroviaria* 9 (2004): 13–21.

Contreras, Camilo, and Moisés Gámez, eds. *Procesos y espacios mineros. Fundición y minería en el centro y noreste de México durante el Porfiriato.* Tijuana: El Colegio de la Frontera Norte, 2004.

Contreras, Carlos, and Gerardo G. Sánchez Ruiz. *Planificación y urbanismo visionarios de Carlos Contreras: escritos de 1925 a 1938.* México, D. F.: UNAM, 2003.

Cook, Sherburne F., and Woodrow Borah. *Essays in Population History, Vol. III: Mexico and California.* Berkeley: University of California Press, 1979.

Cook, Sherburne F. *The Historical Demography and Ecology of the Teotlalpan.* Berkeley: University of California Press, 1949.

Cook, Sherburne Friend, and Woodrow Wilson Borah. *The Indian Population of Central Mexico, 1531–1610.* Berkeley: University of California Press, 1960.

Gayón Córdova, María. 1848. *Una ciudad de grandes contrastes: I. La vivienda en el censo de población levantado durante la ocupación militar norteamericana.* México: Instituto Nacional de Antropología e Historia, 2018.

Corona-Esquivel, Rodolfo, Jordi Tritlla, María Elena Benavides, et al. "Geología, estructura y composición de los principales yacimientos de carbón mineral en México." *Boletín de la Sociedad Geológica Mexicana* 58, 1 (2006): 141–60.

Cosío Villegas, Daniel. *Historia Moderna de México.* 7 vols. México, D. F.: Editorial Hermes, 1973.

Cotter, Joseph. *Troubled Harvest: Agronomy and Revolution in Mexico, 1880–2002.* Westport: Praeger, 2003.

Craib, Raymond B. *Cartographic Mexico: A History of State Fixations and Fugitive Landscapes.* Durham: Duke University Press, 2004.

Cribelli, Teresa. "'These Industrial Forests': Economic Nationalism and the Search for Agro-Industrial Commodities in Nineteenth-Century Brazil." *Journal of Latin American Studies* 45, 3 (2013): 545–79.

Crocker, Marvin D. "The Evolution of Mexican Forest Policy and Its Influence upon Forest Resources," PhD Dissertation, Oregon State University, 1973.

Crosby, Alfred W. *The Columbian Exchange: Biological and Cultural Consequences of 1492*. Westport: Greenwood Press, 1972.

Children of the Sun: A History of Humanity's Unappeasable Appetite for Energy. New York: Norton, 2006.

Cross, Harry E. "Living Standards in Rural Nineteenth-Century Mexico: Zacatecas 1820–80." *Journal of Latin American Studies* 10, 1 (1978): 1–19.

Cuevas, Martha Eugenia Alfaro. "Características de las dos fábricas industriales que Jorge Unna Gerson estableció en San Luis Potosí: la primera en 1889 y la segunda en 1903." *Boletín de Monumentos Históricos* 33 (2017): 87–105.

Daemen, Jaak J. K. "History of Coal Industry," 457–73. In Cutler J. Cleveland, ed., *Encyclopedia of Energy*. New York: Elsevier, 2004.

Dalrymple, Mark. "Deforestation and Land-Use Change in Veracruz, Mexico: A Remote Sensing Analysis," Master's Thesis, University of New Orleans, 2006.

Darmstadter, Joel. *How Industrial Societies Use Energy: A Comparative Analysis.* Baltimore: Johns Hopkins University Press, 1977.

Davis, Diane. "Whither the Public Sphere: Local, National, and International Influences on the Planning of Downtown Mexico City, 1910–1950." *Space and Culture* 7, 2 (2004): 193–222.

Urban Leviathan: Mexico City in the Twentieth Century. Philadelphia: Temple University Press, 2010.

De Vos, Jan. *Oro verde: la conquista de la selva lacandona por los madereros tabasqueños, 1822–1949.* México, D. F.: Fondo de Cultura Económica, 1996.

Vos, Jan de. *Una tierra para sembrar sueños: Historia reciente de la Selva Lacandona, 1950–2000.* México, D. F.: Fondo de Cultura Económica, 2015.

Dean, Warren. *The Industrialization of São Paulo, 1880–1945.* Austin: The University of Texas Press, 1969.

With Broadax and Firebrand: The Destruction of the Brazilian Atlantic Forest. Berkeley: University of California Press, 1997.

Debeir, Jean-Claude, Jean-Paul Deléage, and Daniel Hémery. *In the Servitude of Power: Energy and Civilisation through the Ages.* London: Zed Books, 1991.

DeLay, Brian. *War of a Thousand Deserts: Indian Raids and the US-Mexican War.* New Haven: Yale University Press, 2008.

Denevan, William M. "The Pristine Myth: The Landscape of the Americas in 1492." *Annals of the Association of American Geographers* 82, 3 (1992): 369–85.

Denison, Roger. *Everette Lee DeGolyer, 1886–1056: A Biographical Memoir.* Washington, DC: National Academy of Sciences, 1959.

Diamond, Jared M. *Guns, Germs, and Steel: The Fates of Human Societies.* New York: W.W. Norton & Co., 1998.

Dinius, Oliver. *Brazil's Steel City: Developmentalism, Strategic Power, and Industrial Relations in Volta Redonda, 1941–1964.* Stanford: Stanford University Press, 2010.

Dirección de Investigación y Evaluación Económica y Sectorial. *Panorama agroalimentario: maíz 2016.* México, D. F.: FIRA, 2016.

Domínguez, María del Refugio González. "Notas para el estudio de las Ordenanzas de Minería en México durante el siglo XVIII." In *IV Congreso del Instituto Internacional de Historia del Derecho Indiano* (1976): 157–68.

Dooley, Brendan Maurice. *Energy and Culture: Perspectives on the Power to Work.* London: Routledge, 2016.

Dukes, Jeffrey S. "Burning Buried Sunshine: Human Consumption of Ancient Solar Energy." *Climatic Change* 61, 1–2 (2003): 31–44.

Duncan, Roland E. "Chilean Coal and British Steamers: The Origin of a South American Industry." *The Mariner's Mirror* 61, 3 (1975): 271–81.

Durán, Esperanza. "El petróleo mexicano en la Primera Guerra Mundial." In *Energía en México. Ensayos sobre el pasado y el presente,* 53–75. México, D. F.: El Colegio de México, 1982.

Durand, Leticia, and Elena Lazos. "Colonization and Tropical Deforestation in the Sierra Santa Marta, Southern Mexico." *Environmental Conservation* 31, 1 (2004): 11–21.

Dyrnes, G. V., and A. Vatn. "Who Owns the Water? A Study of a Water Conflict in the Valley of Ixtlahuaca, Mexico." *Water Policy* 7, 3 (2005): 295–312.

Endfield, Georgina. *Climate and Society in Colonial Mexico: A Study in Vulnerability.* Malden: Blackwell Pub., 2008.

Energy, Resources, and the Long-Term Future. Hackensack World Scientific Publishing Company, 2007.

Escorza Rodríguez, Daniel. "El automóvil y la fotografía de sus inicios." *Dimensión Antropológica* 40 (2007): 179–200.

Escudero, Alejandrina. "Carlos Contreras, el urbanista y la ciudad," 41–61. In Catherine Ettinger and Louise Noelle, eds., *Los arquitectos mexicanos de la modernidad: corrigiendo las omisiones y celebrando el compromiso.* Morelia: Universidad Michoacana de San Nicolás de Hidalgo, Universidad Autónoma de San Luís Potosí, 2013.

Escudero, César, and Gloria Camacho, "*Los montes y su desamortización en los pueblos del sur del valle de Toluca, 1880–1917.*" *HiSTOReLo. Revista de Historia Regional y Local* 7, 13 (2015): 76–110.

Espinosa, Rosana. "El Molino de Tuzcacuaco. Antecedentes de la Hacienda Molino de Flores, Texcoco, Estado de México, 1567–1667." *Boletín de Monumentos Históricos* 25 (2012): 94–108.

Etemad, Bouda, and Jean Luciani. *World Energy Production, 1800–1985.* Geneva: Librairie Droz, 1991.

Evans, Sterling David. *Bound in Twine: The History and Ecology of the Henequen-Wheat Complex for Mexico and the American and Canadian Plains, 1880–1950.* Texas: A&M University Press, 2013.

Ezcurra, Exequiel. *The Basin of Mexico: Critical Environmental Issues and Sustainability.* Tokyo: United Nations University Press, 1999.

Ezcurra, Exequiel, and Marisa Mazari-Hiriart. "Are Megacities Viable? A Cautionary Tale from Mexico City." *Environment* 38, 1 (1996): 6–35.

FAO. *Tendencias y Perspectivas del Sector forestal en América Latina y el Caribe.* Estudio FAO Montes 148. Rome: FAO, 2006.

FAO, and Juan Manuel Torres Rojo. *Estudio de tendencias y perspectivas del Sector Forestal en América Latina Documento de Trabajo. Informe Nacional México.* Rome: FAO, 2004.

FAO, and UNECE. Handy Guide to Wood Energy. https://unece.org/forests/h andy-guide-wood-energy.

Farjon, Aljos. *A Natural History of Conifers.* Portland, OR: Timber Press, 2008.

Fernández-Paradas, Mercedes. "El consumo bruto de energía primaria en Andalucía (1870–1930)." *Baetica. Estudios de Arte, Geografía e Historia* 31 (2009): 493–511.

Fischer-Kowalski, Marina, and Helmut Haberl. *Socioecological Transitions and Global Change: Trajectories of Social Metabolism and Land Use.* Cheltenham: Edward Elgar, 2007.

Fischer-Kowalski, Marina, and Fridolin Krausmann. "A Socio-Ecological View on Industrialization in Europe Since the 19th Century." *IHDP UPDATE. Newsletter of the International Human Dimensions on Global Environmental Change,* 2005.

Fitzgerald, Deborah. "Exporting American Agriculture: The Rockefeller Foundation in Mexico, 1943–53." *Social Studies of Science* 16, 3 (1986): 457–83.

Flikke, Rune. "South African Eucalypts: Health, Trees, and Atmospheres in the Colonial Contact Zone." *Geoforum* 76 (2016): 20–7.

Flinn, Michael W. *The History of the British Coal Industry.* Oxford: Oxford University Press, 1984.

Flores, Juárez, and José Juan. "Street Lighting in Puebla and Tlaxcala and Environmental Deterioration in the Forests of La Malintzi, 1820–1870." *Historia Crítica* 30 (2005): 13–38.

Florescano, Enrique, Virginia García Acosta, and Magdalena A. Garcia Sánchez. *Mestizajes tecnológicos y cambios culturales en México. Sociedades, historias, lenguajes.* México, D. F.: CIESAS; Miguel Angel Porrúa, 2004.

Folchi, Mauricio, and Mar Rubio. "El consumo de energía fósil y la especificidad de la transición energética en América Latina, 1900–1930." III Simposio Latinoamericano y Caribeño de Historia Ambiental, Carmona, 2006: 1–27.

Fouquet, Roger. "The Slow Search for Solutions: Lessons from Historical Energy Transitions by Sector and Service." *Energy Policy* 38 (2010): 6586–96.

Fouquet, Roger, and Peter J. G. Pearson. "A Thousand Years of Energy Use in the United Kingdom." *The Energy Journal* 19, 4 (1998): 1–41.

"Past and Prospective Energy Transitions: Insights from History." *Energy Policy* 50, 1–7 (2012): 1–7.

Fournier, Patricia. "Indigenous Charcoal Production and Spanish Metal Mining Enterprises: Historical Archaeology of Extractive Activities and Ecological

Degradation in Central and Northern Mexico," 87–108. In M. Souza, and D. Costa (eds). *Historical Archaeology and Environment*. Cham: Springer, 2018.

Fox, David J. "Man-Water Relationships in Metropolitan Mexico." *Geographical Review* 55, 4 (1965): 523–45.

Frank, Alison Fleig. *Oil Empire: Visions of Prosperity in Austrian Galicia*. Cambridge, MA: Harvard University Press, 2005.

Frank, Marti Jaye. *Carrying the Mill: Steam, Waterpower, and New England Textile Mills in the 19th Century*. Cambridge, MA: Harvard University Press, 2008.

Freeman, J. Brian. "El despertar del camión de carga en México." In Ilse Angélica Álvarez Palma, ed. *Automotores y transporte público. Un acercamiento desde los estudios históricos,*. Toluca: El Colegio Mexiquense, 2017.

"Los Hijos de Ford: Mexico in the Automobile Age, 1900–1930," 214–32. In *Technology and Culture in Twentieth Century Mexico*. Tuscaloosa: University of Alabama Press, 2013.

Freeman, Joshua B. *Behemoth: A History of the Factory and the Making of the Modern World*. New York: W. W. Norton & Company, 2018.

Freese, Barbara. *Coal: A Human History*. Cambridge: Perseus, 2003.

French, Daniel. *When They Hid the Fire: A History of Electricity and Invisible Energy in America*. Pittsburgh: University of Pittsburgh Press, 2017.

French, William E. "In the Path of Progress: Railroads and Moral Reform in Porfirian Mexico." In *Railway Imperialism*. New York: Greenwood Press, 1991.

Friedrich, Johannes, and Thomas Damassa. "The History of Carbon Dioxide Emissions." World Resources Institute. Accessed June 22, 2016.

Froeling, Maria. "Energy Use, Population and Growth, 1800–1970." *Journal of Popular Economics* 24 (2011): 1133–63.

Fulwider, Ben Curtis. "Driving the Nation: Road Transportation and the Postrevolutionary Mexican State, 1925–1960," PhD Dissertation, Georgetown University, 2009.

Funes Monzote, Reinaldo. *From Rainforest to Cane Field in Cuba: An Environmental History since 1492*. Chapel Hill: University of North Carolina Press, 2008.

Galan, Francis. "There Will Be Blood: Oil, Rebels, and Counterrevolution in the Gulf of Mexico Borderlands, 1900–1920," 7–19. In *New Frontiers in Latin American Borderlands*. Newcastle upon Tyne: Cambridge Scholars Publishing, 2012.

Gales, Ben, Astrid Kander, Paolo Malanima, and María Rubio. "North versus South: Energy Transition and Energy Intensity in Europe over 200 Years." *European Review of Economic History II* (2007): 219–53.

Galicia, Leopoldo, et al. "Perspectivas del enfoque socioecológico en la conservación, el aprovechamiento y pago de servicios ambientales de los bosques templados de México." *Madera y Bosques* 24, 2 (2018).

Galloway, James A., Derek Keene, and Margaret Murphy. "Fuelling the City: Production and Distribution of Firewood and Fuel in London's Region, 1290–1400." *The Economic History Review* 49, 3 (1996): 447–72.

Gamboa Ojeda, Leticia. "La Constancia Mexicana. De la fábrica, sus empresarios y sus conflictos laborales hasta los años de la posrevolución." *TZINTZUN, Revista de Estudios Históricos* 39 (2004): 93–111.

García Luna, Margarita, and Xavier I. Esparza Santibáñez. *Los orígenes de la industria en el Estado de México, 1830–1930.* Toluca: Instituto Mexiquense de Cultura, 1998.

García, Magdalena. "El dominio de las 'aguas ocultas y descubiertas': hidráulica colonial en el centro de México, Siglos XVI-XVII." In *Mestizajes tecnológicos y cambios culturales en México.* México, D. F.: CIESAS; Miguel Ángel Porrúa, 2004.

García, Marta. *Querétaro: historia breve.* México, D. F.: FCE, 2010.

García Martínez, Bernardo, and Alba González Jácome (eds). *Estudios sobre historia y ambiente en América, II.* México, D. F.: El Colegio de México, 2002.

García Martínez, Bernardo, and Takako Sudo. *Las carreteras de México, 1891–1991.* México, D. F.: Secretaría de Comunicaciones y Transportes, 1992.

García Ramírez, Bernardo. *Un pueblo fabril del Porfiriato: Santa Rosa, Veracruz.* Ciudad Mendoza: Fondo Mendocino para la Cultura y las Artes, 1997.

García-Romero, Arturo. "Evolution of Disturbed Oak Woodlands: The Case of Mexico City's Western Forest Reserve." *Geographical Journal* 167, 1 (2001): 72–82.

Garza, Adriana. "Guido Moebius y las fábricas Apolo. Un industrial alemán en Monterrey." *Boletín de Monumentos Históricos* 15 (2009): 124–40.

Garza, Gustavo. *El proceso de industrialización en la ciudad de México, 1821–1970.* México, D.F.: El Colegio de México, 1985.

"Dinámica industrial de la Ciudad de México, 1940–1988." *Estudios Demográficos y Urbanos* 6, 1 (1991): 209–14.

"Evolución de las ciudades mexicanas en el siglo XX." *Notas. Revista de Información y Análisis* 19 (2002): 7–16.

La urbanización de México en el siglo XX. México, D. F.: El Colegio de México, 2003.

"Technological Innovation and the Expansion of Mexico City, 1870–1920." *Journal of Latin American Geography* 5, 2 (2006): 109–26.

"La urbanización metropolitana en México: normatividad y características socioeconómicas." *Papeles de Población* 13, 52 (2007): 77–108.

Garza Merodio, Gustavo. "Frecuencia y duración de sequías en la cuenca de México de fines del siglo XVI a mediados del XIX." *Investigaciones Geográficas* 48 (2002): 106–15.

Gauss, Susan M. *Made in Mexico: Regions, Nation, and the State in the Rise of Mexican Industrialism, 1920s–1940s.* University Park: Penn State University Press, 2011.

Gerali, Francesco, and Paolo Riguzzi, "Los inicios de la actividad petrolera en México, 1863–1874: una nueva cronología y elementos de balance." *Boletín Archivo Histórico de Petróleos Mexicanos* 13 (2013): 63–87.

"Gushers, Science and Luck: Everette Lee DeGolyer and the Mexican Oil Upsurge, 1909–19." *Geological Society, London, Special Publications* 442 (December 2016): 413–24.

Gibson, Charles. *The Aztecs under Spanish Rule: A History of the Indians of the Valley of Mexico, 1519–1810.* Stanford: Stanford University Press, 1964.

Giebelhaus, August W. "History of the Oil Industry,"649–60. In Cutler J. Cleveland, ed. *Encyclopedia of Energy.* New York: Elsevier, 2004.

Gillingham, Paul. "Maximino's Bulls: Popular Protest after the Mexican Revolution 1940–1952." *Past & Present* 206, 1 (2010): 175–211.

Glahn, Richard von. "Foreign Silver Coins in the Market Culture of Nineteenth-Century China." *International Journal of Asian Studies* 4, 1 (2007): 51–78.

Gómez Galvarriato, Aurora. "El primer impulso industrializador de México: el caso de Fundidora Monterrey," BA Thesis, ITAM, 1990.

"El desempeño de la Fundidora de Hierro y Acero de Monterrey durante el Porfiriato: acerca de los obstáculos a la industrialización en México." In *Historia de las grandes empresas en México, 1850–1930,* 201–43. México, D. F.: Universidad Autónoma de Nuevo León/FCE, 1997.

La industria textil en México. México, D. F.: Instituto Mora; Colegio de Michoacán; Colegio de México; Instituto de Investigaciones Históricas-UNAM, 1999.

Revolución en la comercialización y producción de textiles en México durante el porfiriato. México: Centro de Investigación y Docencia Económicas, 2001.

"Industrialización, empresas y trabajadores industriales. Del Porfiriato a la Revolución: la nueva historiografía." *Historia Mexicana, Ruggiero Romano, in Memoriam (Fermo 1923–París 2001)* 52, 3 (2003): 773–804.

The Mexican Cotton Textile Industry: An Overview. México, D. F.: CIDE, 2008.

"Networks and Entrepreneurship: The Modernization of the Textile Business in Porfirian Mexico." *The Business History Review* 82, 3 (2008): 475–502.

Industry and Revolution: Social and Economic Change in the Orizaba Valley, Mexico. Cambridge: Harvard University Press, 2013.

Gómez Galvarriato, Aurora, and Jeffrey G.Williamson. "Was It Prices, Productivity or Policy? The Timing and Pace of Latin American Industrialization after 1870." *Journal of Latin American Studies* 41, 4 (2009): 663–94.

Gómez, Patricia, and Héctor Martínez. "Los tranvías eléctricos de la Ciudad de México: Transformaciones urbanas y los conflictos de los tranviarios." In Miriam Zaar, et. al. (eds), Cuarto Simposio Internacional de la Historia de la Electrificación, Universitat de Barcelona. *La electrificación y el territorio. Historia y futuro* (2017): 1-19

Gómez, Víctor. "Los molinos del Valle de México. Innovaciones tecnológicas y tradicionalismo (Siglos XVI-XIX)," PhD Dissertation, UAM-Iztapalapa, 2008.

González, Alejandro. "El patrimonio industrial de la región carbonífera de Coahuila (México)." *Revista de Administração FEAD-Minas* 6, 1/2 (2009): 10–32.

Gonzalez de Bustamante, Celeste, and Richard Cole. *Muy Buenas Noches: Mexico, Television, and the Cold War.* Lincoln: University of Nebraska Press, 2013.

Gonzalez, George A. "The Conservation Policy Network, 1890–1910: The Development and Implementation of 'Practical' Forestry." *Polity* 31, 2 (1998): 269–99.

González Navarro, Moisés. "Las huelgas textiles en el porfiriato." *Historia Mexicana* 6, 2 (1956): 201–16.

González-Abraham, Charlotte, Exequiel Ezcurra, Pedro P. Garcillán, et al. "The Human Footprint in Mexico: Physical Geography and Historical Legacies." *PLoS One; San Francisco* 10, 3 (2015): e0121203.

González-Quintero, L. "Análisis polínicos en la porción austral de la cuenca de México II Tlatengo: Contribuciones al conocimiento arqueobotánico de la cuenca del Valle de México." *Cuicuilco* 3 (1981).

Gortari, Hira de, and Regina Hernández Franyuti. *La Ciudad de México y el Distrito Federal: Una historia compartida.* México, D. F.: Departamento del Distrito Federal/Instituto de Investigaciones Dr. José María Luís Mora, 1988.

Greenberg, Dolores. "Energy Systems and Social Change." *Science* 220, 4603 (1983): 1265.

"Reassessing the Power Patterns of the Industrial Revolution: An Anglo-American Comparison." *The American Historical Review* 87, 5 (1982): 1237–61.

"Energy, Power, and Perceptions of Social Change in the Early Nineteenth Century." *The American Historical Review* 95, 3 (1990): 693–714.

Grove, Richard H. "Conserving Eden: The (European) East India Companies and Their Environmental Policies on St. Helena, Mauritius and in Western India, 1660 to 1854." *Comparative Studies in Society and History: An International Quarterly* 35 (1993): 318–51.

"A Historical Review of Early Institutional and Conservationist Responses to Fears of Artificially Induced Global Climate Change: The Deforestation-Desiccation Discourse 1500–1860." *Chemosphere* 29, 5 (1994): 1001–13.

Groysman, Alec. "History of Crude Oil and Petroleum Products." In *Corrosion in Systems for Storage and Transportation of Petroleum Products and Biofuels: Identification, Monitoring and Solutions*, 221–6. Dordrecht: Springer Netherlands, 2014.

Grübler, Arnulf. "Time for a Change: On the Patterns of Diffusion of Innovation." *Daedalus* 125, 3 (1996): 19–42.

"Energy Transitions Research: Insights and Cautionary Tales." *Energy Policy* 50 (2012): 8–16.

Grunstein, Arturo. "Estado y ferrocarriles en México y EU, 1890–1911." *Secuencia* 20 (May-August 1991): 79–106.

"¿Competencia o monopolio? Regulación y desarrollo ferrocarrilero en México, 1885–1911." In *Ferrocarriles y vida económica en México (1850–1950)*, 167–221. Toluca: El Colegio Mexiquense, 1996.

Guajardo, Guillermo. *Trabajo y tecnología en los ferrocarriles de México: una visión histórica, 1850–1950*. México, D. F.: Consejo Nacional para la Cultura y las Artes, 2010.

Guardino, Peter. "Barbarism or Republican Law? Guerrero's Peasants and National Politics, 1820–1846." *The Hispanic American Historical Review* 75, 2 (1995): 185–213.

The Dead March: A History of the Mexican-American War. Cambridge: Harvard University Press, 2017.

Guerra, Erick. "The Built Environment and Car Use in Mexico City: Is the Relationship Changing over Time?" *Journal of Planning Education and Research* 34, 4 (2014): 394–408.

"The Geography of Car Ownership in Mexico City: A Joint Model of Households' Residential Location and Car Ownership Decisions." *Journal of Transport Geography* 43 (2015): 171–80.

Guerrero, Saúl. "The Environmental History of Silver Refining in New Spain and Mexico, 16 c to 19 c: A Shift of Paradigm," PhD Dissertation, McGill University, 2015.

Guevara Fefer, Rafael. *Los ultimos años de la historia natural y los primeros días de la biología en México: la práctica científica de Alfonso Herrera, Manuel María Villada y Mariano Barcena*. México, D. F.: UNAM, 2002.

Gugliotta, Angela. "Class, Gender, and Coal Smoke: Gender Ideology and Environmental Injustice in Pittsburgh, 1868–1914." *Environmental History* 5, 2 (2000): 165–93.

Guha, Ramachandra. *The Unquiet Woods: Ecological Change and Peasant Resistance in the Himalaya*. Berkeley: University of California Press, 2000.

Gutiérrez, Jorge. *Energía renovable en el siglo XXI*. Monterrey, México: Senado de la República, 2001.

Guzmán del Próo, S. A., et al. "The Impact of the Ixtoc-1 Oil Spill on Zooplankton." *Journal of Plankton Research* 8, 3 (1986): 557–81.

Haber, Stephen H. *Industry and Underdevelopment: The Industrialization of Mexico, 1890–1940*. Stanford: Stanford University Press, 1989.

"Industrial Concentration and the Capital Markets: A Comparative Study of Brazil, Mexico, and the United States, 1830–1930." *The Journal of Economic History* 51, 3 (1991): 559–80.

"Assessing the Obstacles to Industrialisation: The Mexican Economy, 1830–1940." *Journal of Latin American Studies* 24, 1 (1992): 1–32.

How Latin America Fell behind: Essays on the Economic Histories of Brazil and Mexico, 1800–1914. Stanford: Stanford University Press, 1997.

Haber, Stephen, and Victor Menaldo. "Do Natural Resources Fuel Authoritarianism? A Reappraisal of the Resource Curse." *The American Political Science Review* 105, 1 (2011): 1–26.

Haber, Stephen H., Noel Maurer, and Armando Razo. "Economic Growth amidst Political Instability: Evidence from Revolutionary Mexico," n.d.

  The Politics of Property Rights: Political Instability, Credible Commitments, and Economic Growth in Mexico, 1876–1929. Cambridge; New York: Cambridge University Press, 2003.

  "When the Law Does Not Matter: The Rise and Decline of the Mexican Oil Industry." *The Journal of Economic History* 63, 1 (2003): 1–32.

Haberl, Helmut, and Fridolin Krausmann. "Changes in Population, Affluence, and Environmental Pressures during Industrialization: The Case of Austria, 1830–1995." *Population and Environment* 23, 1 (2001): 49–70.

Haberl, Helmut, Marina Fischer-Kowalski, Fridolin Kraussman, et al. "A Socio-Metabolic Transition towards Sustainability? Challenges for Another Great Transformation." *Sustainable Development* 19 (2011): 1–14.

Haines, Michael R., and Richard Hall Steckel. *A Population History of North America*. Cambridge, UK: Cambridge University Press, 2000.

Hakes, Jay. "Introduction: A Decidedly Valuable and Dangerous Fuel." *Journal of American History* 99, 1 (2012): 19–23.

Hale, Charles A. *The Transformation of Liberalism in Late Nineteenth-Century Mexico*. Princeton University Press, 2014.

Hall, Charles, Pradeep Tharakan, John Hallock, et al. "Hydrocarbons and the Evolution of Human Culture." *Nature* 426 (2003): 318–22.

Hall, Linda B., and Don M. Coerver. "Oil and the Mexican Revolution: The Southwestern Connection." *The Americas* 41, 2 (1984): 229–44.

Hammersley, G. "The Charcoal Iron Industry and its Fuel, 1540–1750." *The Economic History Review* 26, 4 (1973): 593–613.

Hart, John M. *Revolutionary Mexico: The Coming and Process of the Mexican Revolution*. Berkeley: University of California Press, 1987.

Hartwell, R. M. "A Revolution in the Chinese Iron and Coal Industries during the Northern Sung, 960–1126 A.D." *The Journal of Asian Studies* 21, 2 (1962): 153–62.

Harvey, H. R., ed. *Land and Politics in the Valley of Mexico: A Two Thousand-Year Perspective*. Albuquerque: University of New Mexico Press, 1991.

Hausman, William J. *Global Electrification: Multinational Enterprise and International Finance in the History of Light and Power, 1878–2007*. Cambridge Studies in the Emergence of Global Enterprise. New York: Cambridge University Press, 2008.

Haussmann, Frederick. "Latin American Oil in War and Peace." *Foreign Affairs* 21 (1943): 354–61.

Hays, Samuel P. *Conservation and the Gospel of Efficiency: The Progressive Conservation Movement, 1890–1920*. Pittsburgh: University of Pittsburgh Press, 1999.

Henriques, Sofia. "Energy Transitions, Economic Growth and Structural Change: Portugal in a Long-Run Comparative Perspective," PhD Thesis, Lund University, 2011.

Hernández-Escobedo, Q., F. Manzano-Agugliaro, and A. Zapata-Sierra. "The Wind Power of Mexico." *Renewable and Sustainable Energy Reviews* 14, 9 (2010): 2830–40.

Hewitt de Alcantara, Cynthia. *Modernizing Mexican Agriculture.* Geneva: United Nations Research Institute for Social Development (UNRISD), 1976.

Hindle, Brooke, and Steven D. Lubar. *Engines of Change: The American Industrial Revolution, 1790–1860.* Washington, DC: Smithsonian Institution Press, 1986.

Hiriart, Gerardo. "Main Aspects of Geothermal Energy in Mexico." *Geothermics* 32 (2003) 389–96.

Hirsh, Richard, and Christopher F. Jones. "History's Contributions to Energy Research and Policy." *Energy Research & Social Science* 1 (2014): 106–11.

Hölzl, Richard. "Historicizing Sustainability: German Scientific Forestry in the Eighteenth and Nineteenth Centuries." *Science as Culture* 19, 4 (2010): 431–60.

Horowitz, Roger, Jeffrey M. Pilcher, and Sydney Watts. "Meat for the Multitudes: Market Culture in Paris, New York City, and Mexico City over the Long Nineteenth Century." *The American Historical Review* 109, 4 (2004): 1055–83.

Hoshino, Taeko. "Industrialization and Private Enterprises in Mexico: Bibliography." *I.D.E. Occasional Papers Series*, 36 (2001): 130–7.

Howard, Philip. "Environmental Scarcity and Violent Conflict: The Case of Chiapas, Mexico." Project on Environment, Population, and Security. Washington, DC: American Association for the Advancement of Science, January 1996.

Huber, Matthew T. "Energizing Historical Materialism: Fossil Fuels, Space and the Capitalist Mode of Production." *Geoforum*, Themed Issue: Postcoloniality, Responsibility and Care, 40, 1 (2009): 105–15.

Hughes, Thomas P. *Networks of Power: Electrification in Western Society, 1880–1930.* Baltimore: Johns Hopkins University Press, 1993.

Hunter, Louis C., and Eleutherian Mills-Hagley Foundation. *A History of Industrial Power in the United States, 1780–1930.* Charlottesville: University Press of Virginia, 1979.

Waterpower in the Century of the Steam Engine. Charlottesville: University Press of Virginia, 1979.

Hunter, Richard William. "People, Sheep, and Landscape Change in Colonial Mexico: The Sixteenth-Century Transformation of the Valle del Mezquital." PhD Dissertation, Baton Rouge, LA: Louisiana State University, 2009.

Ibáñez González, Luis Antonio. "La evolución de las fábricas textiles de Puebla en el corredor Atoyac." *Boletín de Monumentos Históricos* 25 (2012): 37–56.

INEGI. *Estadísticas históricas de México.* Vol. 1. 2 vols. Aguascalientes: INEGI, Instituto Nacional de Estadística, Geografía e Informática, 1999.

Estadísticas históricas de los municipios de Nuevo León. Aguascalientes: INEGI, 2008.

Estadísticas históricas de México: Población. Aguascalientes: INEGI, 2009.

Anuario Estadístico y Geográfico de Querétaro 2017. Aguascalientes: INEGI, 2017.

Iriarte-Goñi, Iñaki. "Forests, Fuelwood, Pulpwood, and Lumber in Spain, 1860–2000: A Non-Declensionist Story." *Environmental History* 18, 2 (2013): 333–59.

Iriarte-Goñi, Iñaki, and María-Isabel Ayuda. "Wood and Industrialization Evidence and Hypotheses from the Case of Spain, 1860–1935." *Ecological Economics* 65 (2008): 177–86.

"Not Only Subterranean Forests: Wood Consumption and Economic Development in Britain (1850–1938)." *Ecological Economics* 77, 77 (2012): 176–84.

Isenberg, Andrew C. "Introduction." In *The Oxford Handbook of Environmental History*, Oxford: Oxford University Press, 2014, 1–20.

Iturriaga de la Fuente, José N. *El medio ambiente de México a través de los siglos: crónicas extranjeras.* México, D. F.: Universidad Nacional Autónoma de México, 2002.

Izazola, Haydea. "Agua y sustentabilidad en la Ciudad de México." *Estudios Demográficos y Urbanos* 16, 2 (2001): 285–320.

Jáuregui, Ernesto. "Climate Changes in Mexico during the Historical and Instrumented Periods." *Quaternary International* 43–44 (1997): 7–17.

Jáuregui, Luis, and Ma Eugenia Romero Sotelo, eds. *La industria mexicana y su historia: siglos XVIII, XIX, XX.* México, D. F.: Universidad Nacional Autónoma de México, 1997.

Jensen, W. G. "The Importance of Energy in the First and Second World Wars." *The Historical Journal* 11, 3 (1968): 538–54.

Jeremy, David J. *Transatlantic Industrial Revolution: The Diffusion of Textile Technologies between Britain and America, 1790–1830s.* Cambridge: MIT Press, 1981.

Jernelöv, Arne, and Olof Lindén. "Ixtoc I: A Case Study of the World's Largest Oil Spill." *Ambio* 10, 6 (1981): 299–306.

Jofré González, José. "Patrones de Consumo Aparente de Energías Modernas En América Latina, 1890–2003," PhD Dissertation, Universitat de Barcelona, 2012.

Johnson, Bob. "'An Upthrust into Barbarism': Coal, Trauma, and Origins of the Modern Self, 1885–1951." *The Journal of American Culture* 33, 4 (2010): 265–79.

Carbon Nation: Fossil Fuels in the Making of American Culture. Lawrence,: University Press of Kansas, 2014.

Jones, Christopher. "A Landscape of Energy Abundance: Anthracite Coal Canals and the Roots of American Fossil Fuel Dependence, 1820–1860." *Environmental History* 15 (2010): 449–84.

"The Social Dimensions of Energy Transitions." *Science as Culture: Forum on Energy Transitions* 22, 2 (2013): 135–48.

Routes of Power: Energy and Modern America. Cambridge, MA: Harvard University Press, 2014.

Jones, E. L. *The European Miracle: Environments, Economies, and Geopolitics in the History of Europe and Asia.* Cambridge, England: Cambridge University Press, 1981.

Jones, Toby Craig. "America, Oil, and War in the Middle East." *Journal of American History* 99, 1 (2012): 208–18.

Joseph, Gilbert M. "From Caste War to Class War: The Historiography of Modern Yucatán (c. 1750–1940)." *Hispanic American Historical Review* 65, 2 (1985): 111–34.

Joseph, Gilbert M., Anne Rubenstein, and Eric Zolov, eds. *Fragments of a Golden Age: The Politics of Culture in Mexico Since 1940.* Durham: Duke University Press, 2001.

Hill, Jr, Jonathan. "Circuits of State: Water, Electricity, and Power in Chihuahua, 1905–1936." *Radical History Review* 127 (2017): 13–38.

"Powerhouse Chihuahua: Electricity, Water, and the State in the Long Mexican Revolution," PhD Dissertation, City University of New York (CUNY), 2018.

Judd, Richard W. "A 'Wonderful Order and Balance': Natural History and the Beginnings of Forest Conservation in America, 1730–1830." *Environmental History* 11, 1 (2006): 8–36.

Kandell, Jonathan. *La Capital: The Biography of Mexico City.* 1st edition. New York: Random House, 1988.

Kander, Astrid. *Economic Growth and the Transition from Traditional to Modern Energy in Sweden.* CAMA Working Paper, no. 65 (September 2013): 1–35.

Kander, Astrid, and Paul Warde. *Number, Size, and Energy Consumption of Draught Animals in European Agriculture.* Working Paper, March 2009.

"Energy Availability from Livestock and Agricultural Productivity in Europe, 1815–1913: A New Comparison." *Economic History Review* 64, 1 (2011): 1–29.

Kander, Astrid, Paolo Malanima, and Paul Warde. *Power to the People: Energy in Europe over the Last Five Centuries.* Princeton: Princeton University Press, 2013.

Kaplan, Jed O., Kristen M. Krumhardt, and Niklaus Zimmermann. "The Prehistoric and Preindustrial Deforestation of Europe." *Quaternary Science Reviews* 28, 27 (2009): 3016–34.

Kehoe, Timothy J., Felipe Meza, Timothy J. Kehoe, and Felipe Meza. "Crecimiento rápido seguido de estancamiento: México (1950–2010)." *El Trimestre Económico* 80, 318 (2013): 237–80.

Keremitsis, Dawn. "Del metate al molino: la mujer mexicana de 1910 a 1940." *Historia Mexicana* 33, 2 (1983): 285–302.

The Cotton Textile Industry in Porfiriato, Mexico, 1870–1910. New York: Garland Publishers, 1987.

Klein, Maury. *The Genesis of Industrial America, 1870–1920.* Cambridge: Cambridge University Press, 2007.

Klepeis, Peter, and B. L. Turner II. "Integrated Land History and Global Change Science: The Example of the Southern Yucatán Peninsular Region Project." *Land Use Policy, Using and Shaping the Land,* 18, 1 (2001): 27–39.

Klooster, Dan. "Campesinos and Mexican Forest Policy during the Twentieth Century." *Latin American Research Review* 38, 2 (2003).

"Forest Transitions in Mexico: Institutions and Forests in a Globalized Countryside." *The Professional Geographer* 55, 2 (2003): 227–37.

Klubock, Thomas Miller. "The Politics of Forests and Forestry on Chile's Southern Frontier, 1880s-1940s." *Hispanic American Historical Review* 86, 3 (2006): 535–70.

La Frontera: Forests and Ecological Conflict in Chile's Frontier Territory. Durham: Duke University Press, 2014.

Knight, Alan. "El liberalismo mexicano desde la Reforma hasta la Revolución (una interpretación)." *Historia Mexicana* 35, 1 (1985): 59–91.

The Mexican Revolution. Volume 1: Porfirians, Liberals, and Peasants. Cambridge: Cambridge University Press, 1986.

The Mexican Revolution Volume 2: Counter-Revolution and Reconstruction. Cambridge: Cambridge University Press, 1986.

Konrad, Herman W. "Tropical Forest Policy and Practice during the Mexican Porfiriato, 1876–1910." In Harold K. Steen and Richard P. Tucker, eds. *Changing Tropical Forests: Historical Perspectives on Today's Challenges in Central and South America.* Durham: Duke University Press, 1992.

Koppes, Clayton R. "The Good Neighbor Policy and the Nationalization of Mexican Oil: A Reinterpretation." *The Journal of American History* 69, 1 (1982): 62–81.

Kourí, Emilio. "Interpreting the Expropriation of Indian Pueblo Lands in Porfirian Mexico: The Unexamined Legacies of Andrés Molina Enríquez." *Hispanic American Historical Review* 82, 1 (2002): 69–117.

A Pueblo Divided: Business, Property, and Community in Papantla, Mexico. Stanford: Stanford University Press, 2004.

Krausmann, Fridolin. "Land Use and Industrial Modernization: An Empirical Analysis of Human Influence on the Functioning of Ecosystems in Austria, 1830–1995." *Land Use Policy* 18 (2001): 17–26.

Land Use and Socio-Economic Metabolism in Pre-Industrial Agricultural Systems: Four Nineteenth-Century Austrian Villages in Comparison. Social Ecology Working Paper, no. 72 (December 2008): 1–40.

Krausmann, Fridolin, Marina Fischer-Kowalski, Heinz Schandl, and Nina Eisenmenger. "The Global Sociometabolic Transition: Past and Present Metabolic Profiles and Their Future Trajectories." *Journal of Industrial Ecology* 12, 5/6 (2008): 637–51.

"A City and Its Hinterland: Vienna's Energy Metabolism 1800–2006," 247–68. In S. Singh, H. Haberl, M. Chertow, M. Mirtl, and M. Schmid (eds), *Long Term Socio-Ecological Research: Studies in Society–Nature Interactions across Spatial and Temporal Scales,* New York: Springer, 2013.

Kull, Christian A. "Deforestation, Erosion, and Fire: Degradation Myths in the Environmental History of Madagascar." *Environment and History* 6, 4 (2000): 423–50.

Kumaran, Ganesh, and Saúl González. "Evolución reciente de la industria de cemento: un estudio comparativo entre México y la India." *Portes: Revista Mexicana sobre la Cuenca del Pacífico* 2, 3 (2008): 165–202.

Kunnas, Jan, and Timo Myllyntaus. "Postponed Leap in Carbon Dioxide Emissions: The Impact of Energy Efficiency, Fuel Choices and Industrial Structure on the Finnish Economy, 1800–2005." *Global Environment*, 3 (2009): 154–89.

Kuntz Ficker, Sandra. *Empresa extranjera y mercado interno: el Ferrocarril Central Mexicano, 1880–1907*. México, D. F.: Colegio de México, 1995.

"The Internal Market and Foreign Connections: The Role of Railways in the Economy of the Porfiriato." *Historia Mexicana* 45, 1 (1995): 39–66.

"La mayor empresa privada del Porfiriato: el Ferrocarril Central Mexicano, 1880–1907)," 39–63. In Carlos Marichal and Mario Cerutti, eds. *Historia de Las Grandes Empresas de México, 1850–1930*. México, D. F.: FCE; Universidad Autónoma de Nuevo León, 1997.

"Los ferrocarriles y la formación del espacio económico en México, 1880–1910." In Sandra Kuntz Ficker and Priscilla Connolly, eds. *Ferrocarriles y obras públicas*. México, D. F.: Instituto Mora; Colegio de México; UNAM, 1999, 105–37.

"Ferrocarriles y mercado de productos agrícolas en el porfiriato el impacto de las tarifas ferroviarias." In Margarita Menegus Bornemann (ed.), *Dos décadas de investigación en historia económica comparada en América Latina: homenaje a Carlos Sempat Assodourian*. México, D. F.: El Colegio de México; Instituto Mora; UNAM, 1999, 467–87.

"Economic Backwardness and Firm Strategy: An American Railroad Corporation in Nineteenth-Century Mexico." *Hispanic American Historical Review* 80, 2 (2000): 267–98.

El comercio exterior de México en la era del capitalismo liberal, 1870–1929. México, D. F.: El Colegio de Mexico, 2007.

"Fuentes para el estudio de los ferrocarriles durante el Porfiriato." *América Latina en la Historia Económica* 7, 13/14 (2014): 137–48.

Historia mínima de la expansión ferroviaria en América Latina. México, D. F.: El Colegio de Mexico, 2016.

Kuntz Ficker, Sandra, and Paolo Riguzzi. *Ferrocarriles y vida económica en México, 1850–1950: del surgimiento tardío al decaimiento precoz*. Toluca: El Colegio Mexiquense: Ferrocarriles Nacionales de México: Universidad Autónoma Metropolitana Xochimilco, 1996.

Labastida, Horacio. *Documentos para el estudio de la industrialización en México, 1837–1845*. México, D. F.: Secretaría de Hacienda y Crédito Público; Nacional Financiera, 1977.

La Botz, Dan. *Edward L. Doheny: Petroleum, Power, and Politics in the United States and Mexico*. New York: Praeger, 1991.

La condición actual de los recursos forestales en México: resultados del Inventario Forestal Nacional 2000. Instituto de Geografía, 2000.

LaFevor, Matthew C. "Sulphur Mining on Mexico's Popocatépetl Volcano (1820–1920): Origins, Development, and Human-Environmental Challenges." *Journal of Latin American Geography* 11, 1 (2012): 79–98.

Landers, John. *The Field and the Forge: Population, Production, and Power in the Pre-Industrial West*. Oxford: Oxford University Press, 2003.

Landgrave, Sinhúe. "El archivo Fotográfico de la fábrica de celulosa en Peña Pobre: una historia gráfica y constructiva." *Boletín de Monumentos Históricos*, 33 (2015): 146–54.

Leal, Claudia, José Augusto Pádua, and John Soluri, eds. *New Environmental Histories of Latin American and the Caribbean*. Munich: Rachel Carson Center Perspectives, 2013.

Lear, John. *Workers, Neighbors, and Citizens: The Revolution in Mexico City*. Lincoln: University of Nebraska Press, 2001.

LeMenager, Stephanie. *Living Oil: Petroleum Culture in the American Century*. Oxford: Oxford University Press, 2016.

Lentz, David L. "Anthropocentric Food Webs in the Pre-Columbian Americas." In *Imperfect Balance Landscape Transformations in the Pre-Columbian Americas*. New York: Columbia University Press, 2000.

Imperfect Balance Landscape Transformations in the Pre-Columbian Americas. New York: Columbia University Press, 2000.

Lenz, Hans. *San Ángel: nostalgia de cosas idas*. México: M.A. Porrúa Grupo Editorial, 1996.

Historia del papel en México y cosas relacionadas, 1525–1950. México: Miguel Angel Porrúa, 2001.

Levi, Enzo. "History of the Drainage of the Valley of Mexico." *International Journal of Water Resources Development* 6, 3 (1990): 201–10.

Li, Xiaobing, and Michael Molina. *Oil: A Cultural and Geographic Encyclopedia of Black Gold*, 2 vols. Santa Barbara: ABC-CLIO, 2014.

Licht, Walter. *Industrializing America: The Nineteenth Century*. Baltimore: Johns Hopkins University Press, 1995.

Lieher, Reinhard, *Empresas y modernización en México desde las reformas borbónicas hasta el Porfiriato*. Madrid; Frankfurt am Main: Iberoamericana; Vervuert, 2006.

Lieher, Reinhard, and Mariano E. Torres Bautista, eds. *Compañías eléctricas extranjeras en México, 1880–1960*. Puebla; Madrid: Benemérita Universidad Autónoma de Puebla; Bonilla Artigas Editores; Iberoamérica, 2010.

Lindsay, Robert Bruce, ed. *Energy: Historical Development of the Concept*. Stroudsburg; New York: Dowden, Hutchinson & Ross, 1976.

Lipsett-Rivera, Sonya. *Gender and the Negotiation of Daily Life in Mexico, 1750–1856*. Lincoln: University of Nebraska Press, 2012.

Lira, Andrés. *Comunidades indígenas frente a la Ciudad de México: Tenochtitlan y Tlatelolco, sus pueblos y barrios, 1812–1919*. Zamora Colegio de México; Colegio de Michoacán, 1983.

"Los bosques en el virreinato (apuntes sobre la visión política de un problema)." *Relaciones* 11, 41 (1990): 117–27.

Liverman, Diana M. "Vulnerability and Adaptation to Drought in Mexico." *Natural Resources Journal* 39, 1 (1999): 99–115.

Llanos-Hernández, Luis. "La odisea de los hermanos Tort y la fábrica de hilados y tejidos La Providencia en Chiapas a finales del siglo XIX." *LiminaR* 11, 2 (2013): 165–79.

Lombardo, Sonia, Yolanda Terán, and Mario de la Torre. *Atlas histórico de la ciudad de México*. México: Smurfit Cartón y Papel de México, 1996.

López, Ana. "Early Cinema and Modernity in Latin America." *Cinema Journal* 40 (2000): 48–78.

López-Alonso, Moramay. "Growth with Inequality: Living Standards in Mexico, 1850–1950." *Journal of Latin American Studies* 39, 1 (2007): 81–105.

López Portillo y Weber, José. *El petróleo de México: su importancia, sus problemas*. México, D. F.: Petróleos Mexicanos, 1988.

López Rosado, Diego. *Historia del abasto de productos alimenticios en la Ciudad de México*. México, D. F.: Fondo de Cultura Económica, 1988.

Losada, H., H. Martínez, J. Vieyra, R. Pealing, and R. Zavala. "Urban Agriculture in the Metropolitan Zone of Mexico City: Changes over Time in Urban, Suburban and Peri-Urban Areas." *Environment and Urbanization* 10, 2 (1998): 37–54.

Lucas, Adam. *Wind, Water, Work: Ancient and Medieval Milling Technology*. Leiden; Boston: BRILL, 2006.

Lucena Giraldo, Manuel, and Luis Urteaga. *El bosque ilustrado: estudios sobre la política forestal española en America*. Madrid: Instituto Nacional para la Conservación de la Naturaleza: Instituto de la Ingeniera de España, 1991.

Lundmark, Hanna, Torbjörn Josefsson, and Lars Östlund. "The Introduction of Modern Forest Management and Clear-Cutting in Sweden: Ridö State Forest 1832–2014." *European Journal of Forest Research* 136, 2 (2017): 269–85.

MacDuffie, Allen. *Victorian Literature, Energy, and the Ecological Imagination*. Cambridge, England: Cambridge University Press, 2014.

Madureira, Nuno Luis. "The Anxiety of Abundance: William Stanley Jevons and Coal Scarcity in the Nineteenth Century." *Environment and History* 18 (2012): 395–421.

"The Iron Industry Energy Transition." *Energy Policy* 50 (2012): 24–34.

Magnusson, Lars. *Nation, State, and the Industrial Revolution: The Visible Hand*. London; New York: Routledge, 2009.

Malanima, Paolo. *Energy Consumption in Italy in the 19th and 20th Centuries: A Statistical Outline*. Rome: Consiglio Nazionale delle Ricerche, Istituto di Studi sulle Società del Mediterraneo, 2006.

"Energy Crisis and Growth, 1650–1850: The European Deviation in a Comparative Perspective." *Journal of Global History* 1 (2006): 101–21.

"Energy Consumption and Energy Crisis in the Roman World." Environmental History Conference, Rome, 2011.

"Energy in History." In Mauro Agnoletti and Simonee Neri Serneri, eds. *The Basic Environmental History*. New York: Springer International Publishing, 2014.

Malm, Andreas. *Fossil Capital: The Rise of Steam Power and the Roots of Global Warming*. London: Verso, 2016.

Malone, Patrick M. *Waterpower in Lowell: Engineering and Industry in Nineteenth-Century America*. Baltimore: Johns Hopkins University Press, 2009.

Marichal, Carlos, and Mario Cerutti. *Historia de las grande empresas en México, 1850–1930*. Monterrey: Universidad Autónoma de Nuevo León; Fondo de Cultura Económica, 1997.

Márquez Murad, Juan Manuel, and Tatiana Cova Díaz. "La Constancia Mexicana: una revisión histórica-arquitectónica." *Boletín de Monumentos Históricos*, 20 (2010): 98–116.

Martínez, Elio, and María Ramos. "Primer intento de construcción de la planta hidroeléctrica de Nexaca." *Boletín de Monumentos Históricos*, Tercera época, 33 (2015): 50–62.

Martínez, Lucía. "Máquinas, naturaleza y sociedad en el distrito de Chalco, estado de México a fines del siglo XIX." In *Tierra, Agua y bosques: historia y medio ambiente en el México central*. México, D. F.: Instituto Mora, 1996.

Martínez Gil, José de Jesús. *Petróleo de México. Breve historia. Su evolución. Su estado actual*. México, D. F.: Porrúa, 2012.

Martins, Marcos Lobato. "A política florestal, os negócios de lenha e o desmatamento: Minas Gerais, 1890–1950." *Historia Ambiental Latinoamericana y Caribeña* 1, 1 (2011): 29–54.

Mas, Jean-François, and Alejandro Velázquez, José Reyes, et al. "Assessing Land Use/Cover Changes: A Nationwide Multidate Spatial Database for Mexico." *International Journal of Applied Earth Observation and Geoinformation* 5, 4 (2004): 249–61.

Mateos, Jimena. "El turismo en México: La ruta institucional (1921–2006)." *Patrimonio Cultural y Turismo*, 2006, 34–43.

Mathews, Andrew S. "Mexican Forest History Ideologies of State Building and Resource Use." *Journal of Sustainable Forestry* 15, 1 (2002): 17–28.

"Suppressing Fire and Memory: Environmental Degradation and Political Restoration in the Sierra Juarez of Oaxaca, 1887–2001." *Environmental History* 8, 1 (2003): 77–108.

Instituting Nature: Authority, Expertise, and Power in Mexican Forests. Cambridge, The MIT Press, 2011.

Matthews, Michael. *The Civilizing Machine: A Cultural History of Mexican Railroads, 1876–1910*. Lincoln: University of Nebraska Press, 2014.

McDaniel, Carl N., and David N. Borton. "Increased Human Energy Use Causes Biological Diversity Loss and Undermines Prospects for Sustainability." *BioScience* 52, 10 (2002): 929–36.

McDowall, Duncan. *The Light: Brazilian Traction, Light, and Power Company Limited, 1899–1945*. Toronto: University of Toronto Press, 1988.

McGrath, David G. "The Role of Biomass in Shifting Cultivation." *Human Ecology* 15, 2 (1987): 221–42.

McGuckin, Alexander James. "La Clase Divina of Puebla: A Socio-Economic History of a Mexican Elite, 1790–1910," MA Dissertation, University of Alberta (Canada), 1995.

McLung de Tapia, Emily. "Prehispanic Agricultural Systems in the Basin of Mexico." In *Imperfect Balance Landscape Transformations in the Pre-Columbian Americas.*, 121–43. New York: Columbia University Press, 2000.

McManus, P. "Histories of Forestry: Ideas, Networks and Silences." *Environment and History* 5, 2 (1999): 185–208.

McNeill, John R. *Something New under the Sun: An Environmental History of the Twentieth-Century World*. New York: W.W. Norton & Company, 2001.

"The State of the Field of Environmental History." *Annual Review of Environment and Resources* (2010): 345–74.

"Epilogue. Latin American Environmental History in Global Perspective." In *A Living Past: Environmental Histories of Modern Latin America*, 266–76. New York: Berghahn Books, 2018.

McNeill, John R., and George Vrtis (eds.). *Mining North America: An Environmental History since 1522*. Berkeley: University of California Press, 2017.

McNeill, John R., and Verena Winiwarter. *Soils and Societies: Perspectives from Environmental History*. Isle of Harris: White Horse Press, 2006.

"Soils, Soil Knowledge, and Environmental History: An Introduction." In *Soils and Societies: Perspectives from Environmental History*. Isle of Harris: White Horse Press, 2006.

Medina, Eden, ed. *Beyond Imported Magic: Essays on Science, Technology, and Society in Latin America*. Cambridge: MIT Press, 2014.

Meléndez Torres, Juana María, and Luis Aboites Aguilar. "Para una historia del cambio alimentario en México durante el siglo XX. El arribo del gas y la electricidad a la cocina." *Revista de Historia Iberoamericana* 8, 2 (2015).

Melosi, Martin V. *Coping with Abundance: Energy and Environment in Industrial America*. Philadelphia: Temple University Press, 1985.

"Energy and Environment in the United States: The Era of Fossil Fuels." *Environmental Review* 11, 3 (1987): 167–88.

Melville, Elinor G. K. *A Plague of Sheep: Environmental Consequences of the Conquest of Mexico*. Cambridge, England: Cambridge University Press, 1994.

Méndez, Matías, and Víctor Magaña. "Regional Aspects of Prolonged Meteorological Droughts over Mexico and Central America." *Journal of Climate* 23, 5 (2010): 1175–88.

Mendoza, Blanca, Virginia García, Víctor Velasco, et al. "Historical Droughts in Central Mexico and Their Relation with El Niño." *Journal of Applied Meteorology* 44, 5 (2005): 709–16.

"Frequency and Duration of Historical Droughts from the 16th to the 19th Centuries in the Mexican Maya Lands, Yucatan Peninsula." *Climatic Change* 83, 1–2 (2007): 151–68.

Merrill, Karen R. "Texas Metropole: Oil, the American West, and US Power in the Postwar Years." *Journal of American History* 99, 1 (2012): 197–207.

Meyer, Lorenzo. *Mexico and the United States in the Oil Controversy, 1917–1942.* Austin: University of Texas Press, 1977.

Micallef, Benjamin Anthony. "The Forest Policy of Mexico," Master's Thesis, University of California, Berkeley, 1955.

Mikulás, Teich, and Roy Porter. *The Industrial Revolution in National Context: Europe and the USA.* Cambridge, England: Cambridge University Press, 1996.

Milanesio, Natalia. "The Liberating Flame: Natural Gas Production in Peronist Argentina." *Environmental History* 18 (2013): 499–522.

Miller, Char. *Gifford Pinchot and the Making of Modern Environmentalism.* Washington, DC: Island Press, 2001.

Miller, Robert Ryal. "Matias Romero: Mexican Minister to the United States during the Juarez-Maximilian Era." *The Hispanic American Historical Review* 45, 2 (1965): 228–45.

Miller, Shawn William. *Fruitless Trees: Portuguese Conservation and Brazil's Colonial Timber.* Stanford: Stanford University Press, 2000.

An Environmental History of Latin America. New York: Cambridge University Press, 2007.

Miller, Simon. "The Mexican Hacienda between the Insurgency and the Revolution: Maize Production and Commercial Triumph on the Temporal." *Journal of Latin American Studies* 16, 2 (1984): 309–36.

Mills, L. Scott, Michael E. Soulé, and Daniel F. Doak. "The Keystone-Species Concept in Ecology and Conservation." *BioScience* 43, 4 (1993): 219–24.

Miño Grijalva, Manuel. *Haciendas, pueblos y comunidades: los valles de México y Toluca entre 1530 y 1916.* México, D. F.: Consejo Nacional para la Cultura y las Artes, 1991.

Miño Grijalva, Manuel, and Edgar Hurtado Hernández. *Los usos del agua en el centro y norte de México: Historiografía, tecnología y conflictos.* Zacatecas: Universidad Autónoma de Zacatecas, 2005.

Miño Grijalva, Manuel, and Mario Téllez González. *Estadísticas para la historia económica del Estado de México, 1824–1911.* Zinacantepec: El Colegio Mexiquense, 1999.

Miño Grijalva, Manuel, and Marta G. Vera Bolaños. *Estadísticas para la historia de la población del Estado de México, 1826–1910.* Zinacantepec: El Colegio Mexiquense; Consejo Estatal de Población, 1998.

Miranda, Sergio. *Tacubaya: de suburbio veraniego a ciudad.* México, D. F.: UNAM, 2014.

Mitchell, B. R. *International Historical Statistics: The Americas 1750–1988.* New York: Stockton Press, 1993.

International Historical Statistics. Basingstoke: Palgrave Macmillan, 2007.

Mitchell, Timothy. *Carbon Democracy: Political Power in the Age of Oil.* New York: Verso, 2011.

Mokyr, Joel, ed. *The British Industrial Revolution: An Economic Perspective.* Boulder: Westview Press, 1998.

Monterroso, A. I. "Simulated Dynamics of Net Primary Productivity (NPP) for Outdoor Livestock Feeding Coefficients Driven by Climate Change Scenarios in Mexico." *Atmósfera* 24, 1 (2011): 68–88.

Montesillo, José. "Rendimiento por hectárea del maíz grano en México: distritos de riego vs. temporal." *Economía Informa,* 398 (2016): 60–74.

Morales Escobar, Claudia. "Los proyectos geográficos de la Secretaría de Fomento, del Porfiriato a la Revolución," 33–48. In José Moncada and Patricia Gómez (eds). *El quehacer geográfico: instituciones y personajes (1876–1964),* México, D. F.: UNAM; Instituto de Geografía, 2009.

Morales, Humberto. "Los molinos de La Asunción y San Miguel en Tecamachalco y Acatzingo, Estado de Puebla (resultados de la arqueología industrial)." *Apuntes: Revista de Estudios Sobre Patrimonio Cultural – Journal of Cultural Heritage Studies* 21, 1 (2008): 136–45.

"Haciendas, molinos y camino a la fábrica en los orígenes de la industria mexicana." *Boletín de monumentos históricos,* tercera época, 18 (2010): 96–112.

Morales Moreno, Humberto, and Oscar Alejo García. "Arqueología industrial y puesta en valor de la primera colonia industrial de América Latina: La Constancia Mexicana (1835–1991)." *Labor e Engenho* 8, 4 (2014): 78–87.

Morelos Rodríguez, Lucero. *La geología mexicana en el siglo XIX: una revisión histórica de la obra de Antonio del Castillo, Santiago Ramírez y Mariano Bárcena.* Morelia; México, D. F.: Secretaría de Cultura del Estado de Michoacán; Plaza y Valdés, 2012.

Moreno Toscano, Alejandra. "Cambios en los patrones de urbanización en México, 1810–1910." *Historia Mexicana* 22, 2 (1972): 160–87.

Moreno-Brid, Juan Carlos, and Jaime Ros. *Development and Growth in the Mexican Economy: A Historical Perspective.* Oxford: Oxford University Press, 2009.

Morse, Kathryn. "There Will Be Birds: Images of Oil Disasters in the Nineteenth and Twentieth Centuries." *Journal of American History* 99, 1 (2012): 124–34.

Morse, Richard M. "Trends and Patterns of Latin American Urbanization, 1750–1920." *Comparative Studies in Society and History* 16, 4 (1974): 416–47.

Mosley, Stephen. *The Chimney of the World: A History of Smoke Pollution in Victorian and Edwardian Manchester.* New York: Routledge, 2008.

Moya, Jose C. "Industrial Development in a Frontier Society: The Industrialization of Argentina, 1890–1930 (Review)." *Journal of Interdisciplinary History* 41, 4 (2011): 670–1.

"Introduction." In *The Oxford Handbook of Latin American History*, 2–24. Oxford: Oxford University Press, 2011.

Muldrew, Craig. *Food, Energy and the Creation of Industriousness: Work and Material Culture in Agrarian England, 1550–1780*. Cambridge: Cambridge University Press, 2011.

Munch, Francis J. "The Anglo-Dutch-American Petroleum Industry in Mexico: The Formative Years during the Porfiriato 1900–1910." *Revista de Historia de América*, 84 (1977): 135–87.

Murgueitio, Carlos. "La industria textil del centro de México, un proyecto inconcluso de modernización económica (1830–1845)." *HiSTOReLo. Revista de Historia Regional y Local* 7, 13 (2015): 43–75.

Murphy, Denis J. *People, Plants, and Genes: The Story of Crops and Humanity*. Oxford: Oxford University Press, 2007.

Musacchio, Aldo, and Ian Read. "Bankers, Industrialists, and their Cliques: Elite Networks in Mexico and Brazil during Early Industrialization." *Enterprise & Society; Wilmington* 8, 4 (2007): 842–80.

Musset, Alain. *El agua en el valle de México, siglos XVI-XVIII*. México, D. F.: Pórtico de la Ciudad de México; Centro de Estudios Mexicanos y Centroamericanos, 1992.

Navarro, Francisco. "'Dejar el casco antiguo': dos casos de modernización urbana en América Latina: Lima y la Ciudad de México, 1895–1910," Master's Thesis, CIDE, 2016.

Negrete, Jaime. "Rural Poverty and Agricultural Mechanisation Policies in Mexico." *Journal of Agriculture and Environmental Sciences* 3 (2014): 22.

Niederberger, C. "Early Sedentary Economy in the Basin of Mexico." *Science (New York, N.Y.)* 203, 4376 (1979): 131–42.

Nikiforuk, Andrew. *The Energy of Slaves: Oil and the New Servitude*. Vancouver: Greystone Books, 2012.

Novelo, Victoria. "De huelgas, movilizaciones y otras acciones de los mineros del carbón de Coahuila." *Revista Mexicana de Sociología* 42, 4 (1980): 1355–77.

"Pequeñas historias de grandes momentos de la vida de los mineros del carbón de Coahuila." *Estudios Sociológicos de El Colegio de México* 12, 36 (1994): 533–56.

Nye, David E. *Consuming Power: A Social History of American Energies*. Cambridge, MA: MIT Press, 1999.

Ochoa, Enrique C. *Feeding Mexico: The Political Uses of Food since 1910*. Wilmington: Scholarly Resources Inc., 2000.

Odum, Howard T. *Environment, Power, and Society for the Twenty-First Century: The Hierarchy of Energy*. New York: Columbia University Press, 2007.

Odum, Howard T., and Elisabeth C. Odum. *Energy Basis for Man and Nature*. New York: McGraw-Hill, 1976.

Olivera, Ruth R., and Liliane Crete. *Life in Mexico under Santa Anna, 1822–1855*. Norman: University of Oklahoma Press, 1991.

Ordoñez, José. "Densidad de las maderas mexicanas por tipo de vegetación con base en la clasificación de J. Rzedowski." *Madera y Bosques* 21 (2015): 77–126.

Ortega, Luis. "The First Four Decades of the Chilean Coal Mining Industry, 1840–1879." *Journal of Latin American Studies* 14, 1 (1982): 1–32.

Ortega Morel, Javier. *Minería y ferrocarriles en la región de Pachuca y Real del Monte durante el porfiriato*. Pachuca de Soto: Universidad Autónoma del Estado de Hidalgo, 2015.

Ouweneel, Arij. *Shadows over Anáhuac: An ecological interpretation of crisis and development in Central Mexico, 1730–1800*. Albuquerque: University of New Mexico Press, 1996.

Pádua, José Augusto. "'Annihilating Natural Productions': Nature's Economy, Colonial Crisis and the Origins of Brazilian Political Environmentalism (1786–1810)." *Environment and History* 6, 3 (2000): 255–87.

Um sopro de destruição: pensamento político e crítica ambiental no Brasil escravista, 1786–1888. Rio de Janeiro: Jorge Zahar Editor, 2004.

"Environmentalism in Brazil: A Historical Perspective." In *A Companion to Global Environmental History*, 453–73. Chichester, West Sussex; Hoboken, NJ: Wiley-Blackwell, 2012.

Páez, Armando. "Energy-Urban Transition: The Mexican Case." *Energy Policy* 38 (2010): 7226–34.

Paine, R. T. "A Note on Trophic Complexity and Community Stability." *The American Naturalist* 103, 929 (1969): 91–3.

Painter, David S. "Oil and the American Century." *Journal of American History* 99, 1 (2012): 24–39.

Palacio, José Luís, Gerardo Bocco, Alejandro Velázquez, et al. "La condición actual de los recursos forestales en México: resultados del Inventario Forestal Nacional 2000." Investigaciones Geográficas, *Boletín del Instituto de Geografía*. UNAM Núm. 43 (2000): 183–203.

Palerm, Angel. *Obras hidráulicas prehispánicas en el sistema lacustre del Valle de México*. México, D. F.: Instituto Nacional de Antropología e Historia, 1973.

Paredes, Raymund A. "The Mexican Image in American Travel Literature, 1831–1869." *New Mexico Historical Review* 52, 1 (1977).

Parra, Alma. "Lord Cowdray y la industria eléctrica en México." In Reinhard Liehr and Mariano Torres (eds.), *Las compañías eléctricas extranjeras en México, 1880–1960*, 107–43. Puebla: Benemérita Universidad Autónoma de Puebla, 2010.

Parsons, Jeffrey R., and Mary Hrones Parsons. *Maguey Utilization in Highland Central Mexico: An Archaeological Ethnography*. Ann Arbor: University of Michigan, 1990.

Pasqualetti, Martin J. "Ancient Discipline, Modern Concern: Geographers in the Field of Energy and Society." *Energy Research & Social Science* 1 (2014): 122–33.

Paun, Ashim, Lucy Acton, and Wai-Shin Chan. "Fragile Planet: Scoring Climate Risks Around the World." London: HSBC Global Research, March 2018.

Pearce, David. "An Intellectual History of Environmental Economics." *Annual Review of Energy and the Environment*, 27 (2002): 57–81.

Peluso, Nancy Lee. *Rich Forests, Poor People: Resource Control and Resistance in Java*. Berkeley: University of California Press, 1992.

Peña, Sergio de la, Teresa Aguirre, and Enrique Semo. *De la Revolución a la industrialización*. México, D. F.: UNAM; Océano, 2006.

Penna, Anthony N. *The Human Footprint: A Global Environmental History*. Chichester, West Sussex: Wiley-Blackwell, 2014.

Pérez, Víctor. "El arribo del ferrocarril a Michoacán y su abastecimiento forestal durante el Porfiriato." *Tzintzun: Revista de Estudios Históricos* 63 (2016): 121–48.

Perló Cohen, Manuel. *El paradigma porfiriano: historia del desagüe del Valle de México*. México, D. F.: Programa Universitario de Estudios Sobre la Ciudad, Instituto de Investigaciones Sociales: M.A. Porrúa Grupo Editorial, 1999.

Pfeiffer, Dale Allen. *Eating Fossil Fuels: Oil, Food and the Coming Crisis in Agriculture*. Gabriola Island, BC: New Society Publishers, 2006.

Pichardo, Beatriz. "La revolución verde en México." *Agraria*. 4 (2006): 40–68.

Pichardo Hernández, Hugo. "La Sociedad Mexicana de Geografía y Estadística y el territorio mexicano, 1902–1930," 15–31. In José Moncada and Patricia Gómez, eds., *El quehacer geográfico: instituciones y personajes (1876–1964)*. México, D. F.: UNAM, 2009.

Pilcher, Jeffrey. "Mexico's Pepsi Challenge: Traditional Cooking, Mass Consumption, and National Identity." In *Fragments of a Golden Age: The Politics of Culture in Mexico since 1940*, 71–90. Durham: Duke University Press, 2001.

   Planet Taco: A Global History of Mexican Food. Oxford: Oxford University Press, 2012.

Pimentel, David, and Marcia H. Pimentel. *Food, Energy, and Society*. Boca Raton: CRC Press, 2007.

Pincetl, Stephanie. "Some Origins of French Environmentalism: An Exploration." *Forest & Conservation History* 37, 2 (1993): 80–9.

Pirani, Simon. *Burning Up: A Global History of Fossil Fuel Consumption*. London: Pluto Press, 2018.

Platt, Harold L. *The Electric City: Energy and the Growth of the Chicago Area, 1880–1930*. Chicago: University of Chicago Press, 1991.

Pletcher, David. "The Building of the Mexican Railway." *Hispanic American Historical Review* 30, 1 (1950): 26–62.

   The Diplomacy of Trade and Investment: American Economic Expansion in the Hemisphere, 1865–1900. Columbia, MO: University of Missouri Press, 1998.

Podobnik, Bruce. *Global Energy Shifts: Fostering Sustainability in a Turbulent Age*. Philadelphia: Temple University Press, 2008.

Pollard, Sidney. *Peaceful Conquest: The Industrialization of Europe, 1760–1970*. Oxford; New York: Oxford University Press, 1981.

   Typology of Industrialization Processes in the Nineteenth Century. New York: Harwood Academic Publishers, 1990.

Pomeranz, Kenneth. *The Great Divergence: China, Europe, and the Making of the Modern World Economy*. Princeton: Princeton University Press, 2000.

"Political Economy and Ecology on the Eve of Industrialization: Europe, China, and the Global Conjuncture." *The American Historical Review* 107, 2 (2002): 425–46.

"Introduction: What Is 'Industrialization' and What Does It Have to Do with the 'Pacific World'?" In *The Pacific in the Age of Early Industrialization*. Farnham, Surrey; Burlington, VT: Ashgate, 2009.

, ed. *The Pacific in the Age of Early Industrialization*. Farnham, Surrey; Burlington, VT: Ashgate, 2009.

Ponce Nava, Diana. *Cien imágenes de la ciudad de México: retrospectiva histórico-ambiental*. México, D. F.: Gobierno de la Ciudad de México; Secretaría del Medio Ambiente, 1999.

Porter, Susie S. *Working Women in Mexico City: Public Discourses and Material Conditions, 1879–1931*. Tucson: University of Arizona Press, 2003.

Potash, Robert A. "El 'Comercio Exterior de México' de Miguel Lerdo de Tejada: Un error estadístico." *El Trimestre Económico* 20, 79 (1953): 474–9.

Mexican Government and Industrial Development in the Early Republic: The Banco de Avío. Amherst: University of Massachusetts Press, 1983.

Pozas Horcasitas, Ricardo. "La evolución de la política laboral mexicana (1857–1920)." *Revista Mexicana de Sociología* 38, 1 (1976): 85–109.

Priest, Tyler. "The Dilemmas of Oil Empire." *Journal of American History* 99, 1 (2012): 236–51.

Purnell, Jennie. "With All Due Respect: Popular Resistance to the Privatization of Communal Lands in Nineteenth-Century Michoacán." *Latin American Research Review* 34, 1 (1999): 85–121.

Radkau, Joachim. "Wood and Forestry in German History: In Quest of an Environmental Approach." *Environment and History* 2 (1996): 63–76.

Nature and Power: A Global History of the Environment. Washington, DC; Cambridge: German Historical Institute; Cambridge University Press, 2008.

Rajan, S. Ravi. *Modernizing Nature: Forestry and Imperial Eco-Development 1800–1950*. Oxford: Oxford University Press, 2006.

Ramírez, Rodolfo. "El aporte del saber científico a la minería de Pachuca y Real del Monte, México, 1849–1864." *Revista Bibliográfica de Geografía y Ciencias Sociales* XXIII,. 28 (2018): 1–26.

Ramos, Gorostiza, José Luís, and Estrella Aznar. "Ideas económicas y gestión forestal en el ámbito ibérico, 1848–1936, España." *Documentos de Trabajo de la Facultad de Ciencias Económicas y Empresariales*, 28 (2001): 1–23.

Ramos, María. "La Compañía Mexican Light and Power Company Limited durante la Revolución Mexicana." In *Memorias del IV Simposio Internacional sobre Historia de la Electrificación sobre la Electrificación del Territorio. Historia y Futuro*, 2017.

Ramos, María, and Juan Saldaña. "Del Colegio de Minería de México a la Escuela Nacional de Ingenieros." *Quipu* 13, 1 (2000): 105–26.

Ramos Medina, Manuel. *Historia de un huerto: historia de la colonia Huerta del Carmen, San Angel, D.F.* Mexico, D. F.: Centro de Estudios de Historia de Mexico, CONDUMEX, 1992.

Ramos-Gutiérrez, Leonardo, and Manuel Montenegro-Fragoso. "La generación de energía eléctrica en México." *Tecnología y Ciencias del Agua* III, 4 (2012): 197–211.

Randall, Robert W. *Real del Monte: A British Silver Mining Venture in Mexico*. Austin: University of Texas Press, 2014.

Rangel, Edgar. "Un comerciante navarro dueño de los bosques de la costa oriental de Yucatán: Faustino Martínez (1889–1909)." *América Latina en la Historia Económica* (September–December 2018): 160–86.

Rankine, Margaret. "The Mexican Mining Industry in the Nineteenth Century with Special Reference to Guanajuato." *Bulletin of Latin American Research* 11, 1 (1992): 29–48.

Razo, Armando. *Social Foundations of Limited Dictatorship: Networks and Private Protection during Mexico's Early Industrialization*. Stanford: Stanford University Press, 2008.

Razo, Armando, and Stephen Haber. "The Rate of Growth of Productivity in Mexico, 1850–1933: Evidence from the Cotton Textile Industry." *Journal of Latin American Studies* 30, 3 (1998): 481–517.

Rees, Peter. *Transportes y comercio entre México y Veracruz, 1519–1910*. México, D. F.: SepSetentas, 1976.

Reina, Leticia. *Las rebeliones campesinas en México, 1819–1906*. México, D. F.: Siglo Veintiuno Editores, 1980.

"Historia regional e historia nacional." *Historias* 29 (1992): 131–42.

Reyes Osorio, Sergio. *Estructura agraria y desarrollo agrícola en México: estudio sobre las relaciones entre la tenencia y uso de la tierra y el desarrollo agrícola de México*. México, D. F.: Fondo de Cultura Económica, 1974.

Reyna, José Luís. "El conflicto ferrocarrilero: de la inmovilidad a la acción." In Olga Pellicer and José Luís Reyna (eds.), *Historia de la Revolución Mexicana, período 1952–1960: el afianzamiento de la estabilidad política*, 157–214. México, D. F.: El Colegio de México, 1978.

Reynolds, Terry S. *Stronger than a Hundred Men: A History of the Vertical Water Wheel*. Baltimore: Johns Hopkins University Press, 1983.

Rhodes, Richard. *Energy: A Human History*. New York: Simon & Schuster, 2018.

Richardson, David M. *Ecology and Biogeography of Pinus*. Cambridge, Cambridge University Press, 2000.

Richter, Burton. *Beyond Smoke and Mirrors: Climate Change and Energy in the 21st Century*. Cambridge, UK: Cambridge University Press, 2010.

Riojas López, Carlos. *Las intransitables vías del desarrollo: el proceso de industrialización en Jalisco durante el siglo XIX*. Guadalajara, Jalisco: Universidad de Guadalajara, 2003.

Ríos, Ricardo, and Esteban García. "Estado actual del manejo forestal en México. Información y análisis para el manejo forestal sostenible: integrando esfuerzos nacionales en 13 países tropicales en América Latina." (GCP/RLA/133/EC). FAO: Chile, 2001.

Rippy, Merril. *Oil and the Mexican Revolution*. Leiden: Brill, 1972.

Robbins, William G. "Federal forestry cooperation: The Fernow-Pinchot years." *Journal of Forest History* 28 (1984): 164–73.

Rocchi, Fernando. *Chimneys in the Desert: Industrialization in Argentina during the Export Boom Years, 1870–1930*. Stanford: Stanford University Press, 2006.

Rodríguez Garza, Francisco. *Protoindustralización, industrialización y desindustrialización en la historia de México*. México, D. F.: UAM Azcapotzalco, 2009.

Rodríguez Sauceda, Elvia Nereyda, Gustavo Rojo, Benito Ramírez, et al. "Análisis técnico del árbol del mesquite (*Prosopis laevigata* Humb. & Bonpl. ex Willd.) en México." *Ra Ximhai* 10, 3 (2014): 173–93.

Rohter, Larry. "Mexico City Journal; Season of Smog in 'Makesicko City.'" *The New York Times*. January 16, 1988.

Rojas, Arturo Carrillo. *Los caballos de vapor: el imperio de las máquinas durante el cañedismo*. Culiacán: Colegio de Bachilleres del Estado de Sinaloa, 1998.

Rojas, Javier. "Conflictos laborales en el despegue industrial de Nuevo León, México: ferrocarrileros y vidrieros." *Ingenierías* XII, 44 (2009): 42–50.

Rojas Rabiela, Teresa. *La agricultura chinampera: compilación histórica*. Chapingo: Universidad Autónoma Chapingo, 1983.

"Ecological and Agricultural Changes in the Chinampas of Xochimilco-Chalco." In *Land and Politics in the Valley of Mexico: A Two Thousand-Year Perspective*. Albuquerque: University of New Mexico Press, 1991.

, ed. *La agricultura en tierras mexicanas desde sus orígenes hasta nuestros días*. México, D. F.: Consejo Nacional para la Cultura y las Artes: Grijalbo, 1991.

Romero, María Eugenia, and Luis Jáuregui. "México 1821–1867. Población y crecimiento económico." *Iberoamericana* III, 12 (2003): 25–52.

Romero, Sergio, Omar Romero, and Duncan Wood. *Energy in Mexico: Policy and Technologies for a Sustainable Future*. México, D. F.: USAID; Wilson Center, Mexico institute; ITAM, 2013.

Romero Lankao, Patricia. *Obra hidráulica de la ciudad de México y su impacto socioambiental, 1880–1990*. México, D. F.: Instituto Mora, 1999.

"Water in Mexico City: What Will Climate Change Bring to Its History of Water-Related Hazards and Vulnerabilities?" *Environment and Urbanization* 22, 1 (2010): 157–78.

Romero Sotelo, María Eugenia. *México entre dos revoluciones*. México, D. F.: UNAM, 1993.

Rosas Becerril, Patricia. "Las sociedades científicas en México." *Eutopía* 18–24 (2012).

Rosas Salas, Sergio. "Agua e industria en Puebla: el establecimiento de la fábrica textil La Covadonga, 1889–1897." *Relaciones. Estudios de Historia y Sociedad* 34, 136 (2013): 223–64.

Rosas Salas, Sergio, and Francisco Rosas. "Inmigración, inversión e industria en Puebla. La trayectoria empresarial de los hermanos Díaz Rubín, 1878–1914." *Tzintzun: Revista de Estudios Históricos*, 53 (2011): 11–46.

Rosenzweig, Fernando. "Las exportaciones mexicanas de 1817 a 1911." *Historia Mexicana* 9, 3 (1960): 377–413.

Ross, Corey. *Ecology and Power in the Age of Empire: Europe and the Transformation of the Tropical World.* Oxford: Oxford University Press, 2017.

Ross, Stanley H. "The Central Business District of Mexico City as Indicated on the Sanborn Maps of 1906." *PROG The Professional Geographer* 23, 1 (1971): 31–9.

Rowe, Patricia M. "Detailed Statistics on the Urban and Rural Population of Mexico: 1950 to 2010." International Demographic Data Center, US Bureau of the Census, 1982.

Rubio, María del Mar. "Oil and Economy in Mexico, 1900–1930s." *Economics Working Papers* 690 (2005): 1–15.

"Energía, Economía y CO2: España, 1850–2000." *Cuadernos Económicos de ICE* 70 (2005): 52–75.

"Contabilidad nacional medioambiental para productores de petróleo. Estimaciones para México y Venezuela (1901–1985)." *Investigaciones Históricas de Historia Económica* 8 (2007): 141–65.

Rubio, María de Mar, and Mauricio Folchi. "Will Small Energy Consumers Be Faster in Transition? Evidence from the Early Shift from Coal to Oil in Latin America," *Energy Policy* 50 (2012): 50–61.

Rubio, María del Mar, César Yáñez, Mauricio Folchi, and Albert Carreras. "Modern Energy Consumption and Economic Modernization in Latin American and the Caribbean between 1890 and 1925." *Economic Working Papers* 1061 (2005): 1–43.

"Energy as an Indicator of Modernization in Latin America, 1890–1925." *Economic History Review* 63, 3 (2010).

Ruddiman, W. F. *Plows, Plagues, and Petroleum: How Humans Took Control of Climate.* Princeton: Princeton University Press, 2005.

Ruedas de la Serna, Jorge A. *Los orígenes de la visión paradisiaca de la naturaleza mexicana.* México, D. F.: UNAM, 1987.

Ruiz de la Barrera, Rocío. "La empresa de minas del Real del Monte, 1849–1906," PhD Dissertation, El Colegio de México, 1995.

Rutter, Paul, and James Keirstead. "A Brief History and the Possible Future of Urban Energy Systems." *Energy Policy* 50 (2012): 72–80.

Rzedowski, Jerzy. *Vegetación de México.* México, D. F.: CONABIO, 2006.

Rzedowski, Jerzy, and Graciela C. de Rzedowski. *Flora fanerogámica del valle de México.* México, D. F.: Compañia Editorial Continental, 1979.

Saavedra Silva, Elvira, and María Teresa Sánchez Salazar. "Minería y espacio en el distrito minero Pachuca-Real del Monte en el Siglo XIX." *Investigaciones Geográficas* 65 (2008): 82–101.

Saberwal, Vasant K. "Science and the Desiccationist Discourse of the 20th Century." *Environment and History* 4, 3 (1998): 309–43.

Sabin, Paul. *Crude Politics the California Oil Market, 1900–1940.* Berkeley: University of California Press, 2005.

"'The Ultimate Environmental Dilemma:' Making a Place for Historians in the Climate Change and Energy Debates." *Environmental History* 15 (2010): 76–93.

Sánchez, María Teresa. "La minería del carbón y su impacto geográfico-económico en el centro-oriente y noreste de Coahuila, México." *Investigaciones Geográficas. Boletín del Instituto de Geografía*, 31 (1995): 93–112.

Sánchez, Rafael A. "El desarrollo de la industria petrolera en América Latina." *Revista Mexicana de Sociología* 60,. 3 (1998): 157–79.

Sánchez Arteche, Alfonso. *Apuntes para la historia forestal del Estado de México.* México: Probosque, 1990.

Sánchez Díaz, Gerardo. "Los orígenes de la industria siderúrgica mexicana: continuidades y cambios tecnológicos en el siglo XIX." *Tzintzun*, 50 (2009): 11–60.

Sánchez Flores, Ramón. *Historia de la tecnología y la invención en México: introducción a su estudio y documentos para los anales de la técnica.* México, D. F.: Fomento Cultural Banamex, 1980.

Sánchez Gómez, Julio. "La lenta penetración de la máquina de vapor en la minería del ámbito hispano." *Arbor* 149 (1994): 203–41.

Sanders, Jeffrey R. "Political Implications of Prehispanic Chinampa Agriculture in the Valley of Mexico." In Herbert Harvey (ed.), *Land and Politics in the Valley of Mexico: A Two Thousand-Year Perspective.* Albuquerque: University of New Mexico Press, 1991: 17-42.

Sanders, William T. "The Agricultural History of the Basin of Mexico," 101–59. In Eric Wolf (ed.), *The Valley of Mexico: Studies in Pre-Hispanic Ecology and Society.* Albuquerque: University of New Mexico Press, 1976.

Sanders, William T., Jeffrey R. Parsons, and Michael H. Logan. "Summary and Conclusions," 161–78. In Eric Wolf (ed.), *The Valley of Mexico: Studies in Pre-Hispanic Ecology and Society.* Albuquerque: University of New Mexico Press, 1976: .

Sanders, William T., Jeffrey R. Parsons, and Robert S Santley. *The Basin of Mexico: Ecological Processes in the Evolution of a Civilization.* New York: Academic Press, 1979.

Santiago, Myrna. *The Ecology of Oil: Environment, Labor, and the Mexican Revolution, 1900–1938.* Cambridge: Cambridge University Press, 2006.

"Culture Clash: Foreign Oil and Indigenous People in Northern Veracruz, Mexico, 1900–1921." *Journal of American History* 99, 1 (2012): 62–71.

"Oil and Environment in Mexico." *Oxford Research Encyclopedia of Latin American History*, 2016.

Saragoza, Alex. *The Monterrey Elite and the Mexican State, 1880–1940.* Austin: University of Texas Press, 1988.

Sariego, Juan Luis. *Enclaves y minerales en el Norte de México: historia social de los mineros de Cananea y Nueva Rosita 1900–1970.* México, D. F.: CIESAS, 2010.

Scarborough, Vernon L. "Agricultural Land Use and Intensification," 541–51. In Deborah L. Nichols and Christopher A. Pool (eds.), *The Oxford Handbook of*

Mesoamerican Archaeology. Oxford; New York: Oxford University Press, 2012.

Schroeder Rodríguez, Paul A. *Latin American Cinema: A Comparative History*. Berkeley: University of California Press, 2016.

Schurr, Sam H., and Bruce C. Netschert. *Energy in the American Economy, 1850–1975*. Baltimore: Johns Hopkins University Press, 1960.

Seager, R., M. Ting, M. Davis, et al. "Mexican Drought: An Observational Modeling and Tree Ring Study of Variability and Climate Change." *Atmósfera* 22, 1 (2009): 1–31.

Secretaría de Agricultura, Ganadería, Desarrollo Rural, Pesca y Alimentación. *Planeación agrícola nacional, 2017–2030. Maíz grano blanco y amarillo mexicano*. México: SAGARPA, 2016.

Secretaría de Comunicaciones y Obras Públicas. *Reseña historica y estadistica de los ferrocarriles de jurisdiccion federal desde agosto de 1837 hasta diciembre de 1894*. Mexico: Tip. de la Dirección General de Telégrafos Federales, 1900–5.

Secretaría del Medio Ambiente del Gobierno del Distrito Federal. *Sistema de Áreas Naturales Protegidas: Plan Rector*. México, D. F.: Secretaría del Medio Ambiente del Gobierno del Distrito Federal, 2012.

Secretaría Nacional de Energía. *Prospectiva de Energías Renovables, 2016–2030*. México: SENER, 2016.

Sellers, Christopher. "Petropolis and Environmental Protest in Cross-National Perspective: Beaumont–Port Arthur, Texas, versus Minatitlan-Coatzacoalcos, Veracruz." *Journal of American History* 99, 1 (2012): 111–23.

SEMARNAT. *Atlas geográfico del medio ambiente y recursos naturales*. México, D. F.: SEMARNAT, 2006.

Semo, Enrique, and Gloria Pedrero. "La vida en una hacienda aserradero mexicana a principios del siglo XIX." *Investigación Económica* (January–March 1973): 129–61.

Shabot Askenazi, Esther. "La Gran Liga de Empleados de Ferrocarril y la huelga de 1908." *Estudios Políticos* 5, 18–19 (2019): 205–43.

Shaw, Frederick John. "Poverty and Politics in Mexico City, 1824–1854," PhD Dissertation, University of Florida, 1975.

Shulman, Peter A. *Coal and Empire: The Birth of Energy Security in Industrial America*. Baltimore: Johns Hopkins University Press, 2015.

Sieferle, Rolf Peter. "The Energy System—A Basic Concept of Environmental History," 9–20. In Peter Brimblecombe and Christian Pfister, eds., *The Silent Countdown*. Berlin; Heidelberg: Springer, 1990.

Sieferle, Rolf Peter. *The Subterranean Forest: Energy Systems and the Industrial Revolution*. Cambridge: The White Horse Press, 2001.

Silva, Andrea. "Fábrica San Rafael. El legado físico de la industria papelera y su valor como tema de estudio, 1894–1910." *Boletín de Monumentos Históricos* 25 (2012): 78–93.

Silva Barragán, Andrea. "Fábrica San Rafael. El legado físico de la industria papelera y su valor como tema de estudio, 1894–1910." *Boletín de Monumentos Históricos* 0, 25 (2012): 78–93.

Simmons, I. G. *Global Environmental History*. Chicago: University of Chicago Press, 2008.

Simón Ruíz, Inmaculada. "Orden y Progreso en la legislación mexicana de aguas, 1910–1930." *Anduli. Revista Andaluza de Ciencias Sociales*, 8 (2009): 191–200.

"Apuntes sobre historiografía y técnicas de investigación en la historia ambiental mexicana." *IELAT-Universidad de Alcalá* (July 2010): 1–30.

"Conflictos ambientales y conflictos ambientalistas en el México porfiriano." *Estudios Demográficos y Urbanos*, 2010: 363–94.

Simonian, Lane. *Defending the Land of the Jaguar: A History of Conservation in Mexico*. Austin: University of Texas Press, 1995.

Simpson, Lesley Byrd. *Exploitation of Land in Central Mexico in the Sixteenth Century*. Berkeley: University of California Press, 1952.

Skirius, John. "Railroad, Oil and Other Foreign Interests in the Mexican Revolution, 1911–1914." *Journal of Latin American Studies* 35, 1 (2003): 25–51.

Smil, Vaclav. "Energy Flows in the Developing World: By Retaining and Improving Many Traditional Uses of Renewable Energies, Developing Nations Can Avoid Excessive Dependence on Fossil Fuels." *American Scientist* 67, 5 (1979): 522–31.

Energy in World History. Essays in World History. Boulder: Westview Press, 1994.

Enriching the Earth: Fritz Haber, Carl Bosch, and the Transformation of World Food Production. Cambridge, MA; London: The MIT Press, 2004.

"World History and Energy." In *Encyclopedia of Energy*. Vol. 6. Amsterdam; Boston: Elsevier, 2004.

Energy in Nature and Society: General Energetics of Complex Systems. Cambridge, MA: MIT Press, 2008.

Energy Transitions: History, Requirements, Prospects. Santa Barbara: Praeger, 2010.

Energy and Civilization: A History. Cambridge: The MIT Press, 2017.

Snoeck, Michele. *La industria de la refinación en México, 1970–1985*. México, D. F.: El Colegio de México, 1989.

Snooks, G. D. *Was the Industrial Revolution Necessary?* London; New York: Routledge, 1994.

Snowden, Simon. "Energy and Culture: Perspectives on the Power to Work." *Area* 41, 3 (2009): 362–3.

Solís Hernández, Oliva, José Ávila, and Alfonso Serna, eds. *Empresa, empresarios e industrialización en las regiones de México, siglos XIX y XX*. Querétaro: Universidad Autónoma de Querétaro, Editorial Universitaria, 2015.

Soluri, John. *Banana Cultures: Agriculture, Consumption, and Environmental Change in Honduras and the United States*. Austin: University of Texas Press, 2006.

"Tierras, montes y aguas: Apuntes sobre energía, medio ambiente y justicia en las Américas." *Revista de Historia*, no. 59–60 (2009): 169–84.

Soluri, John, Claudia Leal, and José Augusto Pádua, eds. *A Living Past: Environmental Histories of Modern Latin America*. New York: Berghahn Books, 2019.

Sordo, Ana María, and Carlos López. *Exploración, reservas y producción de petróleo en México, 1970–1985*. México, D. F.: El Colegio de México, 1988.

Sørensen, Bent. *A History of Energy: Northern Europe from the Stone Age to the Present Day*. Abingdon, Oxon, England: Earthscan, 2012.

Soto González, Fidel. *Hércules, industrialización y clase obrera, 1838–1877*. Querétaro: Consejo Estatal para la Cultura y las Artes, 2003.

Sovacool, Benjamin. "What Are We Doing Here? Analyzing Fifteen Years of Energy Scholarship and Proposing a Social Science Research Agenda." *Energy Research & Social Science* 1 (2014): 1–29.

Spier, Fred. "How Big History Works: Energy Flows and the Rise and Demise of Complexity." *Social Evolution & History* 4, 1 (2005): 87–135.

Spreng, Daniel. "Transdisciplinary Energy Research – Reflecting the Context." *Energy Research & Social Science* 1 (2014): 65–73.

Stahle, David W., J. Villanueva, D. J. Burnette, et al. "Major Mesoamerican Droughts of the Past Millennium." *Geophysical Research Letters* 38, 5 (2011): 1–4.

Stearns, Peter N. *The Industrial Revolution in World History*. Boulder: Westview Press, 2012.

Steen, Harold K., and Richard P. Tucker, eds. *Changing Tropical Forests: Historical Perspectives on Today's Challenges in Central & South America: Proceedings of a Conference Sponsored by the Forest History Society and IUFRO Forestry History Group*. Durham: Duke University Press, 1992.

Steffen, W., J. Grinevald, P. Crutzen, and J. McNeill. "The Anthropocene: Conceptual and Historical Perspectives." *Philosophical Transactions. Series A, Mathematical, Physical, and Engineering Sciences* 369, 1938 (2011): 842–67.

Steinberg, Theodore. "An Ecological Perspective on the Origins of Industrialization." *Environmental Review* 10, 4 (1986): 261–76.

  Nature Incorporated: Industrialization and the Waters of New England. Cambridge: Cambridge University Press, 2003.

Steinhart, John S., and Carol E. Steinhart. "Energy Use in the US Food System." *Science* 184 (1974): 307–16.

Stern, David, and Astrid Kander. "The Role of Energy in the Industrial Revolution and Modern Economic Growth." *The Energy Journal*, 33, 3 (2012): 125–52.

Stirling, Andy. "Transforming Power: Social Science and the Politics of Energy Choices." *Energy Research & Social Science* 1 (2014): 83–95.

Storey, Rebecca. "Population Decline during and after Conquest." In *The Oxford Handbook of Mesoamerican Archaeology*. Oxford; New York: Oxford University Press, 2012.

Story, Dale. *Industry, the State, and Public Policy in Mexico*. Austin: University of Texas Press, 2014.

Studnicki-Gizbert, Daviken. "Exhausting the Sierra Madre: Mining Ecologies in Mexico over the Long Durée," 19–46. In John R. McNeill and George Vrtis, eds., *Mining North America: An Environmental History Since 1522*, Berkeley: University of California Press, 2017.

Studnicki-Gizbert, Daviken, and David Schechter. "The Environmental Dynamics of a Colonial Fuel-Rush: Silver Mining and Deforestation in New Spain, 1522 to 1810." *Environmental History* 15 (2010): 94–119.

Suárez Cortez, Blanca Estela, and Diana Birrichaga Gardida. *Dos estudios sobre usos del agua en México, siglos XIX y XX.* México, D. F.: CIESA, 1997.

Szeman, Imre, and Dominic Boyer, eds. *Energy Humanities: An Anthology.* Baltimore: Johns Hopkins University Press, 2017.

Tahvonen, Olli, and Janne Rämö. "Optimality of Continuous Cover vs. Clear-Cut Regimes in Managing Forest Resources." *Canadian Journal of Forest Research* 46, 7 (2016): 891–901.

Tann, Jennifer, and M. J. Breckin. "The International Diffusion of the Watt Engine, 1775–1825." *The Economic History Review*, New Series, 31, 4 (1978): 541–64.

Teich, Mikuláš, and Roy Porter. *The Industrial Revolution in National Context: Europe and the USA.* Cambridge: Cambridge University Press, 1996.

Tello, Carlos. *Estado y desarrollo económico: México 1920–2006.* México, D. F.: UNAM, 2007.

Tello-Aragay, Enric, and Gabriel Jover-Avellá. "Economic History and the Environment: New Questions, Approaches and Methodologies," 31–78. In Mauricio Agnoletti and Simone Neri Serneri, eds. *Basic Environmental History.* Cham/Heidelberg/New York: Springer International Publishing, 2014.

Terán Trillo, Yolanda. "Maderos impelidos por la fuerza del agua. Molinos del período virreinal." *Boletín de Monumentos Históricos*, 27 (2013): 99–110.

Therrell, Matthew D., David W. Stahle, José Villanueva, et al. "Tree-Ring Reconstructed Maize Yield in Central Mexico: 1474–2001." *Climatic Change* 74, 4 (2006): 493.

Thomson, Guy P. C. *Puebla de Los Angeles: Industry and Society in a Mexican City, 1700–1850.* Boulder: Westview Press, 1989.

"Popular Aspects of Liberalism in Mexico, 1848–1888." *Bulletin of Latin American Research* 10, 3 (1991): 265–95.

Thorsheim, Peter. *Inventing Pollution: Coal, Smoke, and Culture in Britain since 1800.* Athens: Ohio University Press, 2006.

Tinajero, Araceli, and J. Brian Freeman, eds. *Technology and Culture in Twentieth-Century Mexico.* Tuscaloosa: University of Alabama Press, 2013.

Tinker Salas, Miguel. *The Enduring Legacy: Oil, Culture, and Society in Venezuela.* Durham: Duke University Press, 2009.

Toledo, Daniel, and Francisco Zapata. *Acero y estado: una historia de la industria siderúrgica integrada de México.* México, D. F.: UAM Iztapalapa, 1999.

Toloza, Bárbara, and Amanda Osuna. "La fotografía como parte del vestigio de la industria decimonónica en Culiacán. Los casos de El Coloso y La Aurora en la Revolución." *Boletín de Monumentos Históricos.* 33 (2017): 35–49.

Tomás, Estanislau. "The Catalan Process for the Direct Production of Malleable Iron and Its Spread to Europe and the Americas." *Contributions to Science* 1, 2 (1999): 225–32.

Torre de la Torre, Federico de la. *El patrimonio industrial jalisciense del siglo XIX: entre fábricas de textiles, de papel, y de fierro.* Guadalajara, Jalisco: Secretaría de Cultura, Gobierno de Jalisco, 2007.

Torre Villar, Ernesto de la. "La capital y sus primeros medios de transporte: prehistoria de los tranvías." *Historia Mexicana* 9, 2 (1959): 215–48.

"El ferrocarril de Tacubaya." *Historia Mexicana* 9, 3 (1960): 377–93.

Torres, Blanca. *Hacia la utopía industrial.* México, D. F.: El Colegio de México, 2006.

Torres, Juan Manuel. *Estudio de tendencias y perspectivas del sector forestal en América Latina al año 2020: Informe Nacional México.* Rome: FAO, 2004.

Tortolero, Alejandro. *De la coa a la máquina de vapor: actividad agrícola e innovación tecnológica en las haciendas mexicanas, 1880–1914.* México, D. F.: Siglo Veintiuno Editores, 1995.

, ed., *Tierra, agua y bosques: historia y medio ambiente en el México central.* México, D. F.: Instituto Mora, 1996.

El agua y su historia: México y sus desafíos hacia el siglo XXI. México, D. F.: Siglo XXI, 2000.

"'Los caminos de agua en la producción y el comercio en el sureste de la cuenca de México en la segunda mitad del siglo XVIII.' In *Empresas y modernización en México desde las reformas borbónicas hasta el Porfiriato,* 15–44. Madrid; Frankfurt am Main: Iberoamericana; Vervuert, 2006.

Notarios y agricultores: crecimiento y atraso en el campo mexicano, 1780–1920: propiedad, crédito, irrigación y conflictos sociales en el agro mexicano. México, D. F.: Siglo XXI, 2008.

Toynbee, Arnold. *Toynbee's Industrial Revolution: A Reprint of Lectures on the Industrial Revolution in England, Popular Addresses, Notes, and Other Fragments;* Newton Abbot: David & Charles, 1969.

Trujillo Bolio, Mario. "Producción fabril y medio ambiente en las inmediaciones del Valle de México, 1850–1880," 343–60. In *Tierra, agua y bosques: historia y medio ambiente en el México central.* Ciudad de México; Guadalajara, Jalisco, México: Centre français d'études mexicaines et centraméricaines; Instituto Mora; Potrerillos Editores; Universidad de Guadalajara, 1996.

Operarios fabriles en el Valle de México, 1864–1884: espacio, trabajo, protesta y cultura obrera. México, D. F.: El Colegio de México, 1997.

Empresariado y manufactura textil en la ciudad de México y su periferia: siglo XIX. México, D. F.: CIESAS, 2000.

"El empresariado textil de la Ciudad de México y sus alrededores, 1880–1910," 33–48. In Claudia Agostoni and Elisa Speckman, eds. *Modernidad, tradición y alteridad. La Ciudad de México en el cambio de siglo (XIX-XX)*. México, D. F.: UNAM, 2001.

"La manufactura de hilados y tejidos en la historiografía mexicana, siglos XVIII y XIX. Obrajes, protoindustrias, empresariado y fábricas textiles." *Secuencia*, 97 (2017): 30–60.

Trujillo Bolio, Mario A., and José Mario Contreras Valdez. *Formación empresarial, fomento industrial y compañías agrícolas en el México del siglo XIX*. México, D. F.: CIESAS, 2003.

Tuñón, Julia. "El espacio del desamparo. La ciudad de México en el cine institucional de la Edad de Oro y en Los Olvidados de Buñuel." *Iberoamericana* 3, 11 (2003): 129–44.

Tutino, John. *From Insurrection to Revolution in Mexico: Social Bases of Agrarian Violence, 1750–1940*. Princeton: Princeton University Press, 1986.

Making a New World: Founding Capitalism in the Bajío and Spanish North America. Durham: Duke University Press, 2011.

The Mexican Heartland: How Communities Shaped Capitalism, a Nation, and World History, 1500–2000. Princeton: Princeton University Press, 2017.

Tyrrell, Ian. "Peripheral Visions: Californian-Australian Environmental Contacts, c. 1850s–1910." *Journal of World History* 8, 2 (1997): 275–302.

Uekötter, Frank. *The Age of Smoke: Environmental Policy in Germany and the United States, 1880–1970*. Pittsburgh: University of Pittsburgh Press, 2009.

The Turning Points of Environmental History. Pittsburgh: University of Pittsburgh Press, Rachel Carson Center, 2010.

Uhthoff, Luz María. "El nacionalismo petrolero de la Revolución Mexicana." *Historias. Revista de la Dirección de Estudios Históricos*, 71 (2008): 87–100.

"La industria del petróleo en México, 1911–1938: del auge exportador al abastecimiento del mercado interno. Una aproximación a su estudio." *América Latina en la Historia Económica*, 33 (2010): 5–30.

United States Department of Agriculture. "US Forest Resource Facts and Historical Trends." Forest Service, August 2014.

Uribe Salas, José Alfredo, and María Teresa Cortés Zavala. "Andrés del Río, Antonio del Castillo y José G. Aguilera en el desarrollo de la ciencia mexicana del siglo XIX." *Revista de Indias* LXVI, 237 (2006): 491–518.

Urquiza, Juan. "Miguel Angel de Quevedo and the Forest Hydrological Conservation Project of National Watersheds in the First Half of the Twentieth Century, 1900–1940." *Historia Caribe* 10, 26 (2015): 211–55.

Urteaga, Luis. *La tierra esquilmada: las ideas sobre la conservación de la naturaleza en la cultura española del siglo XVIII*. Barcelona: Serbal, 1987.

Valadés, José, C. "El nacimiento de una industria mexicana." *Estudios de Historia Moderna y Contemporánea de México*, 4 (1972): 95–103.

Valverde, Ismael. "Lucas Alamán empresario. Fundación y desarrollo de la fábrica de hilados de Cocolapan, Orizaba, Veracruz, 1837–1842." *Boletín de Monumentos Históricos*, 33 (2015): 23–34.

Van Hoy, Teresa Miriam. *A Social History of Mexico's Railroads: Peons, Prisoners, and Priests*. Lanham: Rowman & Littlefield, 2008.

Van Young, Eric. *Hacienda and Market in Eighteenth-Century Mexico: The Rural Economy of the Guadalajara Region, 1675–1820.* Berkeley: University of California Press, 1981.

Vandergeest, Peter, and Nancy Lee Peluso. "Empires of Forestry: Professional Forestry and State Power in Southeast Asia, Part 1." *Environment and History* 12, 1 (2006): 31.

"Empires of Forestry: Professional Forestry and State Power in Southeast Asia, Part 2." *Environment and History* 12, 4 (2006): 359–93.

Vargas, Fernando, and Susana Escobar. *Áreas naturales protegidas de México con decretos federales (1899–2000).* México, D. F.: Instituto Nacional de Ecología-SEMARNAP, 2000.

Vargas, Gilberto. "Las batallas del hilo. Historia e imágenes de las fábricas textiles de San Ildefonso, La Colmena y Barrón, cuna del movimiento obrero mexicano." *Boletín de Monumentos Históricos* 25 (2012): 19–36.

Vásquez, Belem, and Salvador Corrales. "Industria del cemento en México: análisis de sus determinantes." *Problemas del desarrollo* 48, 188 (2017): 113–38.

Velasco Reynaga, Anabel. *Mariano Santiago de Jesús de la Bárcena Ramos: de minerales, fósiles y plantas.* Guadalajara, Jalisco: Editorial Universitaria, Universidad de Guadalajara, 2007.

Velásquez García, Erik, et al. *Nueva historia general de México.* México, D. F.: El Colegio de México, 2011.

Ventura Rodríguez, María Teresa. "La industrialización en Puebla, México, 1835–1976." Presented at the Encuentro de Latinoamericanistas Españoles (December 2006), Santander.

Vitz, Matthew. "La ciudad y sus bosques. La conservación forestal y los campesinos en el Valle de México, 1900–1950." *Estudios de Historia Moderna y Contemporánea de México* (June 2012), 135–72.

"To Save the Forests." *Mexican Studies/Estudios Mexicanos* 31, 1 (2015): 125–55.

A City on a Lake: Urban Political Ecology and the Growth of Mexico City. Durham: Duke University Press, 2018.

Vizcaya, Isidro. *Los orígenes de la industrialización de Monterrey. Una historia económica y social desde la caída del Segundo Imperio hasta el fin de la Revolución, 1867–1920.* Monterrey: Universidad de Nuevo León, 2006.

Wagner, Philip L. "Natural Vegetation of Middle America," 216–64. In Robert Wauchope and Robert C. West (eds.), *Handbook of Middle American Indians. Volume One: Natural Environment and Early Cultures.* Austin: University of Texas Press, 1964.

Wakild, Emily. "'It Is to Preserve Life, to Work for the Trees.' The Steward of Mexico's Forests, Miguel Ángel de Quevedo, 1862–1946." *Forest History Today* (Spring–Fall 2006), 4–14.

"Naturalizing Modernity: Urban Parks, Public Gardens and Drainage Projects in Porfirian Mexico City." *Mexican Studies/Estudios Mexicanos* 23, 1 (2007): 101–23.

Revolutionary Parks: Conservation, Social Justice, and Mexico's National Parks, 1910–1940. Tucson: University of Arizona Press. 2011.

"Environment and Environmentalism." In *A Companion to Mexican History and Culture*. Blackwell Publishing Ltd., 2011.

Walker, David W. *Kinship, Business, and Politics: The Martinez del Rio Family in Mexico, 1823–1867*. Austin: University of Texas Press, 1987.

Walter, R. C., and D. J. Merritts. "Natural Streams and the Legacy of Water-Powered Mills." *Science (New York, N.Y.)* 319, 5861 (2008): 299–304.

Warde, Paul. *Ecology, Economy and State Formation in Early Modern Germany*. New York: Cambridge University Press, 2006.

"Fear of Wood Shortage and the Reality of the Woodland in Europe, c. 1450–1850." *History Workshop Journal*, 62 (2006): 28–57.

Energy Consumption in England & Wales, 1560–2000. Roma: Consiglio nazionale delle ricerche, Istituto di studi sulle società del Mediterraneo, 2007.

"The Invention of Sustainability." *Modern Intellectual History* 8, 1 (2011): 153–70.

Wasserman, Mark. *Persistent Oligarchs: Elites and Politics in Chihuahua, Mexico, 1910–1940*. Durham: Duke University Press, 1993.

Weart, Spencer R. *The Discovery of Global Warming*. Cambridge, MA: Harvard University Press, 2008.

Wells, Christopher W. *Car Country: An Environmental History*. Seattle: University of Washington Press, 2012.

"Fueling the Boom: Gasoline Taxes, Invisibility, and the Growth of the American Highway Infrastructure, 1919–1956." *Journal of American History* 99, 1 (2012): 72–81.

Wendt, Carl J., and Ann Cyphers. "How the Olmec Used Bitumen in Ancient Mesoamerica." *Journal of Anthropological Archaeology* 27, 2 (2008): 175–91.

Wenzel, Jennifer, and Patricia Yaeger. *Fueling Culture: 101 Words for Energy and Environment*. Edited by Imre Szeman. New York: Fordham University Press, 2017.

West, Robert C. *The Mining Community in Northern New Spain: The Parral Mining District*. Berkeley: University of California Press, 1949.

, ed. *Handbook of Middle American Indians, Volume 1: Natural Environment and Early Cultures*. Austin: University of Texas Press, 1964.

Westoby, Jack. *Introduction to World Forestry*. Oxford: Wiley-Blackwell, 1991.

White, Leslie. "Energy and the Evolution of Culture." *American Anthropologist* 45, 3, Part 1 (1943): 335–56.

White, Richard. *The Organic Machine*. New York: Hill and Wang, 1995.

Whitmore, Thomas M., and B. L. Turner. *Cultivated Landscapes of Middle America on the Eve of Conquest*. Oxford; New York: Oxford University Press, 2001.

Williams, James C. *Energy and the Making of Modern California*. Akron: University of Akron Press, 1997.

Williams, Michael. *Deforesting the Earth: From Prehistory to Global Crisis*. Chicago: University of Chicago Press, 2010.

Williamson, Jeffrey G. *Industrial Catching Up in the Poor Periphery, 1870–1975*. NBER Working Paper No. 16809, JEL No. F1,N7,O1 (February 2011).

Wionczek, Miguel S. "The State and the Electric-Power Industry in Mexico, 1895–1965." *The Business History Review* 39, 4 (1965): 527–56.

Wionczek, Miguel S., and Lorenzo Meyer. *Energía en México: ensayos sobre el pasado y el presente.* México, D. F.: Colegio de México, 1982.

Wirth, John D., ed. *The Oil Business in Latin America: The Early Years.* Washington, DC: Beard Books, 2001.

Wolf, Eric R., ed. *The Valley of Mexico: Studies in Pre-Hispanic Ecology and Society.* Albuquerque: University of New Mexico Press, 1976.

Wolfe, Mikael D. "Drought and the Origins of the Mexican Revolution." *Oxford Research Encyclopedia of Latin American History,* 2017.

Watering the Revolution: An Environmental and Technological History of Agrarian Reform in Mexico. Durham: Duke University Press, 2017.

World Bank. "Population of Vehicles in Mexico City's Metropolitan Area and Their Emission Levels." The World Bank, January 1, 2010.

Worster, Donald. *Nature's Economy: A History of Ecological Ideas.* Cambridge: Cambridge University Press, 1994.

Wright, Angus. *The Death of Ramon Gonzalez: The Modern Agricultural Dilemma.* Austin: University of Texas Press, 2005.

Wright, Richard, and Dorothy F. Boorse. *Environmental Science: Toward a Sustainable Future.* Boston: Benjamin Cummings, 2010.

Wrigley, E. A. *Continuity, Chance and Change: The Character of the Industrial Revolution in England.* Cambridge, UK: Cambridge University Press, 1988.

Energy and the English Industrial Revolution. Cambridge, UK: Cambridge University Press, 2010.

Wu, Shellen. "The Search for Coal in the Age of Empires: Ferdinand von Richthofen's Odyssey in China, 1860–1920." *The American Historical Review* 119, 2 (2014): 339–63.

Wu, Shellen X. "Coal, Oil, and Diplomacy: Fueling the American Empire?" *Diplomatic History* 40, 3 (2016): 566–9.

Yergin, Daniel. *The Prize: The Epic Quest for Oil, Money, and Power.* New York: Simon & Schuster, 1991.

Zuleta, María Cecilia. "La Secretaría de Fomento y el fomento agrícola en México, 1876–1910: la invención de una agricultura próspera que no fue." *Mundo Agrario* 1, 1 (2000).

Index

CPSIA information can be obtained
at www.ICGtesting.com
Printed in the USA
LVHW040937240523
747884LV00002B/36